NEW STUDIES IN

HEGEL'S
philosophy

EDITED BY **WARREN E. STEINKRAUS**

State University College, Oswego, New York

HOLT, RINEHART AND WINSTON, INC.

New York   Chicago   San Francisco   Atlanta
Dallas   Montreal   Toronto   London   Sydney

193
St 3n
75961
Oct 1971

COPYRIGHT ACKNOWLEDGMENTS

Presses Universitaires de France, Jean Hyppolite, "Hegel's Phenomenology and Psychoanalysis," translated by Albert Richer. Translated from *La Psychanalyse*, 3 (1957), 17–32, by permission of the publisher.

George Allen & Unwin Ltd., G. W. F. Hegel, excerpts from *Phenomenology of Mind*, translated by J. B. Baillie (London, 1931, rev. ed.). Reprinted by permission of the publishers.

New Directions Publishing Corporation, Paul Valéry, excerpt from *La Jeune Parque*, from *The Selected Writings of Paul Valéry*, translated by Jackson Matthews. Copyright 1950 by New Directions Publishing Corporation.

The Open Court Publishing Company, John N. Findlay, "Hegel's Use of Teleology." Reprinted from *The Monist*, Vol. 48, No. 1 (1964) with permission of The Open Court Publishing Co., La Salle, Illinois.

W. Kohlhammer GmbH, Karl Löwith, "Mediation and Immediacy in Hegel, Marx, and Feuerbach," translated by Kenley Royce Dove, from *Vorträge und Abhandlungen zur Kritik der christlichen Überlieferung* (Stuttgart, 1966). Translated by permission of the publishers.

Macmillan & Company Ltd. and St. Martin's Press, Frederick C. Copleston, "Hegel and the Rationalization of Mysticism," from *Talk of God*, ed. Vesey (New York, 1969). Reprinted by permission of The Royal Institute of Philosophy.

Doubleday & Company, Inc., and Weidenfeld & Nicolson Ltd., Walter Kaufmann, "Hegel's Ideas about Tragedy," from § 42 and § 55 of *Tragedy and Philosophy*. Copyright © 1968 by Walter Kaufmann. Reprinted by permission of the publishers.

PREFACE

There is a kinship among Hegel scholars which bridges time and space, but it is an elusive kinship. It is not based on intellectual concord nor on hero worship. There is hardly any fundamental agreement as to what precisely Hegel taught on many basic questions. From the earliest days, Hegel scholars were divided—even into left- and right-wing inter-pretations. Furthermore, there has never been an inkling of a personality cult, for Hegel the man had little charm, was an undramatic person and a dull lecturer. Moreover, there has never been a trace of "scholasti-cism" or a line of orthodox exegetes. Nevertheless a rapport exists among today's students of Hegel just the same and it is based on the fertility and germinating force of Hegel's ideas. This stimulating power of Hegel has influenced or motivated thinkers as diverse in their views as Karl Marx, Bernard Bosanquet, Benedetto Croce, John Dewey, Alfred North Whitehead, and Jean-Paul Sartre.

One might gather from the recognition of such variations in philosophy resulting from this influence that the thinker who spawned them must either be a fund of ambiguity whose thought is subject to diverse interpretations or an eclectic who had something to say for everybody because he rode off in several directions at once. But though there are difficult passages in Hegel, he is not a compendium of ambiguity, and though he has something to say about almost every aspect of human experience—from estrangement to magnetism, from phrenology to marriage, and from the syllogism to religion—his impact is not due to these things. It is rather due to the richness and suggestive power of his philosophy. There is structure and system in Hegel, but it is broad structure and a wide-ranging system, and it is hard for any scholar to encompass the whole simply because there are few minds today that can claim the universality and breadth of a Hegel. As a result, scholars stress facets and implications of his thought, unearthing some gem of insight here, some jewel of wisdom there.

The reader of this book will not find any striking unity of interpretation of Hegel in these essays. Indeed, there is disagreement on such simple things as the meaning of *Geist* and on such basic things as the importance of the dialectic. Surely some contributors to this volume could write critical essays on their colleagues' interpretations. And there would no doubt be rejoinders. But this is partly due to the genius of Hegel. Throughout the volume there is a common enthusiasm for Hegel, an effort to come to terms with his thought, and a recognition of the grandeur and depth of his mind. His views on a wide variety of topics are discussed, and his relations to other movements and thinkers are explored. But one can immediately think of what has been left out— what Hegel himself called "the labor of the negative."

All the essays herein were in some way especially prepared by their authors for this volume. Nine of them are completely new and were written expressly for this book; two appear for the first time in English translations from earlier French and German versions (IV and VIII); three essays were selected specifically by their authors in consultation with the editor as appropriate representations of their current thought on Hegel and were worked over, revised, added to or adapted slightly by them for this volume (VI, XII, and XIII). Professor Walter Kaufmann's essay, for example, does not appear as such anywhere else but is a union of separate sections of a larger whole.

Like my *New Studies in Berkeley's Philosophy* (Holt, Rinehart and Winston, 1966), this volume is international in scope and the result of a cooperative endeavor. It is the first volume of its kind on Hegel. Scholars from eight different countries have essays in this volume—France,

Germany, Great Britain, Ireland, Israel, Italy, Switzerland, and the United States. In securing contributions for this book, many of the established Hegel scholars throughout the world were consulted. Unfortunately, it was impossible to obtain an essay from a philosopher in the Soviet Union. During the preparation of the book, three Hegel scholars who shared interest in the project passed away: Jean Hyppolite, Alexandre Kojève, and Jacob Loewenberg. Fortunately, Professor Hyppolite saw and approved the translation of his essay and prepared captions and new footnote material before he died. Professor Kojève expressed interest in the volume in a letter as late as May 15, 1968, writing that he had "unfortunately, nothing that would be ready or suitable." Professor Loewenberg had tentatively agreed to write a foreword because his advanced years forbade his preparing a new essay, but his passing occurred before the studies were fully assembled.

Scholars such as G. R. G. Mure, Sidney Hook, Loyd Easton, and Dieter Henrich were consulted on various matters, and expressions of interest came from Emil Fackenheim, W. H. Walsh, F. Nicolin, and Abigail Rosenthal. Those who must be singled out for special thanks for advice and assistance are Sir T. M. Knox, Professors A. A. Luce, Karl Löwith, Risieri Frondizi, and Walter Kaufmann. Of course, all the essayists must be thanked for their cooperative spirit and for their patience. In each instance of translation, the original authors have seen and approved the English versions of their essays. Dr. Dove's translation of Chapter VIII was commissioned and has been approved by Professor Löwith. The translator is indebted to Professor Löwith for several editorial clarifications and to Christa Dove for a critical proofreading of the entire translation. In addition, Professor Hyppolite instructed me to express his gratitude to Dr. Jean Laplanche for assistance with his article, and I wish to acknowledge my gratitude to Professor Enrico Mustacchio for special assistance in the preparation of Professor Lombardi's article. Recognition is also due to Dr. Kenneth Culver, now retired from Holt, Rinehart and Winston, for encouraging the preparation of the volume in the first place.

Oswego, New York
September 1970

WARREN E. STEINKRAUS

Note on Abbreviations

Unless otherwise specified, all page citations to the works of Hegel preceded by *Werke* and a volume number refer to the twenty-volume *Sämtliche Werke*, edited by Hermann Glockner (Stuttgart, 1927–1930). Generally, parallel references to English translations are indicated by the English title and the translator's name.

Wherever possible, section numbers are indicated instead of pages, for these are the same in all languages. The designation *Enc.* refers to the *Encyclopädie der Philosophischen Wissenschaften* (*Encyclopedia of the Philosophical Sciences*), which has appeared in several editions since Hegel's last version of 1830. (Hegel's 1817 version has different section numbers, and these are specially noted where necessary.) The term *Zusatz*, which sometimes occurs after a section number citation to the *Encyclopedia*, refers to additions to Hegel's original text inserted by later editors. These additions are passages of material garnered from students' notes of Hegel's lectures. Later printings tend to include more students' notes as well as critical apparatus.

PR refers to the *Philosophie des Rechts*, which is also divided into sections. The English translation by Sir Malcolm Knox, *Hegel's Philosophy of Right* (Oxford, 1942) has become standard. PH refers to the *Philosophy of History*.

The abbreviation *Phen.* always refers to the *Phänomenologie des Geistes*, but the edition or translation used varies somewhat with the preference of the individual authors, and this is indicated in each case. The only complete English translation is by J. B. Baillie (London, revised 1931), though portions of it have been translated by others.

The first part of the *Encyclopedia*, the *Logic*, is sometimes referred to in this book as the "smaller" or "lesser *Logic*" to distinguish it from the separately issued *Wissenschaft der Logik* (*The Science of Logic*), which is sometimes called the "larger *Logic*." Until 1969, the only English translation of this latter work was by W. H. Johnston and L. G. Struthers (London, 1929). Most of the essayists cite that edition, though in a few instances references are made to the 1969 Miller translation (London).

CONTENTS

vii

i

A PLEA FOR HEGEL

Sir T. Malcolm Knox

The shadow of Hegel looms over the modern world to a greater extent than many people realize. The impact of Marx on social and political life, and, as some believe, on philosophy too, is obvious enough. In a very different sphere, namely theology, the influence of Kierkegaard is no less pronounced. I suppose that far more people in the world today are followers of Marx or Kierkegaard than those who study Hegel, and yet these two were eager students of Hegel, and what they wrote is a reaction from him, not really intelligible without some knowledge of his work. The time has come for a reaction from the teaching of these false prophets and for a return to a study of the master whose genius towered above that of his contemporaries and still towers over that of his successors. It was easier to revolt against him than to understand him and this may still be true.

To read many of the philosophical journals in English-speaking countries today is to find many, if not most, of the articles written by very ingenious people who unfortunately know little and care less about the history of philosophy before the late nineteenth century. They are preoccupied with modern linguistic usage; whether they are always aware of the presuppositions of their enterprise I do not know, but their teachers had adopted a view of philosophy which I call "positivist." This means presupposing that the truth about the world is provided by some discipline other than philosophy; those who denied any supranatural realm thought that the truth about the world was to be found, if at all, in the natural sciences; those who recognized a supranatural realm believed, with Kierkegaard, that the truth of that realm was provided by theology. Philosophy was left with the task of criticizing scientific or theological language or of expounding, clarifying, and curing ordinary language. If those who accept such a view are to approach the study of Hegel, they must enter a new world altogether.

In the first place, although Hegel made most strenuous efforts to make into an intelligible whole what contemporary scientists told him about the physical world, he took the measure of nature and knew that, however necessary the mastery of nature was to man, the really important problems lay elsewhere. The stars, which excited awe in Kant, were for Hegel only a "rash,"[1] and the mountains of the Bernese Oberland he found equally unimpressive.[2] He was ready to grant that the sciences provided truth about nature, but what sort of truth was this, and what was nature?

Second, Hegel was a deeply religious but profoundly unorthodox man. All philosophies rest on faith or "absolute presuppositions." A philosophy, like Hegel's, with religious presuppositions at its heart must be utterly alien to someone who has no religion but natural science, and it must be rejected by a dogmatic theology which spurns philosophy and denies its warrant to criticize or rationalize dogma.

In addition, Hegel would have had little time for the modern linguistic philosophy. Language, he said, is, as it were, the body of thought, and the philosopher might well criticize the thinking which language embodied. (*Enc.* § 145, *Zusatz*) But to focus attention on linguistic expressions themselves as something given, and to speculate, for example, on why in English we speak of "false" teeth but "arti-

---

[1] This remark was made in conversation and I have been unable to trace the reference, but Hegel's contempt for the stars is evident enough (for example, see *Werke*, VII, 92 and 461, Glockner edition).

[2] J. Hoffmeister, *Dokumente zu Hegels Entwicklung* (Stuttgart, 1936), for example, 236.

ficial" limbs would in his view be an empiricism, the sort of thing, as he would say, that passes for philosophy in England but is not really worth the name of philosophy at all. (*Enc.* § 7) It would be the study of an object, conducted on no principle different from that which a scientist might use in recording the "sixty species of parrots or the one hundred and thirty seven varieties of veronica,"[3] conducted therefore not by a philosopher but by a grammarian or a philologist. Hegel was interested not in how people spoke about justice but in what justice was, and he ever regarded philosophy as the critic of common sense and not its slave.

Kant drew a distinction between the empirical and the speculative researcher:

> Those who are especially speculative are . . . always on the look out for the unity of the genus . . . those on the other hand whose mentality is especially empirical are constantly trying to split nature into such a multiplicity as almost to force us to give up hope of ever being able to judge its phenomena on universal principles.[4]

In this sense Hegel's philosophy is speculative. He did try to understand the whole realm of human experience by grasping it as the manifestation of *Geist*. *Geist* means both "mind" and "spirit," and it may not always be clear whether Hegel is thinking of mind as a philosophical concept, or of spirit, a theological one. But in the last resort he identifies the two, because his philosophy is his religion crystallized into thought.

If this general outlook is to be made intelligible, let alone acceptable, we must think of its background. Hegel's philosophy takes its immediate rise from Kant, but it is Kant seen through the spectacles both of an intensive study of Plato and Aristotle and of a religious conviction that has rejected orthodoxy. If Aquinas is the philosopher who, soaked in Aristotle, produced the *Summae*, which since 1879 have been the official philosophy of the Roman Catholic Church, Hegel is the philosopher who, under Greek inspiration too, produced the philosophical matrix of the Modernist movement, which flourished from 1890 to about 1925 and is now as dormant as dogmatic theology was during that period. It must, therefore, be hard for anyone to understand Hegel's system if he lacks an intelligent appreciation of Greek philosophy and Kant and has no sympathy with or interest in Christian theology. This is what makes it difficult to get a hearing for Hegel today. Another difficulty, but a far slighter one, is Hegel's literary style. He is an easier author than Kant, and a far more exciting one

---

[3] G. W. F. Hegel, *Werke*, V, 143; *Science of Logic*, trans. Johnston and Struthers (London, 1929), II, 320.
[4] I. Kant, *Critique of Pure Reason*, A, 655.

than Locke or Hume. He had an amazing gift of epigram, and in his exposition of the various levels of consciousness in the *Phenomenology*, and in many places elsewhere, his descriptive power in sketching modes of consciousness from within was masterly. And it disclosed a literary gift that his readers may wish that he had always exercised. Some of his earliest publications, namely some of the essays in a periodical which he issued along with Schelling, occasionally imitated Schelling's peculiar latinized language, but it was not long before he gave earnest attention to terminology and framed his own on the principle of "making philosophy speak German."[5] He did not think that any peculiar terminology was required.[6] He followed Aristotle in adopting and adapting words in common use in his own language, and the terminology so framed is not really difficult for those who read German. However, even if Hegel is easier in German, a reader of the English translations of the numbered paragraphs in the textbooks that he wrote for his lectures (*Encyclopaedia of the Philosophical Sciences* and *Philosophy of Right*) can hardly fail to admire their vigor, conciseness, and clarity.

Hegel was born in 1770, the son of an obscure civil servant in Stuttgart. He died in 1831 as Professor of Philosophy in Berlin, the uncrowned king of philosophy in all the German countries. His life ought to be an encouragement to those who in youth find everything against them. He was forty-six before he attained a salaried post in a university.[7]

A philosopher cannot be understood unless he is read in the context of his own age. Some say that this is nonsense because arguments are timeless and that the logic of Plato's arguments, for example, can be assessed by someone completely ignorant of ancient Greece. This might be true of some arguments in the *Cratylus* or the *Parmenides*, but philosophical argument rests almost always on presuppositions which are taken for granted, and its acceptance or rejection rests, in the long run, on our attitude to its presuppositions, and these always have an historical context.

Thus philosophical arguments are dated, and it follows that we cannot get to grips with Hegel unless his biography is known and unless it is understood against the background of his time.

Except Sir Karl Popper, who says that he does not think that Hegel was even talented,[8] no one, so far as I know, who has read

---

[5] *Briefe von und an Hegel,* ed. J. Hoffmeister (Hamburg, 1952), I, 100.

[6] G. W. F. Hegel, *Werke,* III, 12; *Science of Logic,* I, 40.

[7] For Hegel's biography, see Walter Kaufmann, *Hegel* (New York, 1965), which makes use of all the material which has come to light since 1844 when Karl Rosenkranz published *Hegels Leben.*

[8] Karl Popper, *The Open Society and Its Enemies* (London, 1945), II, 30.

Hegel or considered his influence would be prepared to deny that he was a man of exceptional ability, endowed with an extraordinary range of scholarship and learning. In his school days he had the great good fortune to have a stimulating teacher of Greek and Latin. This gave him the firm foundation which enabled him to become such an able expositor of Plato and Aristotle. Today we read these authors with the aid of nineteenth- and twentieth-century commentaries and translations, many of them inspired by Hegel, but he had to work with sixteenth-century folios, and, whatever Sir Karl Popper may say, I cannot understand how any scholar who examines Hegel's lectures on the history of philosophy or considers the impact of Plato and Aristotle on his other works could do other than hail Hegel's contribution to this field as that of not merely talent but genius.

I return to the schoolboy. Equipped with a thorough knowledge of Latin and Greek, and already endowed with wide-ranging intellectual curiosity and a special interest in history, he goes to the University of Tübingen to read philosophy and then theology. He arrives there one year after the publication of the second edition of the *Critique of Pure Reason* and one year before the French Revolution. At Tübingen he clearly bestraddles eighteenth-century rationalism and the romantic movement. He was an exact contemporary of Wordsworth, and it is not surprising that these two men of genius were *begeistert* by the French Revolution, nor surprising that with more experience they began to have doubts about the worth of absolute democracy. What must not be minimized is the impact on a young German's mind of the French Revolution and Kant's philosophy.

At Tübingen he did well in philosophy, but this was but a propaedeutic to theology. This did not necessarily mean that he was to be a cleric; he had distinguished predecessors and contemporaries who never took orders. But he revolted against the orthodoxy of his teachers, and this is important, because some of them based themselves on Kant in a way similar to what is happening in some quarters today. Kant had to limit knowledge to make room for faith; so today, as I have mentioned, we are asked to leave to faith a supranatural realm explored by dogmatic theology. Hegel was not prepared to accept a dogmatism of this kind. He believed passionately in human reason, not because it was human, but because the spirit of man is the candle of the Lord.

For seven years after taking his degree at Tübingen, Hegel acted as a private tutor, first at Bern and later at Frankfurt. During that period he wrote, but did not publish, some remarkable essays, partly on Christian origins and partly on politics, a dominating interest throughout his life. Of the theological essays the most brilliant is *The Spirit of Christianity*. Dilthey said that Hegel never wrote anything finer.[9] He may have been thinking of the style. The importance of the essay for Hegel's development may lie in his remark, after finishing it, that his task was now to cast his thought in a philosophical form.[10] Reason, he had argued in these early writings, was prefigured in love, but there it was veiled in feeling. The unity of opposites achieved in love must somehow be translated into conceptual terms so that cleavages which religion could never reconcile, as, for instance, those between "church and state, worship and life, piety and virtue,"[11] could be reconciled by a thinking which had risen above the categories of religion to become explicit self-consciousness in philosophy. *Geist* remained as a religious presupposition, but the notion of spirit (*Geist*) could become transparent to itself only by the exercise and advance of mind (which is *Geist* also), only by a hard struggle beyond subjective religious experience to philosophical self-knowledge and so to absolute truth. Whatever may be thought of this attempt to attain absolute knowledge through the philosophical grasp of religion's essence, Hegel never departed from his original conviction. In his inaugural lecture in Berlin he said: "In religion the spirit becomes present to spirit. In religion man abandons his limited and temporal aims, the pressure and delight of the present, and his essence becomes free by itself; the inner God is one with the outer."[12] This may be Modernism and not orthodoxy, but only a religious man could have said it.

Of the early political essays the most important is *The German Constitution*. Germany, Hegel maintains, has ceased to be a state: the old Imperial constitution survives, but it is a dead letter; Germany has fallen asunder into a mass of independent states, and their reunification could be brought about only by some genius like Machiavelli's Prince, and probably only by his methods. Anyone who supposes that Hegel is a dry logician, the manipulator of abstractions by a rigid method of dialectic, will be quickly disillusioned if he will read *The Spirit of Christianity* or *The German Constitution*, for in these essays he cannot fail to recognize the great incisiveness of mind allied to a depth of feeling which amounts to passion.

The writer of these early essays knew where he stood; by writing them he had cleared his own mind. He was ready to embark on the teaching of philosophy. His opportunity came in 1800 when he in-

[9] Wilhelm Dilthey, *Gesammelte Schriften* (Berlin, 1925), IV, 68.
[10] *Briefe von und an Hegel*, ed. J. Hoffmeister, I, 59.
[11] G. W. F. Hegel, *Theologische Jugendschriften*, ed. Herman Nohl (Tübingen, 1907), 342; *Hegel's Early Theological Writings*, ed. T. M. Knox (Chicago, 1948), 301.
[12] *Berliner Schriften, 1818–1831*, ed. J. Hoffmeister (Hamburg, 1956), 13.

herited a small patrimony and was thus enabled to take the risk of starting at Jena as a *privat-dozent*. His audience was never large. At no time did he excel as a lecturer. His delivery was slow and painful, and, to the end of his life, his matter was often too obscure for some of his hearers. Perhaps the most lasting fruit of his Jena experiences was his friendship with Goethe. Was Goethe likely to make a friend of a man who was not even talented?

Unfortunately his philosophical career was cut short after only six years when the university was closed by the advent of Napoleon. He had to leave the town and work for a year as a newspaper editor in Bamberg, and then for eight years as headmaster of a grammar school in Nüremburg. Not until 1816 did he succeed (at Heidelberg) in obtaining the university chair which had been his ambition. After two years there he was called to Berlin where he died from cholera at the age of sixty-one.

The long articles which Hegel published at Jena show us his philosophy germinating, especially as he defines his position by reference to the contemporary philosophies which he rejects. Just after leaving Jena he published a book long enough and obscure enough to make the reputation of any German philosopher. It also happened to be a work of genius. I refer to *The Phenomenology of Spirit*. He described it in later life as his "voyage of discovery";[13] it is an elaborate exposition of the stages through which the mind has progressed from mere sensation to absolute knowledge. Like most of Hegel's major works, this is really a history, a history of mind's progress to full self-consciousness and a partial history of European civilization. The curious thing is that Hegel so often speaks almost contemptuously of history. "This is purely an historical question," he will say, always with the implication that it is of no importance for the philosopher. The historical event, like the phenomena of nature, is only the external and contingent guise in which the genuine reality, mind or spirit, appears. When he was a headmaster he published his immense *Science of Logic*, a work that it is advisable to tackle only after assimilating what is called the smaller *Logic*, namely the first part of the *Encyclopedia of the Philosophical Sciences*. (The translation of this part by William Wallace is by far the best of all the English translations of Hegel, and may be the best introduction to Hegel for English and American readers.) This *Encylopedia* was first published as a textbook for lectures at Heidelberg, but two later editions were published in Berlin, the last of them considerably enlarged. The book summarizes Hegel's system of philosophy in its three distinct parts, Logic, Nature, and

[13] In Karl Rosenkranz, *Hegels Leben* (Berlin, 1844), 204.

Spirit (or Mind). In Berlin, apart from review articles and an interesting essay on the English Reform Bill of 1830, his only other published work was the *Philosophy of Law*.[14]

From lecture notes taken by Hegel's pupils many volumes were published after his death—on Aesthetics, Philosophy of Religion. Philosophy of History, History of Philosopy—and much extra material was added to the *Encyclopedia* and the *Philosophy of Law*. Much of the material thus added to the Hegelian corpus is of great value, but some of it has to be used with caution because some pupils are not always reliable note-takers. It is therefore safer to judge Hegel on what he himself published and on manuscripts written by himself and published posthumously.

As a student of Greek philosophy, Hegel remembered the precept: Become what you are. In other words, you have potentialities, realize them. You were born on the animal level and so are not what you ought to be, for, as a human being. you are mind or spirit. Thus you have potentiality, as the ants and bees have not, of rising. by self-transcendence and the negation of your beginnings, to the higher intellectual levels of *Verstand* and *Vernunft* (understanding and reason). This distinction between the animal, or natural, level and the intellectual, or supranatural, level is cardinal in Hegel's whole system. I do not affirm that it originated with him; I do not deny that he exaggerated to the extent of impiety the scope of the higher reaches of man's mind. But he did argue with a power that no successor has surpassed, and that no successor has refuted, that there is a distinction between the natural and the supranatural, that man is rooted in the natural but has potentialities which are not natural at all and which it is the aim and glory of human life to realize, and, I would add, as he did not, which it is the shame of human life never to realize completely. Men have feet of clay, and Hegel did not always sufficiently allow for that fact.

It would not be unreasonable to maintain that one key concept in Hegel is freedom. In his view the whole course of history has been a gradual approximation to this end; and he believed that the gradual advance of mind to full self-consciousness was an advance to freedom, where subject was no longer dominated by object, but where subject, conscious of itself in and through the object, was free. If freedom, however, is the goal of the process, the governing concept of the process

14 This is the work which appears in two English translations as the *Philosophy of Right*—an unintelligible phrase and a dubious translation. When the second of the two English translations was to be published, the translator pleaded for *Philosophy of Law* as the title, but he was overruled on the ground that the book was known in English as the *Philosophy of Right* and that a different title might mislead.

is development, the development of the original potentialities of the subject.

Hegel's system of philosophy is a description of development from bare abstract categories, the revelation of God, he makes so bold as to say,[15] before the creation of nature and a finite spirit, and so from a sort of skeleton which is to be clothed with flesh through the inadequate embodiment of the categories in nature, to their fuller embodiment in man and in history, and ultimately to their full concrete realization in man's intellectual achievement in art, religion, and philosophy. In philosophy, mind becomes conscious of itself as mind; subject and object coalesce into one. Finite mind, though rooted in nature, is in truth at one with the infinite with whose thought the process began. The process of creation culminates in man, and man comes to full self-consciousness through his experience of nature and history, art, religion, and philosophy. This self-consciousness is ultimately man's consciousness of himself as not merely finite, but as the dwelling place of the infinite; and only because the infinite has been dwelling in him from the start has he been spurred on to this development from the natural level on which his life began to the intellectual or spiritual life which is his true life and his heritage.

What, however, is this development of which Hegel speaks? How is it conceived?

I have mentioned a "spur." What is this? Hegel's answer is: the power of the negative. This is one of his most characteristic doctrines. For positivism, the negative is something which supervenes on the positive from the outside. This is the outlook for which what is real is nature, and the prime characteristic of nature is that everything in it is external to everything else. Mind or spirit is the reverse of this. Thoughts are not external to one another, and the negative is a necessary moment within mind itself.

This inherent negativity is neglected by educationists who would bid us to allow the child to develop "naturally" or by anthropologists who counsel us to study savagery if we wish to understand civilization. If the child is to develop into the man, he must put away childish things; negation by discipline is essential. To become actually what he is potentially, man must reject present achievement and rise to higher things on the stepping-stone of a dead self, a self rejected and negated. This development of civilization from savagery is not a purely positive process, the addition of new features to an unchanging core. Civilization is achieved only by the rejection of savagery, and the reason for this is that the negative is there from the start, intrinsic to spirit from its very beginnings. The spur to intellectual and spiritual

[15] G. W. F. Hegel, *Werke*, III, 36; *Science of Logic*, I, 60.

advance is a divine discontent, a consciousness of an internal clash between potentiality and achievement. The experience of temptation is felt as painful only because the clash of, for example, duty and desire lies within consciousness. To imagine the tempter as external to the self is a mistake, because the external tempter has no power until the self is conscious of itself as tempted and so, as itself, tempting.

Another way of describing this spur is to call it the consciousness of limitation, or a sense of inadequacy, or a determination to do better. Hegel is never tired of pointing out that to be conscious of a limit as a limit is already to be conscious of what lies beyond it. Consciousness of our finitude is only possible for us because we are infinite too. No opposite is intelligible except in conjunction with its counterpart. A scientific account of the world is a knowledge of objects, so that a science of psychology must distort its subject matter by turning it into an object too. But philosophy should never forget the subject which does the observing and constructs scientific theories. And when the subject becomes conscious of himself as theorizing, he becomes conscious of the duality within himself and of his limitations. The clash between his theory, to which he ascribes full adequacy at his peril, and the ideal of truth at which he aims, is a clash within himself, and this it is which makes him self-critical and presses him on to revise his theory, to realize and make explicit the infinite, the ideal, implicit within himself as mind or spirit. The finite spirit yet has the infinite immanent within it, and this clash of negative and positive is the spur to development. The development is a process of self-transcendence.

This process has three phases, repeated at various levels. The first phase is that of immediacy or undifferentiated unity or feeling or intuition. It is the innocence of childhood. The second phase is the negative of the first, that is, the phase of alienation from nature, the phase of mediation, difference and understanding, the analytical intellect. It is also the phase in which man masters nature by work. Here he raises himself above the animals who do not work but appear simply to enjoy their quest for food. (A critic may ask whether the building of anthills does not involve work.) The third phase, reason, the synthetic mind, is the negative of the second, a return to the unity of the first phase, but the unity is now enriched by difference. It is a unity which has incorporated difference and not just canceled it. It is a concrete unity of opposites, not an abstract unity.

The history of a successful marriage may provide an example of Hegel's meaning. At first the marriage is a unity of feeling: the lovers are conscious of unity in love. But they are both persons and therefore minds, and a consciousness of difference arises and the marriage may be exposed to strain. The strain is overcome when each recognizes the other as other and yet as partner and as united. The immediacy of passion has passed; but the difference that has supervened has been overcome, and a moral unity of opposites in love has been achieved. Utilitarian ethics, a child of the scientific intellect, never gets beyond the second phase, the phase of difference. Marriage becomes a contract between two persons, voidable, like other contracts, in the interest of the supposed happiness of one or both partners. Shakespeare knew better:

> So they loved, as love in twain
> Had the essence but in one;
> Two distincts, division none;
> Number there in love was slain.

Intuition, Understanding, Reason—the triad comes straight from the *Critique of Pure Reason*, where there is the suggestion that categories fall into triads, the third being the synthesis of the first two. Thesis, antithesis, synthesis—how often Hegel has been accused of using this pattern mechanically! In fact it is used but seldom, and never mechanically.

Kant limited knowledge to the understanding, the scientific or analytic intellect. He correctly identified the fundamental concepts of the science of his day, but, in Hegel's view, he did not see that the consequence of his own teaching was that the higher range of intellect, which he recognized as reason, was a source of knowledge too, and that the contradictions of the understanding led on to it of necessity. The understanding operates in and with the categories of what Hegel called essence, that is, with dualities like inner and outer, substance and accident, cause and effect, means and end. (*Enc.* §§ 112–159) And operations of this kind lead inescapably to antinomies, as Kant showed. Which is the more important, heredity or environment? Which produces the excellence of the cake, the mixing or the baking? Antinomies such as these are the inevitable product of what Hegel calls the Either-Or of the understanding. The Understanding can never reach finality in these terms. The arguments on both sides are equipollent and endless. There is no way out save by taking higher ground and finding in reason the synthesis involved in Both-And. The difference intrinsic to the level of Understanding is a difference for the mind which is aware of it. The realization of this is an advance in self-consciousness and so is the self-transcendence of the Understanding. The opposing differences are seen to be partial, or complementary to one another, and it is this which makes it possible to overcome the antinomy by grasping the opposites together as a unity. The process of development or self-transcendence which I have tried to describe may also be termed dialectical. Dialectic, which originally means conversation, is a process of thought. Consider, for example, the beginning of Hegel's *Logic*, the three concepts, Being, Nothing, and Becoming. It is only by thinking these concepts that it is possible to proceed from one to the other. Try to think the notion of pure being, and you will find that, in doing so, the notion turns into its opposite— nothing. Pure being, empty of all content, of all characterization or determinacy, turns out to be just nothing. Yet try to think the notion of nothing, and you find that your mind is not empty of all content, you are thinking that nothing *is*, and so thinking "being" all over again. But your thinking thus has two concepts on its hands, being and nothing; each negates the other and turns into the other as you try to think it. However, the power of mind or thought, which is ever the overcoming of externality, grips the two opposites together, sees them collapsing into one another, and thus conceives them as elements or moments in a new single concept of becoming, for becoming just is the unity of is and is not, precisely as a curve is the unity of the opposites concave and convex. It is because dialectic is a process of thought that a dialectical materialism is a contradiction *in adjecto*.

The unity of opposites achieved through dialectic is the route by which the fundamental antithesis of subject and object is overcome. But it can be overcome only by giving primacy to the subject. To give primacy to the object, as in materialistic theories, is to forget that it is the subject which is giving the primacy. Matter is matter only by contrast with mind and therefore *is* for mind alone. By asserting that Hegel's dialectic "stands on its head," and by implying that he was putting it the right way up, Marx made nonsense of Hegelianism, without providing sense of his own. If the primacy is given to matter and not to mind, then mind and its activity of thinking becomes a mere epiphenomenon, determined in some way by a material world. But this is a theory about thinking, and it claims truth. How can the claim be justified if the thinking is only the product of an environment and not the free apprehension of that environment and its essence?

The primacy of the subject may be illustrated in another way. It is in and through its own objectification that the subject comes to knowledge of itself or indeed to explicit reality. Thus Hegel argues, for example, that the subject reaches consciousness of himself as person only through property; what a man calls his are objects into which he has put something of himself; they embody his personality, but the personality itself is actualized and characterized only in and through the process of acquisition. Similarly, a nation's political institutions are the embodiment and expression of its own political genius, and this genius becomes actual only in and through the working of the institutions which are its expression. The outer embodies the inner.

It is impossible to start with the outer, because outer is not known as outer except in contrast with inner. It is outer for me only insofar as I am conscious of it as outer. It is but one element in a complex where the inner side, consciousness in all its forms, must come first.

By starting his system with the categories of logic and showing how the thinking in them gradually comes to self-consciousness and freedom through the stages of nature and mind, and by an occasionally incautious use of words like "deduction" and "derivation," Hegel has often given the impression that he believed that, starting with pure thought, he could deduce its embodiments in nature and history. Even in his own lifetime he was taken up on this point by W. T. Krug who challenged him to deduce the pen with which he wrote his challenge. Hegel treated this with well-merited sarcasm,[16] but he is still unfairly accused of adopting an a priori attitude to nature and history. This is a complete misunderstanding. In his view the task of philosophy is to understand what is. For knowledge of what *is* in nature and history he depended on natural scientists and historians. Philosophy's task was indeed to get to the bottom of what they reported, but it could not alter their report or substitute anything for it. His *Philosophy of Nature* might have been more highly regarded if it had explicitly adopted a theory of evolution; no theory could better have fitted Hegel's own views, but it was not the theory of the scientists who were his contemporaries, and this debarred him from speculation along that line.

To philosophize about nature and history was to get at the heart of things, to discern the rose in the cross of the present, to discern the categories or the rational heart of what is. While nature and history are embodiments of mind's stages in its advance to self-knowledge, their inner core is reason. Their outer configuration is just show or appearance, the insubstantial and the transient. It is in the light of this that we must understand a well-known passage in the preface to the *Philosophy of Law:*

> Philosophy is its own age apprehended in thought. It is . . . absurd to fancy that a philosophy can transcend its contemporary world. . . . When philosophy paints its grey on grey, then has a shape of life grown old. By philosophy's grey in grey it cannot be rejuvenated but only understood. The owl of Minerva spreads its wings only with the falling of the dusk.[17]

Philosophy is simply concerned to understand what spirit has achieved up to this point and it must accept the description of that

---

[16] G. W. F. Hegel, *Werke*, XVI, 56ff.
[17] G. W. F. Hegel, *Werke*, VIII, 19–21; *Philosophy of Right*, trans. T. M. Knox (Oxford, 1942), 11–13. "The rose . . . etc." comes from the same passage.

achievement by scientists and historians; that is, it must accept the facts, but it has the duty of penetrating to the heart of the facts and finding there the concepts in the light of which alone the facts become through and through intelligible. It follows that, despite what critics have so often said, Hegel could not and did not claim finality for his philosophy. As he says at the end of his *Philosophy of History:* "Thus far has knowledge advanced."[18] The changes which he foresaw as inevitable after the Napoleonic wars would produce a new civilization, and philosophy would have to make a further advance in due course in order to get to the bottom of (*begreifen*) that new form of spiritual achievement.

This, at any rate, was Hegel's mature view; but I am bound to add that when he wrote his voyage of discovery he may have been more optimistic. The *Phenomenology* ends with a chapter on Absolute Knowledge and the inference is that this, the final stage in spirit's advance, is one which is attainable in human life, and which has apparently been reached by Hegel himself. The fact that this chapter is so short, so tantalizing, and so unsatisfactory is not to be excused by Hegel's statement in a letter to Schelling that he completed it in a hurry on the eve of the battle of Jena.[19]

It is because Hegel's mature view is to be preferred to his earlier optimism that it would be altogether false to Hegel's own spirit for anyone today to be a Hegelian in philosophy. So far as I know, there is no one nowadays who could be called a Hegelian in the sense of being a defender of Hegel's whole system. Students of Hegel are more apt to think that the task of philosophy is to go beyond him in one sense while thinking that in another he went too far. His description of the stages of mind's advance from sense-perception to reason, his conception of self-transcendence, his vindication of the realm of spirit and his defense of freedom are all permanent philosophical gains. But science and history may have no inner core for philosophy to descry and expound.

We may be equally dissatisfied with Hegel's views on religion, and since these views dominated so much of his life it may be worth saying a little more about them. As a theological student he accepted Kant's view that the purpose of religion was to support morality and that what Jesus taught was simply a "pure morality," that is, one based on pure reason and the categorical imperative. To test this exegesis of the New Testament, Hegel wrote a life of Jesus. This was an enterprise which at that date had had hardly any predecessor. In

[18] G. W. F. Hegel, *Werke* (2d ed.), IX, 546; *Philosophy of History*, trans. J. Sibree (New York, 1900), 456.
[19] The letter was dated May 1, 1807. A translation occurs in Kaufmann, *op. cit.,* 319ff.

this life, Jesus speaks with the accent of Kant. For example, he is represented as saying: "Heaven and earth may well pass away, but not the demands of the moral law or the duty to obey them. . . . You are not to be satisfied with the letter of the law but must act in the spirit of the law out of reverence for duty."[20] The life is carefully elaborated; it contains no reference to miracle; but it did not take Hegel long to see that this Kantian interpretation of Jesus was wrong. A few years later, in his essay *The Spirit of Christianity*, which was mentioned above. Kant is discarded. and Jesus appears as teaching a morality and a religion based on love. In this essay Hegel records a conviction which he had learnt from Lessing and from which he never afterwards departed, namely that faith cannot rest on historical events or be affected by the results of any historical enquiry. "Make what you like of Jesus historically or exegetically, it is the idea that matters."[21]

This dismissal of the historical problem made it possible for Hegel to say: "I am a Lutheran and will so remain." He adds that the Lutheran faith is not a historical one, but the "original faith" of the Apostles.[22] What did he take this to be? After the death of Jesus the disciples received the gift of the Spirit which led them to the truth, namely to a realization of the unity of the divine and the human, the infinite and the finite. Christianity is not to be found in the Gospels or indeed in the New Testament; it was the early Fathers who worked out the doctrine of the Trinity. The Son is distinguished from the Father and yet is one with him, these two distincts being united by love or the Spirit. This language is obviously metaphorical; philosophy has at length been able to translate metaphor into plain prose. Man's essence is to be a thinker; thought advances to self-consciousness by the process of particularizing the universal and then uniting the universal and particular. The negative which, as we have seen, is the spur to this process is, like the finite. one essential moment in the life of God. The Cross is a symbol of infinite grief—the thought, as Luther said, that God is dead. But this is canceled in the Resurrection, whereby the Son rises in glory to be one with the Father. "The Resurrection" is figurative. "To consider the Resurrection as an event is to adopt the outlook of the historian, and this has nothing to do with religion."[23]

[20] G. W. F. Hegel, *Theologische Jugendschriften*, ed. Herman Nohl (Tübingen, 1907), 83. Cf. *Matthew*, 5:18–20.

[21] G. W. F. Hegel, *Werke*, IX, 395ff.; *Philosophy of History*, 325.

[22] G. W. F. Hegel, *Werke*, XIII, 89. *History of Philosophy*, trans. E. S. Haldane (London, 1892), I, 73.

[23] G. W. F. Hegel, *Theologische Jugendschriften*, 334; *Hegel's Early Theological Writings*, edition cited, 292.

How far this exposition of Lutheranism was acceptable to Hegel's fellow Lutherans may admit of doubt. But there is no doubt about Hegel's meaning. Christianity and philosophy, that is Hegel's philosophy, teach exactly the same message; only the form is different. For the symbolical and metaphorical language of religion, philosophy substitutes conceptual thinking. Either this makes religion unnecessary, or else it offers us religion for the masses and philosophy for the *cognoscenti*. Neither alternative may be acceptable.

Those called Hegelians in histories of English philosophy were very different in temperament and achievement. Bradley, a philosophical genius, was so deeply dyed in English common sense and utilitarianism that he could never escape altogether from this tradition, and he ended, like McTaggart, in a *Schwärmerei* which was far from the spirit of Hegel. Caird, or rather the two Cairds, were nearer Hegel's spirit, and Edward Caird's book on Hegel is still the best short book on the subject in English. Bosanquet also was nearer to Hegel than his master Bradley was, but the writer in English who really was a Hegelian is Lord Haldane. His work was not so original as Balfour's, the politician on the other side, but the work of these two men has perhaps not yet had the study it deserves from some first-class graduate student. Instead of reading Hegelians, however, it would be better to read Hegel himself. He has had a bad press. Go to the fountainhead.

Hegel's defects have nowhere been so brilliantly sketched as in Mr. G. R. G. Mure's *Study of Hegel's Logic*.[21] But the trouble is that his merits have not yet been assimilated by our modern philosophers. English philosophy languishes in empiricism and has hardly gone far beyond Hume. The loss of faith in Europe has plunged philosophy into positivism or into an existentialism derived from Kierkegaard, who had not the character, and perhaps not the brains, to understand his master.

There are some contemporary writers who would try to persuade us that, after centuries of darkness, philosophy came into the daylight with—is it Frege, or Russell, or Wittgenstein, or Ryle, or Ayer, or Austin? They are blind guides. Their standard of judgment may seem odd until we remember that, while Hegel's philosophy is the child of the same age which produced Beethoven's music (which Hegel never mentions), their own work is all of a piece with, for example, the music of Bartok, the painting of Picasso, the sculpture of Moore. Its renunciation of metaphysics goes along with a widespread indifference to religion. Its assertion that moral statements are exclamations or expressions of emotion accompanies both a change in moral standards, and also the advocacy in many academic or even ecclesiastical quarters,

[21] Oxford, 1950.

of a naturalness of behavior which would invite us to desert civilization for savagery and animalism. This may suggest that these philosophers are guilty of the *Trahison des Clercs*. Perhaps they are, but I must defend them by quoting another saying of Hegel's: "As for giving instruction about what the world ought to be, philosophy always comes on the scene too late to give it. As the thought of the world, it appears only when actuality is already there cut and dried after its process of formation has been completed."[25] This is the best case I can make for the philosophers whose teaching is now dominant in so many of our English-speaking universities.

I have offered them a Hegelian defense. I wish I thought it would make them study Hegel for themselves. But I am not here able to take what Hegel says at its face value. We must examine his meaning. He is far from the materialism which would make philosophy a mere product of the environment. Philosophy has to apprehend its own age, he would say; it is the thought of the world. But on Hegel's own principles, it ought to follow that this apprehension is already the transcendence of the present and so the defense of ideals which are manifested, but only imperfectly, in what is. Philosophers can and ought to descry the corruption of their time and argue for the ideals or the ways of life that, in a time of corruption, their contemporaries repudiate. Hegel did this himself in his *Philosophy of Law* which, for its time, is a defense of a reasonable liberalism, far removed from the autocracy of the Prussian government under which he lived and which forced him to postpone the book's publication for a couple of years and censored and denied publication to the last section of his essay on the English Reform Bill. Moreover, so far was he from being a tool of the Prussian government, as has so often been alleged, that more than once, as his correspondence shows, he defended his assistants in Berlin when they came under government suspicion.

No short summary, such as this, can convey much of the greatness of Hegel, of the breadth, the range, the penetration, the depth of his mind. He lifts us above time and sense to the grandeur of the spiritual life. Kant and Hegel are, respectively, the Plato and Aristotle of the modern world.

[25] G. W. F. Hegel, *Werke*, VIII, 20; *Philosophy of Right*, edition cited, 12–13.

THE INTERDEPENDENCE OF THE PHENOMENOLOGY, LOGIC, AND ENCYCLOPEDIA

Gustav Emil Mueller

1. Die Phänomenologie des Geistes

Already the title of this richest and most obscure book in the history of philosophy is untranslatable! How should we render Hegel's *Geist?* "Mind" is too intellectual, too rational; and "spirit" in English has a too narrow, too "spiritual" a meaning. This difficulty is not merely terminological or one of translation. It is deeply rooted in the subject matter itself. No identifying term will suffice, because *Geist* is an identity of a concrete manifold; which maintains its unity in a process. In this adventure *Geist* becomes for himself what he was potentially in himself.

One might translate *Geist* as soul, especially since Hegel put a word from Heraclitus on the title page: "The soul (*psyche*) is that which augments itself out of itself." The "soul" in its immediacy belongs to the organic life of preconscious nature. It wakes up to consciousness which transforms its former subconscious self into its own object or "other." As consciousness the soul develops itself together with all intentional contents of all its functions. It mirrors a living and concrete whole of reality, world-itself, or as Hegel calls it, "Substance." World-itself, as a whole, is wholly present in each shape of consciousness; "substance becomes subject." These definite, concrete shapes of consciousness are what Hegel calls *Begriffe;* they are remembered by the soul as having contributed to its educational growth.

How is world-itself, nature and history, mediated in the medium of human consciousness? This is the question of the *Phenomenology*.

Each "Concept" is a world viewed together with all practical, theoretical, artistic, and religious approaches and levels of viewing it. All those representations are individual expressions of the universal life of the whole. Each represents the whole or is a moment of truth. The Absolute is present in every one of its nonabsolute or relative aspects *in* the world, none of which is the world-itself.

This relativity of each position *in* the world necessarily becomes felt, and is thus known in the anguish of self-examination, despair, experience of limits, and disappointments; *The Phenomenology* describes the "way of doubt and despair" (*Zweifel und Verzweiflung*). In the medium of soul as consciousness, truth appears in the breakdown of all of its limited certainties; but they are, also, preserved in larger visions. Thus, everywhere we see rising *levels* of consciousness. That which is experienced changes together with the subject experiencing it.

The first part of the *Phenomenology* recapitulates the history of modern subjective philosophy from empiricism, the immediate experience of the sensuous consciousness, together with its percepts or sense data; through the modern sciences of mathematical measurements correlated to general laws of object-behavior, through rationalism as the standpoint of scientism, through the criticism of Kant to Fichte. In Fichte's dialectic of I and other, I and not I, the underlying dialectic of this whole development is condensed and summarized. In §§ 331–332 of the 1817 edition of the *Encyclopedia*, Hegel hints at this historical parallel to his first movement of the *Phenomenology*.

In the second part, called Self-consciousness, the "Other" of the "I" is not an alien object, but another Soul. The underlying dialectic here is, therefore, the problem of how to achieve unity and harmony in the face of the many individual souls, partly estranged from each other through their physical appearance to one another. This mutual estrangement ties them at the same time of the previous dialectic of I and other as object.

"Comprehension" (*Vernunft*), as existing in the subjective mind, is the concrete identity of its object-consciousness and its free self-consciousness."[1] In self-comprehension (*Vernunft*) each individual recognizes in the other the same ultimate dignity as human *Being:* In the successful mutual I-thou recognition "the I has become a We, and We are present in each of us."

In Hegel's *Encyclopedia* of 1817, only these two first movements of the "Subjective Mind" are retained under the title *Phenomenology*.

This implies a self-criticism. In his letters from the time of publishing the *Phenomenology* Hegel says that the book has no structure, composition, or form; that it is loaded with accidental stuff; that the same themes are treated under different titles; that there is no order, but themes crisscross without warning; that there is no necessity to the sequence—all in all a very regrettable piece of a careless, disorderly writer![2]

Hegel knew that he had written and mixed two different books; and he consequently wrote two different introductions to these two books. One is called the *Preface*, the other the *Introduction*. Both may be considered as concluding the series of "essays" published in the *Critical Journal of Philosophy* in Jena. The Introduction was written first and sent to the publisher with the first half of the manuscript. The Preface, which is first in the book, was written after the whole book was written. The Introduction expresses the original intention to describe the experience which human consciousness as soul or subjective mind makes with itself in reaching the comprehensive standpoint of philosophy. The Preface, overlooking the whole production, imparts to it an aesthetic unity which the whole story acquired quite unintentionally.

All this is perfectly understandable, if one knows that Hegel wrote the whole *Phenomenology* in a few summer months of 1806. It can be compared to nothing less than an eruption of a volcano. After writing about half of it, he lost his original plan and began to pour all kinds of historical, contemporary, and personal problems into the flow of his writings; for example he includes the most recent publication of Goethe, a translation of Diderot's *The Nephew of Rameau;* or he vents his wrath on the, then fashionable, romantic movement. No wonder his world-historical, unfinished, symphony needed a new Preface!

Only the first part of it is systematic. Later, when the reader expects to enjoy the triumph of comprehensiveness (*Vernunft*), the

---

[1] G. W. F. Hegel, *Encyclopedia of Philosophy*, trans. and annotated by G. E. Mueller largely from 1817 edition (New York, 1959), § 359 (*Werke*, VI).
[2] *Briefe von und an Hegel*, ed. J. Hoffmeister (Hamburg, 1952), I, 156, 161, 200.

world comes crashing down in rubble, as if a bomb had hit it. The major theme in the middle part of Hegel's book is the grim and pessimistic critique of the incompetence of man. In principle ("in itself") comprehension understands reality as a beloved and loving, organic whole, in which all individuated forms of life would be known in their contribution to this "we that is I." But, alas! in practice, comprehension (*Vernunft*) fails most miserably. It only "observes" vague analogies to itself in external teleological relations; or in equally vague interpretations of physical appearance, body types, bone structures as clumsy expressions of soul or life. The opaqueness of the physical "other than I" baffles and frustrates comprehension to find itself in it.

But this irrevocable failure of comprehensive "observation" is still a harmless affair compared with all the enormous failures of practical reason. To meet this failure or express it, various forms of despair and of escape develop: the Epicurean idyllic privacy; the Stoic indifference and formal duty for duty's sake; and the Skeptical nihilism. All these deficiencies gather in the Christian "unhappy consciousness," having lost trust in world and in man, and having the Absolute only in the form of an unattainable "Beyond."

But this moral incompetence continues unabated in the "modern world." The Faustian man ventures out to conquer the world and establish his unity with nature. But his "Law of the Heart" turns into the "Frenzy of Self-Conceit." The world-course does not regard virtue, and virtue does not improve the world-course. Man finds himself in a universal situation (*geistiges Tierreich*) of mutual self-deceptions.

In this universal self-estrangement, language serves our self-deception: the language of *meanness* (*niederträchtiges Bewusstsein*) describes everyone as being as mean as the speaker feels he is; the language of *optimism* (*edelmütiges Bewusstsein*)—man good by nature—prettifies and camouflages; the language of *indignation* (*empörtes Bewusstsein*) blames everyone else, the speaker excluded—by destroying the "class-enemy" he bolsters his self-esteem.

The relation of state and church is one misery; and so is the corresponding battle between superstitious faith and iconoclastic reason. Religion camouflages injustice and makes membership in the church an unjust condition of citizenship.

Finite reason wins this fight, but does not understand that it has attacked its own belief in objective facts as ultimate. Reason is no less superstitious than the superstitions it attacked.

The bloody terror of freedom and of revolution turns into the cold terror of the new party to maintain its power. Capitalism and political power denounce each other as corrupters and praise themselves as benefactors. This confusion enjoys its own vanity and takes pride in being confused; the hope that we can escape from this sorry scheme entire is the illusion of "beautiful souls" and the helplessness of aesthetics.

The finishing touches are applied when Hegel shows the self-contradictions in the moralism of Kant and Fichte, prepared by the essays in the *Journal*. One contradiction of moralism is this: if the world would become as I think it ought to be, then I would have eliminated myself as moralist; there would be no longer the pleasure of being morally indignant at other people's pleasures. Happiness and moral integrity fall apart.

Another contradiction holds between the abstractness of reason in its moral law and the individual agents with their concrete interests. The two sides are not mediated. No individual value-content is capable of becoming a general law for all. The impersonal moral law depends on the same individual agents which it wants to eliminate from its consideration. The moral law can do nothing but convince man that there is no escape from his incompetence. He has to learn to accept it and live with it.

This is the beginning of the *Absolute Spirit*. The absolute spirit has shown itself already as ruthless critic of all moralisms and their deceptions. The absolute spirit is "the infinite sorrow," which has chosen individual agents in religious, artistic, and philosophical forms of self-knowledge. It is rooted in the truth that there is no absolute wisdom in this world. Hegel's *Phenemonology* is the philosophy of a latent human-moral crisis which has become actual in the twentieth century.

Seeing the *Phenomenology* as a whole and at the same time understanding it as a document of Hegel's development, one can easily see in it his desperate struggle with himself. It is the life of the spirit not to shun his own devastations, but to face them with absolute honesty.

Guided by the Preface, one may see the *Phenomenology* as a great work of art, an immense world-historical stage play. On the stage appears one form of human consciousness after another, each together with what it believes in, its value. Each makes a disappointing experience with its certainty and is replaced by another one which enjoys and suffers the same fate. At the end all these various characters will have contributed their share to the whole play. The audience at the same time become aware that all these roles are their own roles. They see their own fable before their eyes and minds.

Or to put it in Aristotelian terms, man is potential *Geist;* that is, what he is *in* himself must become and must be worked out *for* himself. At the same time he is also the bricklayer, the worker, working at himself. Third, he is the architect and planner. But he comes to know only at the end what he was really planning. While he is building his destiny, he is constantly changing himself together with the plans of his construction, just as the author did in writing this book.

Man cannot find out what he can be apart from finding out what he has done; on the other hand, his experiences and actualizations sink back into the shadowy realm of perennial human possibilities. Hopes and projections are tied to work and disappointments, anguish and suffering. Hegel's *Phenomenology* is just as essential as it is *existential*. Man is essentially temporal or mortal; this truth and its knowledge is absolute and not merely temporal. In this absolute truth man has reached "absolute knowledge."

Let us turn from this program of the Preface to the original intention condensed in the Introduction. The long Preface of the *Phenomenology of Mind* is followed by thirteen pages, now called Introduction, which contains sixteen sections. I shall quote them thus numbered. The original manuscript had no title for this piece; it followed immediately after the title which was not *Phaenomenologie des Geistes* but *Wissenschaft der Erfahrung des Bewusstseins*. These pages, then, are something like a long subtitle explaining the meaning of the title, which is still meant to be the title of the book in section XV.

The literal English translation of the original title as *Science of Experience of Consciousness* would be rather misleading, because *Wissenschaft* is not *Science*, *Erfahrung* is not *Experience*, and *Bewusstsein* has in its "-sein" an ontological weight, which the more psychological "consciousness" lacks.

Such a translation would suggest that there is an object, such as mental processes, of which there is a science. But Hegel's title contains no such object-reference. The subject of the title is not *Wissenschaft*, but *Erfahrung*. This word is taken in its literal meaning: a venturing out, an adventure (*fahren*) which arrives somewhere, comes to rest or achieves a result (*er*-fahren). This result achieved is *Bewusst-sein*. What I am, I must learn in risking myself. *Bewusst-sein*, Being-conscious, is constituted in the process of my own *Er-fahrung*. And the *Wissenschaft* is the wisdom in which that which I am is expressed and formulated. This wisdom is constituted by a desperate struggle and painful process of *Erfahrung*, whose stations are various forms of consciousness.

That this *Erfahrung*, which the soul makes out of itself and with itself, is the central term of the original title, is also indicated in the Heraclitus quotation which is used as a motto on the title page of the *Phenomenology*: "The soul's meaning is self-augmenting."

I shall now try to state the sixteen theses of the Introduction as briefly as possible.

1. Philosophical knowledge is neither a practical tool, by which the Absolute could be handled, nor a theoretical medium of reception. Both forms of empirical knowledge postulate a separation between an object known and empirical subjects knowing it. The Absolute is both Being in itself and Subject for itself. Truth is the ontological consciousness of Being in us, the One becoming aware of itself in many beings.

2. Our fear of error and untruth is a testimony to the presence of the absolute consciousness in our existence.

3. The Absolute is the only truth, and only truth is absolute. The absolute whole is presupposed (*vorausgesetzt*) by and in all empirical informations. To "know all" is not knowledge of wholeness or integrity. This ground of philosophy is at the same time the goal of its self-development.

4. Philosophy is not one position among others; it cannot withdraw to an inner certainty, a sentiment, a voluntaristic choice, an arbitrary faith, or an intuitive hunch. It has to go through all essential positions of consciousness to show them their own limitations; and in their limitations their values.

5. One might see this way through the stations of the appearing consciousness as an ascent toward the Absolute. This Platonic image is misleading, if it is not remembered that each station of this passion-way is in itself an appearing phase of the Absolute; in all seemingly fixed or one-sided positions, the Absolute's own negations must be recognized.

6. For the varieties of the natural or empirical consciousness this realization of their limits seems to be a horrifying and desperate experience. The truth explodes all finite certainties. This way of doubt and despair must not be confused with mere riddles; the scientist can return to his position unscathed after his riddle has been figured out; but he is a changed man, after philosophical critique has convinced him of his relativity *in* the world.

7. This self-realizing (*sich vollbringend*) skepticism must further not be identified with the particular position of skepticism as one of the one-sided forms of consciousness. That one-sided skepticism is merely the negative result of having seen through the metaphysical ultimacy of sense-certainty and object-realism of natural consciousness. It remains negatively tied up with the dogmatic assumptions from which it abstains.

8. The dialectical process is on all levels a living dialogue between the absolute world-itself and the relative consciousness of it in us. Every empirical subject-object dualism, every finite fixation is secretly aware of death as that power which overwhelms it. Against this feeling of being overwhelmed (*Gefühl der Gewalt*) and against the anguish in the omnipresence of the Absolute, the finite positions cling all the

more stubbornly to their comforts. This is the misery of unauthentic existence, which can be cured if existence is willing to appropriate its own "death" as means of bringing itself into its true Being.

9. There seems to be, then, in all levels of existential knowledge a discrepancy between absolute truth as measure, and the certainties of standpoints as that which is measured; of Being in itself beyond consciousness, and Being-for consciousness; transcendence and immanence.

10. This dialectic is the essential nature of consciousness itself. Every consciousness distinguishes that which it intends and its own awareness of intending.

11. We who know consciousness as this existential dialectic are involved in the same dialectic which we seem to be observing. Philosophy is self-knowledge, dialectical self-reflection, and self-realization.

12. Philosophical knowledge, therefore, distinguishes itself from all other types of knowledge in that its observed object is the same sort of thing as that which does the observing. In apprehending the other I characterize myself. That which is evaluated is also that whereby it is evaluated. Empirical, natural consciousness intends to know objects as if they were independent of this consciousness. In understanding this kind of object-consciousness we understand a mode of existence which we are if and when we practice it. Empirical consciousness, thus, exists in and for itself as that which it is for us in philosophy. Truth and certainty, that which consciousness is in itself and that which it is for itself, are one and the same appearing dialectical process.

13. Consciousness itself is this process of comparing its own two sides, that of which it is aware and its being aware of it. Philosophical "science" (*Wissenschaft*) is pure *theoria* (*reines Zusehn*). The process of experience (*Erfahrung*) thus knows and criticizes itself in its limitations.

14. This dialectical movement, in which consciousness is forced to take one position after another in the correlations of knowledge and its intentional object, is the experience (*Er-fahrung*) which it makes with itself. Consciousness constitutes itself in and by this experience.

15. The unity and coherence of the process itself is the ontological truth of world-itself ("*to on*") in and of the limited ontic positions ("*onta*") in the world. The absolute whole establishes itself in the buildup and breakdown of all of its own limited positions. To reach this *Wissenschaft*, consciousness is forced through a series of conversions (*Unkehrung*).

The result of the phenomenological development will be categories of truth to be studied by a logic of philosophy; but since the result cannot be thought apart from the process of arriving at truth, the *"Wissenschaft der Erfahrung des Bewusstseins"* is itself a necessary prerequisite of the *Logic*.

16. The realm of truth is inseparably one with our tentative and provisional trials of existence; there is not a moment of truth which is not also a shape of living consciousness.

At the end of the *Phänomenologie des Geistes*, Hegel says that the world-consciousness as developed in the medium of the soul is a preparation for *Logic*.

2. Logic

In 1812 the first volume of Hegel's *Logic* appeared; the second volume was published in 1816. His school and his new family life kept him busy during the days. The *Logic* is the work of his nights.

The *Logic* is, like the *Phänomenologie des Geistes*, a new creation, a miracle of achievement. And, as in the case of the latter, there are a number of long and careful comments and reproductions, notably those of the orthodox Hegelians Kuno Fischer[3] and Johann Edward Erdmann.[4] But those elegant reproductions of Hegel's *Logic* are no less artificial than the original; their sequence of categories is not less arbitrary, and many transitions are just as forced. Fortunately, I do not have to join their company.

Hegel meant to develop Logic as ontology. He intended to unfold the categories of Being itself, present in and pervading all beings, and all of its regional dimensions such as nature and history. He kept working on this theme to his last days. The *Logic* never satisfied him.

Hegel apologizes because his table of contents gives the reader a false impression of a perfect whole. These titles are merely "provisional" products, or an external reflection, "of no systematic value, but of an historical interest"[5] only. From all this it follows that one cannot read Hegel's *Logic* as if the sequence of the chapters were a necessary, logical, coherent development, let alone as a rationalistic machinery of "thesis, antithesis and synthesis." The book simply becomes unreadable if it is forced into this Procrustes bed of Marxist

---

[3] Kuno Fischer, *System der Logik und Metaphysik* (3d ed., Heidelberg, 1909).
[4] J. E. Erdmann, *Grundriss der Logik und Metaphysik* (Halle, 1864). See also his *Geschichte der Neueren Philosophie* (Stuttgart, 1931), VII, 435–475.
[5] G. W. F. Hegel, *Wissenschaft der Logik*, *Werke*, IV, 52. The translation is by the present author; *Science of Logic*, trans. Johnston and Struthers (London, 1929), I, 65.

fabrication. Hegel sighs in the *Preface* about a total revision which he had planned before his sudden death—that it *would* be desirable to have a logically coherent development of logic, but that he had to give it up.[6]

Hegel frequently uses a mythical, personifying language, borrowed from Christianity, which does not fit his *Logic* but muddles it up, for example, when he says that his *Logic* describes the thought of God before he created a world;[7] or when he says that the absolute spirit decides to leap into Nature or to create a world.[8] Erdmann puts it this way: "If Hegel had kept the impersonal term 'the Absolute' instead of personifying it, then he would not have muddied the clarity of thought with mythical images."[9] If one looks twice, one can clearly see that nature is not a "product" or a "creature" of the "IDEA," but one category or "Concept" of reality-as-a-whole, world-itself, dialectically limited.

Such defects put together detract from, but do not destroy, the incomparable value of this immense work. A grandiose vision is carried out through dialectical masterpieces in every part. In the Prefaces the *Logic* as the *logic of philosophy* is seen to emerge from other meanings of the term.

Pragmatic logic in everyday use is embedded in a dense matrix of practical needs and technical manipulations. Its standard is: does a hypothetical assumption "work"? It is after this logic of practical existence has done its work, helping man to a more comfortable standard of life, that a higher level of thought emerges.

This thinking, which is no longer merged with immediate practical interests, is described by Aristotle's *formal logic*. General classes and formal relations between them are distinguished from the perceptual data of immediate experience; inductive generalizations are interwoven with deductions from general theories. This is the *logic of reason* (*Verstand*) with its principles of formal identity and noncontradiction, which is valid for analyzing finite and given objects. It is the logic of object-thinking. It is *not* the *speculative logic* of philosophy, to which we now turn.

The personal tone of the first Preface in 1812 is surprisingly similar to the one of 1830. The logic of philosophy, Hegel says in 1812, can never be popular. It is necessarily confined to a few lonely or solitary souls (*die Einsamen*) who are exiled from the world, sacrificed by their own people, in order that there be *in* the world the service

---

[6] *Ibid.*, 32 (Preface to the 2d ed.); *Science of Logic*, 49.
[7] *Ibid.*, 46; *Science of Logic*, 60.
[8] *Ibid.*, 75; *Science of Logic*, 83.
[9] J. E. Erdmann, *Geschichte der Neueren Philosophie* (Stuttgart, 1931), VII, 475.

of truth, the contemplation of world-itself. The dialectical logic of philosophy takes the place of what formerly used to be called metaphysics
in which man has gathered the treasures of what was and still is
and must be that which is of ultimate reality and importance to him.
Every category in the *history* of philosophy is a definition of the Absolute, both in its affirmative or creative as well as in its annihilating,
negative aspects or manifestations. The *Logic* of philosophy strips these
valid cores of every essential world-view of its phenomenological appearance in souls or conscious individuals and presents them in their
metaphysical essence, as categories or concepts of world-itself. Without
this logic of philosophical contemplation, without metaphysics, the
pragmatic and formal logics, with all their finite advantages, are like
a marketplace around a temple which is empty, is without the *Holy*.

Similarily in the Preface of 1831, Hegel speaks of the accelerated
modern civilization, of industry and commerce, preoccupied by political and economic excitements. He doubts whether the clamors of the
day and the twaddle of momentary importance will still leave open
the possibility of participation in the passionless calm of contemplation.
Serving the truth is an absolute, a religious imperative, which must
be obeyed regardless of whether this service is popular or not. It is
done in behalf of all and is a "blessing" (*Segen*) for all.

In the first Preface, Hegel also placed his *Logic* between the
Phenomenology and the coming *Encyclopedia* which was in prepara-
tion in the painful lecture notes for his classes at the University of
Jena and the simple *Propädeutik* for his high school students in
Nürnberg. The first edition of the *Encyclopedia* was published in
Heidelberg in 1817, a year after the second volume of the *Logic*.

In the *Phenomenology* the whole philosophy is discovering itself
in the voyage and adventure which the human soul undertakes to
become aware of its world and of itself in itself. Every step and phase
of this human consciousness discovers in itself a perennial human possibility, both in ascending, as well as in descending directions. Its failure
and incompetence are just as real and important as its triumphs and
achievement. At the end, human consciousness has gained the absolute
self-understanding that all of its shapes or forms belong to its remembered life and recur as fighting mutually limiting positions and standpoints within its totality.

The *Logic* develops the same "Concept" of reality in the form
of thought. Every possible world-view that has emerged in the history
of metaphysics has grasped a truth which can be stated as such without
the factual flesh and blood of its historical representatives. Each standpoint calls forth, and is limited by, its own *opposite* truth. To think
the whole of Being as this concrete and living whole of opposite aspects,
grasped in the various philosophical standpoints of "isms," is the total

vision of Hegel's *Logic*. It is the whole of world-itself as the unity of identities and differences in the medium of thought.

Hegel's dialectical *Logic* of philosophy carefully appreciates the logic of reason as valid in all sciences. These sciences think finite objects in their selection and abstraction from the whole. As soon as reason tries to think this whole by its formal logic of identity and excluded middle, it gets entangled in necessary contradictions or antinomies; for the whole cannot be thought in abstract either/or isolations. It is not either eternal or temporal; either finite or infinite; either quali- tative. individual. or quantitative-mathematical; either only appearance or only a "thing-in-itself"; either object apart from subject or subject apart from being real. All those and many more necessary opposites can only be thought together. both in their difference and in their validity as well as in their necessary complementariness. so that one alone makes no sense without its complementary other; for exam- ple, the negative pole in a magnet is nothing apart from its positive pole. Abstractly isolated they are antinomies.

Hegel distinguishes many types of oppositeness, such as difference, complementary contraries, and contradictions; and consequently devel- ops many types of dialectics with two or more participants.

His *Logic* as a whole moves through four levels in which the Absolute (Being) manifests itself. The first part. called *Being*, shows itself as that sovereign self-determination which is both free and neces- sary. It is necessary because it is what it determines itself to be, know- ing nothing outside of itself; this necessary self-determination is identi- cal with its freedom.

Qualitatively it is infinitely individuated, or it is finite and infinite at the same time. Its individuation is also *alienation*, so that all life appears to itself externally or physically. This is the ontological cate- gory preparing the philosophy of irrationalism in nature. If this quali- tative Being is treated *as if* it were nothing but externally given. we then see it as mathematics sees it, as quantitative. This struggle be- tween the living qualitative Being and its quantitative externality, establishes Being again as the omnipresent. concrete unity of such opposites. This unity of quantity versus quality Hegel calls "measure." Being is thus the identity of identity and difference as well as the difference of identity and difference; such is its dialectical *Essence,* the second part of the *Logic.*

Reality appears. Reality is not identical with its appearance, but is nothing without it. Appearance. likewise, is also disappearance. But in spite of this negativity it is not the appearance of nothing, but of reality.

The *Logic* of Essence justifies the truth of negatively or irration- ality (categories: *das Begrifflose, Zufall, schlechte Unendlichkeit,* and so on) which we saw so painfully and dominantly at work in the incompetencies of the human consciousness in the *Phänomenologie des Geistes*.

Essence exists. And personal existence has essential dialectical structures; existence is as necessary as its essence. Essence is not prior to its own existence, and existence is not prior to its essential character; but both together form a dialectical whole, different and inseparable.

Being is thus essentially or in-itself dialectical. It becomes for-itself what it is in itself in human consciousness; Hegel calls this thinking, existential subject, aware of its dialectical essence, the *"Concept,"* the third movement of his *Logic*. In the "Concept," man, the subject of all this thinking, knows himself to be essentially real, actual (*wirklich*); and reality as dialectical is known to be the essential background of the dialectical subject; Reality, or "Substance," has subject character. "Concept" means that actuality becomes a conscious-being (*Bewusstsein*); if we translate "Concept" with man as philosopher, then this man finds himself in the world, and finds world in himself.

In giving himself to the objective contents and values of the world, man gives them personal existence and representation. The subject, on the contrary, gains objective meaning and value, overcoming man's private immediacy as natural soul. In practice he desires to be desired, to be loved and to be recognized by the other, just as he loves and recognizes in turn.

The fourth and last part, entitled *Idea*, or "absolute spirit," is the awareness that all movements of the whole are also present in the nonlogical forms of art and religion. The *Logic* mirrors its own "speculative Concept" in the nonlogical media of art and religion.

Thus this dialectical logic thinks nonlogical forms of the whole *Idea* logically. The dialectical logic of philosophy thus transcends itself in its own medium and in the direction of a third focus of Hegel's philosophy: The *Encyclopedia*.

3. The Encyclopedia

Hegel published his first systematic outline of philosophy as a whole in May 1817. The essentials of his *Logic* and of his *Phenomenology* now become particular spheres or "circles" of reality-as-a-whole, world itself. Its symbol is the infinite circle. Nicolaus Cusanus saw in the "infinite circle" the symbol of philosophy; it symbolizes the "coincidence of all opposites," because in it all geometrical lines coincide: [10] all lines coincide because all lines are either straight or curved;

[10] Nicholas of Cusa, *Of Learned Ignorance*, trans. G. Heron (New Haven, 1954), 28.

and the infinite circle must be both thought as curved and also as straight in a given section. Hegel accepted this "infinite circle" as the symbol of his philosophy. This infinite circle of circles is the literal meaning of the Greek word *"Encyclopedia,"* which is an "encircling culture" or "All-around education," in contrast to its usual form as an alphabetically arranged aggregate of informations.

> Since philosophy must be comprehensive wisdom, therefore each of its disciplines is in turn a philosophical whole; but in each this philosophical idea is in a particular medium of self-determination. The particular circle therefore breaks through the limitation of its medium on account of its totality-character, and so becomes the ground of a wider sphere. *The whole presents itself as a circle of circles,* of which each is a necessary movement. The system of all essential media produces itself as the whole IDEA and is present wholly in each as well.[11]

But not only Logic or Phenomenology can serve as centers of philosophy.

In principle each of these "circles" or disciplines of systematic philosophy, not only soul as consciousness, *Phenomenology,* or the world-categories of *Logic,* is capable of being the focus or medium which develops the whole in contrasting itself with the other "circles." Hegel's *Aesthetics,* for example, introduces the reader no less to the whole of philosophy than his Ethics (*Philosophie des Rechts*), his *Philosophy of Religion,* his *Philosophy of History,* or even his *Philosophy of Nature.*

The "circle" is the "symbol of true infinity"[12] because in it every point is the result of the preceding point as well as the start of the succeeding one; and the end reached in its movement was at the same time the beginning. (*Phen.* 613) It is the image of philosophical mediation in which every immediate beginning is also the result of the whole movement which returns to it (*Enc.* § 12) and then realizes it as an abstract point within its concreteness. In the circular movements of the "celestial spheres" of the stars and in the circular processes of organic reproduction Plato and Aristotle saw symbolic images of the presence of eternal Being, "time as the moved image of eternity" (Plato), and the unmoved mover (Aristotle).[13]

What are the "Circles" in philosophy? They are what the former rationalistic metaphysics (*Verstandesmetaphysik*) treated under the titles of World, Soul, God; or Nature, History, and the totality of

[11] G. W. F. Hegel, *Werke,* VI, § 6 (1817 *Encyclopedia*); emphasis added. Also, *Enc.* § 15 (*Werke,* VIII).
[12] G. W. F. Hegel, *Werke,* IV, 173; *Science of Logic,* 162.
[13] G. W. F. Hegel, *Werke,* XVIII; Plato, 225–265; Aristotle, 328–330.

Being, the Absolute present in the "shapes" (*gestalten*) of life reflected in the philosophical sciences; systems of "ought" versus "is," such as morality and law and concrete ethics; of art and of religion. They are the concrete content of the IDEA; its wholeness is not separate or abstract Absolute outside or apart from all its own self-differentiations. The absolute whole in the medium of *Logic* is thought in abstraction from its worldly contents; it is, therefore, both the whole and *not* the whole; it is only a "realm of shadows." Philosophy is the consciousness or reflection on the value of what we are in the *many* dimensions of the *One* reality.[14]

In philosophical comprehension, all those "circles" of Being become articulate; they exist both in and for themselves.[15] Insofar as each "circle" mediates the others, or in the "infinite circle," each is a part of a total movement; at the same time its totality accomplishes its eternal and unmoved presence in every phase or moment of itself. Philosophical comprehension and its circle of circles may be compared to a "syllogism" in which each of the three spheres—Nature, Man, the Whole—may be thought of as serving in analogy to a middle term of formal logic, linking the two others as its extremes.

> The objective and final (*überhaupt*) meaning of the figures of the syllogism (*Schluss*) is this: that all comprehensiveness turns out to be a threefold "conclusion" in such a way that each of its members may both take the position of an extreme as well as that of a mediating middle. This is especially so in the case of the three members of philosophy, i.e. logical Idea, Nature, and Spirit.

The *same* Absolute is present in *every* partial manifestation of itself; they do not follow first a one and *then* afterwards another. Time, world itself as temporal, is one of those manifestations.

> If nature is taken as the middle and mediating totality, then it unfolds its meaning in the extremes of logical Idea on the one hand, in the spirit on the other hand. Spirit is spirit only in being mediated through its struggle with nature, and through its orientation towards the Absolute.
>
> In the same way "Spirit" can be the "Middle"; it is that which is known to itself as the individual and active reality for whom nature and the logical idea are extremes. If spirit in the medium of logical self-reflection is the Middle, then Logic mediates the whole categories present in nature *and* spirit.[16]

[14] G. W. F. Hegel, *Werke*, VI, § 5, §§ 14–24 (1817 *Encyclopedia*). See also *Werke*, VII (*Philosophie des Rechts*), §§ 30–32.
[15] *Ibid.*, § 187.
[16] *Ibid.*

The whole circular movement of the comprehensive "Concept" always presents the *universal* whole in *particular* spheres and in *individual-active* self-realizations. The basic systematic categories prove one another in that each is the premise and the conclusion of the others; as immediate they are undefinable because they do the defining.

"It is therefore quite wrong (*unrichtig*) and clumsy (*ungeschickt*) to think of the three circular movements as if one were 'before' or prior to the two others,"[17] as if they were abstract and distinct chunks of the One and only reality. "This is a mere rationalistic and external notion (*Vorstellung*) which applies its habits of external, spatial knowledge to the fluid movements of philosophy as if they were juxtaposed parts outside of one another." (*Enc.* § 18)

"The current opinion," Hegel writes to his disciple Hinrichs,

> that the Absolute has only comprehended itself in my philosophy would need a lengthy comment; a brief comment is this: that if one speaks of philosophy as such, one does not speak of "my" philosophy because every philosophy is comprehension of the Absolute—not an alien object, but a comprehension which is at the same time a self-knowledge. Religion and theology have always declared the same intention. But misinterpretations are impossible to prevent in those people who, in such ideas, can never eliminate from their heads the private person in themselves or in others.[18]

The whole of reality, the universe of philosophy, is both eternal and temporal, infinite and finite, One and Many, Being and process—this is its concrete dialectical "Concept." Man within this whole relates himself to himself and to the whole. Reality is his ground as well as his goal of comprehension and of participation. But this is, as we know from the *Phenomenology of Mind*, a slow and laborious process. Consequently, in each of the circles, spheres, or dimensions of reality, there are essential degrees or levels of insight and self-realizations, different "attitudes of thought." (*Enc.* §§ 26–83)

[17] *Ibid.*, § 11.
[18] *Briefe von und an Hegel*, ed. J. Hoffmeister (Hamburg, 1953), II, 216. (Translation by the present author.)

HEGEL'S PHENOMENOLOGICAL METHOD*

Kenley Royce Dove

There is probably no aspect of "Hegelianism" which has attracted more attention and occasioned more confusion than the so-called dialectical method. Every university student has doubtless heard at least one lecture on this "secret" of Hegelianism, whether in terms of the notorious triad—thesis-antithesis-synthesis—or in some more sophisticated terminology. This is particularly noteworthy, not only because it misrepresents Hegel, but because Hegel's *Phenomenology of Spirit*

* All page references to the *Phenomenology* are to the edition prepared by Johannes Hoffmeister (Hamburg: Meiner, 1948), and are indicated in the text by the designation *Phän*. A new translation of the "Introduction" to Hegel's *Phenomenology* by the present author has been published in Martin Heidegger's *Hegel's Concept of Experience* (New York, 1970). References to this translation will be indicated by "HCE."

was probably the first philosophical treatise whose method was radically and consistently nondialectical.[1]

What, then, is the method of Hegel's *Phenomenology* if it is not dialectical? Insofar as it can be characterized in a word, it is *descriptive*. The study of science, in Hegel's sense, requires that the student, through a tremendous effort of restraint, give himself completely over to the structural development of that science itself. This, I take it, is what Hegel means by the famous phrase *"die Anstrengung des Begriffs"* ("the effort of the concept"). (*Phän.* 48) The true philosopher must strenuously avoid the temptation of interrupting the immanent development of the subject matter by the introjection of interpretive models; he must, rather, give up this instinctively felt prerogative or "freedom" and "instead of being the arbitrarily moving principle of the content," his task is "to submerge this freedom *in* the content and let the content be moved through its own nature, that is, through the self as the self of the content, and to observe the movement." (*Phän.* 48)

But if the phenomenological method must not interfere with the movement of the subject matter, it must also abstain from a purely negative attitude vis-à-vis all content, for example, the stance of the disengaged analyst who removes all life from the content, going straight after its truth value by a more or less elaborate and systematic employment of the formal criterion of tautologyhood. This methodological device, which is of unquestionable value in the mathematical sciences, is totally inadequate in the field of philosophy. The abstract affirmations and negations evinced by a two-valued logic of tautological truths versus nontautological falsehoods *eo ipso* exclude from consideration the characteristics of negation inherent *in* the subject matter itself. And it is precisely this internal negative movement which the Hegelian phenomenological method seeks to describe.

Since this method excludes the central criterion of formal or mathematical logic, it is natural to ask what sort of standard Hegel proposes to put in its stead. His answer to this question, which constitutes the theme of the brief but all-important "Introduction" to the *Phenomenology*, is also the clearest indication of his radical departure from the previous history of Western philosophy. He acknowledges

---

[1] Although scores of commentators, from Trendelenburg to Findlay, have denied that Hegel employed a consistently dialectical method (claiming on the contrary that his thought only attains its apparent dynamic through surreptitious appeals to experience), Ivan Iljin was, so far as I am aware, the first to develop the insight that "Hegel in his philosophical method was no dialectician." (*Die Philosophie Hegels als kontemplative Gotteslehre* (Bern, 1946), 126. Iljin's argument, persuasive though it is, does not focus on the *Phenomenology*, but deals rather with Hegel's authorship as a whole.

that if the *Phenomenology* were to be regarded as an exposition in which science is *related* to knowledge as it appears, or as an inquiry into the nature of human understanding or reason, then it would indeed require, after the manner of a Locke or a Kant, some sort of fundamental presupposition which could serve as a standard of measurement. (*Phän.* 70; HCE 18) But instead of adapting himself to this classical philosophical orientation, Hegel (to borrow a phrase from Kierkegaard) has found a way of "going beyond Socrates"—and Kant as well.[2] Unlike that of any previous philosophy, the method of Hegel's *Phenomenology* takes the "paradox of learning" of Plato's *Meno* (80d) in complete seriousness: "But here, where science makes its first appearance, neither science nor anything else has justified itself as the essence or as the In-itself." (*Phän.* 70; HCE 18).

The argument of the "Introduction" divides itself at this point into three compact and organically inseparable moments. The *first* concerns the abstract distinction between knowledge and truth on which all previous epistemological theories have turned. This distinction is based upon the observation that consciousness itself "distinguishes from itself something to which it at the same time relates itself." (*Phän.* 70; HCE 19) The *determinate* aspect of this interrelationship, the something which is said to be for consciousness, the "being-for-another," is called knowledge. But, on further consideration, we also notice the side of that which is determined, namely the *determinable*. Or, to employ the expression of Brentano, consciousness is always consciousness *of*. This aspect of "being-in-itself," whether regarded as a material thing, an abstract entity, or a thing-in-itself has tended to be associated in philosophical theory with *truth*, and philosophers have accordingly sought to establish criteria for determining the truth of knowledge.

It is particularly important to notice that Hegel does not join in this time-honored enterprise. From the viewpoint of the *Phenomenology*, the question of the truth *of* knowledge is not a matter of direct concern; it is, in the modern idiom, "bracketed." The only object with which the *Phenomenology* is concerned is knowledge as it appears, already organized in the form of a "science" involving some systematic distinction between knowledge and truth.[3] If, on the contrary, we were to concern ourselves with the truth *of* knowledge, that is, with what

---

[2] Cf. Nicolai Hartmann, *Die Philosophie des deutschen Idealismus*, II. Teil: *Hegel* (Berlin, 1929; 1960).

[3] The term "science" is not to be taken merely in the restrictive sense of the natural sciences or any other formally organized discipline—although these too will come into view. What Hegel means by *Wissenschaft* here is a specific shape or *Gestalt* of consciousness or spirit which is itself constituted by a systematic mode of relating form and content, certainty and truth, subject and substance. Thus "*die Sittlichkeit*" is just as much a science as "psychology."

knowledge is in itself, then we should have to provide some standard whereby that truth could be determined. But it is clear that the truth thus attained, if indeed any such knowledge could be acquired, would not be the truth of knowledge, its being-in-itself; it could at most be *our* knowledge of it or its being-for-us. Moreover, as Hegel observes, the standard would be *our* standard and that for which our standard was to serve as a determinate "would not necessarily have to recognize it." (*Phän.* 71; HCE 20)

The *first* moment of Hegel's methodological exposition therefore serves as a preliminary elucidation of what is implied by undertaking a phenomenological description of knowledge as it appears. (*Phän.* 66; HCE 13) Since the object of our inquiry is knowing, any distinction on our part between subject and object would be a playing with mere abstractions. *Our* object is at once and inseparably both the object-knowing subject and the object known-by-the-subject. Thus our object, consciousness or spirit, contains this subject-object distinction within itself and requires no further distinction by us.

The *second* moment of Hegel's argument is equally far-reaching and revolutionary, though its philosophical significance can be no more than adumbrated here. It directly concerns the Concept (*Begriff*),[4] but it also involves a radically new insight into the perennial problem of time and eternity. Just as the object of knowledge is seen to fall *within* the object of *our* inquiry, Hegel also makes the unprecedented move of regarding the Concept as something completely within the temporal process of the consciousness or spirit under investigation.[5] Thus the Concept is not regarded as, in the Parmenidean tradition, identical with timeless eternity, or, after the manner of Plato or White-head, as an eternal object which "participates" or "ingresses" in the tem-poral realm of human experience or "actual occasions." It is also to be distinguished from the Aristotelian and Nietzschean interpretation of the Concept as something which, although falling within time, for ex-ample, as a "natural kind," nevertheless undergoes a cyclical process of eternal recurrence within time itself. For Hegel the Concept *is* time, and time is "the existentially embodied Concept itself." (*Phän.* 558)[6]

[4] In view of the radical novelty of Hegel's use of the term *Begriff*, it is tempting to avoid translating it as "Concept," the most obvious choice. Wallace and Baillie have presented cogent arguments for the term "notion." It has the advantage of suggesting a kinship with the Greek "*nous*" and it has a systematic precedent in Berkeley's *Siris*. Unfortunately the term carries with it irrepressible connotations of vagueness and imprecision.

[5] For a discussion of the Concept *qua* known by the philosophical "we," see p. 44ff. of the present chapter.

[6] Cf. also *Phän.* 38: "As to time . . . it is the existentially embodied Concept itself." Both these passages are given an extensive and illuminating interpretation in A. Kojève, *Introduction à la Lecture de Hegel: Leçons sur la Phénoménologie de l'Esprit*, ed. Raymond Queneau (Paris, 1947).

Since the Concept is seen to fall within the knowledge we are investigating, it follows that "consciousness provides itself with its own standard, and the investigation will accordingly be a comparison of consciousness with its own self." (*Phän.* 71; HCE 20) To understand how this comparison takes place we must observe that just as consciousness or spirit was seen to be at once both "subjective" and "objective," this same duality holds true for the Concept: consciousness itself distinguishes between (a) the Concept *qua* knowledge and (b) the Concept *qua* object. Hence there is within consciousness not only something which is taken to be *for it;* consciousness also assumes that that which is for it, is in-itself or has an independent status as well. Accordingly, we see that the Concept has two moments. If we take the Concept to be knowledge, then the standard for this Concept *qua* knowledge will be its object or what is said to exist in-itself. In this case the comparison will consist in seeing whether the Concept corresponds to the object, that is, what consciousness regards as the standard of truth. But, on the other hand, if we take the Concept to be the object as it is essentially or in-itself, then the Concept itself will be the standard for the Concept *qua* known, that is, the Concept as object of knowledge. Here the comparison consists in seeing whether the Concept *qua* known or *qua* object corresponds to the Concept itself.[7]

Although both aspects of the Concept must no doubt be taken into account in any adequate description of the knowing process—and an emphasis on one or the other has traditionally served as the touchstone for a realist or idealist epistemology[8]—Hegel's descriptive method seems, in this second moment of its explication, to be in danger of losing its purely descriptive character in virtue of the necessity of *our* determining which aspect of the Concept is to serve as the standard.

His answer to this problem is as simple as it is convincing, especially when the reader has followed the presentation through the section called "Consciousness." He observes, namely, that both of these processes are the same. The standard is selected by consciousness itself and, since both moments of the process fall within our object, that is, knowledge as it appears, any selection of standards on *our* part

---

[7] Hegel has in this analysis developed an important insight into the problematical relationship between the positive and negative senses of the Kantian Thing-in-itself: that is, of the Thing-in-itself as object (that which according to the "Transcendental Aesthetic" is said to be known) and the Thing-in-itself as noumenon. From the perspective of the *Critique of Pure Reason*, there is no unambiguous answer to Jacobi's well-known charges that Kant tried, against his own strictures, to have it both ways.

[8] For Hegel's most explicit discussion of this question, see his Jena lectures of 1803–1804, first published as *Jenenser Realphilosophie I* (Hamburg: Meiner, 1932). See 214ff.

would be superfluous.[9] Needless to say, the adoption of such a purely descriptive stance does require a great deal of restraint; it is not the traditional way of "doing" philosophy.

The *third* moment in the development of Hegel's phenomenological method is guided by the observation that consciousness not only selects its own standard but is also the *comparison* of its knowledge with its own standard. This is based on the fact that consciousness is "on the one hand, consciousness of the object, on the other, consciousness of itself; it is consciousness of what to it is the true, and consciousness of its knowledge of this truth." (*Phän.* 72; HCE 21) Consciousness is therefore both consciousness of something, and consciousness of its self.[10] In view of this characteristic feature of consciousness, it is at the same time conscious of its standard of truth and conscious of its knowledge of the truth in question. Since both the standard and the knowledge are for the same consciousness, their comparison is a fundamental feature in the movement of consciousness itself.

It is indeed true that consciousness' standard of truth is only a standard insofar as it is known by consciousness, as it is *for* consciousness and not as it is in itself. This observation has driven many less descriptive philosophers to some form of skepticism, for the presumptive standard does not really seem to be what it "ought" to be (namely something independent of knowledge). Hence it seems incapable of serving as a criterion of knowledge. But for Hegel, whose attention is steadfastly focused on the experience of knowledge as it appears, all such talk about "capacities" and "intentions" is beside the point.[11] The crucial point is that consciousness, in all the shapes of its appearance, *does* draw a distinction between its standard, or what the object *is* in itself, and its knowledge, or the being of the object *for* consciousness. (*Phän.* 72; HCE 22) If, in the course of the comparison, con-

---

[9] In view of the endless polemics among Marxists and critics of Marx on the question of the "Hegelian method," it is interesting to note that this "method" is quite different to the rival claims of idealism on the one hand and realism on the other.

[10] This second aspect of consciousness must not be simply identified with that of the *Phenomenology* explicitly called "Self-consciousness." As a moment of human knowing, self-consciousness is a factor, however much explicitly emphasized, throughout the entire course of experience from "Sense-certainty" to "Absolute Knowledge." But this aspect of human experience is not grasped by the reader of the *Phenomenology* before he has followed the argument *through* the chapter on *Verstand*. (N.B. *Phän.* 128) As we shall see, an understanding of this characteristic feature of the *Phenomenology* is essential for a demystification of the philosophical "we"; or, which is another way of expressing the same problem, it is essential to the intelligibility of the *Phenomenology* as a philosophical work.

[11] For a complementary formulation of this important methodological issue, see Hegel's Jena lectures of 1803–1804, *op. cit.*, 200.

sciousness should find that its standard and its knowledge do not correspond, it will, on the basis of its own assumptions, have to change
its knowledge in order to make it correspond to its standard.

But it also follows from these assumptions that a change in consciousness' knowledge *eo ipso* involves a change in its standard, for
the standard was based upon the object, indeed, the object as known.
Hence with a change in the knowledge for the sake of truth, the standard of truth is itself changed. Consciousness thus discovers that the
process in which it placed its knowledge in *doubt*, all the while certain
that it held a firm criterion for what the object of its knowledge was
in-itself, turns out to be a movement in which it loses its own truth;
the "path of doubt" (*Zweifel*) is transformed into "the way of despair"
(*Verzweiflung*). (*Phän.* 67; HCE 14) Moreover, this despair is not
something arbitrarily imposed on consciousness from without; it is
immanent in the very movement of consciousness itself. Thus, in
Baillie's poignant translation, consciousness "suffers this violence at
its own hands."[12]

The positive aspect of this third moment of Hegel's method is
that the process of examining knowledge, which of necessity involves
a standard, is actually (and equally necessarily) an examination of
the standard as well. And with the emergence of a new standard,
consciousness is confronted by an object which is for it new and now
true. At this point in the exposition, one is, nevertheless, compelled
to ask, "Whence this new object?" or, more skeptically, "Isn't Hegel
here attempting to justify that sleight-of-hand trick for which his
dialectical method is so notorious?"

If this "new object" is in fact the product of Hegel's "dialectical
method," the traditional charge against him is completely justified.
But Hegel's method is radically *un*dialectical. It is the experience of
consciousness itself which is dialectical, and Hegel's *Phenomenology*
is a viable philosophical enterprise precisely to the extent that it merely
describes this dialectical process. The "new object" therefore must not
be introduced by the philosopher; it must arise out of the course of
the experience described—and not merely *as* described, but through
itself.

Experience itself is therefore described as dialectical to the extent
that it generates new objects for itself. But the "new object" seems
to be no more than a reflection on the part of consciousness, a reflection
which is not based on anything objective, but merely on its knowledge
of its first object. The term "reflection," however, is misleading; it
tends to suggest something which takes place immediately. But experi-

[12] See Baillie's translation of the *Phenomenology* (London, 1931), 138.

ence is a *process*, something which takes time; and the process of experience is *constituted* by the alteration of its first object, and therewith its first standard. The alteration, in turn, must be seen as a negation of the *appearance* of the first object within consciousness' experience. Thus the negating process of alteration is not an immediate, empty, or abstract negation; the appearance which is negated has content and the alteration is a *determinate* negation (*Phän.* 68; HCE 16), which as the result of the negated appearance, also has a *content*.

Thus the "new object" is not simply the product of an immediate reflection; it is constituted by the process of negating the first object; "it is the experience constituted through that first object." (*Phän.* 73; HCE 24) But Hegel's concept of determinate negation can only be grasped through a careful analysis of (1) the role of appearance in experience and (2) why "we" must describe the experience of consciousness as a phenomenon.

Hegel's concept of experience is both more restrictive and at the same time far more inclusive than what is usually understood by the word. The intelligibility of the entire *Phenomenology* hinges upon a firm grasp of what phenomenal experience, knowing as it appears, consists in. In the first place, phenomenal experience is more restrictive than other philosophical interpretations of experience because experience, to be described as a phenomenon, must *appear*. Thus mere intentions, capacities. dispositions, meanings, etc., do not, as such, constitute experience. Insofar as such "mental entities" are recognized as the real content of experience, the attempt at phenomenological description is condemned to acknowledge the validity of Prufrock's claim: "That is not it at all, that is not what I meant, at all"; or the equally enigmatic "meaning" which is presumably expressed in the assertion "The present King of France is bald."

For Hegel, on the contrary, genuine experience *is* a self-revealing process, and philosophy is conceived as a description of this process, not as a systematic analysis of a presumed relationship between meanings and assertions. Experience is constituted by an *act*, something actually said or done. Experience is therefore revealed in language and work and what is so revealed can be *described:* it is an *act*, "and it can be *said* of it, what *it is*." (*Phän.* 236) In the act the "inexpressible meaning" is simply abolished, that is, it is expressed.

But if this restriction of experience to that which can be described appears to be a narrowing of what philosophers have usually understood by the term, the wealth of human experience[13] actually described in the *Phenomenology* is a most eloquent demonstration that Hegel's method is far more "empirical" than that of the philosophers who call themselves "empiricists."[14]

There are basically two kinds of phenomenal experience described in the *Phenomenology:* first, the acts of individual men considered in abstraction from their social and linguistic "world," and, second, the interaction of individuals within a community or a "world" in the course of its development. (*Phän.* 315) This emphasis on the forms of experience in terms of the nature of the acting subject suggests a systematic division of the *Phenomenology* into two parts.[15] The first, covering the sections called "Consciousness," "Self-Consciousness," and "Reason," is a phenomenological description of man as individual or "natural consciousness," in the various shapes (*Gestalten*) of his theoretical (in language) and practical (through labor and work) struggle for truth. The second, spanning the sections from "Spirit" through "Religion" to "Absolute Knowledge," concerns the sequence of shapes assumed by man in his life with other men, or, man as Spirit. Although Hegel himself is not entirely consistent in his account of the relations between "Spirit" and "Religion" (Compare *Phän.* 476 with 557), it is clear that the entire second half of the *Phenomenology* deals with the development of associated humanity. "All of the previous shapes of consciousness are abstractions from Spirit. . . . This abstractive isolating of such moments presupposes Spirit and requires Spirit for its subsistence." (*Phän.* 314)

We have seen that the most critical precondition for a phenomenological description of experience is the actual *appearance* of experience itself. But the term "appearance" has two distinct usages in the

[13] Richard Kroner suggests that *"Erleben"* would be a more adequate term for what Hegel describes as experience. Cf. his *Von Kant bis Hegel*, Vol. II: *Von der Naturphilosophie zur Philosophie des Geistes* (Tübingen, 1924), 374.

[14] This argument is forcefully developed by George Schrader in "Hegel's Contribution to Phenomenology," *The Monist*, 48 (1964), 18–33.

[15] The structure of the *Phenomenology* is so complex that nothing short of a detailed commentary could possibly do it justice. It is interesting to note that Hyppolite's well-known commentary on the work divides into the two parts indicated above. Cf. Jean Hyppolite, *Génèse et Structure de la Phénoménologie de l'Esprit de Hegel*, 2 vols. (Paris, 1946), 40 *et passim*. But Hyppolite's contention on page 55 that "the *Phenomenology* was for Hegel, consciously or unconsciously, the means to deliver to the public, not a complete system, but the history of his own philosophical development," seems to commit that intentional fallacy which Hegel subjected to such a devastating criticism. (*Phän.* 227–301) The most elaborate structural interpretation of the *Phenomenology* is given in the third appendix to Kojève's lectures, *op. cit.*, 574–595. These pages are now available in an English translation by Kenley and Christa Dove in Alexandre Kojève's *Introduction to the Reading of Hegel* (New York, 1969), 261–287.

Phenomenology, and Hegel's phenomenological method is bound to seem either exotic or capricious if these two usages are not distinguished. The first of these concerns the appearance of experience; the second concerns appearance *in* experience. A great deal of what is unique, and consequently "unfamiliar" about Hegel's method is based on his insight into and his consistent awareness of this twofold character of appearance throughout the *Phenomenology*. The appearance *of* experience is the condition necessary for the possibility of a phenomenological description. It is the basic presupposition of the *Phenomenology* as a philosophical work. This presupposition must also be shared by the reader. We shall discuss this problem of the appearance *of* experience in Section B below. Here attention will be directed to the problem of appearance as it is revealed *within* experience.

The experiencing subject, either as an individual or a community, tacitly or explicitly presupposes a distinction between appearance and reality (*Wesen*), between its knowledge and its standard. Appearance as such is taken to be something involving time; reality is felt to be something which is at least in principle timeless or somehow eternal. (cf. *Phän.* 558) But as long as this sense of the unchangeable remains a mere feeling, there is no experience in the proper sense of the word. Human experience must involve action. It must involve an expression of the inwardly felt reality—which as such is no reality. This is what Hegel means by an *act:* it is the revelation of "reality" through the process of letting it appear. Action, in turn, has two basic phenomenal forms: language and work.

Both forms of action entail an objectification of what is otherwise merely "meant," "intended," or "presumed" to be. Consequently the subject who actively expresses himself in the world of appearance puts himself at the same time under the *risk* that his sense of reality will be altered or perverted. (*Phän.* 237) The risk, however, is inevitable for the experiencing subject; the only seeming alternative is a solipsism of the present moment. But this is only theoretically conceivable as a "philosophical" stance which one tacitly 'intends' or 'means' to assume. As Hegel demonstrates in his opening chapter on "Sense-Certainty," it is impossible for this solipsism to say what it "means" because any saying involves *language*, and language is a form of expression or objectification. But as objectified, such a "meaning" is patently contradicted: the solipsist's "here and now," once it has been written down, becomes a "there and then." In its actual appearance, in language, "meaning" must mix with time; and by this process its semblance of atemporal reality is simply negated.

But a negation of meaning-solipsism in no way entails a negation of that sense of eternal reality for which the language of sense-certainty is merely the most immediate expression. The entire course of human experience, both individual and collective, can be viewed as a series of progressively less immediate or more mediated expressions of this quest for certainty and truth, in the form of something which will not, like Chronos, be devoured by Zeus.

Thus, with the negation of meaning-solipsism the process of letting appear begins once again. But this beginning of appearance within experience is not the same as its antecedent. The experiencing subject has changed; it has become a new subject through its objective activity. Perhaps it itself does not explicitly know this, but "we" do—and not because we have some special access to the inner recesses of its consciousness akin to that of the "omniscient narrator," which was once such a popular device of novelists.

The *Phenomenology* is not a work of that sort; in method of presentation as well as in subject matter it is far more comparable to a dramatic work.[16] Like all literature, it is an expression in language; but unlike "ordinary language" and the language of pre-Hegelian philosophers, it is purely descriptive. The course of the dramatic development is only describable because it has appeared: because there have been actual appearances within experiences and because these appearances are susceptible of being discussed and have been discussed. Under these circumstances the development of human activity and the continual dialogue about human activity can be *comprehended* by those who have a descriptive guide and who are able to master the art of reading scientific descriptions. The guide in question is the *Phenomenology*. We shall now turn to the problem of its readers.

2

The reader's most obvious source of difficulty stems, of course, from the external literary form of the *Phenomenology*. It is at best a very peculiar kind of *Lesedrama*. But the dramatic development itself is systematically interrupted by what may be described—in the felicitous phrase of Brecht—as a *Verfremdungseffekt* (estrangement-effect).[17] Every reader of the *Phenomenology* has doubtless puzzled over the significance of the *"wir"* and the *"für uns"* which periodically come into view and break up the flow of experience described. In the Preface, before the actual drama gets under way, it is clear that

---

[16] Among existing works of drama, the one which immediately suggests itself for comparison is Goethe's *Faust*. An elaboration of this comparison between the *Phenomenology* and Faust may be found in Georg Lukács, *Goethe und seine Zeit* (Bern, 1947), and in Ernst Bloch, "Das Faust-Motiv in der *Phänomenologie des Geistes*," *Hegel-Studien*, 1 (1961), 155–171.

[17] Cf. Bertold Brecht, *Schriften zum Theater* (Frankfurt, 1957).

the "we" is to be taken in the sense familiar to readers of almost any philosophical work, namely, we philosophers who are following the argument in question.

The "Introduction" may be viewed as a transition from the ordinary philosophical usage of an editorial "we" to the problematical usage of the work itself. Here Hegel comes closest to giving an explicit account of how the term "we" is to be understood in the sequel. Yet even at this juncture the reader is forced to ask himself: "Who are 'we'?"

The problem seems to become critical at two points in particular. The first concerns the determination of what shall serve as a standard within experience: object or Concept. (at *Phän.* 71; HCE 20) Hegel at first seems to suggest that "we" make the selection. But as the previous discussion has shown, he provides an answer which, in principle, preserves the purely descriptive character of his method. The second difficulty (at *Phän.* 74; HCE 24) is, unfortunately, not so easily answered.

We have already seen the general relationship of consciousness to its object, the twofold character of the Concept, and how in the course of experience consciousness brings about both an examination of its standard and emergence of a new object. All of this is intelligible as a process which takes place within experience. We have also seen that experience itself involves, by its very nature, action and appearance. Thus the process of experience is not constituted by any hidden or "inner" meanings or intentions. It is in principle describable. The problem which now emerges is that what is *for* consciousness a new object is *for us* a new attitude toward objectivity, a new shape or *Gestalt* of consciousness or Spirit. In other words, whereas consciousness itself merely seems to be related to a new object appearing *within* experience, from *our* point of view, the description of the appearance *of* experience, consciousness, the active protagonist, has itself changed.

"This way of observing the subject matter is *our* contribution; it does not exist for the consciousness which we observe. But when viewed in this way the sequence of experiences constituted by consciousness is raised to the level of a scientific progression." (*Phän.* 74; HCE 24) On the one hand, therefore, "we" seem to be merely describing what the active experience of consciousness presents for phenomenological description. On the other hand, however, "our" observation is also seen to be an act ("*unsere Zutat*") which plays a constitutive role in the drama as a whole. Moreover, as Hegel adds, without "our contribution," the drama of human experience could only have a skeptical conclusion, or rather no conclusion at all.

In view of these considerations, the descriptive character of the whole *Phenomenology* seems to become paradoxical, if not impossible.

For if our observation is regarded as totally determined by the subject matter, the development of appearance within experience, then "we" may indeed observe the coming to be and passing away of various objects of experience, but the upshot would be no more than a chronicle tracing a formless flow of phenomenal content. Insofar as the description concerned historical phenomena, our viewpoint would be that of a skeptical relativism or historicism. This has in fact been a popular characterization of what Hegel's mature philosophy of history—minus the Absolute Idea—implies. When we consider the radical temporalizing of the Concept in the *Phenomenology*, together with the conspicuous absence of talk about the Absolute Idea, the method of this work seems to entail a distinctively relativistic orientation for the "we."

If on the other hand our description of the sequence of objects experienced is raised to the level of a scientific series simply because of the fact that it is "we" who do the describing, that the description is "*unsere Zutat*," then "we" seem to be nothing short of the Absolute itself. Either our description would be carried out *sub specie aeternitatis*, or "our" addition would have the significance of an arbitrary positing, or both.

Hegel's phenomenological method, for all its cogency in the treatment of appearance *in* experience, thus seems to entail an impossible dilemma with respect to the no less important and complementary question of the appearance *of* experience. Between the Scylla of relativism and the Charybdis of constructive metaphysics there seems to be no safe passage. In view of the critical nature of this problem, it will be worthwhile to consider at this point what Hegel scholars have had to say about the "we" in the *Phenomenology*.

As one might expect, Hegel's use of the term "we" in the *Phenomenology* has been recognized by most of his commentators as, in one way or another, in need of an explanation.[18] The explanations usually provided are, however, remarkably laconic. It will therefore be feasible to expedite our brief survey of these explanations by presenting and commenting on a selection of relevant quotations from the literature. In several cases the passages cited are coextensive with the total direct discussion of the problem in the work referred to:

> *Herbert Marcuse:* The reader who is to understand the various parts of the work must already dwell in the "element of philosophy". The "We" that appears so often denotes not everyday men but philosophers.[19]

---

[18] The problem of the "we" has, however, received scant attention in Marxist-oriented studies dealing with the *Phenomenology*. It is, for example, not even mentioned by Bloch, *Subjekt-Objekt: Erläuterungen zu Hegel* (Frankfurt, 1951; 1962).

[19] Cf. Herbert Marcuse, *Reason and Revolution* (Boston, 1960), 94.

Georg Lukács: The characteristic mode of exposition consists in always clarifying for the reader that connection of the objective and subjective categories which remains hidden to the individual "shape of consciousness" then under consideration. . . . The dualism exists only for the "shapes of consciousness," not for the philosopher and consequently not for the reader. When Hegel . . . says that the decisive connections between the objectivity and subjectivity are opaque for the "shapes of consciousness" but transparent *for us,* he means for the philosophical reader, who observes this process of evolution of the human genus from a higher plane.[20]

Nicolai Hartmann: With the term "we" Hegel means the accompanying philosophical comprehension. And therein lies the possibility for philosophy, in tracing the origination [of a new shape of consciousness], to grasp its necessity as well. For it is in virtue of this possibility that "this road to science is itself already a science", a science of the experience of consciousness.[21]

Jean Hyppolite: That is why the necessity of the experience which consciousness undergoes presents itself under a double light, or rather that there are two necessities, that of the negation of the object, brought also by consciousness itself in its experience, in the examination of its knowledge, and that of the appearance of the new object which is formed through the earlier experience. (This necessity could be called *retro*spective). This second necessity only belongs to the philosopher who re-thinks the phenomenological development; there is in it a moment of the in-itself or "for us" which is not to be found in consciousness. . . . (The *Phenomenology* is *theory of knowledge* and at the same time *speculative philosophy;* but it is speculative philosophy only for us . . . which means that Hegel's *Phenomenology* is at the same time a *description* of phenomenal consciousness and a *comprehension* of this description by the philosopher). . . . (The succession of the "experiences" of consciousness is thus contingent only for phenomenal consciousness. As for us who are gathering these experiences, we discover at the same time the necessity of the progression, which goes from the one to the other. The *Phenomenology* demonstrates the immanence of all experience in consciousness. Moreover, it must be recognized that this (synthetic) necessity is not always easy to grasp and the transition sometimes appears arbitrary to the modern reader. This transition also poses the problem of the connection between history and the *Phenomenology.*)[22]

Richard Kroner: In the *Phenomenology* there are thus two moving series running parallel to each other: that of the observed object, the

---

[20] Cf. G. Lukács, *Der junge Hegel: Über die Beziehungen von Dialektik und Ökonomie* (Zürich and Vienna, 1948). The translation of this passage and the others through the Heidegger excerpt are by the present author.

[21] Hartmann, *op. cit.*, 317.

[22] Hyppolite, *op. cit.*, 29–30. Cf. also 81 and 104.

wandering "soul" which passes from experience to experience, and that of the observer who surveys this progress from the end of the road and comprehends it as the self-actualization of the Absolute. Each step which "natural" consciousness advances thus becomes a doubly necessary one; or *the necessity of each step appears under a double light.* On the one hand consciousness is urged forward on the basis of its own experience, . . . on the other hand, however, the necessity of the first self-movement is placed into the light of Absolute Knowledge and is comprehended as a necessity by the observer who has already reached that goal towards which consciousness directs itself and which in truth attracts the wandering ego to itself.[23]

Martin Heidegger: Who are the "we"?

They are those who in the inversion of natural consciousness let it persist in its own meaning and opinion but at the same time and expressly look at the appearance of the appearing. This looking-at, which expressly watches the appearance, is the watching as which the skepsis fulfills itself, the skepsis which has looked ahead to the absoluteness of the absolute and has in advance provided itself with it. That which comes to light in thoroughgoing skepticism shows itself "for us", i.e. for those who, thinking upon the beingness of being, are already provided with Being. . . .

The contribution accordingly wills the will of the absolute. The contribution itself is what is willed by the absoluteness of the absolute. . . . The contribution gives prominence to the fact that and the manner in which we, in watching, are akin to the absoluteness of the absolute.[24]

The passages here assembled provide an instructive spectrum of possibilities for envisaging the "philosophical we" but they also show how an interpretation of the "we" tends to govern—or be governed by—one's view of the *Phenomenology* as a whole. The following discussion will thus enable us not only to survey the field of Hegel scholarship through the prism of this vital issue; it will also afford an occasion for systematically developing the argument of this essay.

The first point of critical importance which, consciously or unconsciously, divides these scholars is the degree of significance they attach to the inverted commas which they place around the "we" or "for us." Only Marcuse and Lukács draw explicit attention to the fact that the "we" refers to the readers of the *Phenomenology*. Thus the problem of the intelligibility of the dramatic activity to the "audience" is elevated to a position of prominence. When the "we" is understood to denote readers such as "you or I," then the *Verfremdungseffekt* serves to remind us first that we are the public, the audience, and second, that *what* we as audience are seeing or have seen in an appearance

[23] Kroner, *op. cit.*, 369–370.
[24] Heidegger, *Holzwege* (Frankfurt, 1950), 173 and 175.

in public space.[25] This prevents us from losing our descriptive perspective by, for example, becoming absorbed in the public action of the play as if it were the private experience of a protagonist.[26] It does not, on the other hand, estrange us from the standpoint of description, tacitly or explicitly suggesting that the "we" stands for some extraordinary intelligence which we readers see through a glass but darkly.

Marcuse's observation that the intelligibility of the *Phenomenology* is only open to those readers who "already dwell in the 'element of philosophy' " is clearly incontestable, but it is not clear from his remarks just what this "element" is. In a subsequent passage, he suggests that this "element" is the philosophy of transcendental idealism. But this is also problematical since, as Hartmann points out, transcendental idealism is not accepted in the *Phenomenology* as a thesis but is rather treated as a historical phenomenon, one of the stages of consciousness described.[27] Although Hyppolite mentions the peculiar difficulties faced by "the modern reader" in following the translation in the *Phenomenology*, as well as the problematical relationship of the *Phenomenology* and history, his extensive study has little to say about the specific preconditions for intelligible reading, whether in 1946 or 1807.[28]

---

[25] The most frequent contexts for the appearance of "we" in the main body of the *Phenomenology* are "Jetzt sehen wir" or "wir sehen."

[26] Jacob Loewenberg's imaginative proposal that the "we" engages in an alternating process of "histrionically impersonating" consciousness and experiencing its "comic denouement" systematically encourages this misunderstanding. The argument is formulated in Loewenberg's introduction to the Scribner edition of *Hegel Selections* (New York, 1929), in his two *Mind* articles (October 1934 and January 1935), and in *Hegel's Phenomenology: Dialogues in the Life of Mind* (LaSalle, Ill., (1965). Emil Fackenheim suggests that the reader of the *Phenomenology* is not the "we" but "must" as it were, hover *between* the viewing and the viewed standpoints." (*The Religious Dimension in Hegel's Thought* [Bloomington, Ind., 1967], 36). Unfortunately the notion of "hovering" is never clearly formulated in Fackenheim's interesting book.

[27] Hartmann, *op. cit.*, 338.

[28] Hyppolite does, however, offer a clue to answering this problem in a subsequent remark which does not directly deal with the problem of the philosophical "we." He writes: "But it is only the *universal individuality*, that which has been able to lift itself to absolute knowledge, which must find again in it and develop in itself the moments implied in its becoming. It is the same consciousness which, having reached philosophical knowledge, turns back upon itself and which, as empirical consciousness, goes upon the phenomenological itinerary. In order to indicate to others the road of absolute knowledge, it must find it back in itself. . . . That which for it is reminiscence and interiorization, must be for the others the road of their ascension. But this individuality itself, as far as it is individuality, carries necessarily elements of particularity; it is bound to time and for it the French Revolution or the period of enlightenment have more importance than other historical events. Isn't there an irreducible contingency in this?" (Hyppolite, *op. cit.*, 50. Cf. 80). [See Professor Hyppolite's remarks in Chapter iv of the present volume.—Ed.]

The only writer who directly deals with the problem is Lukács. He suggests that the appearance *of* the various "shapes of consciousness is intelligible for the philosophical reader because he (the "we") observes the developmental process of the human genus from a "higher plane." The higher plane is said to be that of "objective Spirit" or the perspective of history.[29] This historical approach to the problem of the "we" is very suggestive, but in Lukács' discussion it has two distinct shortcomings as a general hypothesis: (i) the specific nature of the historical preconditions for the "we" is not developed (for example, in connection with Hegel's references on pages 15ff. of his Preface to "our age," ca. 1806, as a "new world"), and (ii) Lukács expressly limits this interpretation of the "we" to what he calls the "first part" of the *Phenomenology*, "Subjective Spirit."[30] For the second and third parts of his triadically divided *Phenomenology* he offers no explanation for the "philosophical we"—which nevertheless continues to appear.

The citation from Hartmann adds to this discussion a recognition of the problem of "our" grasping the "necessity" in the sequence of consciousness' experiences, thus enabling "us" to raise this sequence to a scientific series, "a science of the experience of consciousness." But it is only Kroner and Hyppolite who develop the problem of the *structure* of "necessity" in the *Phenomenology*. In the terminology of this study, both scholars recognize that there is (a) a process of necessity *within* experience, the process in which consciousness judges its knowledge by its own standard and consequently tests its standard and alters its object, as well as (b) the necessity *of* experience as a noncontingent series observed by us. As the foregoing discussion has shown, it is this second kind of necessity which is most problematical and crucial for an understanding of the philosophical "we."

It is noteworthy that, of the two, only Hyppolite speaks of this second necessity in terms of *appearance*. But it is an appearance of a peculiarly "retrospective" nature. The "we" or the philosopher is said to be already (and not merely implicitly) at the level of "speculative philosophy" and, on Hyppolite's reading, the appearance *of* experience seems to provide the philosopher something like an *occasion* to rethink the phenomenological development, which he has presumably already, in some sense, experienced. In view of the historical preconditions for "our" phenomenological comprehension suggested by Hegel in his Preface, this is at least a partially plausible assumption. One is, however, led to ask Hyppolite whether the standpoint of "speculative philosophy" is itself attainable without having *first* rethought the phe-

---

[29] Lukács divides the *Phenomenology* according to the Triad of Spirit in the *Encyclopedia*.
[30] Cf. Lukács, *op. cit.*, 602.

nomenological development presented in the *Phenomenology*. This surely would seem to follow from Hegel's description of the *Phenomenology* as an *introduction*, and a necessary introduction, to speculative philosophy or, since for Hegel they are equivalent, to Logic. (*Phän.* 33)[31] Hegel observes that the *System der Erfahrung des Geistes* ("System of the experience of Spirit") only embraces the *appearance* of this experience (*Phän.* 33), and he clearly does not set down systematic philosophy as a precondition for grasping the systematic character of this experience. It is manifest that the reverse of this is proposed.[32]

If then our critique of Hyppolite has hit its mark, Kroner's interpretation of the philosophical observer, or "we," is even less viable. Not mentioning the problem of the *appearance of* experience, he asserts that the "we" grasps the necessity in the sequence of natural consciousness' experiences from the standpoint of the goal toward which it is striving, from the *end* of its pathway, which the "*we*" recognizes as the "self-realization of the Absolute." Kroner's version of the "we" has already arrived at the level of Absolute Knowledge. But if this interpretation were accepted, one could give no plausible answer to Hegel's "rhetorical" question: "one might simply dispense with the negative as something *false* and thus demand to be led to the truth without further ado; why bother oneself about that which is false?" (*Phän.* 33)

The most detailed and provocative interpretation of the "we" problem in Hegel's *Phenomenology* is found in Heidegger's essay, *Hegel's Concept of Experience*. He alone explicitly poses the question "Who are the 'we'?", and his answer to the question constitutes the heart of his proposal for a reading of the entire book.[33] Like the other commentators, Heidegger assumes that the "we" has some kind of privileged access to the Absolute. But the superiority of the "we" over natural consciousness is not attributed to its "higher" historical standpoint (Lukács) or to its ultimately mystical and irrational intuition (Kroner). Heidegger's account is distinguished by the claim that the

---

[31] Hyppolite makes up the question of the relationship of the *Phenomenology* to the *Logic* in the last chapter of his commentary. His discussion includes for this reader a novel argument showing how the *Logic* may be regarded as the standpoint "*für uns*" in the *Phenomenology* and the *Phenomenology*, reciprocally, as the standpoint "*für uns*" in the *Logic*. Cf. Hyppolite, *op. cit.*, 560ff. But this discussion also leaves unanswered the problem of the philosophical "we" *qua* reader in the *Phenomenology*.

[32] Cf. also *Phänomonologie des Geistes*, 25ff. and *Wissenschaft der Logik*, I, 30 (Lasson edition, Leipzig, 1923).

[33] Heidegger, *op. cit.*, 188. An English translation appears in Heidegger's *Hegel's Concept of Experience* (New York, 1970), 149. References to *Holzwege* in the following paragraphs will be indicated by *Holz.* and to the English translation by HCE.

"we" is akin to the Absolute through the fact that it lets consciousness be, that it keeps its own standards out of the self-investigation of consciousness. No one has seen more clearly than Heidegger that "our contribution" consists in the act of restraint in the face of the appearance *of* experience, that "our contribution" is the omission of all contributions. (*Holz.* 174; HCE 128)

The peculiarity of Heidegger's interpretation is found in his tendency to identify the "we" of the *Phenomenology* with the fundamental ontologist of his own writings. Thus he refers to the consciousness described in the *Phenomenology*, natural consciousness, as "ontic consciousness" (*Holz.* 161; HCE 105), whereas the "we" is said to think "the Beingness of being" and to be therefore "already provided with Being (*Sein*)." Heidegger accordingly reads the *Phenomenology* as "a dialogue between ontic and ontological consciousness" (*Holz.* 185; HCE 144), or between natural consciousness and absolute knowledge. (*Holz.* 186; HCE 146) This dialogue is precisely what he regards as Hegel's concept of experience. The "we" is said to be receptive to that ontological dimension of consciousness' experience which remains invisible for natural or ontic consciousness because what appears *within* this experience excludes the appearance *of* experience for consciousness. But the "we," in its "thoroughgoing skepticism," does not interfere with the appearance *within* consciousness' experience and thus lets the "new object," and therewith the Being of experience itself, appear.

Heidegger's interpretation rests upon his contention that the term "Being" may be used to refer to what Hegel calls Spirit. (*Holz.* 142; HCE 69) But Hegel's sense of Being (Spirit) is said to suffer from the forgetfulness characteristic of post-Socratic metaphysics in that Being is implicitly regarded as *will*. (*Holz.* 187f.; HCE 148f., and *Holz.* 120; HCE 30) The ontological knowledge of the "we" is therefore defective because (i) it has not yet made explicit and radicalized the traditional metaphysics of Being as will (an achievement Heidegger attributes to Nietzsche's writings on the will-to-power), and (ii) it has not yet grasped the necessity of systematically destroying traditional metaphysics (the task which Heidegger himself claims to have undertaken). But Heidegger's interpretation of Spirit in the *Phenomenology* as Being, and Being as Will, rests upon his interpretation of the "we" as a mode of consciousness. For him, "Everything depends upon thinking the experience mentioned here [in the *Phenomenology*] as the Being of consciousness. (*Holz.* 171; HCE 121)

The safest generalization about Heidegger's essay is that it uses the Introduction to the *Phenomenology* as a touchstone for elucidating some important elements of his own fundamental ontology. As such it is a valuable document for the student who seeks to grasp the relationship between *Sein und Zeit* and the "late" Heidegger. And while it is in many respects a stimulating exercise for the Hegel student. it can be singularly misleading if taken literally as a commentary on the *Phenomenology*. For the *Phenomenology* is *not* an ontology (Hegel's *Logic* may be properly spoken of as his ontology);[34] it is a *phenomenology* and can only be understood if it is read as such.[35]

The most remarkable feature of Heidegger's interpretation of the philosophical "we" is that it focuses upon the dark passage in the next last page of the "Introduction" dealing with "*unsere Zutat.*" (*Phän.* 74; HCE 24–25) But perhaps this is not so remarkable after all, for when we look closely at the studies of Kroner. Hartmann, and Hyppolite, we find that their definitive utterances on the "we" also take the form of analyses of *Phän.* 74. It seems to this writer a matter of no mean consequence that four of the six scholars cited tend to so limit their attention in defining a term on whose comprehension intelligibility in *reading* the *Phenomenology* hinges. If, in addition, one recalls Hegel's frequent critical comments on prefaces and introductions to philosophical works. it is reasonable to assume that he too would be highly skeptical of a general definition which is based on a passage where, in the language of contemporary semantical theory the term is, from the viewpoint of the work as a whole, metalinguistically "mentioned" rather than dramatically "used."

In point of fact, the term "we" and its variants are *used* repeatedly throughout the *Phenomenology*. Rather than adding any further speculations on the 'real' meaning of "*unsere Zutat,*" perhaps it might be more fruitful to arrive at a comprehension of who "we" are through the process of "working the matter out." In the following paragraphs certain working hypotheses will be stated. but these can only be provisional; their only verification can be an enhanced comprehension on the part of a reader who works his way through the *Phenomenology* itself.

First. let us gather together the helpful suggestions which have emerged from our view of Hegel scholarship.

(1) Following Marcuse, our attention must be fixed on the problem of *intelligibility* in the *Phenomenology* and (2) with Lukács this intelligibility is to be sought, insofar as possible, in connection with the specific prerequisites for comprehension by "us" as intelligent (but also human) *readers*. (3) As Hyppolite has pointed out, certain of these prerequisites are *historical*. (4) All the while, we must not forget

---

[34] Cf. Heidegger's discussion of the *Logic* in his *Identität und Differenz* (Pfullingen, 1957).

[35] Cf. T. W. Adorno's critique of Heidegger's Hegel interpretation in his *Drei Studien zu Hegel* (Frankfurt, 1963), 69.

that, as Hartmann observes, "we" must grasp the *necessity* in the development of the described consciousness' experiences. It will be of singular importance to comprehend just what this necessity consists in. (5) But our comprehension of this necessity will be clouded if we neglect to distinguish between the *two* parallel processes of necessity at work in the *Phenomenology*, as Kroner indicates.

The first and absolutely essential stage in the actualization of the reader's already implicitly philosophical (in Hegel's sense) comprehension (that is, the first of the two processes of necessity) is found in working through the section called "Consciousness." (*Phen.* I–III) It is here that Hegel shows that the "we," contra Heidegger, cannot be understood as a mode of consciousness, for in his explication of the result of "Consciousness" (*Phän.* 133–140) the "we" comes to see that the "I" of consciousness is first *constituted* through the interaction of the "we" and that the unity in question in the *Phenomenology* is not (as in Heidegger) the unity of consciousness and Being but the "spiritual unity" in reciprocal recognition. It is this "spiritual unity" which constitutes the Concept of Spirit. (*Phän.* 140–141) But the way out of consciousness' meaning-solipsism cannot be simply "pointed out"; it must be worked through. In doing so, the reader must note Hegel's peculiar use of the word "we" in this section. For it is only in "Consciousness" (and in subsequent references back to *Phen.* I–III) that the "we" is seen to play the role (*zum Bei-spiel*) of the consciousness presented, to *speak* for it and *write* for it (*Phän.* 81), immediately and passively *observe* for it (*Phän.* 85), as well as perceive for it (*Phän.* 95), and actively participate in its Concept (*Phän.* 103).[36] Moreover, "we" are able so to relate ourselves, not because it is some primordial experience and the "we" "is the Absoluteness of the Absolute" (with Heidegger), or because the "we" is a speculative Hegelian philosopher (with Hyppolite), or because the "we" enjoys the privileged access of Absolute Knowledge (with Kroner). Both the consciousness in question and "we" ourselves are already in the element of *pre*-Hegelian philosophy.[37] Indeed, the section called "Consciousness" is the most clearly philosophical of the entire work—when philosophy is understood as the theory of knowledge. And

---

[36] This is the only section of the *Phenomenology* which presents any *prima facie* grounds for Loewenberg's interpretive notion of "histrionic impersonation." It is perhaps worth noting that Loewenberg's *Mind* articles, mentioned above (footnote 26), written thirty years before his commentary on the *Phenomenology* as a whole, developed the "histrionic" thesis in connection with an analysis focusing on *Phenomenology*, I–III.

[37] The term "pre-Hegelian" is to be understood in a systematic and not merely a chronological sense.

this is so because it must enable its readers to get beyond "philosophy," beyond the "love of knowledge" and thus to begin to know. (*Phän.* 12)

Hegel, contrary to many a legend, demonstrates in the *Phenomenology* a great respect for his readers. This, rather than his reputedly esoteric and didactic style, is a more probable source of "unintelligibility" to the readers of the *Phenomenology*. He recognized that the individual reader has "the right to demand that science at least provide him with the ladder to this standpoint [the element of philosophy], and show him this standpoint within himself." (*Phän.* 25) The ladder which Hegel extends in the opening three chapters of the *Phenomenology* is a "ladder language" quite unlike that of Wittgenstein's *Tractatus*. It *does* enable "our" theoretical orientation to rise above the level of solipsism, mystical or otherwise, because it destroys the "myth of meaning" underlying the "paradox of learning" which has plagued philosophical thought since Socrates.

In these chapters Hegel shows that meaning remains a myth and learning remains paradoxical as long as the ultimate subject is taken to have the egological structure of consciousness. Consciousness *is* dialectical because it presumes to give an account of its experience in terms of the ego and its other. But by playing the role of consciousness, *we* come to see at the end of Chapter III of the *Phenomenology* that consciousness' attempt at self-explication results, when pushed to the limit, in an inversion of consciousness and its world. (*Phän.* 121ff) To see this inversion is "our contribution," an act of restraint through which we are finally able to relinquish the standpoint of consciousness.

We may agree with Heidegger that the *Phenomenology* presents us with a dialogue. But the protagonists are not the ontic and ontological modes of consciousness' experience. They are rather consciousness and Spirit. The dialogue itself is consciousness' (not Hegel's) voyage to the discovery that it *is* Spirit. For *us*, this dramatic dialogue begins when the Concept of Spirit reveals itself to us (*Phän.* 140), when we no longer take ourselves to be substitution instances of the protagonist consciousness. Heidegger's brilliant exposition of the "Introduction" founders on just this issue. He fails to see that the Concept of Spirit is inexplicable in terms of consciousness or its ontic and ontological modalities of experience. The "I" of consciousness must rather be grasped as constituted through the "we" of Spirit. And when "we," the readers of the *Phenomenology*, grasp this, the "we" becomes, for the first time, "we" in Hegel's distinctive sense of the word. As such, "we" are able to witness the dialogue between consciousness and Spirit through which consciousness works out in concrete detail (*Phen.* IV–VIII), what "we" have come to grasp merely *ex negativo* and in principle. (*Phen.* I–III)

In the concluding paragraph to the "Introduction," Hegel says

consciousness will reach a point (*Punkt*) at which it casts off the semblance of being burdened by something alien to it, something which is only *for* it and which exists as an other. In other words, at that point where its appearance becomes equal to its essence, consciousness' presentation of itself will therefore converge with this very same point in the authentic science of Spirit. (*Phen.* 75; HCE 26)

The suggestion which follows from the argument of this essay is that the "point" referred to is the transition to Chapter IV of the *Phenomenology*. "In self-consciousness, as the Concept of Spirit, consciousness has for the first time reached its turningpoint (*Wendungspunkt*)." (*Phän.* 140)

These texts suggest that the *method* of Hegel's *Phenomenology* is developed in two stages. The first (*Phen.* I–III) is a dialogue between consciousness and the "we" in which the "we" participates. The result of this dialogue is that consciousness, through its inversion, comes to present itself to us as the appearance *of* experience, whose essence (Spirit) *we* no longer distinguish from its appearance. Since we no longer interfere with consciousness (as at *Phän.* 81, 85, 95, 103), "our contribution" *becomes* "the pure act of observation." (*Phän.* 72; HCE 21) The second stage (*Phen.* IV–VIII) is accordingly "the authentic science of Spirit," the *Phenomenology of Spirit* rather than consciousness. At this point *we* have grasped the essence of consciousness.

The "Introduction" ends with these words: "And finally, when consciousness itself grasps this its essence, it will indicate the nature of absolute knowledge itself." (*Phän.* 75; HCE 26)

iv

HEGEL'S PHENOMENOLOGY AND PSYCHOANALYSIS*

Jean Hyppolite

The title of this article may seem by itself strange and enigmatic. Relating Hegel's phenomenology to psychoanalysis seems to break all historical laws and the principle of the irreversibility of time. We must admit that there was no historical influence of Hegel on the founder of psychoanalysis. Seemingly, Freud had not read Hegel. May we not relate this "gap" in such a broad education to Freud's telling in confidence that in order to avoid the risk of letting himself be influenced in the originality of his own discoveries, he had refused to read Nietzsche in spite of the gratifications he might have received from this reading?

On the other hand, common sense, so it seems, does not allow

---

* Translated from the French by Albert Richer.

us to speak of retrospective influence, a sort of influence going upstream in time from Freud to Hegel. However, I would like first of all to justify such absurdity, because it involves some truth, which is *retrospection*. Bearing this in mind, I shall recall Freud's wonderful text in *The Science of Dreams*[1] where he tells us Oedipus' tragedy, showing him to us as he is racing to his destiny, and where he says all of a sudden, in one of those profound observations which lend a delightful charm to reading Freud (I do not say Freudians, with a few exceptions): "But this is psychoanalysis!" This unfolds like a psychoanalysis; psychoanalysis is a type of drama, just like the gradual discovery Oedipus makes of himself. I shall also compare with this, the text in which Freud tells us that a psychoanalysis ends in a sentence such as: "I have known this all the time"; the very moment the psychoanalyzed himself recognizes this, his analysis is over.

Well, we shall try to view Hegel's phenomenology in an interpretation which is, properly speaking, retrospective and in a sense which is not really different from that of Freudian psychoanalysis in such texts. To reread phenomenology in this way would consist in viewing the totality of this difficult and meandering work as the true Oedipus tragedy of the entire human mind, except that the final revelation—what Hegel calls "absolute knowledge"—will remain ambiguous and enigmatic.

How can we recapture, within a relatively limited space, the totality of *The Phenomenology of Mind* from a certain aspect? As a guideline for our interpretation, we shall choose the following proposition: The notion of truth as a revelation is established by the intercommunication of human self-consciousnesses, by mutual recognition, and by language which replaces the problem of God. Perhaps we should go back to Rousseau to find the source of this new way of stating the problem of truth. Whereas for Cartesians, for example, consciousness in its solitude appeals to God in order to guarantee its truth and then, armed with divine evidence, returns to its own kind, for Hegel, on the contrary, universal self-consciousness is elaborated and truth is revealed in the sole play of intercommunication between consciousness, and in language. This problem is developed through the entire phenomenology, but is repeated on various levels. We intend to recapture four of these stages.

1. The Itinerary of Consciousness, Its Misknowledge of Itself

The first stage which corresponds to the Introduction of the *Phenomenology* might be called the *unconsciousness—or the uncon-*

[1] Sigmund Freud, *The Interpretation of Dreams, Works*, trans. J. Strachey (London, 1953), IV, 261–264.

scious—of consciousness. In this text[2] (on which Heidegger has given such an admirable and biased commentary—for only minds with a great bias are great minds), Hegel presents to us the consciousness which he calls *natural* (we do not say that it is naïve). It may be the consciousness of the man in the street as well as that of scientists who are engaged in psychoanalysis. It is a natural consciousness which, by the way, cannot help being natural: consciousness ignorant of itself which, in one of its fundamental traits, is radically unconscious.

A radical unconsciousness of self might be called a *function of unconsciousness of consciousness.* Consciousness sees and yet does not see itself. Consciousness, in the process of knowing, fails to recognize. But do not let us forget that to fail to recognize is not completely equivalent to not to know; to fail to recognize is to know in order to be able to recognize and say one day: "I have known this all the time." He who fails in a certain way to recognize himself knows himself. Thus, whereas natural consciousness is fundamentally unconsciousness of self, it is also in a certain manner, by failing to recognize itself, enabled one day to recognize itself.

We have perhaps here a key to the problem of the unconscious; it is not a thing behind a thing, but fundamentally a certain spirit of consciousness, a certain inevitable way for natural consciousness to be itself. Hence, we might speak of a certain ontological unconsciousness of consciousness.

> Natural consciousness will prove itself to be only knowledge in principle or not real knowledge. Since, however, it immediately takes itself to be the real and genuine knowledge, the pathway on which it travels has a negative significance from its point of view; what is a realization of the notion of knowledge means for it rather the ruin and overthrow of itself, so to speak; for on this road it loses its own truth. Because of that, the road can be looked on as the path of doubt, or more properly, a highway of despair.[3]

[2] See Heidegger's treatment of Hegel's concept of experience in his *Holzwege* (Frankfurt, 1952). Heidegger has commented on the introduction to Hegel's *Phenomenology* by referring to his own philosophical works such as *Sein und Zeit* and *Was ist Metaphysik?*. In his work, Heidegger seeks the *meaning of being*, the fundamental ontology which presupposes an analysis of our existence of the *Dasein*, that we are. He sought to separate the presuppositions of all Western metaphysics from the pre-Socratics to Nietzsche, who announces the end of metaphysics. Dr. Jacques Lacan has translated one of Heidegger's texts into French in the *Revue de Psychanalyse* 1 (1956).

[3] G. W. F. Hegel, *La Phénoménologie de L'Esprit*, trans. J. Hyppolite (Paris: Aubier, 1939–1941), I, 69; *Phen.* 135. [Citations to Hegel's *Phänomenologie des Geistes* which follow will be from this two-volume French translation by Professor Hyppolite. Additional notations preceded by *Phen.*, as above, refer to pages in the English translation by Baillie.—Ed.]

This is precisely the path of Oedipus' tragedy. It is the way of self-discovery, in this self-unconscious consciousness. So there is a kind of itinerary, and consciousness is embarked all at once on a voyage which is called experience. And the very theme of Hegel's *Phenomenology* is the presentation of this voyage as a voyage.

The beginning of our quotation illustrates this function of unconsciousness of consciousness: "Natural consciousness will prove itself to be only knowledge in principle." So it *is* something in its unconsciousness. It has already some glimmer of itself. We do not say that it is subconscious, which would only mask the contradiction. Ontologically speaking, consciousness does not see itself. However, it can only be a consciousness, because it sees itself to a certain extent. Otherwise it would see nothing. It sees only through a veil, in a state of nonseeing. In this failure to recognize, it is already capable of recognizing itself some day, and that is what Hegel claims "to be only knowledge in principle," that is, an anticipation of knowledge; and for being an anticipation of itself and for being at war and astray, it is an experience and an itinerary. It would like to stop, but it cannot, because it is more than a natural consciousness. However, as a natural consciousness, it naturalizes again each truth that it discovers. This is basically the fate of all great discoveries, whether those of Freud, or in Freud himself. This is to say that there exists a kind of natural transposition of an original discovery which cannot see itself anymore and cannot stop, nevertheless. In this sense Hegel's "natural consciousness" is necessarily the form in which whoever thinks to have arrived at the end, presents himself.

There still remains one enigma in this Introduction to Hegel's text. Who is the "we" which sees so clearly in a consciousness that does not see itself? Phenomenology taken as a whole is precisely an answer to that question. We shall have to find this "we," whereas it is presented at the beginning as a "being for us." This "being for us"—or, say, this "philosopher" in the Introduction of the *Phenomenology*—may be understood within a very concrete frame of reference, that of "educational novels" the first of which was the *Emile* of Rousseau. (And it would also be exciting to read *La Nouvelle Héloïse* as a psychoanalysis.) There are two characters in *Emile*. The one is essentially consciousness which experiences; the other (with a great deal of patience, by the way) watches our experiencing subject. There is the tutor and there is the other.

Now the problem is to know the relationship which exists between this "we," this tutor who, to a certain extent, is the descendant of God, and natural consciousness, on the other hand, which is always ontologically ignorant of itself. If "we" see clearly in this consciousness and already know its truth, is it not enough to relate immediately what it really is to what it believes itself to be? For Hegel, this solution, this kind of shortcut to phenomenology, is radically impossible. In fact, "what we should assert to be its essence would rather be, not the truth of knowledge, but only our knowledge of it."[4] This is a very profound statement. If the psychoanalyst believes he can read the history of his patient by his symptoms and informs him of his discovery, he will fail. In fact, his patient would not recognize this truth, since it would be read to him, so to speak, without his reading it within himself. And by this very token, this truth would be an error.

> The essence or the criterion would lie in us [in us, the philosophers] and that which was to be compared with this standard, and on which a decision was to be made as a result of this comparison, would not necessarily have to recognize that criterion.[5]

Thus there is no other way of truth for our natural consciousness than this long journey which leads it to read its own truth.

2. Self-Consciousness, Its Mirror in the Alter Ego—I and the Other

We do not yet foresee all the detours of this journey. Is progress toward knowledge for a consciousness ignorant of itself not simply a discovery of its own self by turning round to itself? Thus, phenomenology would include two chapters: natural consciousness and self-consciousness. Now, Hegel's famous theme of "self-consciousness"—"Lordship and bondage" (master and slave) appears only as a stage in the very first chapters of his *Phenomenology*. I would like to give some idea as to the key to this enigma by proposing a title for this dialectic stage, which will "speak" to Dr. Lacan's audience while expressing exactly the drama performed in this very abstract Hegelian text: *Self-consciousness as a mirror play*.[6]

Now, this chapter by Hegel is also a chapter on life. It is paradoxical for us, since a human self-consciousness is not only a living consciousness, a desire to live, for this desire does not actually presuppose a fundamental otherness. We are thinking of the theme of Paul

---

[4] *Ibid.*, I, 73; *Phen.* 140.
[5] *Loc. cit.*
[6] Dr. Jacques Lacan is a French psychoanalyst who has prepared an interpretation of the complete works of Freud, often attaining insights from the philosophers. His seminars have exerted an influence on contemporary French youth. His writings have recently been collected in a volume: *J. Lacan; Ecrits* (Editions du Seuil, 1966). Dr. Lacan has stressed the spoken word and language in psychoanalysis and the "mirror phase" (*"stade du miroir"*) in the development of consciousness.

Valéry's *La Jeune Parque*, as she recalls the time previous to all injury:

> Blent with desire, I was obedience's
> Self, imminent on candid knees;
> My wishes were fulfilled by impulses
> So quick my cause was hardly quick as they!
> Toward luminous senses swam my fair clay,
> And as in ardent natural peace I dreamed,
> All these infinite stops eternal seemed.
> Until, O Splendor, the enemy at my feet,
> My shadow . . .

. . . but something looms up here which is already otherness. One can see in this the relation between life and the consciousness of life—which implies the meaning of death.

Hence, vital desire does not really know otherness, or transcends it, as in sexuality. "Life" Hegel says, "refers to something else than what it is."[7] It refers to the meaning of life; but the meaning of life is tested in something else than life, in the formation of an Alien Ego.

"The I is another." Maybe Rimbaud did not attribute to this sentence all the meaning we have given it. Self-consciousness exists as Ego only if it sees itself in another self-consciousness; phenomenology presents us here in abstract terms the scheme of otherness, where the "mirror" relationship is essential. We might say that the double (Hegel says "duplication") is fundamental in self-consciousness. Understand by this that self-consciousness is not confined somewhere within a biological organism. It is a relation, and a relation to the other. But it is related to the other on condition that the other be I; related to me on condition that I be the other. This is what Hegel calls *the infinite*, characterized by a double meaning, which is expressed in the contradiction of the double, the *alter ego*, with *alter* and with *ego*.

"For self-consciousness." Hegel begins to say, "there is another self-consciousness. It presents itself to it as coming from *the outside*."[8] This is indeed fundamental: to exist as Ego, I have to *find* another—emphasizing the word "to find"—for if I do this, it is no more another. Now, this involves us in the play of the double meaning: "Self-consciousness has lost itself, for it finds itself to be *another* essence"; if I find another Ego, I am lost, since I find my Ego as another. But the double meaning is that consciousness "has by this very fact sublated *the other*, for it does not see the other as an essence, but what it sees in the other is *itself*." So, there is a kind of endless race in which

---

[7] Hegel, *op. cit.*, I, 152; *Phen.* 224.
[8] *Ibid.*, I, 155; *"La conscience de soi doublée"*; *Phen.* 229.

self-consciousness, as distinguished from life, never reaches itself. If it now attempts to sublate the other, this has again a double meaning. First, it must set itself to sublate the *other* independent being in order thereby to acquire its self-certainty as a true being. Secondly, it thereupon proceeds to sublate its own self, for this other is itself.

And we can easily see how this seemingly abstract dialectic is the scheme of the "absent-present" play which Freud talks about.[9] In the play of presence and absence, the child who has perhaps lost his mother or the person in charge of him, has even done much worse. He has lost himself by placing himself below the mirror. For in the end, by making the other disappear, I also make myself disappear. But by making the other appear, I also lose myself, I am out of myself, in a certain sense, since I see myself as another.

Now Hegel's real discovery is that there is no sense speaking of an Ego outside this relationship. Not only that, this relationship, in spite of the chain of double meaning, is still too one-sided to form an Ego: "This movement of self-consciousness in its relationship with another self-consciousness has therefore been represented as the *operation of one* of the self-consciousnesses"; now *the operation* itself must be two-sided; it must be double, shared and mutual operation of each consciousness. In order to recognize the other as Ego, I must see him do to myself what I see myself do to him.

We grasp the interplay of two consciousnesses which not only see themselves in each other, but also *see themselves as seeing themselves* in each other, and missing each other at the same time, is a reciprocity expressed in the following words: "They recognize themselves as mutually recognizing each other."[10]

We will not insist here on the sequence of a text which is well-known, the struggle for life and death between the opposed self-consciousnesses, and "master and slave." We shall bring out only the two implications of this dialectic, which are apparently quite opposed.

The first is that at the end of this struggle we have the impression that self-consciousness has fallen back upon itself, that, to a certain extent, it has made otherness disappear. It is the *unhappy consciousness*. Consciousness is unhappy because it has engaged in labor and sorrow. It has changed what is considered to be the master into something which is there and which it does not reach, unchanging consciousness. Otherness has become the Superego. This god has been produced by consciousness which, as a result, judges itself only guilty and buries itself in its guilt, transplanting into itself the relationship between

---

[9] S. Freud, *Beyond the Pleasure Principle*, *Works*, trans. J. Strachey (London, 1955), XVIII, 15f. See Dr. Lacan's paper given at the 1953 Rome Convention and published in *La Psychanalyse*, 1 (1955), 162ff.
[10] Hegel, *op. cit.*, I, 157; *Phen.* 231.

lordship and bondage. And a whole theme could be taken up in the formation of sinning consciousness, or of guilty.[11]

But the mirror play of self-consciousness in this movement of Hegelian consciousness does not come to a dead end. We might say that the abstract scheme we presented is the fundamental experience required to form a human self-consciousness. And first of all, human self-consciousness must be formed as a "mirror," so that history itself will be possible. The concrete figures that we shall deal with are possible only in *the element* of self-consciousness (in the meaning implied when one speaks about the sea element, for example), and this element could be defined in the following words: The essence of man is to be mad, that is, to be himself in the other, to be himself by this very otherness.

3. The Alienation of Self-Consciousness, the Law of the Heart and Delight

In this repeated tragedy (not in the sense of a Freudian mnesic repetition, but as a deepening), we pass on now, on a more concrete level, to a social world where *the alienation of concrete self-consciousness* reproduces itself. Although it may be concrete, our self-consciousness has nevertheless an imaginary, still unrealized object, which is itself.

Its first attempt at self-realization is that of desire.[12] Its desire is first to test itself in another self-consciousness which is also concrete. One has just to be happy, taste pleasure—why not?—and enjoy happiness rather than make it. One has just to pluck life as a ripe fruit is plucked and would be taken, though it is hardly ripe. Self-consciousness could taste this pleasure immediately and so it would experience in enjoyment the intuition of the unity of two self-consciousnesses. Now what it experiences is not this unity, but an inevitable frustration which it does not understand at all. It calls this "the encounter of necessity." Enjoyment clashes with fate, with a frustration that has no meaning. Consciousness sees itself here without understanding itself in a fate which is not consciousness. It survives itself without being able in this survival to make the history of its own origin. On the

---

[11] Something rather striking about Hegel is that he is not a moralist. We feel that moral science, properly speaking, does not preoccupy him as it did Kant, for example, or even Nietzsche. At the same time Hegel constantly studies the conditions of moral consciousness. The sinning consciousness, consciousness of guilt, and the forgiving consciousness are the forms he analyzes. This, by the way, goes much further than all moral discourses.

[12] Hegel, *op. cit.*, I, 297f.; *Phen.* 384f.

sole level of lived experience, it is not yet capable of discovering what will however be the only thing to give this lived experience a meaning, a truth which will be promoted by language. What it experiences refers to a future which it does not experience yet; the meaning of what it experiences presently will be like this future.

And that is why what this consciousness encounters assumes the form of poorest necessity: "This *transition* of its living being into lifeless necessity appears to it a perversion which is mediated by no agency at all";[13] that is, what this enjoyment and frustration lack is precisely significance. And the individual simply finds the purest nonsense in this lack of significance which strikes him. This is what appears as fate to him.

> The mediator should be that in which both sides would unify, therefore, it should be consciousness which would know one of the moments in the other, i.e., it would know in fate its aim and its operation.[14]

That is, it would be capable not only of discovering its own frustration, but also of understanding in its own life, the meaning of this life. This is precisely impossible for this consciousness because of its peculiar demands.

> Thus, in an experience which should develop its truth, consciousness has rather become an enigma for itself; the consequences of its operations are no more for consciousness its own operations; what is happening to it is not *for it* the experience of what it is *in itself*.

The second transition is what Hegel calls "the law of the heart" and "the frenzy of self-conceit" and in which we might see (in the third transition as well, something of Quixotism) the form of paranoiac knowledge as a fundamentally human structure.[15]

In fact, consciousness is no longer at this elementary level we have just described. It is no longer just a consciousness eager to pluck life and enjoy it which notices that at the moment it thinks it is plucking life it is facing death. It is a consciousness which facing this enigma has taken necessity upon itself. That is what it calls "the law of the heart." It is a consciousness which believes itself to be perfectly pure, but finds that the world is ill-made. This consciousness wants to realize the law of its own heart in the world. It wants to realize not only its heart, but *the law of this heart;* it wants not only to realize its enjoyment, its desire, but a desire that would at the same time be universally valid.

All men, it thinks, are caught in a dilemma. Either they realize

---

[13] *Ibid.*, I, 301; *Phen.* 388.
[14] *Ibid.*, I, 301–302; *Phen.* 388f.
[15] *Ibid.*, I, 302; *Phen.* 391.

their desire, their heart, but are deprived of the consciousness of their own excellence, or, they realize the law, but live deprived of enjoyment. Thus, what is there left to be done except than to put pleasure and the law on the same side. This is the law of the heart.

Unfortunately, when an individual wants to realize the law of his heart, it becomes something alien for him in which he does not recognize himself. He fails to recognize himself in the man that *he becomes in others and for others*. And this drama is the beginning of a madness through which man is unable not to pass (as a man).

> The law of the heart, by the very fact of its actualization, ceases to be the law of the *heart*, for it receives in this actualization the form of *being* and it is now a universal power to which this particular heart is indifferent. So, by *exposing* its own order, the individual finds it no longer as its own.[16]

This theme will develop more deeply in so far as—and this corresponds to the title of *frenzy of self-conceit*—the individual who wanted in this way to realize the law of this heart does not recognize himself in his own operation which is turning against him. He feels a deep upheaval within himself and he rejects it by casting it out of himself. This *projection* is fundamental. And this might properly be called man's inherent madness. Hegel analyzes this madness in Schiller's famous character, Karl Moor, in *The Robbers*. Dr. Lacan also finds it in Alceste who is not the virtuous man, but really a madman.[17] For it is quite obvious that Alceste carries in his own heart the evil he notices. He casts it out of himself in order not to see it in himself. And this projection (Hegel's term) is not a special psychological phenomenon. It is man's inner self. It realizes concretely the scheme which appeared as an abstract duality on the level of "self-consciousness."

Hegel tells us that the heart-throb for the welfare of mankind

> passes into the rage of frantic self-conceit, into the fury of consciousness to shield itself against its own destruction; and to do so by casting out of its life the perversion which it really is, and by straining to regard and to express that perversion as something else.[18]

For the fundamental thing here is that consciousness is deranged within itself. It is an internal derangement of which Hegel, a great admirer of Pinel, says that it is a characteristic of madness. For there would

---

[16] *Ibid.*, I, 305; *Phen.* 393.
[17] See his discussion on psychic causality in his *Problème de la psychogenèse des névroses et des psychoses* (Bruges: Desclée de Brouwer, 1950), 39ff.
[18] Hegel, *op. cit.*, I, 309; *Phen.* 397.

be no madness if a madman was not at the same time reasonable, as there would be no patient if a patient was not at the same time a healthy person. Otherwise he would be unquestionably dead.

So there is a profound duality in a madman. To defend himself against this he sees it outside of himself as something contingent. One would only have to destroy all of this on the outside and all would be well. And here is the truly paranoiac representation that certain revolutionaries had of the world:

> Fanatical priests, corrupt despots helped by their minions [and this was not altogether wrong] who seek to indemnify themselves for their own degradation by degrading and oppressing in their turn, supposedly had invented and practiced this distortion to the nameless misery of deluded mankind. Consciousness denounces in its frenzy *individuality* for being the principle of this folly and of this perversion. However, this individuality is alien and contingent.[19]

4. Consciousness Which Acts and Which Judges.
Evil and Its Pardon and the " We."

We will not dwell here on the third form to which frenzy leads, Quixotism, in order that we may pass on to the resolution of this kind of interplay of self-consciousness in the final phase of the phenomenology, namely "Evil and the forgiveness of it."[20] It shows us again the two characters whom we have met all the time and who always present, in a dual sense, a double-meaning operation.

But those two consciousnesses are realized here in the most concrete manner. The one assumes the form of a consciousness that we might call creative, acting consciousness. Hegel calls it *Gewissen*, and I have translated it with a bit of audacity as *bonne conscience* (good consciousness). Indeed, when we act, we always have to be, with some hypocrisy, a good consciousness. In fact, Hegel says that moral consciousness is dumb; the acting one is concrete; it invents what must be done, and justifies it afterwards. It justifies all the time. If it did not, it would make the blunder of being immoral. For it can always justify itself. In a famous text of his *Provincial Letters* (#14), Pascal raises the question whether a man really has the power of life and death over another man. He says that the Jesuits believe when a man's honor is brought into question, that he may after all. . . . Pascal goes very far, even to say that no one has the power of life and death

---

[19] *Loc. cit.*
[20] *Ibid.*, II, 190ff.; *Phen.* 667ff.

over another man. Only God does. However, from time to time, God will have to delegate this power to some sovereign.[21]

Let us also remember Tartuffe in the play *Le Tartuffe* by Molière. The wife of Tartuffe's friend and scapegoat Orgon objects to Tartuffe's scruples with a totally feminine malice:

"Must one not be afraid of Heaven's wrath?"

He replies:

> Madam, forget such fears and be my pupil,
> And I shall teach you how to conquer scruple.
> Some joys, it's true, are wrong in Heaven's eyes,
> Yet Heaven is not averse to compromise;
> There is a science . . .
> . . . whereby any wrongful act you care to mention
> May be redeemed by purity of intention.
>
> (Act IV, Scene 5)

Perhaps he himself believes in his justifications. When you steal, it is to feed your family; if you kill it is to avenge your honor or defend your country. Immorality is, in short, the clumsiness of not being able to justify oneself. We know many of these consciences which know how to be lax. And they all are, for otherwise action would be impossible.

Well, the consciences we have here are of that order. Both are Jesuitic. We cannot help it. Jesuitism has something eternal, unavoidable by itself. The consciousness which acts invents what it has to do and justifies itself. But *it has a need to justify itself*. This is its basic need. It needs to justify itself to another self-consciousness. And the other self-consciousness judges the first. They seem to be asymmetrical. The one will be judging consciousness and the other the judged consciousness.

Notice the concrete stage where we are in the reenactment of the same drama which leads us to say: Where is this "we"—this "we" which appears on the level of the most concrete relationship, the need to be judged. This need does not abandon man; it is a need for recognition, "an appeal to history." As Péguy said: "We must appeal to history."[22] Men are called upon, people even write in order to be judged after death.

---

[21] The opposition of Pascal to the casuistry of the Jesuits is brought out by Hegel in his *Philosophie des Rechts*, § 140. In the last paragraph of this section, Hegel refers to the text of his *Phänomenologie des Geistes* on the topic of the consciousness of good and evil. (Cf. *Phen.* 663ff.)

[22] Charles Péguy has spoken at length about history and about the judgment of history in his works, especially *Clio*, a dialogue of history with the pagan soul. It was written shortly before World War I, in which he was to die.

> "Happy are those who died for sensual earth
> Provided that it is a just war."

"History will judge" the saying goes, but the question is which character will ultimately judge the other. At the beginning. it is the one who does not act. Are we dealing with the relationship of the psychoanalyzed to the psychoanalyst? Perhaps so, if the countertransferences were given the same weight as the transferences. For, according to the scheme of master and slave, we have here an exchange. Consciousness which is noble becomes base, and the base consciousness becomes noble. It so happens that the truly sinning consciousness is the judging consciousness, and the consciousness which basically dissolves or resolves its knot in the other comes to see itself in the other. Moreover, it sees itself there the more so as the other is just as guilty.

And why is the judging consciousness a sinning consciousness? Because for Hegel. judging consciousness is basically hypocritical. It does not act and it wants to have its judgment passed for an action. But there is a more profound reason. In order to be able to perceive in its own light the evil and partiality of the other, and the inequality of the other, it must carry them already within itself. We know this projection. We know that kind of people who all their lives have denounced outside of themselves what proves to be the infernal desire they could not realize in their own lives. This is the evil which judging consciousness carries in itself. And in this connection. Hegel quotes the following words by Napoleon which are already in the *Nouvelle Héloise:* "A great man does not exist for his valet." Not that there is no great man. but because there are menservants. The judging consciousness of the valet is morality. There is no great man that is not liable to be viewed from a valet's perspective. To cast light on a man from a manservant's perspective. to serve him as a mirror of his perspective is to carry within oneself the evil which is denounced in him.

So the roles are reversed between the consciousness which could be universal and dissolve the knot. and resolve within itself the acting consciousness, and the latter which feels a need for justification, recognition and calls for a meaning that can only be realized in a dialogue and in a language. Hegel says this in appropriate words: "So once more we see language manifest itself as the being there of mind"; it is a "universal self-consciousness";[23] it is in language, a language of meaning, and in this intercommunication that the problem of "we" is solved.

But, as you see, this *we* is neither in the consciousness which would claim to judge nor in the consciousness which is judged. Everything emerges from mutual recognition. since each consciousness is at the same time acting and judging, projecting evil and being evil, and a consciousness in need of recognition.

---

[23] Hegel, *op. cit.*, II, 184; *Phen.* 660.

However, the emergence of this "we" may still suffer an ultimate failure—a frightful failure due to what might be called the death instinct of him who does not wish to be cured, that is, who does not wish to speak anymore.[24] When it happens that one of the consciousnesses— and Hegel describes this last stage[25]—withdraws to itself and rejects all communication, this supreme schizophrenia, this total breakdown of relationship, cannot be understood as a benefit of illness, but as a total refusal to be cured.

On the contrary, in the communication emerging between judging consciousness and judged consciousness, in this movement which is again a kind of mirror play, since sinning consciousness says: "I am evil, but you are as well," and since the other says: "I see evil, but I also am evil," there appears a "we" which is no more the one Hegel posited abstractly at the beginning. This "we" which looked like a transcendence and pierced through a consciousness which failed to recognize itself, emerges here as the forever unending movement of a history where *the problem of meaning is being solved*, and of absolute knowledge, a "we" which is such that one can say in the end: it is not without us.[26]

---

[24] Or at least, if he still has a petrified language he refuses speech.

[25] Hegel, *op. cit.*, II, 188–189; *Phen.* 665f.

[26] EDITOR'S NOTE: The substance of this paper was originally presented orally at the French Society for Psychoanalysis on January 11, 1955. It was transcribed by Jean Laplanche and later published by Professor Hyppolite in *La Psychanalyse* 3 (1957), 17–32. The right of translation has been generously granted by the Presses Universitaires de France. Shortly before his death, in a letter to the editor dated April 19, 1968, Professor Hyppolite made certain emendations, added subtitles, and provided additional explanatory notes for this translated version of his paper. He suggested that the following report of a postlecture conversation between himself and Dr. Lacan be included as a note "because it illuminates this so important problem of the 'we' which goes beyond the 'I' and the 'thou.' "

In the discussion following the paper, Dr. Lacan asked Professor Hyppolite what is meant by this "we"—not only as an encounter of two consciousnesses, but as making the encounter possible, and realizing, therefore, a sort of revelation which is beyond man. In this connection, Dr. Lacan recalled Heidegger and pointed out the philosophical significance of Freud's discoveries, beginning with the death instinct.

Professor Hyppolite admitted the problematical situation arising from this going beyond the mere dialogue and responded to Dr. Lacan by asking Dr. Lacan what psychoanalysis in its practice may contribute to the third term which appears in the interaction of two consciousnesses.

As the discussion continued, the question was raised again and again concerning the duality of consciousness and the significance that this going beyond could have both on the positive level where the field of consciousness appears as a kind of impersonal multiplicity, and on the ontological level where original speech, a primordial "logos" might be revealed. The problematical nature of this revelation, both in Freud's psychoanalysis and Hegel's phenomenology, is at the center of the issue. Naturally, the question of the philosopher or of the analyst being beyond such discussion was inevitably raised.

HEGEL'S THEORY
OF FEELING

Errol E. Harris

At the end of the nineteenth century and in the early decades of the twentieth, Hegel was perhaps the most influential, the most revered, and the most closely studied philosopher of the western world. Today he is probably one of the most despised and neglected. He is despised and neglected by the logical empiricists, as a purveyor of metaphysical obscurity, and by the existentialists, as the architect of a cramping and suffocating system. Even by Marxists, who owe him so much, he is disdained as an inveterate idealist. He is studied by only a few exceptional scholars whose interest is mainly academic, some of whom have concentrated upon the *Logic*, some on the *Phenomenology of Spirit*, and others on the *Philosophy of Law* and the *Philosophy of History*. What has received least attention, many may think deservedly, has been the *Philosophy of Nature* and that portion of the *Philosophy of Mind* which falls outside the *Phenomenology* forming a kind of transition from *Naturphilosophie* to *Geistesphilosophie*. In my opinion this neglect is regrettable. Although many of the relevant scientific ideas of his day were grossly incorrect, Hegel's philosophical insights were exceptional and often far in advance of the contemporary science, sometimes prophetic of later discoveries, and with rare exception they are illuminating even in contemporary contexts.

The purpose of this paper is to examine that part of the *Philosophy of Mind* which bears most directly upon the problem of mind-body relationship, a question on which the wider connection between nature and mind obviously bears. The details of the *Philosophy of Nature* fall beyond its scope, but some discussion of the relations between Notion, Nature, and Mind will be needed at the outset, partly because Hegel's treatment of this matter has been subjected to severe criticisms in the past (based, often upon misunderstanding), and partly because of its patent relevance to our main topic.

1. Dialectic

A proper understanding of this, or of any other, issue in Hegel's philosophy is impossible without a clear grasp of the nature and working of the dialectic, which, if not ridiculed out of hand as a monstrous texture of sophistry, is commonly misunderstood as a quasi-mechanical juggling with opposites—a triadic Procrustean bed into which Hegel forces every subject matter he chooses to handle. The same critics who make this accusation often complain that Hegel at times fails to apply his triadic structure strictly, that the alleged theses and antitheses are forced and unnatural, and that the pretended necessary transitions are arbitrary and artificial.

The truth of the matter is that Hegel regarded dialectic as the normal and proper movement of thought which was the immanent principle of all movements, all activity, and (especially) of all development. (*Enc.* § 81, *Zusatz*) The real, for him, was a continuous developing process in which, as it proceeded, the principle of movement also developed in a definite and characteristic manner. It is not, therefore, always wholly reducible to the same clear-cut paradigmatic formula, and what, at one stage, can be presented as a stark antithesis of abstract moments subsequently resolved in a synthesis not much less abstract, at other stages becomes complicated and involved, displaying overlaps and anticipations which defy presentation as a simple triad.

For Hegel the activity of thought is one of construction, and what it constructs is a concrete universal or system—a world, which is a single totality comprised of a multitude of internal differences. This kind of union of differences is organization, and that involves distinction and relation between elements which is impossible without negation. Distinction and discrimination require the identification of "this-not-that" and the combination of both within one complex by correlation. The negative, therefore, plays an essential part in the process of thought or dialectic. But what is negatively distinguished from what is other than itself ranks, in that negation, as its opposite, and the distinction and subsequent correlation therefore present themselves as thesis, antithesis, and synthesis. The structure is triadic because the negative relation is essentially dipolar whether or not the negated other is simple or complex.

Hegel was far from mistaking distinctions for opposites or confusing the two—as Croce contended.[1] In the logic he deals with distincts in their proper place. But more significant than this is his realization that the idea of a group of coordinate species of a genus which rank as distincts is an abstraction imposed by science—or what he calls the Understanding—upon a structure which never quite answers to the imposed form. The species are never really coordinate. They are invariably in some measure serial (or dialectically related), so that in some way one is prior to another, they constitute a progression of some sort.[2] Wherever this occurs the extremes of the series are opposite poles, and however you limit or truncate the series its members become related (qua members of a series) as opposites. Distincts and opposites, therefore, are not strictly distinct. If they are treated as such, they become, immediately, opposing characterizations of difference and their identity becomes patent.

The opposition, inherent in negation, accounts for the triadic form of Hegelian "deduction," but this deduction is never a derivation of equivalent propositions by stipulated transformation rules. It is always a development of implications which displays each result as a phase in a progressive series. It follows that the kind of opposition that obtains at one end of the series is not necessarily the same kind as obtains at the other; the kind of opposition between adjacent members is not necessarily the same as that between members more widely separated; and while we may expect some degree of similarity in the relationships,

---

[1] See B. Croce, *What Is Living and What Is Dead in the Philosophy of Hegel*, trans. D. Ainslie (London, 1915).

[2] The Aristotelian or the Kantian tables of categories are cases in point, or Plato's distinctions between the forms of knowledge on the Divided Line, or his classification of states. Numbers, however classified, always constitute series and geometrical figures, because of their close relation to numbers, have a similar tendency (cf. the regular solids, conic sections, and the like).

we must not be surprised to find the dialectical process displaying differences at different points and in different phases.

Further, Hegelian "deduction" is no merely formal linear illation. It does not begin from some arbitrarily posited hypothesis or fortuitous premise. Nor is it a sort of intellectual creation *ex nihilo*. It is a constant effort to characterize the universal which is its goal. Every such effort, therefore, is a more or less vague or provisional, definition of the concrete universal—the Absolute. Thus the whole which is the ultimate conclusion is implicit at the start. The process is analogous to that of focusing a picture projected by a lens onto a screen. At first it is a mere blur, though in the blur all the elements of the picture are already adumbrated and as the focus sharpens these elements become progressively more distinct. But the universal, which is the goal of reflective thinking, is unlike a picture in that it is not just a static pattern which might be built up piecemeal out of simple units. It is an activity of systematization or self-differentiation that reveals a complex world, not merely as a dead lump, but as a developing process which turns out to be continuous with the very process of thinking which seeks to know. The object of thought thus reveals itself ultimately both as the world and as the thinking self-awareness, a statement which should not surprise us because the final goal of thought is generally admitted to be both the comprehension of its object as a self-differentiating and self-differentiated system and of its own procedure.

The object of knowledge is the world which, while it is the content of experience, is also a world of which the subject who thinks is aware of himself as a member. Reflective thought, therefore, always presupposes (more or less tacitly) the whole of experience, and (as we shall presently see more fully) that experience in its turn presupposes the world, both as its content and as its source. It follows that the dialectical process is one of increasing self-knowledge and in those levels at which its self-consciousness becomes explicit, the object of each succeeding phase is the one immediately prior (and, through it, the preceding process). At these levels also we can, in consequence, expect a noticeable overlap between stages. Some overlap is implicit at every stage, but in the higher and more developed stages it becomes more evident.

2. Logic and Nature

If we understand the dialectical process in this way, we shall be able to grasp the connections guiding Hegel's transitions and may be able to interpret successfully some of the more obscure passages in his exposition. The most important transitions, and those often considered the most obscure, are those between the major divisions of the *Encyclopaedia*—from the Absolute Idea to Nature, and from Nature to Mind or Spirit. These are, in fact, key turning points in the dialectic. Yet what, we may wonder, could be more obscure than Hegel's conclusion of the *Logic?*

> The Idea, which is for itself, treated in accordance with this its unity with itself, is intuition; and the intuitive idea is Nature. But as intuition, the idea is set in the one-sided determination of immediacy or negation through external reflection. The absolute freedom of the idea, however, is not merely that it goes over into life, nor lets life appear in itself in the form of finite knowledge, but in the absolute truth of itself it decides freely to release from itself the moment of its particularity or of the first characterization and other-being, the immediate idea as its reflected image—itself as Nature. (*Enc.* § 244)

Yet if we realize that the logic is the philosophical reflection upon the whole range of common experience and science, and is the explication of the categories inherent in that experience, we must recognize three facts: (i) that this relatively unreflective awareness of a common sense world and the partially reflective understanding of it in science are presupposed by the logic as earlier stages in the activity of thought;[3] (ii) that common sense consciousness itself is the product of a long evolutionary development in nature (Hegel was clearly aware of this even though, in his day, the biological theory of evolution had barely been suggested) (Cf. *Enc.* § 384); (iii) that, as a result of all this, the logic, in spite of its proper claims to "concreteness," is in the last resort an abstraction. (See *Enc.* § 19 and § 247, *Zusatz*.) The Idea, which is its final phase, is the self-reflective philosophical awareness that the finite knowledge of the world is the awareness of the very principles of existence of the world itself. (Cf. *Enc.* § 38, *Zusatz*.) That our knowledge is an activity, one with that immanent in nature and is the stage of its development at which it becomes conscious of itself (in and through its Other) is not recognized either by common sense or by science, but is revealed only in philosophical reflection. It is not revealed, therefore, prior to the end of the logic and is its final discovery. Consequently, it is only at this stage that the mind, recognizing its identity with its object, becomes aware that this object (the world) is no more nor less than a manifestation of thought's own categories, and turns to a fresh study of nature—not the abstract study of the understanding, still less the "unmediated" view of common sense, but a philosophical study.

The philosophical attainment of the Idea is an act of the human

---

[3] Cf. *Enc.* § 2 and the Preface to the second edition of *Wissenschaft der Logik*, *Werke*, IV, 24f.; Miller translation (London, 1969), 34f.

mind. But that is an embodied individual entity—a member of the world it knows. The logical Idea is both less and more than this: less in that it is abstract, more in that it embraces the intelligible essence of the whole of reality. But the form in which it *exists* is man's mind—an embodied personality. And this is a natural creature contained in and continuous with the rest of Nature. The degree of self-awareness reached at the final stage of the logic, therefore, is one at which the mind recognizes nature as itself, "in the form of other-being," in the self-external form of *partes extra partes*. The Idea may thus be said to go over into other-being, or, so to speak, to free the implicit moment of immediacy from itself as mere idea. Thus it is seen not merely as the finite awareness of man but as the whole of nature, within which the organism arises that develops that awareness.

Yet, again, the awareness possessed by the finite organism is itself a sublation (*Aufhebung*) of nature—a knowledge of the world, or more correctly the world come to consciousness—which is the idea. And so a further transition comes about, from nature to mind, in which the self-externality of nature is internalized in and as subjectivity. It is this transition with which this paper is primarily concerned, with the form and character of this subjectivization of external nature in its earlier phases.

3. Nature and Mind

Hegel is commonly accused of volatilizing nature away into an idea or logical construction in some mind, either God's or man's; but nothing could be a greater travesty of what he has actually written. He is aggressively realistic in his affirmation of nature as the precondition of the existence of the human mind. The Absolute, of course, is logically prior to everything finite, but its actualization as Absolute Mind is not to be found in nature or prior to it in the dialectical series, for as we have said, the logic and its absolute Idea are relatively abstract and Absolute Mind is not fully realized in them. "The mind of God before the creation of nature and finite Spirit"[4] is itself a relative abstraction, for God is not simply a concept. "The Divine Idea is precisely this: to disclose itself, to exhibit this Other produced from itself and to take it back into itself again in order to become subjectivity and spirit." (*Enc.* § 247, *Zusatz*) The realization of subjective mind requires the "creation" of the world or, to use less symbolic language, the externalization as nature of the rational principle immanent in

---

[4] G. W. F. Hegel, *Werke*, IV, 46; *Science of Logic* trans. Johnston and Struthers (London, 1929), I, 60; Miller translation, 50.

all reality. For Hegel, then, nature is the actual process of becoming through which mind is realized. His conception of reality is both realistic and essentially teleological, the nisus of the process throughout being the dialectical push toward self-completion.

The entire natural process is one in which the self-externality of the spatiotemporal world is progressively overcome, as each successive grade of natural being reflects more adequately the entire system. This is evident first in the merely mechanical interdependence of physical entities; next in the interrelation of organism (both vegetable and animal) and environment, and the increasing efficiency of the organism in dominating its environment; finally, in sentience, the whole of this natural interconnectedness focused in the animal organism is "inwardized" in subjectivity.

Mind thus comes to be both as the product of nature and as its sublimation in feeling and awareness; it is the form in which nature becomes aware of itself, in a natural organism. Nature provides the vehicle and instrument of consciousness in and through which it becomes known. Thus the relation of nature to idea is epitomized in the relation of the organism (the natural body) to its mind. Idea is the conceptualization of that activity operative throughout nature, which develops the organic from the mechanical and the psychical from the organic; and this actually takes place in the living body as (through the mediation of its physiological processes) it becomes aware of itself and its world. The mind-body relationship is therefore the focus and the key to the understanding of the relation between idea and nature. Again, the crucial point of the transition from nature to mind is the emergence of sentience, constituting what Hegel calls "the soul," the origin and basis of everything in consciousness.

4. Body and Soul

The Cartesian doctrine of two substances inexplicably related in the human mind-body nexus Hegel rejected as emphatically as any of the modern rebels against dualism, while at the same time he allowed for those aspects of the contrast between mind and body that make dualistic theories seem plausible. His protest against "the so-called Rational Psychology or Pneumatology" is unequivocal. This, he says, concerns itself with abstract general characteristics, with a putative essence lacking any manifestation (*erscheinungslos*) or evidence. It raises futile questions whether the soul is a single immaterial substance, and regards it as something fixed and unchanging; whereas spirit, he declares, is absolute unrest, pure activity—not an already complete being hiding itself behind the mass of its appearances, but one which

is truly actualized only through the determinate forms of its own necessary self-revelation—not a "ghost-thing" (*Seelending*) in external relation to the body, but integrally involved with the body, through the
utility of the concept. (*Enc.* § 378, *Zusatz*)

The body is the medium of the soul's "necessary self-revelation"
and the "absolute restlessness" and "pure activity" is an activity which
takes place in and through the body. There the physiological functions,
reflecting widespread influences of nature are focused and integrated
into a single unity, which is *felt*, and in feeling sublated (*aufgehoben*),
subjectivized, and idealized as sensation. Primitive sentience belongs
to the soul, the "dark" or preconscious stage of mental development;
but the restless activity of organizing, distinguishing, correlating, and
ultimately objectifying its own sentient content, continues and develops
into intelligent awareness and reason, which is the activity of mind
proper.

It is only when the soul is pictured as a thing set over against
matter as something *true* (*ein Wahres*)—an intelligible and self-com-
plete reality—that the question of the immateriality of the soul can
have any interest. But on the one hand even the physicists have found
matter becoming "imponderable," and the biologists fail to identify
"vitality" with anything solid, while on the other hand mind is the
intelligible utility which constitutes "the truth of" the self-externalism
and self-alienation of matter. (*Enc.* § 389) Today the "imponderables"
of the physics of Hegel's time have been replaced by the immaterialism
of the relativity and quantum theories, and the vitalism of the earlier
biology by systems theories and the organismic approach, but Hegel's
philosophical insight remains valid and his treatment of body-mind
relationship is in principle still appropriate.

This relationship, he says, is an utterly incomprehensible mystery
so long as we (falsely) insist on treating soul and body as absolutely
antithetical and independent of each other. (*Enc.* § 389) His own
treatment of the topic is very different and is closely bound up with
his conception of the relation between the particular and the universal
and that again with the antithesis between immediacy and mediation.
These terms, like so many others in Hegelian dialectic, have relative
application. The purely immediate, the totally abstract, what is utterly
devoid of mediation, is pure being, empty and contentless, and anything
with any degree of definition or determinateness is at once mediated
by an antithesis to what it is not—what defines and determines it.
It is mediated by the structural principle and design of some system
within which it has definitive position. But as this system develops
and is further elaborated, what at an early stage appears as relatively
mediate, at a later stage appears relatively immediate. We may say
that in general the immediate is what is simply presented (*Dasein*),

even though its presented character may involve implicit and unexpressed mediation, and that it is mediated as these tacit implications are explicated and set out to view. The unified structure the explication of which is the process of mediation is, for Hegel, the (concrete) universal, and the presented element or moment in this structure, presented without explicit elaboration of its defining relations, is the particular. The body, as a mere material entity, simply given or presented is immediate, only a particular. The explication in idea of its relation to the natural world and to the total scheme of reality is mind or spirit, the mediate universal.

But within the process of this explication there are many phases which, compared with what supervenes upon them, are only immediate, though compared with that upon which they have supervened are themselves universal. So we find Hegel speaking of "immediate mind" (*der unmittelbare Geist*), and of sentience (*Empfindung*) as immediate, though also in a sense universal. ("In virtue of sentience, the soul has thus come to the point at which the universal constituting her nature becomes for her an immediate determination."[5]) Consciousness, which emerges from sentience as a further development, is the explicit grasp of this universality or unity-in-and-through differences; and the mind, of which the sentient soul is the first inchoate form, is the universal "for-itself," which the body, a mere particular within the system of nature is "in itself." Hence "mind came into being as the *truth* of nature." (*Enc.* § 388) But this principle of holism come aware of itself is no new separate immaterial entity; it is, as Hegel says, the general immateriality (universality or idealization) of nature. (*Enc.* § 389) We shall see that it is equally proper to say that it is similarly the idealization of the body.

5. The Awakening of Mind in Nature

Nature is a whole of interrelated parts and processes such that, at any level at which we consider it—physical, chemical, or biological—each part in some degree reflects the whole. Physical interdependence of material entities had been recognized by Leibniz, and the dependence of the chemical on the physical and the biological on the chemical was already widely recognized in Hegel's day. The self-external character of material nature is to this extent counteracted even before the biological and psychological phases are reached. But, as

---

[5] *Enc.* § 399, Zusatz. "*Durch das Empfinden ist somit die Seele dahin gekommen, dass das ihre Natur ausmachende Allgemeine in einer unmittelbaren Bestimmtheit für sie wird.*"

Hegel would say, this expression by the part of the whole is, at levels below mind, only "for us" (who reflect upon it) and not for the natural entity itself whose dependence on its environment constitutes this expression. In it, the unity of interrelationships is only implicit (*nur an sich*). As this unity becomes progressively more integral and complete it is more fully internalized in the entity concerned, so that in living forms (even in plants) their behavior is more explicitly responsive to other things and events external to them. The process of "inwardizing" has already begun. In such reaction to environmental influences plants are less organic than animals. Their own parts are not so fully dominated by the character of the total vegetable organism as are the bodily parts of animals by their animal organism, in which the vital interchange with environment is more intimately focused and concentrated. Organic reaction is commonly thought of as sensitivity, and with it we are already verging upon sensibility. When that emerges, it is the more intense unification or reflection into self in the animal organism of the scattered self-external profusion of nature:

> We have learnt from the philosophy of nature how nature sublates her externality step by step, how already at the material level weight nullifies (*widerlegt*) the independence of multiple singularities, and how this nullification begun through weight and still more through the indivisible simplicity of light, is completed by animal life and the sentient [organism]. For this reveals to us the pervading presence of the single soul at all points of its corporeity and thereby the sublated reality of mutual externality of material parts.[6]

The subjectivization of nature's self-externality is thus, at the same time the felt unity of the bodily organism in the primitive phase of mind which Hegel designates the soul.

It is, however, no world-soul like that which Plato describes in the *Timaeus*. Hegel explicitly repudiates hylozoism. (Cf. *Enc.* § 391.) Soul emerges in a multiplicity of individual organisms, "like light in an endless multitude of individual stars." (*Enc.* § 390, *Zusatz*) Those of its characteristics which express natural qualities most directly, representing its most rudimentary phase, are from the beginning characteristics of individual living beings. They are not, as Findlay thinks, "a sort of psychic life diffused throughout wide segments of Nature and not yet parcelled off into separate individual Souls."[7] There is no evidence of this in the text. But the effects of climate, the changes of the seasons, and the differences of times of day do express themselves in the sensitive character of man, beasts, and plants. The types of life and the differences of human temperaments appropriate to tropical,

[6] *Enc.* § 389. Cf. also § 390, *Zusatz*.
[7] J. N. Findlay, *Hegel: A Re-examination* (London, 1958), 291.

temperate, and polar regions of the earth are actualities; the moods reflective of the different seasons are well known and universally expressed—the gaiety of the spring, the relaxation of the summer, the invigoration of autumn, and the tendency in the severe cold of winter to congealed inactivity (corresponding to the hibernation of animals). These are not just outward behavioral manifestations but also psychical qualities *felt* by individual animals. Similarly we are all familiar with the different feeling tones accompanying the various periods of the day; and these again vary with climatic conditions and the season of the year. We see here, as we shall see further anon, the overlap of different kinds of feeling tone corresponding to different natural conditions, those of morning, noon, and evening with those of climatic and seasonal differences. In this way, it is true, wide segments of nature are subjectivized, but not in some pervasive soul-substance for which no evidence is forthcoming, but in the felt-experience of actual individuals, for it is as actual individual minds that the universal idea *exists*.

These more general expressions of natural conditions are specified in racial and national characteristics, again in part determined climatically and in part by local circumstances. Hegel draws attention, for instance, to the differences in national character between mountain- and plain-dwelling peoples. Once more, all these naturally conditioned mental characteristics are individualized in persons and express themselves in their moods, temperaments, dispositions, and aptitudes, and physically in their bodily types and appearance. What Hegel is concerned with here is really one set, not three, of mental traits, but they are expressive of nature in three different ways reflecting (a) geographic, (b) biological or racial, and (c) personal characteristics. These are degrees of specification and also contrasting aspects. For the merely geographical conditions are largely physical and mechanical, the biological more teleological in quality, and the two are synthesized in the personal traits of the individual which give them actual expression. So the dialectical form is still in evidence, not as a synthesis of starkly opposed abstractions, but rather as a concrete realization of two interdependent though nevertheless contrasted aspects of a single phase of psychical life.

6. The Mind's Embodiment

The point to be stressed at this stage is the inseparability of mind from body. All these natural qualities are as much bodily as mental and find expression equally in either form. Accordingly, the physical changes and varieties of biological form occurring in the animal organism also represent forms of soul or psychical determinations: the periods of life from infancy to youth, from youth to maturity, and from maturity to age, the difference between sexes, and the alternation of sleeping and waking. Here there certainly is no dialectical rigidity, and the list of forms seems at first sight quite haphazard and fortuitous. What "logical" connection, we may ask, has the difference between male and female with the ages of man, on the one hand, or with sleep and waking, on the other? Yet they are all differences in one way or another of psychical and physical condition and they are by no means unconnected. The stages of animal life might well be represented simply as stages of sexual maturation, and corresponding to them the sentient life of the individual is variously divided between sleep and waking. The infant sleeps the greater part of the time, having, as it were, barely awakened from the continuous sleep of gestation. As the individual matures, waking takes precedence over sleep; and as age increases to senility, the proportion of sleep to waking is once again reversed.

Sleep is the psychical state in which the unconscious processes of the body are present without explicit awareness; yet it is no mere physiological condition, for dreams give evidence of a sentience of some obscure kind which, as it emerges into a higher cognitive form, takes on fantastic and symbolic significance. The waking state, as Hegel says, is that in which the soul finds, as a "given," the contents of its subconscious sleeping condition and becomes explicitly aware of them. (Cf. *Enc.* § 399.) Every stage of psychical life takes on these two alternating forms at all ages, thus they are an aspect of all the other psychophysical conditions listed. Further, all the psychophysical differences characteristic of the life-periods of the individual are duplicated in the two sexual forms. So that all these natural alterations are interrelated, all aspects of the same organic life, and all forms of psychical as well as physiological functioning.

Sexual differences involve separate individuals, while differences of age occur in one and the same individual. Sex is also a persistent bodily and mental form, while with age both mind and body constantly change. Both sets of alterations are obviously combined in the alternate forms of sleep and waking. Nevertheless the negation by one of the other, as seen in other phases of the dialectic, is not sharp or obvious here, though the sex differences themselves form an opposition and so do sleep and waking even if the form of their reconciliation is not clearly defined. Further, all these physical alterations are specific and affect the individual directly, as opposed to the generality of the natural qualities of the prior group. And both sets are united in the sentient life of the individual organism. If the dialectic is here somewhat loose and lacks the "necessity" that Hegel constantly claims for it, it is still true that what is being described is a continuous process of emergence of mentality, the phases of which are mutually disposed in a dialectical type of relationship.

The main significance of this section is the recognition by Hegel of a subconscious psychic life which emerges into consciousness with a particular degree of integration of physiological functioning. This is the great contribution of his theory of feeling, in a measure anticipating Freud, and we must now pass on to consider the main discussion of sentience, neglecting many interesting and perceptive remarks that Hegel makes about physical alterations, which could be properly treated only in a voluminous commentary.[8] These omissions may perhaps be the more readily excused because Hegel's discussion here admittedly assumes much that belongs only to a later stage of the dialectic. As he frequently points out, one can treat of the sentient characteristics of the mind for the most part only as they are known and recognized in the more developed forms of consciousness, which must therefore be in a sense illegitimately anticipated by the reflective study.

This is especially noticeable in the succeeding sections of the exposition, for the distinction between sleep and waking brings us to a level of awareness which is not yet fully explicit consciousness (*Bewusstsein*) but which also is not mere oblivion and total unconsciousness. It is sentience (*Empfindung*), a phase which spans the frontier between the unconscious and the conscious. For sentience of a sort exists in sleep and at subconscious levels of mind, while no awareness however clear is devoid of it. For Hegel, consciousness requires explicit recognition of an object set over against a subject, an opposition which is not characteristic of sentience. Yet the objective as well as the subjective elements in explicit consciousness are both derived from sentience and are, so to speak, made out of what is felt, as a sort of primary (physical) "matter."

7. Sentience

Sentience is the immediate unification at once of the processes of the body and of the whole of nature. It becomes mediated in consciousness as the awareness of self and of the world. How it unifies and sublates the variety of nature we have already seen from the account given of natural qualities, and its integration of bodily states is indicated in the account of physical alterations. Hegel treats it ini-

[8] In particular his perspicacious comparison of the mental characteristics of youth and age and his unerring solution of Descartes' problem of the distinction between dream and waking. See *Enc.* § 396, *Zusatz* and § 398.

tially as the manifold of sensations (outer and inner), summing up all that has been outlined above, and then passes to the essential unity of self-feeling (*Die fühlende Seele*), first as purely immediate, then as self-distinguishing, and finally as realized in active (habitual) unity of body and soul, each precisely and without conflict expressing the state and condition of the other. It is, in fact, this intimate unity of the two aspects which Hegel repeatedly stresses throughout his exposition.

On the one hand, the immediacy of natural forms and conditions becomes "ideal" in being felt (while as merely felt it remains sensibly unmediated). On the other hand, what is "inwardized" and belongs essentially to the incipient ego is incorporate and has bodily form and expression. Everything that enters into consciousness belongs to the waking life of the individual with which he identifies his personality; and at its lowest psychical level it is the feeling or sensation of all those physiological states and processes which reach a sufficiently high degree of organized unity. These are all present in sleep at the pre-conscious level (*an sich*), so that sleep and waking in a peculiarly appropriate way represent the relation of body and soul.

The dialectical advance involved in the transition from sleep and waking to sentience consists (Hegel tells us) in the fact that the un-differentiated "being-in-self" of the organism represented by the sleeping state is displayed in waking sentience as a manifold demanding concrete unification. This cannot be effected simply by the alternation of sleep and waking, but is realized in the sentient soul as an immediate "given." The manifold determinations are absorbed (*versenkt*) into the universality of the soul and so idealized. (*Enc.* § 399, *Zusatz*) The point seems to be that the diversity of merely physiological, un-conscious processes is unified in sentience in such a way that under the later effect of conscious attention and correlation—the activity of the single subject—it can be explicitly and manifestly organized as a concrete universal system.

But the bodily states and processes are themselves organic integra-tions of and adjustments to natural influences reflecting wide areas, if not the whole, of nature. Consequently, all nature comes to be summed up and consummated in the sentient awareness of the indi-vidual organism. The "object" of waking consciousness is the bodily unity and through its nature; and the contents of sentience subse-quently become the objects of consciousness in which they are distin-guished, identified, related to one another, and defined as external and independent.

"Sentience in general," Hegel says, "is the healthy community (*Mitleben*) of the individual mind with its corporeity." (*Enc.* § 401) The variety of corporeal influences are specified in the external senses, the internal reactions, no less expressed in and through corporeal processes, are specified as inner emotional states.[9] To be felt, they must at one and the same time be received as the effects of alien causes and identified with the subject as his own inner states. Therefore, these affections must be embodied and have a physiological aspect.

> If we speak of the inner determinations of the feeling subject, without reference to its corporeality (*Verleiblichung*), we deal with it as it is merely *for us*, but not as it is for itself, as it feels its own determinations in itself. . . . This somatization of the manifold of inner feelings defines a circle of corporeality within which they proceed in sequence. This circle, this limited sphere, is my body, which defines itself as the sphere of sentience, as much for the inner as for the outer determinations of the soul. The vitality of this, my body, consists in the fact that its materiality is not able to be for itself. It can offer me no resistance, but is subordinated to me, permeated throughout by my soul, for which it is something ideal. It is through this (psychical) nature of my body that it becomes possible and necessary for my feelings to be corporally manifested[10] and the movements of my soul become immediately movements of my body. (*Enc.* § 401, *Zusatz*.)

This passage has a remarkably modern ring. In the first place it anticipates the modern neurophysiological and psychological doctrines of the body-image which play so large a part in contemporary theories of localization of sensation and perception—but Hegel avoids the error of conceiving this "image" as a replica in the brain to which sensations are referred.[11] For him the body-image is the felt unity and order of the physiological processes. His doctrine is in effect that which R. G. Collingwood reasserts in *The New Leviathan* (Chapters II and III), that there is at least one sense of the word "body" in which it means simply "feeling." Hegel makes the point that so far as the body is alive (*lebendig*) it is in this sense (of "feeling") that

---

[9] Hegel's detailed treatment of the external senses (*Enc.* § 401, *Zusatz*) must here be passed over, for our main concern is his account of the body-mind relation which he brings out more directly in discussing inner affective states. In his treatment of the five senses an apparent application of the Procrustean bed occurs. The five senses are classified as three groups corresponding to the moments of the Idea: (a) sight and hearing corresponding to psychical ideality, (b) scent and taste—real difference, and (c) touch—terrestrial (solid) totality. However artificial this classification may appear at first sight it does not lack perspicacity. Sight reveals only evident surfaces, hearing only inner conditions (resonance, hollowness, harshness and the like), smell and taste make us aware of forms of chemical process; but all go together to make the solid body which is grasped and felt by contact. The two dualities are synthesized severally and together in the final synthesis of touch.

[10] I have tried by this circumlocution to convey Hegel's sense of the word *Verleiblichung*.

[11] W. Russell, *Brain, Mind, Perception and Science* (Oxford, 1957), 17.

the word is properly used. The unity (*Mitleben*) of body and soul, referred to above, is here further illuminated in such a way as to exclude any suggestion of dualism. The body as physical is permeated with soul (or feeling) inasmuch as it is "quickened" and alive, for sentience is the sublation of the physiological process. The theory is not unlike that set out by Susanne Langer in her most recent works.[12] It is a doctrine which renders the traditional theories of body-mind relationship futile and obsolete—as Collingwood calls them, old wives' tales—what they have been ever since Hegel wrote.

The subsequent account which Hegel gives of the bodily counterpart of felt emotional states is, on the one hand, marred by the primitive state of the scientific knowledge of psychology and psychiatry in his day, and includes the old wives' tales then current concerning psychosomatic effects. On the other hand, he recognizes and himself asserts that the true facts of the matter had been obscured by centuries of error and misunderstanding (*Enc.* § 401, *Zusatz*), and his own descriptions, in spite of their occasional fantasies, are full of anticipatory insights adumbrating the James-Lange theory of emotion and the modern understanding of psychosomatic phenomena.

8. The Feeling Soul and the Unconscious

We said earlier that each category of the dialectic was a provisional definition of the whole. So we find in the *Geistesphilosophie* that each phase gives one view or aspect of mind as such, and, at the level in which we are directly interested, this is soul. What we have reviewed so far has been the character of its content at the sentient level, and sentience because of its immediacy and mere givenness is particular and transient. (*Enc.* § 402) But this does not apply to the soul as subject of sentience. All sensed content belongs to and is felt by the single individual subject and so is of necessity gathered into one experience which the individual feels as himself (not as clearly and intellectually identified in contradistinction to a not-self, but as a single totality of feeling in which the distinction of self and not-self is merely potential). This is the soul in another aspect which Hegel calls the Feeling Soul.

[12] See Susanne Langer, *Philosophical Sketches* (Baltimore, 1962), 9, and *Mind, An Essay on Feeling* (Baltimore, 1967): "What is felt is a process, perhaps a large complex of processes. Some vital activities of great complexity and high intensity, usually (perhaps always) involving nervous tissue, are felt; being felt is a phase of the process itself. A phase is a mode of appearance and not an added factor." (21) "One may say that some activities, especially nervous ones, above a certain (probably fluctuating) limen of intensity, enter into 'psychical phase'. This is the phase of being felt." (22)

Hitherto we have used the words "feeling" and "sentience" as equivalent with no attempt to distinguish between the German words *Empfindung* and *Fühlen*. Hegel here uses the latter to refer to the feeling soul as a totality. Sentience (*Empfindung*), he says, implies passivity, but feeling (*Fühlen*), though he does not go so far as to call it active, implies to a greater extent an awareness of self (*Selbstichkeit*). The distinction, he admits, is not one usually made, yet we speak of "a feeling of rectitude" or "self-feeling" and not of "a sensation of rectitude" or "a sensation of self." The term does indeed connote some degree of activity, for Hegel uses it to refer to forebodings and experiences of second sight—the sort of thing of which one says, "I feel it in my bones," not as a mere physical sensation but as an implicit judgment.

The feeling soul is intermediate between the immediacy of sentience and the explicit consciousness of a surrounding world of objects, in which (as Hegel puts it) what is immediately sensed is just a point in the comprehensive interrelatedness of things[13] in the objective world. This intermediate phase is hard to describe. Hegel uses the phrase "*die ahnende Seele*"—intuitive, foreboding, having vague, inexplicable, nondiscursive awareness—and in his detailed account of this phase of mental life, he is undoubtedly dealing with what nowadays we call the Unconscious. He includes under it dreams, the mental life (such as it is) of the embryo in the womb, the subconscious self or genius of the individual, various forms of extrasensory perception (*das fühlende Wissen*), hypnotism ("animal magnetism"), somnambulism, and the like. What was known of these psychological phenomena in his day was vague, unsystematic and, so far as it could be called scientific at all, groping and speculative. So were the current accounts of insanity, which Hegel also treats in a later section under this heading. Many of the errors and vagaries current at the time are reflected in his writing, for Hegel is always careful to follow what the current science had accepted as established. In dealing with matters of empirical fact he scrupulously held to the available evidence and refused (even when it would suit his philosophical position better) to accept theories which were then mere speculations. Consequently, he adopted many explanations of psychological phenomena which to us are obsolete and seem ludicrous and made valiant efforts to render them reasonable. But the errors can hardly be held against him, for we cannot expect him to divorce himself wholly from his own age, and what is remarkable about his thought is the extent to which it is in advance of his times.

---

[13] "*Zugleich ist diess Empfundene aber für mich ein Punkt in dem allgemeinen Zusammenhange der Dinge.*" (*Enc.* § 402, *Zusatz*)

Claims to clairvoyance, extrasensory perception, and suchlike experiences Hegel treats seriously and he attributes them to a level of mind which is below that of consciousness and cognition proper. They are forms of intuitive awareness which can give no rational account of themselves and are simply "felt." Their source is precognitive and is thus subconscious. He commends Plato for associating divination with the liver and for ascribing it to the irrational part of the soul. Clairvoyance, he considers, is far from "clear," but rather is confused with accidental fancies and extraneous suggestions, so that it is difficult to distinguish between genuine prevision and self-deception. Least of all is it justifiable to treat this kind of experience as an elevation of the spirit capable of giving access to higher truths. (*Enc.* § 406) At best it is a psychical manifestation typical of a pathological condition.

Some may dispute the interpretation which attributes to Hegel a theory of the unconscious, but there are passages which can hardly be otherwise understood.

"Every individual," he says,

> is a treasury of sensations, ideas, pieces of information, thoughts, etc., but the ego is nevertheless entirely simple, a featureless pit in which all this is stored, without existing. Only if I recall an idea (*Vorstellung*) do I bring it out of that interior to existence before consciousness. It happens in illness, that ideas and information, said to have been forgotten years ago because they had not been brought to consciousness for such a long time, come again to light. We were previously not in possession of them and no more come to possess them by such reproduction of them as occurs in illness, yet they were in us and continue to remain in us. So a person can never know how many items of knowledge he actually has in him, once he has forgotten them; they do not belong to his actuality, his subjectivity as such, but to his implicit being (*an-sich-seienden Sein*). (*Enc.* § 403)

Again, he says of the feeling self that it is mind in "the stage of its darkness," and it is to this dark, featureless pit that he traces back, not only things recovered in delirium, but also the phenomena of dreams and somnambulism, psychic *rapport*, and noninferential prescience mentioned above. One can hardly consider the level of *Fühlen und Ahnen* as anything but preconscious, for although there is some awareness of their products it is an awareness which strictly belongs to a more developed and explicit stage of mind (the treatment here as elsewhere is proleptic), and Hegel quite unmistakably places it below the level of consciousness for which he reserves the term *Bewusstsein*.

The feeling self is presented under three heads as the feeling self in its immediacy, self-feeling, and habit. Once again there is much which we must pass by for lack of space, and a brief comment on

Hegel's treatment of insanity is all we shall permit ourselves. Self-feeling is that stage in which the soul identifies itself as subject of its feelings, yet as one with them. This appears to be the stage at which the Ego distinguishes itself from the Id (in Freudian terms). Modern psychologists, whether of the analytic school or not, have given definite recognition to this emergence of a self.[14] It becomes the center of subsequent phases at which, with the explicit distinction of itself from the objects of its experience it attains to consciousness proper, the awareness of an ordered world of interrelated objects. But if at this later stage the self becomes so obsessed with some special element of its feeling life that it loses the sense of the proper relation of that element to the rest so that it becomes disproportionately engrossing, the element thus selected assumes the role of a dream encapsulated, as it were, in waking life, and is thus a mental derangement. Again the root source is the feeling (subconscious) life of the soul, but now disproportionately and illegitimately invading the sphere of higher consciousness.

In his attitude to insanity Hegel is again in advance of his time. He declares that the mentally ill must be regarded not as devoid of sanity but simply as suffering *de*rangement. The conscious, rational, individual is one who has subjected the content of the soul at the level of feeling to order and rule. The relaxation of this control by the organizing activity of thought and the reversion of the mind to the lower level, by allowing the felt content of the soul to play a disproportionate role in its consciousness, is insanity. But neither is the feeling soul insane nor does the insane altogether lack rationality. The lunatic is a rational person in whose consciousness some element of feeling has usurped the dominant place. Treatment of the ailment, therefore, must depend upon and assume the basic rationality of the patient, as the physician bases his cure upon the normal functioning of the body. It must be humane and considerate of the individual as essentially a responsible person.

9. Habit and the Actualization of Soul in Body

It is not, however, only the abnormal that is to be attributed to subconscious sources. Hegel has given plentiful evidence of his awareness of the influence upon our ordinary waking life of causes which have deeper roots than we are conscious of. Moreover, our conscious practices may also affect, or find lodging in, the subconscious underpinning of the mind, and may reduce deliberate action or thought to automatic, unconscious habit.

[14] K. Koffka, *Principles of Gestalt Psychology* (London, 1955), 319ff.

This reduction of overt action and experience to unconscious automatism is a necessity for higher mental development in that it releases the mind from attending to particular details and enables it to direct itself to the more general and universal aspects of things. The vehicle of this unconscious automatism is again the body in which repetition and practice engender a "second nature." So the body becomes completely molded and dominated by the soul and is in fact and actuality the soul's existence. Thus the feeling soul is actual as the body; they are identical, the soul being but the psychical aspect of the same natural entity of which the body is the physiological aspect. But the identity is not such as to restrict the mind to mere feeling,. and is one which equips it for activities higher in degree of organization and more explicitly complex unification, which it accomplishes in properly conscious activities of knowing and doing. The modern neural-identity theory obscures these differences in degree of complexity, organization, and holism, and restricts the correlation of psychical and physical to brain processes, similarly neglecting the holism of physiological activity. Hegel avoids the dualism against which the modern theories inveigh while he consistently preserves the distinctions between nature and mind, physiology and psychology, feeling and explicit consciousness, the awareness of which persuade the dualist of the inadequacy of narrowly materialistic doctrines. The soul, and subsequently the mind, are presented as successive phases of integrating, idealizing activity, the effect of which is progressively higher degrees of organization and diversified unity. What is unified and idealized is primarily the organic process of the body, for body and mind are not two substances in external relation but one in which different dialectical phases of concrete organization are manifested. The more explicit and integral sublate (cancel, while they preserve in more developed form) the more immediate and implicit. The process of advance is one in which unconscious organic functioning becomes preconscious sentient apprehension and thence emerges into clear awareness as the activity of discrimination, opposition, and interrelation of elements proceeds.

Today, phenomenologists like Merleau-Ponty are returning to a position similar to this. They seek to get back to an original experience prior to the presupposition of a formed world of external objects and a recorded "knowledge" of that world in the mind. They rebel against the picture of a soul as a thing set over against matter (or the world) as *ein Wahres*.[15] They find the knowledge of the world inseparably bound up with the direct awareness (feeling) of the body and its organic functioning; and they regard attention as the primary activity

---

[15] See page 78, of the present essay.

of thought, creating its own objects in a dialectical process which moves in consequence of the stimulating drive that results from vagueness and contradiction, the problematic character of the object presently discovered. "It is precisely by overthrowing data [what Hegel would call *Aufhebung*] that the act of attention is related to previous acts, and the unity of consciousness is built up step by step through a 'synthesis of transition.' "[16] It is the object which "gives rise to the 'knowledge-bringing event' which is to transform it, only by means of the still ambiguous meaning which it requires that event to clarify."[17] So writes Merleau-Ponty, and he quotes Valéry as saying that "the work of the mind exists only in act." Hegel has told us that it is absolute unrest and pure activity. But the phenomenologist, while he brackets the assumption of the existing world (as *ein Wahres*), nevertheless asserts that that assumption is prior to our theorizing. He leaves it either undefended or by implication deducible from our consciousness. The relation remains obscure which Hegel through his dialectical procedure succeeds more satisfactorily in explaining. So far as the phenomenologist fails to make good his claim to transcend the antithesis of idealism and realism, Hegel has already advanced beyond him; so far as phenomenology succeeds, it has been anticipated by Hegel.

10. Conclusion

The cumbrous style of Hegel's writing, the dense obscurity of his involved and often elliptical exposition, as well as the inclusion in his discussions of ideas about physiological phenomena long since disproved, contribute to discourage students from giving close attention to this part of Hegel's philosophical system. Nevertheless, it repays study because of its many suggestive insights and illuminating analogies (for example, "Habit is the mechanism of self-feeling, as memory is the mechanism of intelligence." (*Enc.* § 410) It anticipates so many later developments and presents them often in forms so superior to their modern versions that the results of neglecting his teaching give testimony to the truth of Collingwood's judgment: "The philosophy which ignores its own history is a philosophy which spends its labor only to discover errors long dead."

[16] Maurice Merleau-Ponty, *The Phenomenology of Perception*, trans. Colin Smith (London, 1962), 30.
[17] *Ibid.*, 30–31.

VI

HEGEL'S USE
OF TELEOLOGY

John N. Findlay

I wish to devote this paper to considering an aspect of Hegel's thought, which, I think, enables us to understand him better than any other, i.e. the thoroughgoing teleology of his manner of thinking. No other philosopher has approached him in this regard, with the sole exception of Aristotle, who is perhaps also the greatest single influence in Hegel's inspirational background.[1] If one regards Hegel as an Aristotle in whom teleology has been carried to the limit, so that it becomes transformed into something else, one will perhaps have achieved a good way of regarding him. The teleology of Hegel's thought

[1] For a study of the relation between Hegel's thought and Aristotle's, see G. R. G. Mure's *An Introduction to Hegel* (Oxford, 1940).

differentiates him from all the philosophers, however idealistic, whose procedure is what I may call axiomatic, all philosophers who start with a clear body of formulated principles and who deduce elaborate and detailed consequences from it. It sets him infinitely far apart from Spinoza, and it sets him infinitely far apart from the dogmatic rationalism of the Bradley who wrote the second part of *Appearance and Reality*. For Hegel the true, the philosophically adequate account of things is an account that emerges out of a great deal of transformed inadequacy and error, which has no content whatever without such inadequate, erroneous preliminaries, which in a sense preserves them all in the ultimate result, and is in fact nothing beyond the fact of their ultimate transformed preservation. (I should argue further, with some evidence to back me, that Hegel means by the ultimate result the provisionally ultimate result.) Hegel's teleology sets him infinitely far apart from all those idealistic or spiritualistic philosophers who put mind, spirit, rational subjectivity at the *origin* of things, who make it the ontological background for whatever exists or appears to exist, whether they do so in the manner of scholastic theism or in the manner of Berkeleian idealism or in the complex qualified manner of Kantian phenomenalism. For Hegel the spiritual, the ideal, the self-conscious which is the ultimate meaning of everything, does not lie at the beginnings of thought and being, but rather at their end: we may decide that it is the logical and ontological Alpha of the cosmos, but only after it has first emerged as its logical and ontological Omega. All this means that at the *origins* of philosophical truth lie much necessary thought that is abstract and formal and mechanically analytic—the thought of the British analytic school will do admirably as an illustration—whereas at the origins of being lie many states of things that are inert, external, purposeless, mechanical, contingent, irregular, empirical and brutally real. The spirituality that arises out of them all is a painfully educed, glorious result. I should like to say that, if Hegel's system is rightly described as one of absolute idealism or spiritualism, it is also rightly described as one of dialectical materialism: it is in fact the true dialectical materialism of which the dialectical materialism of Marx and Engels may be said to be an incompetent, amateur travesty. These sweeping assertions require, however, a good deal of backing, which I shall now endeavor to give.

I shall first seek to apply these teleological perspectives to the dialectic, the peculiar self-critical, self-transcendent method of thought which hardly anyone has learnt from Hegel, and which distinguishes his philosophy from any other. The dialectic is in my view primarily a method of persistently reapplied higher-level, or metalogical, or second-order comment, in which we pass from a situation where we merely employ a concept to a situation where we consider the content and operation of a concept from *outside* as it were, and assess its success in doing whatever it sets out to do. It is also, secondarily, a method where we use such metalogical thought-transitions to understand a series of strata or layers of being in the world, or a succession of phases in personal biography or in world-history.

That Hegel's method is reiteratively metalogical no one who studies him closely can for a moment doubt. We consider, e.g., the thought-stance involved in a mere assertion of *being*, and see that, while purporting to be rich in content, it is utterly empty and abstract, and undistinguishable in what it really covers from the thought-stance which asserts the total *absence* of anything. We then see that in our whole previous procedure we have been experiencing the inherent instability of abstract concepts, in other words their *becoming*. Modern semantics suffices to show us that novelties of principle persistently emerge as we proceed to comment on what went before. What was unformulable or unprovable in an object-language may be formulable and provable in a metalanguage and so on. And quite apart from modern semantics, common-sense shows us that what is true *of* an idea differs from, and is often opposed to, the content of the idea itself. The idea of the concrete is very abstract, the idea of beauty is not beautiful at all, the notion of moral worth is itself devoid of moral worth, and the absence of any of our family and friends at Christmas is not itself absent but woefully near and present, the Wittgensteinian arguments that one cannot talk about one's own or other people's private experiences show a perfect understanding of what it is to be, or to have, just such a private experience, a behavioristic analysis of mental life perhaps points by its sheer brilliance and synthetic comprehensiveness to the existence of what is not behavioral, etc. Most of the current objections to Hegelian dialectic rest on the persistent assumption that it is thought that operates on one level, rather than persistently revisionary thought that is always commenting on and criticizing itself.

I now wish to connect the various steps in Hegel's dialectic with the notion of teleology, and to suggest that they always involve comment on a notion and its content and operation from the standpoint of an *aim*, a *Meinung* or intention which the notion secretly involves, and that this comment assumes at least three standard forms: (a) The notion does not at all achieve what it sets out to perform. While it sets out to be the thought of X, it is such as not to strike its target at all, but as much, or even rather, a target opposed to X. The notion in short breaks down under metalogical scrutiny. This breakdown is itself dysteleological—we do not frame concepts in order that they should *not* do their work—but it clears the deck for a mere positive teleology. (b) The notion, in not achieving what it sets out to perform, intrinsically points to another notion which effects what the first only tries to effect. It can be regarded as a confused, implicit form of the latter notion, and the latter is the notion we are trying to frame when we frame the former. This type of step is plainly teleological; an inadequate notion is seen not merely as inadequate, but as being inadequate in a respect which implies consciousness of a corresponding adequate notion. (c) The notion, while not seeming adequate, none the less can be seen by the removal of a few confusing demands and suggestions to be in all essentials adequate. This, the most characteristic teleology of all in Hegel, and the one least understood by his students, is the sudden finding of oneself at one's goal for the very reason that at first seemed to place one far from it. It is the solution of one's problem by turning the problem into its own answer, and resembles falling in love with a woman for the very qualities that at first made her unattractive. I shall now give cases of each of these three dialectical transformations.

Of the first, the breakdown of a notion as achieving the opposite of what it claims to achieve, the above-mentioned passage from Being to Nothing is a good example. Pure Being is a would-be concrete notion, but it does nothing to substantiate its claim. What it sets before us, an object that is and no more, and which is without definite character, is also indistinguishable from the absence of an object which it claims to exclude. Another example is the transition in the *Phenomenology* from absolute revolutionary freedom, which by forcefully abolishing every difference of status which enables men to tyrannize over one another, itself becomes an absolute tyranny, in which the guillotine is the ultimate leveller and equalizer. These then are moves involving a dialectical breakdown: a notion collapses and nothing positive as yet takes its place.[2]

Of the second type of move in which a notion reveals itself as an implicit form of a more adequate notion, there are countless examples. (*Enc.* §§ 86ff.) The empty senseless Being which simply is, reveals itself as an inadequate attempt to think the Definite Being which involves contrast in itself, which is Being-there-and-thus, and involves content and opposition. The notion of a genus as a type capable of being abstractedly present in the mind of a scientist who surveys and studies that world. The abstract difference of objects which, as it seems, have nothing to do with one another, is likewise seen to

[2] G. W. F. Hegel, *Werke*, II, 449–459; *The Phenomenology of Mind*, trans. Baillie (London, 1931), 599–610. The translations from the German are by the present author.

be an inadequate expression of the kind of polar difference in which each thing presupposes its opposite, and has it in a sense built into itself.

And of the third type in which we suddenly find ourselves at our goal by a sort of reversal of aim and perspective, I can find no better example than that of the transition, continually repeated in various forms, from the so-called Bad Infinite to the True Infinite. The Bad Infinite is a notion exemplified in any logical progression or series where each term introduces a next term which continues the progression, and where the frustrated yearning emerges to complete a series which can never be completed, to achieve the infinite by merely passing on to a wider finite.[3] This Bad Infinite swings over into the True Infinite, not by any mystical flight beyond finitude, but when the essential futility of trying to outsoar finitude emerges, when one realizes that in each term and step of the series one in principle has all, when one replaces the shackling finite that merely exchanges one set of bonds for another by the freely variable finite which in all its variations is self-same and free. Finite existence in the here and the now, with every limitation of quality and circumstance, is, Hegel teaches, when rightly regarded and accepted, identical with the infinite existence which is everywhere and always. To live in Main Street is, if one lives in the right spirit, to inhabit the Holy City, a view that will be deeply surprising and shocking to many of Hegel's transcendental interpreters. Another example of the arrival at a goal by the simple removal of a false perspective and the substitution of a better one, is the famous transition at the end of the *Logic* where the content of the Absolute Idea, the goal of the dialectic, is simply said to be "the system of which we have been hitherto studying the development," i.e. dialectic itself, where the end of the journey is simply seen to be the journey itself, and the method that has been followed on the journey. (*Enc.* § 237, *Zusatz*) It is by the capacity to understand and accept this last type of dialectical transformation that the true Hegelian is marked off from his often diligent and scholarly, but still profoundly misguided misinterpreter, who still yearns after the showy spectacular climax, the Absolute coming down in a machine accompanied by a flock of doves, when a simple arrest and return to utter ordinariness is in place.

To have indicated the threefold use of teleology in the dialectic, in respectively breaking down, in positively transforming, and in quietly stabilizing our notions, is quite insufficient unless one shows the steady operation of a teleological *nisus* in the system considered

---

[3] See *Werke*, IV, 164; *The Science of Logic*, trans. Johnston and Struthers (London, 1929), I, 155.

as a whole. I want therefore to say something about the implicit role of teleology in the three parts of Hegel's official system: the *Logic*, the *Philosophy of Nature*, and the *Philosophy of Spirit*. I shall say nothing about its role in the *Phenomenology of Spirit* though all that I say would find abundant illustration there as well. In the *Logic*, teleology is throughout implicit in that the Notion, with its basic principle of Totality—the principle that *every* aspect of a thing is built into *any* aspect of it, so that complete separateness of aspects is everywhere unthinkable—the Notion with this principle of Totality can, I say, be seen retrospectively to have been obscurely at work in the two "spheres" of Being and Essence which lead up to the sphere of the Notion. In the sphere of Being, Totality is anything but explicit: the categories of Being give themselves out as surface-categories, categories of quality and quantity, none of whose applications implies any other. To say that *A* is like this does not seem to involve that it is also like that, or that anything else is like this or that, and it does not seem to allow that *A* can pass gradually from being like this to being like that without sacrificing its identity altogether: its quantity or amount is likewise wholly irrelevant to its quality, and can be increased or diminished without let or stint. The effect of Hegel's dialectical comment in the Doctrine of Being is to show that this sort of surface independence of aspects is really unthinkable; qualities only qualify in relation to other qualities which are in a sense part of themselves, and which show their internal dependence by perpetual change into one another, qualities likewise are nothing except as involving quantitatively variable determinables, which link them intelligibly with other qualities, while the quantity which these determinables exemplify is nothing except as marked off by, and recognizable in, qualitative change, and so on. In the end the whole brave atomistic Humean structure with which we started lies in ruins and its residuum of truth is sought and found in a sphere of absolute relativism and interdependence, where *A* points to *B* as its necessary correlative, while *B* correspondingly points to *A*. What is found in this sphere, the so-called sphere of the categories of Essence, is however a wrangling relationship, in which everything seems to be limited by something *else*, precisely because the built-in unity of the correlatives is not manifest. The manifest quality refers back to the permanent essential disposition as the latter reveals itself in the former, the phenomenon points to the law or the force behind it, and the law or force points to the phenomenon. The cause looks to the effect and the effect to the prior cause, and so on. What is implicit in all this is precisely the Notion in which this insensate taking in of one another's washing ceases, in which the various conditioning and conditioned aspects of things come to be regarded as "the same thing seen from different angles," which is therefore unconditioned and free. It is the free notion of each and everything which determines what it causes and what causes it, what it outwardly manifests and what it secretly is, what impinges on it from without and what springs to meet this from within.

It is worthwhile stressing at this point the thoroughly teleological character of this central Hegelian concept, that of the *Begriff* or Notion. It is simply the Form of Aristotle conceived as a final cause which is also the full actuality and the achieved goodness of a thing. It only differs from the Aristotelian Form in that the individual, as well as the genus and the species, is part of it: it is the essence of each general form or type to have individual expressions, and Hegel further suggests, in the section entitled "The Judgment of the Notion," that the perfection which each type involves is such as to have its individual, as well as its specific differentiations. (*Enc.* §§ 178–180) We all recognize that Buddha and Socrates (say) achieved a perfection of manhood peculiar to *themselves*, and the same applies in the aesthetic field to the perfection of representation or expression achieved by works like Shakespeare's *Romeo and Juliet*, Giorgione's *Concert* and so on. The teleological character of the Notion is likewise shown in the fact that it is not necessarily exemplified in what a thing *actually* does or expresses (in the ordinary sense of "actually"): a thing can always deviate from, or fall short of, its notion, can be a poor and bad, and therefore, in the Hegelian sense, "untrue" version of its kind, or even of itself. What Hegel counsels us to do in the sphere of concepts is not simply to study things as they are, and to collect concepts which more or less cover their peculiarities, but rather to see in them approximations to rather full, rich types which they do not adequately represent at all. I may say that I for my part believe that this stress on imperfectly exemplified, normative universals, rather than on painfully discerned, necessary and sufficient conditions for calling something this or that, is of infinite fruitfulness in every philosophical enquiry and that the sustained triviality of certain modern linguistic investigations indirectly testifies to this fact. We may note further that the Hegelian Notion, like the Aristotelian Form, has an objective as well as a subjective status: it may exist immaterially in the mind, but it is also genuinely immanent in outer things, and constitutes the essential inner nature which comes out in all they do and undergo.

Teleology, however, becomes explicit in the last part of the Hegelian Logic, and yields the step which enables us to pass to the last stage of that Logic, the Absolute Idea: we shall not have a glimmer of what that Absolute Idea is, unless we understand the thoroughgoing teleology which it involves. It is the form of the Notion which explains all that went before precisely because it expresses the absolutely comprehensive purposiveness in which all other explanatory and interpretative positions find their place and their sense: it expresses the absolute finality which alone leaves not residuum of unexplained otherness outside of itself. The teleology from which we make our ascent to the Absolute Idea, which *is* in fact the Absolute Idea itself, is not, however, the ordinary finite teleology which we experience in our conscious practical pursuit of personal ends, nor is it even the finite teleology we see evinced in various unconscious performances of organisms, e.g. eating and digesting this or that type of food. It is, Hegel says, an *infinite* rather than a finite teleology, and we shall have the key to the whole thought of Hegel if we know what infinite, as opposed to finite, teleology really is. What is this infinite teleology which is so essential to Hegelianism, and how does it differ from the ordinary finite teleology which we all recognize? Finite teleology obtains where there is a definite result to be achieved, a definite situation in which this result is to emerge, definite means through which the result is to arise, and a definite process of actualizing the result in question, and where result, situation, means and process all differ profoundly in content. Thus, if a University invites me as a Visiting Professor at a certain point in their history and does so by making me an offer by cable, we have a case of finite teleology, and the same would obtain if an amoeba were to devour some food by flowing around it and enclosing it. Such finite teleology is by its nature always variable: as soon as a particular end is achieved by particular procedures or acts, it immediately becomes part of the situation, and is replaced by other ends. Explanation in terms of such finite ends is likewise never finally satisfactory, but points backwards and forwards without end. This bad infinity can only be overcome by postulating the true infinity of a *causa finalis sui*, a *Selbstzweckmässigkeit* which pervades the whole endless process, and which is totally present in its successive phases. This infinite teleology has not specific content, or rather its content is freely variable: one can say that its end is simply purposive organizing activity as such. In this infinite teleology there are various specific ends, but these specific ends are mere orientation-points of self-organization, necessary because one cannot be self-organizing without being so in a specific direction. In the same way, in infinite teleology there is an objective situation which fails to satisfy in some aspect, and so calls forth purposive scheming and trying, but this objective situation can be looked on as subserving, and as therefore a part of, infinite purposiveness, since infinite purposiveness would have nothing to concern itself with if everything were well adjusted. In infinite teleology there are likewise many definite means and many definite practical proceedings which must also be treated as "moments" of the infinite teleology since it would be impossible without them. The concept of infinite teleology is therefore, in the first place, one of purposive activity undertaken for its own sake and, in the second place, one in which all internal and external conditions of such purposive activity are, by the removal of special finite content from the end, made part of purposive activity itself. Such infinite purposiveness is seen at its most immediate in life. In a living organism all circumstances and available instruments are as much part of its life as are the activities it turns upon them; in all forms and guises of its activity its aim is only itself. Whatever it does or has or works on is part of its living and it lives only in order to live. And the imperfect expression of infinite teleology carried out in the successive generations of perishable organisms has a more perfect expression in the rational thinking life of the conscious person. Here too all activity, and all objective material of activity, can be said to be thinking, and nothing but thinking, and we think in order to think. The Aristotelian inspiration of these crucial Hegelian ideas will be evident.

This doctrine of infinite teleology is even more definitely expounded in those penultimate paragraphs of the *Logic* where Hegel deals with the Idea of the True and the Idea of the Good, the two opposed and complementary embodiments of the Absolute Idea. (*Enc.* §§ 213ff.) The Idea of Truth is the Idea of an Objective order which completely meets the demands of the probing intelligence by being at all points dominated by universals, at all points explained in terms of generic patterns and laws which simply *are* intelligence itself, so that intelligence will simply see in the world a mirror-image of its inherent rationality. The Idea of Truth involves, however, an inherent inadequacy: it *demands* the realization of something which it also implies *cannot* be fully carried out. It demands the final explanatory liquidation of the individual, and this it also demands and implies cannot be completed, since it is of the essence of knowledge to want something hard and individual to confront it which it cannot wholly make or unmake, which is simply *there* for its scrutiny and its explanation. However far the net of explanation may reach, there will always be individual details that slip through its meshes, and this is not merely a lamentable accident, but something demanded by the very nature of knowledge itself. The inadequacies of knowledge and truth now point to a more radical overcoming of the gulf between subject and object, the ideal of a practice which achieves what is good. This ideal, it seems, does stretch down to explain the individual, for what is practice but the transformation, not of mere notions, but of individual existence? Here, again, however, a seeming flaw variates the perfect understanding we seem to be gaining: for rational practice, though it may stretch down to the individual, still demands a gulf between the existent state of the individual and the ideal it seeks to impose on it. If rational practice is to be possible, the individual must not be *wholly* as it should be. and yet rational practice consists simply in making the individual as it should be.

We seem therefore to be frustrated in our attempt to conceive the world in terms of infinite teleology, as being in all its details nothing but an aspect of mind's rational activity: rational activity seems to be impossible without an element of inexplicable individual contingency which it seeks to explain, and must also involve an element of irredeemable irrational badness which it seeks to transform. Here, however, where we seem infinitely removed from our goal. a sudden swing of the dialectic brings us to it. We simply see that, since the gulf between contingent individuality and explanatory universality, and the gulf between such individuality and organized rational practicality. not only cannot, but *should* not, be eliminated in the interests of rational explanation and organizing practice themselves, both gulfs are from a higher point of view already bridged. Since there *ought* to be such gulfs between what is and what ought to be, there are, from a higher point of view, no such gulfs at all: everything from a higher point of view (we may parody Wittgenstein) is in order as it is.

The ultimate step in Hegel's *Logic* is therefore a step of the kind classified above as (c): a consolidating. quietistic step, one which achieves its goal by suddenly coming to see its goal in what previously seemed only an infinite, hopeless struggle towards it. It is the step we all take in those major moments where we realize that in exerting ourselves to the last for ideals not perfectly attainable against odds that tax our strength to the utmost, and which will never be overcome, we have in a sense reached our goal; we have become one with an infinite activity, with the life of God. if you like, which accepts the difficulties which crucify it as teleologically necessary to itself. This is why Hegel in this sort of context employs a language of illusion: the infinite End is achieved when the illusion vanishes which makes it still seem unachieved, when it no longer stands in its own light by its own wrong view of itself,[4] when we no longer see the absolute Good as something to be achieved but as something actually achieving itself and already achieved. when we realize that the nonachievement of the Absolute Good is, as it were. a shadow cast by its own light, a shadow cast in order only that it may be removed, and that we may see rational intelligent life as the all-in-all of everything. What Hegel teaches in these crucial passages is that an element of ineliminable irrationality, of recalcitrant externality. is teleologically necessary for the life of reason. and that this irrationality, this externality becomes rational, explained, eliminated precisely because it is thus teleo-

[4] G. W. F. Hegel, *Werke*, V, 326; *Science of Logic*, II, 465.

logically necessary. It is the old Christian message that the evils of life are there to try us, and that a cross gladly borne will sustain its bearer. How disappointing this simple declaration must be to all who expect absorption in a timeless Absolute or into a timeless society of spirits, to whom Hegel only gives a new look upon the tribulations of this transitory life! The astringent realism of Hegel's final solution is, however, precisely what renders it acceptable to many who find flights of transcendental otherworldliness nothing but a nauseous opiate.

Infinite teleology is therefore the central notion of the Hegelian *Logic*. How does it operate in the *Philosophy of Nature* and the *Philosophy of Spirit*, the remaining parts of the Hegelian system? Here it might seem that the transition from the Absolute Idea to the concrete sphere of Nature and Spirit was precisely *not* teleological, for does not Hegel say that the Absolute Idea freely releases its moment of particularity, thereby giving rise to the concrete, intuitive idea of Nature, and does not all this suggest the generation of the world by a ready-made, pre-existent perfection, which generation has all the purposeless gratuitousness of Thomistic creation, and is infinitely far from setting the "truth" of the matter at the end rather than at the beginning. Hegel certainly tried hard in this passage and in some others to mislead his readers into believing that he held something like Christian theism, a doctrine that is not through and through teleological, that explains things by their origin rather than by their ultimate goal. He provides, however, the materials for his own demythologization, and this can be abundantly found, e.g., in the treatment of the creation-story in the *Phenomenology*[5] and in several passages in the *Philosophy of Nature*. He there makes perfectly plain that the transition at the end of the *Logic* really involves the breakdown of an abstraction rather than a creative advance to anything more comprehensive. We simply see that the idea of infinite teleology to which we have advanced, is so far a *mere* idea, an abstract *logical shadow*, rather than an actual concrete achievement, and that it is only in so far as it can *also* be a concrete achievement that it can be a *genuine* idea at all.

As Hegel puts it in the *Phenomenology:*

> The Spirit as declared in the element of pure thought is itself essentially this, not to be only in this element but also *actual*. . . . The merely eternal or abstract spirit therefore becomes an other to itself and enters existence, and immediately enters immediate existence. It therefore creates a world. This creation is an imaginative locution

[5] G. W. F. Hegel, *Werke*, II, 587ff.; *The Phenomenology of Mind*, edition cited, 769ff.

for the Notion in its absolute movement, for the fact that the thought asserted to be absolutely simple and pure is, because it is abstract, rather the negative and therefore the opposite and other to itself.[6]

Or more explicitly in the *Philosophy of Nature:*

How did God reach the point of creating a world? God as an abstractum is not the true God, but it is only as the living process of positing his Other, the world . . . and only in unity with his other, in Spirit, is God a subject. (*Enc.* § 246)

Or

the knowledge contained in the simple Logical Idea is only the concept of knowledge as thought of by us, not the knowledge which exists in its own right, not actual spirit, but merely its possibility. (*Enc.* § 381, *Zusatz*)

Hegel tells us that the realm of logic is the realm of shadows, of thought-forms stripped of sensuous concretion. The Absolute Idea may be the noblest shadow in the realm of shadows and for a shadow the most concrete. It is however nothing at all except as worked out in the realm of nature and man. In a sense, therefore, the Hegelian system *starts* with the *Philosophy of Nature,* and this gives a crucial central importance to some of the things said in this much neglected book. And the system is teleological in the sense that it starts with inert material objects in Space and Time, and only at the end yields us objects which have life and mind and spirit.

It is here instructive to stress how far the Philosophies of Nature and Spirit, the concrete part of Hegel's idealism, anticipate what is now called a philosophy of emergent evolution. Thus there is in Hegel no notion that Spirit and Mind lie at the origins of the world, or that they engineered the world by some exercise of creative imagination, both of them notions that dominate Kant and Fichte, and that one might expect to find in Hegel. Hegel the Aristotelian denies explicitly that Space and Time, the forms of the intuitive idea he calls Nature, are the projections of any sort of intuiting subjectivity. "When we have said," he remarks,

that our sensation receives the form of the spatial and temporal from the intuiting spirit, this proposition should not be understood as if Space and Time were merely subjective forms: . . . the things themselves are in reality spatial and temporal. This two fold form of mutual externality is not one-sidedly imposed on them by our intuition, but is imposed on them from the beginning by the infinite Spirit which has being in itself, by the creative, eternal Idea. (*Enc.* § 448, *Zusatz*)

[6] *Ibid.,* 336.

If anyone is tempted to construe this passage as teaching that the Idea is the infinite subject responsible for Space and Time, let him remember that the Idea is the mere possibility, not the reality of cognition, and that it is in beings like ourselves, and ourselves alone, that cognition becomes a reality. And we must note further that Hegel does not place his emergence of conscious life at the origin of the world: the facts of the geological record, which were becoming well-known at that time, forced him to admit that the earth had a sort of life and a sort of history before what is properly organic and conscious arose on it. As Hegel expresses it in a passage dating from his Jena period but retained in his later exposition, the earth had "a life which, fermenting in itself, possessed its own internal time." It was a life in which "the Earth-spirit, not yet risen to opposition" enjoyed "the movement and dreams of a sleeper, until it awoke and reached consciousness in man, and was set before itself as a stable formation."

Hegel imagines the emergence of various types of organism as taking place in the life of the Earth in a series of lightning changes: he lends his authority to the Mosaic creation story: "To-day the plants arose, to-day animals, to-day man." The emergence is also compared to the sudden emergence of Minerva from the forehead of Jupiter. (*Enc.* § 339, *Zusatz*) Whatever one may think of this strange mythology, it at least disposes of any notion that Hegel held a Berkeleian or a Kantian view of the natural world in space and time. This natural world is spiritual in its ultimate destiny and purpose—it is only there to make the emergence of spiritual life possible—it is not spiritual in the sense of having covertly been manufactured by our spirit or by any spirit. If Spirit already existed in full reality there would be no need for Nature to exist at all. And the categories and forms and laws we find in Nature are present in Nature as organizing principles *before* we abstract them and think them: they exist there as a sort of frozen, petrified or alienated intelligence, but they are none the less really there.

If we now turn to the actual content of the *Philosophy of Nature*, it is through and through teleological. Nature exhibits what Hegel calls *die seiende Abstraktion*, the apparently separated, independent existence of aspects that cannot really exist separately and independently: its development is a steady elimination of this *seiende Abstraktion* until it acquires all the totality, the built-in unity of the Notion. From consisting of phases which lie outside of each other in space and time, and which have a merely inert, self-contained being and an indifference to each other's existence, it comes to consist of phases organically linked with one another and reflecting each other's existence. In other words it comes to embody the infinite immanent teleology of the Idea in the form of Life, and in this form it is ready to move inward to the form of Conscious Spirit. Hegel gives magnificent accounts of what he calls Nature's naiveté, its attempts to express various subtle logical entailments in the form of separately observable existences, like a child transforming abstractions into pictures. In so doing he seems to me to have done more to illuminate natural existence than any other philosopher. Nature we may say embodies Whitehead's fallacy of simple location even when it strives beyond it: thus the necessary unity of the two opposed poles of a magnet appears in a definitely located special indifference point between them (*Enc.* § 312), and the necessary presence of everything to everything else in the world is revealed in the special phenomenon of light. Like a child nature has made a category mistake, and turned a conceptual necessity into a quasi-material stuff. (*Enc.* §§ 275–276) One way, however, very much regret that palaeontological study had not advanced far enough in Hegel's day for Hegel to give his Philosophy of Nature an explicitly evolutionary guise. For him spiritual phenomena evolve in time, but merely natural phenomena only involve a *logical* evolution, whose various stages and phases exist side by side in space. I do not think we can doubt that, if Hegel had lived a little later, he would have given us an evolutionary, teleological theory of Nature as he did in mind in history. He would have done with brilliant competence what Darwin, Spencer, and also Marx and Engels, did in an extremely incompetent manner.

I have neither the space nor the need to prove the teleological character of Hegel's Philosophy of Mind or Spirit. It starts with Mind immersed in Nature, and in the deepest rapport with its body and its environment, and shows us Mind gradually liberating itself from this bondage, and achieving the free universality of thought, which enables it to return to Nature and put *it* into chains, rendering it intelligible by science, and rendering it completely malleable to its purposes by the rational technology which springs from science. If Marx spoke of man overcoming the alienation of nature he was merely plagiarizing from Hegel, and plagiarizing without understanding the import of what he plagiarized. From the conquest of material nature man proceeds to the conquest of his own raw wants and needs, and to their organization in the rational aims of social living: a second rational Nature is reared in the open clearing made by the destruction of the first. Finally Spirit becomes absolute in Art, Religion and Philosophy, where rational conscious life realizes and enjoys itself as the final meaning, the accomplished end of everything in the world. Everything exists in order to promote rational conscious life, and the highest forms of rational conscious life are precisely the forms in which this is consciously realized: the life of the artist, the life of the religious devotee, and the life of the Hegelian philosopher. If the bringing in of religion in this connection still rouses some association of Kierkegardian otherness and transcendence, let us remember that for Hegel God is only self-conscious in man, and in man's consciousness of God. (*Enc.* § 564) The religion recommended by Hegel is one in which it is good for God as a separately conceived being to die, and to be resurrected and live evermore as the shared spirit of the religious community.

I wish to conclude my inadequate treatment of Hegel's immensely complex teleological idealism by raising a few questions and sounding a few doubts. These are not the questions and doubts connected with most idealistic systems: Hegel does not believe in subsistent Platonic types, nor does he believe that *esse* is *percipi*, nor that all relation and unity in the world is the work of a constructive synthetic Mind, whether divine or human. What we have to ask in connection with Hegel is whether his queer brand of infinite teleology is acceptable. Is everything in the world explained by being shown to be a necessary condition for the emergence of self-conscious spiritual life? Does not the thesis readily permit of an inversion: that self-conscious spiritual life, far from being the explanatory focus of the world, is rather entirely dependent on that world for its existence and intelligibility, is perhaps only a negligible offshoot of it? That rationality depends on the irrational might be held to prove the irrationality of rationality, rather than the rationality of irrationality. Does not, we may further ask, the thesis prove too much? Could we not say of *every* phenomenon in the world that, since its necessary conditions are to be found in all reaches and levels of being, it too is the sense of the world, the thing for which the aeons labored! Cannot Dinkelsbühl or Popocatepetl be regarded as the absolute end for whose realization everything is as it is, or was as it was? And what finally is the nature of the teleology which is not the work of a definite organizing agent—for that the Idea is no agent we have seen—but is somehow obscurely inherent in the constitution of things? Is such a teleology more than the regulative teleology of Kant, a particular way of reflectively regarding the facts of the world?

To these questions I am not able to give a finally satisfactory answer except to say that I think Hegel's infinite teleology will be an acceptable thought-scheme only to the extent that we really believe in a strong, increasingly dominant trend in the world towards enhanced self-consciousness and rationality. I do not myself think that it is enough to cherish Hegelian teleology as a sort of rational faith necessarily implied by our various higher enterprises: one must be willing to give that faith some sort of metaphysical, ontological justification. Hegel thought that the facts of nature and history evinced a steady progress towards liberated, self-conscious rationality, but some might feel that these facts can be given a different, less optimistic interpretation. I myself would accept something like Hegelianism only with a considerably wider sweep of knowledge, perhaps demanding penetration into spheres of being lying beyond the confines of this transitory life. But whether or not one accepts Hegel, the interest of his problems, of his solutions and of his methods remains unique. He has certainly set before us the richest intellectual feast in the world if it is perhaps also the most difficult of all to digest.

vii

CONSCIOUSNESS AND HISTORY: LIST DER VERNUNFT IN HEGEL AND MARX

Shlomo Avineri

From his definition of history as progress toward the consciousness of freedom Hegel derives his criteria for the periodization of history.[1] The stages of historical development are the stages through which man becomes conscious of himself in the objective world, and it is only at the last stage, in Christian-Germanic Western civilization that "the subject discovered in objectivity the consciousness of his subjective freedom and rationality."[2] Though it has been repeatedly pointed

---

[1] Hegel, *Philosophy of Right*, trans. T. M. Knox (Oxford, 1942), §§ 341–343; Hegel, *Reason in History*, trans. R. S. Hartman (New York, 1953), 11–19.

[2] Hegel, *Vernunft in der Geschichte*, ed. J. Hoffmeister (Hamburg, 1955), 256–257. Translation by the author.

out that this process has to be viewed as a cumulative one and thus never attains absolute dimensions, it is still quite clear that Hegel sees his own contemporary age as the apex of historical development.[3]

Two questions seem to present themselves in this context: if history is progress toward the consciousness of freedom, the question has to be asked, How much is the historical actor himself aware of this? Second, if the present stage of history has achieved the level about which one can say that "what is rational is actual and what is actual is rational,"[4] what are the perspectives of further historical change and how do they affect Hegel's vision of history as a dialectical process? It is my aim in this essay, to discuss these two problems within the context of Hegel's own philosophy of history and to suggest that their impact can be found in Marx's thought as well. More precisely, I shall try to argue that Marx's attempt to solve these problems is directly related to some difficulties in the way these issues were settled by Hegel.

The first question, then, is the problem of the self-consciousness of the historical actor. The main dilemma here is raised by Hegel's separation between subjective intent and objective historical results. To Hegel, world historical events are not necessarily the consequence of the conscious intention of the historical actor. The "Cunning of Reason" (*List der Vernunft*) works through this dialectic of intent and consequence which makes the "world-historical individual," the historical hero, into a mere vehicle for the realization of reason in history.

Thus history for Hegel is never a linear, causal outcome of the forces at work at any given historical time; there always is a deeper, almost hidden meaning that has to be discovered. Moreover, subjective intentions should never be considered at their face value; hence Hegel's *caveat* against the romantic subjectivism of Fichte, Fries, and Schleiermacher, who overlook the dialectic of intent and consequences and limit themselves to a mere moralistic evaluation of subjective motivations.[5] Hegel's view of the hero in history has a double aspect: on the one hand, the world-historical individual has a central place in historical development as an agent of change, innovation and transformation; on the other, he is a mere instrument in the hands of superior forces and his own views or ideas are of little importance, nor

[3] Cf. F. Rosenzweig, *Hegel und der Staat* (Munich and Berlin, 1920), Vol. II; E. Weil, *Hegel et L'État* (Paris, 1950), 100–104; W. Kaufmann, *Hegel* (Garden City, N.Y., 1965), 254–286.
[4] PR, Preface, *Werke*, VII, 33; Knox translation, 10.
[5] PR, *Werke*, VII, 22–29; Knox translation, 3–7; See also §§ 126, 140, and Hegel's *Lectures on the History of Philosophy*, trans. Haldane and Simson (London, 1895) Vol. III, 508–511.

is it they that are being realized in history.[6] As a matter of fact, what a Caesar or a Napoleon have been motivated by, might have been petty ambitions rather than an overall view of historical destiny; yet the hidden hand of Reason managed to fit this into a wider perspective. Passions, ambition, greed, and so on, are thus viewed as the handmaids of reason working in history. Consequently, there is a basic difference in the way in which Hegel views the historical hero as compared with Carlyle or Spengler, since the vehicle of reason—the hero—is to be judged according to Hegel, not by his subjective spiritual qualities, but on the merits of deeds accomplished by him sometimes without his own recognition of their import. The personal fate of the world-historical individual is also of secondary importance:

> Once their objective is attained, they fall off like empty hulls from the kernel. They die like Alexander, they are murdered like Caesar, transported to Saint Helena like Napoleon. . . . They were fortunate in being the agents of a purpose which constituted a step in the progress of the Universal Spirit. But as individuals . . . they were not what is commonly called happy, nor did they want to be.[7]

This dramatic scenario contains however an epistemological difficulty which frustrates much of its brilliance. We have already seen that Hegel calls the world-historical individual an "agent" and an "instrument," and this goes hand in hand with the assumption that these individuals may not only have been motivated by considerations far inferior to the ultimate ends of history, but also that they may not have been aware at all of the historical importance of their work. But the textual evidence that suggests that this is Hegel's view is slightly inconclusive, and it seems that Hegel had difficulties in constructing a model of a historical agent who is *totally* unaware of the historical significance of what he is doing. Thus we have at least three different variations on this theme in Hegel's discussion of the world-historical individual:

> (a) The historical men, world-historical individuals, are those who grasp . . . a higher universal, make it their own purpose, and realize this purpose in accordance with the higher law of the spirit.[8] . . . The world-historical persons, the heroes of their age, must therefore be recognized as its seers.[9]

[6] Sidney Hook, *The Hero in History* (Boston, 1955), 59–66, does not always take account of this dialectical relationship.
[7] *Reason in History*, trans. Hartman, 41. A similar fate is envisaged by Hegel for the world-historical nations, whose principles gained wide acceptance, but they themselves may perish politically, like ancient Israel or Germany. Cf. *Hegel's Political Writings*, ed. Knox and Pelczynski (Oxford, 1964), 206.
[8] *Ibid.*, 39.
[9] *Ibid.*, 40.

(b) Caesar was motivated not only by his own private interest, but acted instinctively to bring to pass that which the times required.[10]

(c) Such individuals have no consciousness of the Idea as such. They are practical and political men.[11]

We thus find Hegel describing the world-historical individual as, alternatively, (i) wholly conscious of the idea of history and its development, (ii) only instinctively conscious of it, and (iii) being wholly unaware of it. With all the possible allowance for the varieties of expression and nuance, no adequate explication can be given to what must in the last resort be viewed as contradictory statements. And though it is obvious that the basic argument of Hegel—that the progress of history is being mediated through subjective motives totally unrelated to the *telos* of history—is apparent in all the variations on the theme cited above, the crucial problem of how much the world-historical individuals are aware of the significance of their deeds remains unsolved in Hegel.

This could have been a minor epistemological problem had not Hegel's scheme of history been based on the notion of self-consciousness. Since it is the development toward the consciousness of freedom, that is, self-consciousness, that is the main theme of Hegel's philosophy of history, the subjective awareness of the significance of historical action is of prime importance. Moreover, the degree of self-consciousness should change over time, and the more recent world-historical individuals should be more conscious of their role than those of earlier periods, since latter periods represent a higher stage of self-consciousness. Yet there is nothing in Hegel to suggest that there is such a development over time of the historical consciousness and self-awareness of the historical actor.

This must lead to the obvious question: Who, then, *is* aware of history's progress if the historical figures themselves are, to say the least, in such an ambivalent position as we have just noted? Further, if the perception of the historical figure is constant and does not undergo any change from one period of history to another, a serious doubt may be raised about the whole set of criteria used by Hegel for historical periodization.

We have thus arrived at a double paradox: on the one hand, the brilliant construction of the Cunning of Reason working through world-historical individuals never really solves the dialectical relationship between subjective motivation and objective historical role; on

[10] *Ibid.*, 39. Cf. PR, § 318, *Zusatz:* "The great man is the one who can put into words the will of his age, tell its age what its will is, and accomplish it. . . . He actualizes his age."

[11] *Ibid.*, 40.

the other, while the succession of historical periods is considered by Hegel as representing a progress in consciousness, the world-historical individuals labor under unchanging conditions. Even if these conditions are, as we have seen, somewhat unclear, there is no indication that they change. The crux of the paradox is that the only aspect of historical development that is not undergoing change is the nature of the vehicle of historical change itself—the world-historical individual. At the root of Hegel's view that man is what he historically makes himself there seems to be a strong a-historical element.

Hegel tries to solve these problems by postulating the philosopher, as distinguished from the historical actor, as one capable of understanding the historical process. This comes out most clearly in the Preface to the *Philosophy of Right:* here Hegel warns against a philosophy that tries to give "instruction as to what the world ought to be." On the contrary, philosophy can only "paint its grey on grey," it is true *Nachdenken*—afterthought. Thus the philosopher who cannot shape the world and should not try to change it, has the task of understanding that which is and shape out of the actual the "ideal [that] apprehends this same real world in its substance and builds it up for itself into the shape of an ideal realm."[12]

But this leaves the gap between subject and object wide open. Those who act in history do not understand it, and those who understand it do not act upon it. Though the philosopher is able to offer a synthesis, it still is external to the subjective element in history, and it always remains an open problem whether anyone except the philosopher shares the consciousness of progressing toward the consciousness of freedom.

It is my belief that Marx's introduction of the idea of *praxis* into historical debate is the point at which his philosophy of history tries to achieve a major breakthrough in bridging the gap left open by Hegel between action and consciousness in history. It is, of course, true that the idea of *praxis* can be traced down to Cieszkowski and Hess and sometimes even to Ruge and Feuerbach.[13] But it was mainly Marx who made it into a distinctive feature of the historical process. It is also immaterial in my view whether Lukács was right in denying that this reintroduces a strong Fichtean element into Marx:[14] the point is, that the idea of *praxis* tries to solve the paradox that had been left open by Hegel.

In a most subtle way, Marx preserved Hegel's idea about the

---

[12] PR, Preface, *Werke*, VII, 36; Knox translation, 13.
[13] See S. Avineri, *The Social and Political Thought of Karl Marx* (Cambridge, 1968), 124–134, and J. Gebhardt's *Politik und Eschatologie* (Munich, 1963).
[14] G. Lukács, *Moses Hess und die Probleme der idealistischen Dialektik* (Leipzig, 1926), 3–8.

Cunning of Reason, but added two modifications: first, for Marx, *List der Vernunft* works not through individuals but through collective entities, classes. Secondly, while history according to Marx has been progressing until now through the tortuous path of *List der Vernunft*, Marx introduces the proletariat as the first historical subject that is able to emancipate itself from the dialectic of ignorance and false consciousness implied in a view of historical development based on a Cunning of Reason.

Marx's description of past historical developments abounds in illustrations to the dialectic between motivation and consequences. In *The Communist Manifesto*, he points out that

> the weapons with which the bourgeoisie felled feudalism to the ground are now turned against the bourgeoisie itself. . . . Not only has the bourgeoisie forged the weapons that bring death to itself; it has also called into existence the men who are to wield those weapons—the modern working class. . . . The development of modern industry cuts therefore from under the bourgeoisie's feet its own foundation. . . . What the bourgeoisie, therefore, produces, above all, is its own gravediggers.[15]

This is even more pronounced when Marx discusses the impact of British rule on India; while criticizing British colonial expansion, he is well aware of the world-historical significance of these events which cannot be reduced to the mere motivation of British economic interests:

> England, it is true, in causing a social revolution in Hindostan, was actuated only by the vilest interests, and was stupid in her manner of enforcing them. But this is not the question. The question is, can mankind fulfill its destiny without a fundamental revolution in the social state of Asia? If not, whatever may have been the crimes of England, she was the unconscious tool of history in bringing about that revolution.[16]

While such a dialectic characterizes the interplay of social forces until now, the proletariat, according to Marx, introduces a new element. According to him, it possesses an adequate insight into the historical process, is therefore the first historical force to possess such an understanding, and is thus able to achieve purposive historical action through being conscious of its role in the productive process. Therefore,

[15] K. Marx and F. Engels, *Selected Works* (Moscow, 1962), Vol. I, 40ff.
[16] K. Marx, "The British Rule in India," in *Karl Marx on Colonialism and Modernization*, ed. S. Avineri (Garden City, N.Y., 1968), 89.

Communism, to Marx, "is the solution of the riddle of history and *knows itself to be this solution*."[17] Class consciousness has thus a crucial role in Marx's system, for it is the point at which subjective consciousness meets the objective role of the working class in modern society.

The language of Marx's eleventh *Thesis on Feuerbach* strongly suggests that he was fully aware of the theoretical difficulty which had confronted Hegel and which ultimately caused him to make the philosopher into the only kind of person capable of understanding world history.[18] Similarly and even more explicitly, Marx characterizes the proletariat in his *Introduction to the Critique of Hegel's Philosophy of Right* as being related to this conception of philosophy while at the same time introducing an active element into it:

> Just as philosophy finds its material weapon in the proletariat, so the proletariat finds its intellectual weapon in philosophy. . . . Philosophy is the head of this emancipation and the proletariat is its heart. Philosophy can only be realized by the abolition [*Aufhebung*] of the proletariat, and the proletariat can only be abolished by the realization of philosophy.[19]

This self-conscious proletarian *praxis* implies that the proletariat changes itself in the process of changing its circumstances. The goals of historical action thus develop simultaneously with the self-evolution of the proletariat, and therefore Marx always points out that it would be erroneous to try and project the nature of Communist society in advance. This is the epistemological reason behind Marx's contention that the proletarians have "no ready-made utopias" and know that "they will have to pass through long struggles, through a series of historical processes, transforming circumstances and men."[20] In the same passage in *The Civil War in France*, Marx goes on to say that the proletarians "have no ideals to realize, but to set free the elements of the new society with which the old collapsing bourgeois society itself is pregnant." The proletariat to Marx is the collective world-historical individual, possessing "the full consciousness of its historic mission . . . and the heroic resolve to act upon it."[21] The language here may be slightly rhetorical, but the substance relates to the traditional Hegelian dilemma of consciousness and action implied in the dialectics of the Cunning of Reason.

[17] K. Marx, *Early Writings*, ed. T. B. Bottomore (London, 1963), 155. Italics added.
[18] K. Marx, *Selected Works*, Vol. II, 405.
[19] K. Marx, *Early Writings*, 59.
[20] K. Marx, *Selected Works*, Vol. I, 523.
[21] *Ibid.* It can be argued that historical developments frustrated Marx's postulate about the *self*-emancipation of the proletariat and that Leninist elitism goes back to the Hegelian dichotomy, where subject and object are still separate.

While the postulate of the "realization of philosophy" poses a host of questions of its own, it should be borne in mind that Marx's development of the class consciousness of the proletariat is, in its way, an answer to the dilemma about the self-awareness of the world-historical figure of the significance of his own actions, a dilemma raised by Hegel's notion of *List der Vernunft* and left open by him.

The second problem suggested at the onset of this essay raises an issue of different dimensions, though it is inherently related to the first one. Given the Hegelian system, the present stage of historical development represents the highest stage of the attainment of self-consciousness. But what about the future?

Though Hegel has been criticized by Cieszkowski for not dealing with the dimension of the future in his system,[22] it is not altogether true that this has been completely neglected by him, since he did try to face the problem of future development as an integral part of his philosophy.

Hegel is very explicit on the systemic aspect of the problem. As a concept, history has been grasped in its totality for the first time in his own contemporary age, once the meaning of the historical process has been integrated into the system of speculative philosophy. It is in this respect, and this respect only, that history has reached its culmination. On the level of future developments, however, "there is still much work before us,"[23] though the exact nature of these developments is never spelled out by Hegel, nor could it have been discussed in detail given his basic premises. Since philosophy always paints its grey on grey and the owl of Minerva spreads its wings only at the falling of dusk, no philosopher can imagine or construct the future. "Every individual is a child of his time. . . . It is just as absurd to fancy that a philosophy can transcend its contemporary world as it is to fancy that an individual can overleap his own age, jump over Rhodes."[24]

Hence in his *Philosophy of History*, Hegel very clearly steers away from any attempt at prediction. Yet there are at least two instances, both of them extremely interesting, where his systematic caution is almost thrown overboard; this happens when he deals with Russia and America.

In his introductory remarks about the modern, Germanic-Christian world, Hegel puts in a few marginal remarks about the Slavs. They are dismissed in a short note, since they did not have, according to Hegel, any impact on world history, though he acknowledges their

[22] August von Cieszkowski, *Prolegomena zur Historiosophie* (Berlin, 1838), 8–9.
[23] Hegel, *Vernunft in der Geschichte*, ed. J. Hoffmeister (Hamburg, 1955), 257.
[24] PR, Preface, *Werke*, VII, 35; Knox translation, 11.

part in stemming the tide of the Turkish invasions. Then he goes on to say:

> Yet this entire body of people remains excluded from our consideration, because hitherto it has not appeared as an independent element in the series of phases that Reason has assumed in the world. Whether it will do so hereafter, is a question that does not concern us here; for in History we have to do with the past.[25]

Though the *caveat* against "jumping over Rhodes" is maintained, the possibility of the Slavs becoming a moment of world historical development is not dismissed altogether. In a letter to a Russian Baltic baron who had earlier attended his lectures at Heidelberg, Hegel is more explicit:

> You are lucky, Sir, to have a fatherland that occupies a conspicuous place in the realm of World History and which has undoubtedly an even higher vocation. It looks as if the other modern states have already passed the pinnacle of their course and their position has become static. Russia, on the other hand, which is perhaps already the strongest power of all, carries in its womb an immense possibility of developing its intensive nature.[26]

A similar set of remarks is made by Hegel about America. In his lectures on the philosophy of history, Hegel points out that in the New World a new culture is being formed, based on a mixture of European, Amerindian, and African elements.[27] In another place he says that "America is clearly the world of the future, which still is in process of becoming."[28] And on yet another occasion he goes into more detail, though again even here he is kept back at the last moment by considerations of systematic caution:

> America is the land of the future, where world-historical significance will manifest itself. It is a land sought by all those who are bored with the historic junkheap of Europe. Napoleon is said to have remarked: *Cette vieille Europe m'ennuie.* . . . What happened [in America] until now is nothing else than the echo of the Old World and is the expression of alien occurrences. And as the land of the

[25] Hegel, PH, trans. J. Sibree, ed. C. J. Friedrich (New York, 1956), 350. For a more detailed discussion in a similar vein, not included in Sibree's translation, see Hegel's *Vorlesungen über die Philosophie der Weltgeschichte*, ed. G. Lasson (Hamburg, 1968), IV, 758, 780.

[26] Hegel to Boris von Uexküll, November 28, 1821. In *Briefe von und an Hegel*, ed. J. Hoffmeister (Hamburg, 1953), II, 297–298. Translation by the present author.

[27] Hegel, *Vernunft in der Geschichte*, 203.

[28] *Ibid.*, 265.

future it does not concern us here. The philosopher has no business with prophecy. Rather we have to deal with that which happened and with that that is.[29]

This is, of course, a remarkable statement coming from Hegel, and his closing remarks attest that he knows that he may be crossing the boundaries his own philosophy has set on historical knowledge. Thus one may conclude that while Hegel considered history as the process of man's progress toward self-consciousness as having attained its apex in his own contemporary age, he was well aware that the future was still open in terms of the development of new cultures. How far these new cultures, or "worlds," the Russian and the American, would signify new "principles" of world history, it is difficult to say, since the text itself is silent on this. It should, however, be realized that contrary to some of the accepted views about Hegel, he did not wholly absolutize his own contemporary world in the sense in which the dialectic was cut off from further developments. Though the world has already achieved its self-consciousness, the fact that Hegel describes history as the progress *toward* the consciousness of freedom always leaves some openness to the future as a potentiality. There are therefore far more ambiguities in Hegel's views about the future than the traditional view, that sees Hegel as absolutizing his own contemporary world, would have allowed.

On the surface, it would seem that Marx's philosophy of history, being explicitly future-oriented, would be free of these ambiguities. Yet it should be recalled that Marx was always very careful about not making statements about the future. While he postulated the *Aufhebung* of capitalist society because of what he considered to be its inherent contradictions and tensions, he was extremely careful not to try and make apodictic statements about where precisely the revolution is going to break out first, what form it is going to take. Nor did he try his hand in sketching a detailed picture of the structure of the future socialist society. Most of his criticism against the utopian socialists was motivated by his opposition to what he considered their wild and unfounded statements about the minutiae of life under socialism. In this he seems to follow very closely Hegel's reluctance to discuss the future. His detailed discussion about possible future devel-

---

[29] *Ibid.*, 209–210. What is characteristic of America, according to Hegel, is that the political state has not yet emerged there, everything is just mere "civil society": "A real state, and a real political government, can evolve only when class differences have already been developed, when richness and poverty assume large proportions and there appears such a relationship, that a great mass cannot satisfy its need in the hitherto accepted way." (*Ibid.*, 207) The existence of free land is the reason why this stage has not yet been reached in the United States. The similarity between this analysis and Marx's views on America is striking.

opments in Russia makes it clear that he was aware of the methodological dimension implied in his position.[30]

There is however at least one instance in Marx where the broader problem posed by Hegel comes up again. That Marx did not wish to commit himself to details about the structure of future society or the way it is going to come about is one thing. It is a totally different matter to find that Marx seems to have had some lingering doubt whether communism is the *final* stage of human society, that is, whether one can absolutize even the communist stage of human development. In his *Economic-Philosophical Manuscripts*, Marx says after having outlined some of the characteristics of communism:

> Communism is the phase of negation of the negation and is, consequently, for the next stage of historical development a real and necessary factor in the emancipation and rehabilitation of man. Communism is the necessary form and the dynamic principle of the immediate future, but communism is not itself the goal of human development— the form of human society.[31]

Perhaps not too much should be read into this passage, and it certainly is unique within the corpus of Marx's writings. It still is an index to the degree that Marx must have been aware of the dilemmas of the Hegelian system about the limits of historical consciousness. In his vision of future society, Marx seems to have attempted to overcome these dilemmas: in the passage just mentioned, they appear again. The complexity and ambivalence of Hegel's views on history are thus far from having been *aufgehoben:* the problems set by the Hegelian *List der Vernunft* remain unsolved, not only in Hegel's own writings, but also in the thought of his most radical critic.

---

[30] Marx to the Editors of *Otechestvenniye Zapiski*, November 1877, in Marx and Engels, *Selected Correspondence* (Moscow, n.d.), 376–379.
[31] K. Marx, *Early Writings*, 167.

MEDIATION AND IMMEDIACY
IN HEGEL, MARX
AND FEUERBACH

Karl Löwith*

1. The Consummation of Philosophy through Hegel and Its Abolition through Marx

Hegel completes the history of spirit in the sense of an ultimate plenitude gathering all previous events and thoughts into the unity of the philosophy of history and the history of philosophy. At the same time, however, Hegel's completion also has the sense of an eschatological end, in which the history of spirit finally comprehends itself.

* Translated from the German by Kenley Royce Dove. The translation has been commissioned and approved by Prof. Löwith. The translator is indebted to Prof. Löwith for several editorial clarifications and to Christa Dove for a critical proof reading of the entire translation.

The end as well as the beginning of his lectures on the history of philosophy show that Hegel has comprehended his own standpoint as that of philosophical completion and that he has brought the realm of thought to its conclusion. According to his schematization of the history of philosophy, his own system stands at the end of the third epoch, in the "old age of spirit." And in agreement with this system of epochs, Hegel's history of spirit is not given a merely provisional termination at a random point; it has been definitively and consciously "concluded." On this historical basis its logical form is also "syllogistic," a merging of beginning and end. This conclusion of the history of philosophy is—like the end of the *Phenomenology*, the *Logic*, and *Encyclopedia*—no mere arbitrary arrival at some place, but an arrival at a "goal" and therefore a "result." Like Proclus, Hegel unified the world of the Christian logos with the absolute totality of the concretely organized idea, thus concluding all three epochs. Only from this eschatological point of view can Hegel's conclusion of the *History of Philosophy* be understood in its full pathos and gravity:

> The world spirit has now arrived at this point. The final philosophy is the result of all that has gone before; nothing has been lost, all principles are retained. This concrete idea is the result of the struggles of spirit through almost 2500 years [Thales was born in 640 B.C.] of spirit's most serious labor to become objective to itself, to recognize itself: *Tantae molis erat, se ipsam cognoscere mentem.*[1]

The ambiguity of Hegel's "consummation," meaning both fulfillment and conclusion, is revealed in the *transformation* of Vergil's "*Romanam condere gentem*" into "*se ipsam cognoscere mentem.*" The sense of this reformulation is that the founding of the Roman Empire then demanded the same effort as is now demanded for spirit to found itself in its own realm.

Ten years after Hegel's death, in a dissertation on Epicurus and Democritus, the twenty-three year old Marx sought to come to terms with the situation created by Hegel. He asks: How is it still possible, after Hegel, to establish a philosophical standpoint which is neither imitative nor arbitrary? His answer: only by a fundamental examination of philosophy in its totalized, Hegelian form, and by an "abolition" of this philosophy which is, at the same time, its "actualization." Philosophy is always at such a "nodal point" when its abstract principle has become totally concrete, as once before in Aristotle and now again in Hegel. The possibility of continued development is then interrupted; a full circle has been completed. Consequently, whoever does not see this necessity will have to deny that man can continue his spiritual

[1] G. W. F. Hegel, *Werke* XV (1844 edition), *Geschichte der Philosophie*, 617ff.

life after such a philosophy. Only this insight makes comprehensible how, after Aristotle, a Zeno, Epicurus, and Sextus Empiricus, and after Hegel "the largely baseless, impoverished experiments of recent philosophers could come to the light of day." In contrast with the Young Hegelians, who only sought a partial reformation of Hegel, Marx gained from history the insight that philosophy *as such* was at stake. In his dissertation, Marx writes: "At such times, the half-hearted ones [meaning philosophers like Ruge] hold opinions contrary to that of strong generals. They think they can recoup their losses through a reduction of forces, through . . . a peaceful compromise with the real demands, whereas when Athens [that is, philosophy] was threatened with destruction, Themistocles [that is, Marx himself] induced the Athenians to leave their city and to found a new Athens [that is, a new kind of philosophy which in the old sense is no longer a philosophy at all] at sea, in another element," that is, in the element of political and economic practice, which must now be understood as "what is." And one must not forget that the age following such catastrophes is an age of iron,

> fortunate if marked by the clash of Titans, but deplorable if like the centuries that drag on after great artistic epochs, for these busy themselves with copying in plaster and copper what was first born in Carrara marble.

Rightly and wrongly, Feuerbach stands in the shadow of Marx and Hegel. Rightly, because the conceptual articulation of his naturalism falls far behind Hegel's philosophy of spirit and also behind Marx's philosophy of labor; wrongly, because the primitiveness of his naturalistic thought derives an advantage over Hegel and Marx from the very fact that—under the title of "nature"—it makes a return to something immediate and elementary. For to ascend from the immediate and elementary to something mediated and derived is easier than the opposite: to find one's way back from the multifariously mediated to something simple and immediate. However, since Feuerbach, as a disciple of Hegel, could make his way back to the immediateness of nature only via a detour, namely a critique of mediation, we must begin with a discussion of dialectical mediation in Hegel and Marx.

Marx deserves the credit for having developed and expressed the insight that the philosophy of the future can no longer be philosophy in the traditional sense of the word if Hegel's metaphysics fulfills the legacy of all previous philosophy and if this fulfillment represents an irrevocable end. Philosophy becomes something entirely different: it becomes Marxism or scientific socialism, or, more generally, a theoretically guided practice designed to bring about a radical alteration of human society. Hegel's theoretical pathos, expressed in the phrase "to recognize what is" (instead of postulating what should be) is irreconcilable with Marx's thesis that the real task is to *change* the world and not simply to *interpret* it in various ways. This decisive difference cannot be relativized by pointing out that the practice which sets out to change the world implies and necessitates a theoretical understanding and a critique of that which is. It is impossible to be a Marxist in the spirit of Marx and at the same time a philosopher in the spirit of the tradition that was valid up to Hegel. When Marx, in the early philosophical manuscripts, speaks about the "abolition" of philosophy in Hegel's double sense of the term and about the abolition of the contradictions in civil society which Hegel himself pointed out, he is, to be sure, using Hegel's language; yet what he really means and intends is not the preserving and at the same time annihilating elevation of these contradictions into a higher comprehensive unity, but—very undialectically—their total removal.[2] Marx takes over the task of the philosophy which ended with Hegel and puts revolutionary Marxism, as reason becoming practical, in the place of the whole previous tradition. And this tradition has indeed come to an end when the priority of theory over practice acknowledged from Aristotle to Hegel reverses itself and when social-historical practice unmasks theory as ideology.[3] Only the utopian Marxism of a Marcuse, a Horkheimer, or an Adorno, which instead of making any practical decisions cultivates a permanent critique of all that is, can labor under the illusion of operating upon the basis of Hegel's dialectic and at the same time sustaining Marx's concern in a sublimated manner.

But despite the fundamental irreconcilability of philosophical and Marxist thought, one must not fail to notice that Marx's critical-revolutionary program was philosophically built on Hegelian conceptions and that Marx in his own way remained a disciple of Hegel even after he had "settled accounts" with his philosophical conscience and written *Das Kapital*. The analysis of the fetishist character of com-

---

[2] Marx's dialectic is no longer dialectical in the Hegelian sense; its moving principle is merely the negation of the negation without that aspect whereby what is negated in abolition [*Aufheben*] is also preserved. The aim of Marx's dialectic is the total "annihilation" of estrangement, religious as well as political-economic. Hegel's ambiguous philosophy of religion is replaced by a resolute atheism in the form of secular humanism: the annihilation of God as the annihilation of human self-estrangement. Cf. *Marx-Engels Gesamtausgabe*, hereafter cited as MEGA (Berlin and Moscow, 1927–1935), Sec. I, Vol. III, 164, 166, 168. Cf. also K. Bockmühl, *Leiblichkeit und Gesellschaft* (1961), 212ff.

[3] Cf. my *Gesammelte Abhandlungen* (Stuttgart, 1960), 247ff., and M. Riedel, *Theorie und Praxis im Denken Hegels* (Stuttgart, 1965), where it is established for the first time that, for Hegel, theory and practice share an equal primacy, since spirit as will is a will to freedom and freedom is the origin of all historical practice.

modities is a prime example of Hegelian dialectics.[4] The question is: In what sense did Marx remain a disciple of Hegel? Certainly not by schoolboy imitations or historico-philological interpretations of the master which make a great display of scholarly accuracy but take no independent position. Nor did he proceed from the "experience of consciousness" in order finally to bring skepticism to its fulfillment in the absolute knowledge of the absolute. His starting point was rather the experience of the social relations of production and his goal was a communist society. The two fundamental and correlated presuppositions which Marx shares with Hegel and which differentiate him from Feuerbach are, first, the *historical consciousness of history*, and second, the *dialectical method of mediation*.

2. Historical Consciousness and Dialectical Mediation in Historical Materialism

First: The unifying whole of Marx's theory, the framework which holds it all together, is a definite idea of *history* and the belief in this idea. Marx's thinking is no more oriented within the world of nature than Hegel's; its horizon is rather that of world-history and of human nature transforming itself historically. The communist of the classless society is the new man of a new historical world in relation to which all previous history is mere "pre-history."

In the first part of the *German Ideology*, Marx has sketched out his basic conception of history in a few pages. The first sentence reads: "We know only one science, the science of history." It is the only science because it is the all-embracing revelation of human nature; it is also "the true natural history of man" because nature as such does not determine man as a societal, generic being. "The nature which comes to be in human history is the real nature of man."[5] Marx not only rejects the belief in a revelation of God through history, in history as a process of salvation, he also expressly outrules the history of nature. Nature is for him merely the "other self" and is represented in geographical and climatic conditions as a subordinate precondition of the historical activity of man. A precedence of nature over human history exists only "on some Australian coral islands of recent origin," as Marx sarcastically formulates it. What Marx finds interesting in

---

[4] Since human intercourse becomes a means for the traffic of commodities, the commodity is humanized and man, the producer, is thingified. In this *quid pro quo* the formal structure of the interrelation of consciousness and object is mirrored in a concrete economic fashion. Just as consciousness and object reciprocally alter one another, man as a producer of commodities corresponds to the social fetishism of commodities.

[5] MEGA, Sec. I, Vol. III, 122.

an apple is not the fact that there are fruit-bearing trees in nature, but that at a certain time and because of certain economic relations this product of nature was imported into Europe, where it was treated as a commodity in exchange for money. From this radically historical point of view, it is unimportant that man, who in cultivating nature is historically productive, is also a creature of nature and not a self-made *homunculus*. The overshadowing truth is rather that the self-production of the historical world by human labor actually changes the world of nature.

> One can distinguish men from animals in terms of consciousness, religion, or whatever. Men begin to distinguish themselves from animals as soon as they begin to *produce* their material life itself. . . . The first act is therefore the creation of means for the satisfaction of these needs, the production of life itself, and this is indeed a historical act, the daily and hourly fulfillment of an elementary historical condition, which is just as necessary today as it was millennia ago, simply to keep men alive.[6]

This mode of production is not merely a reproduction of physical existence; it is a definite kind of activity, a historically determined way of life. Individuals are what they express about their lives in the active production of something. "What they are coincides with what and how they produce." With the spread of various modes of production and transportation, history becomes world-history, which corresponds to a world market.

Two years after writing the *German Ideology*, Marx published the *Communist Manifesto*. Like the earlier work, it is based entirely upon a philosophical concept of history. Its central thesis is that the course of human history consists in a process of perpetual antagonism, in which the struggle between rulers and ruled is so sharpened and intensified, that it must finally be resolved through the clash of the capitalist bourgeoisie and the propertyless proletariat. At the end of this struggle there is, for Marx, the eschatological expectation that communism will prepare an end for the rule of man over man by eliminating private property. Communism is nothing less than the "riddle of history solved." Marx is no longer astonished by those things which are by nature what they are and cannot be otherwise. Instead, he is indignant because things are not different in the historical world. He therefore wants to change the world, a demand which can be met if, and to whatever degree, the "world" as such is a world of man, "a nature coming to be man." Marx particularly liked to quote Hegel's remark that the most criminal thought is more magnificent and sublime than all the marvels of the firmament because the criminal,

---

[6] *Ibid.*

as spirit. is conscious of his thought, whereas nature knows nothing of itself and is exteriority itself. In a similar vein, Hegel says in his lectures on Aesthetics that. from a formal point of view, even a bad idea in the mind of man is more lofty than any product of nature, for spirituality and freedom are always present in such an idea.

Hegel and Marx are also at one concerning the history of *philosophy*, even though historical materialism, contrary to Hegel. does not regard it as "the innermost core of world-history." Yet Marx is not alone in standing under the spell of Hegel's philosophical conception that world-history and the history of philosophy reveal a necessary progression toward a predetermined goal. Equally Hegelian is Heidegger's conception of the history of Being, for which the innermost core is the thought of Being, thus paralleling Hegel's conception of the movements of thought. The only difference is that Heidegger conceives of progress as something negative. as a history of progressive decay, looking back to an unexhausted beginning and forward to "another beginning" whose way is to be prepared by the question of Being.

It was said at the outset that Marx deserves the credit for having seen the implications of Hegel's completion "if" Hegel's philosophy actually is the consummation of the entire previous tradition. But is this really the case? The model governing Hegel's universal-historical conception of philosophy is actually only a very specific and limited epoch, namely the road leading from Kant via Fichte and Schelling to Hegel himself.[7] In addition. the direct, personal succession of these philosophers and the academic character of their work constitute an exceptional case in the history of philosophy. The philosophy from Kant to Hegel is a philosophy of German professors. F. Bacon and Descartes, Spinoza and Leibniz, Hobbes, Locke and Hume were not philosophers who taught from a public lectern and their thought resists compression into the familiar "from x to y" schema. What has been completed with Hegel is not *the* history of *the* philosophy, at whose end Marx begins afresh; what has been completed is only the history of German idealism.[8] And thus evaporates the charm of radicalness in which the young Marx sought historical legitimation by reference to Hegel's consummation; it vanishes as soon as one questions Hegel's interpretation of spiritual history as a complete course of necessary development and instead proceeds soberly and historically, taking a

---

[7] Cf. L. Feuerbach, *Sämtliche Werke* (Leipzig, 1846), II, 193ff., 207, and 215ff.

[8] The peculiarity of German idealism is indicated by the fact that a mathematician and philosopher as significant as A. N. Whitehead could entirely disregard this great movement because it was not effectively in touch with science. Instead, Whitehead refers primarily to Descartes, Leibniz, Locke, and Hume. See his *Science and the Modern World* (New York, 1925), chap. IX.

philosopher's appraisal of his relationship to real and presumed predecessors of two millennia for what it really is: an *ex post facto* historical
projection designed to justify his own undertaking. The history of philosophy no more completes itself with Hegel than world-history reaches
its preordained end in the *Communist Manifesto*. And this by no
means excludes the fact that the *Manifesto* has been a most effective
prophetic document and that post-Hegelian philosophy has brought
forth nothing comparable to Hegel in depth and breadth, in conceptual
articulation and sophistic art.

Second: Together with historical consciousness, the *dialectical
mediation* between historically productive man and his age and environment assumes for Marx a fundamental significance. This can
be seen especially clearly, albeit indirectly, in his "Theses on Feuerbach." Marx's critique of Feuerbach's a-historical materialism is based
upon the teachings of Hegel. To be sure, the writings of Feuerbach
are for Marx the only ones since Hegel which contain "a real theoretical revolution," but the only thing that Marx adopts from Feuerbach
is his critique of religion, that is, the reduction of metaphysical onto-
theology to social anthropology. As a Hegelian, however, Marx, like
Marxists and Hegelians of today, was unable to understand that Feuerbach freed himself from the magic circle of Hegel's system of total
mediation precisely because he had got behind the reflective level of
his teacher. In his introduction to Feuerbach's writings on Hegel, W.
Harich declares that Feuerbach remained hopelessly behind the "progressive movement" of the 1840s.[9] H. G. Gadamer states that none
of Hegel's critics were able to break the compelling power and truth
of the philosophy of reflection without either contradicting themselves
or abandoning philosophy as such.[10] In return one could ask: What
is the philosophical and not merely historical criterion for this progres-
siveness, this compelling superiority of the dialectical movement of
reflection? For Harich, as a Marxist, the criterion is progress toward
a community without estrangement, that is, a community which stands
in total mediation with nature and society and thus fulfills what the
young Marx postulated: the mediation of "humanism" and "naturalism."[11] Gadamer sees Hegel's superiority in that there is no position
possible which could not be included in the reflective movement of
"consciousness coming-to-itself." To be sure, Gadamer wants to avoid
the hybrid conclusions of speculative idealism and to take seriously
the critique of the Young Hegelians. Even though his thought lacks
the onto-theological foundation of speculative mediation, Gadamer's

---

[9] L. Feuerbach, *Zur Kritik der Hegelschen Philosophie* (Berlin, 1955), 10. [This
essay appears also in Feuerbach's *Kleine Schriften* (Frankfurt, 1966), 78–123, K.R.D.]
[10] H. G. Gadamer, *Wahrheit und Methode* (Tübingen, 1960), 324ff. and 472ff.
[11] MEGA, Sec. I, Vol. III, 144.

idea of universal hermeneutic as a superior and uniquely true method corresponds in principle to Hegel's idea of historical-dialectical mediation. But Hegel's concept of truth as that which is in-and-for-itself accordingly dissolves into the ever-changing perspectives of a truth which is for us.

Although it is indeed beyond dispute that the "Archimedean point" from which Hegelian thought might be overturned is not to be found "within the realm of reflection"—were that possible, it would be no Archimedean point—, this point may nevertheless be found outside that realm. And what reason might there be for regarding a position outside of reflection as unphilosophical, unless, of course, philosophy itself were to be identified with the transcendental and speculative philosophy of reflection and its tendency toward total mediation? Gadamer maintains that Feuerbach's reliance upon the immediate is self-refuting because the appeal to the immediate is not an immediate attitude but rather a reflective act. And in the same spirit he says, with reference to my position, that the appeal to nature and its naturalness is itself neither nature nor natural. But this proposition only expresses the tautology that every reflection is an act of conscious thought and is, as such, no immediate product of nature. This, however, in no way rules out the possibility that nature itself is the measure of all things natural and that even our conscious attitude to it is a power of human nature which produces, discovers, and thinks in us.[12] Reflective consciousness is neither independent nor fundamental and reflection is not initiated by a decision to reflect; it begins rather through a return from the world of things to ourselves.[13]

The priority of nature in its immediacy—insusceptible to dialectic because it does not speak to us—rests upon the fact that it, in contrast to all products and creatures of man, is not constituted by our produc-

---

[12] The step from organic nature to consciously reflective man constitutes no *absolute* differentiation from the prehuman forms of life. For how could man, as a creature of natural production, invent and produce something if nature herself were not already productive and inventive, making a thousand experiments before producing something new. As Teilhard de Chardin has said, a vertebrate that spreads and feathers its limbs to glide in flight, and man who builds airplanes with craft and reflection both testify to the fact that *Physis* has a *Logos*—with or without consciousness.

[13] "We awake through *Reflection*, i.e., through a necessitated return to ourselves. But a return without resistance or a reflection without an object are simply unthinkable." (F. Schelling, *Werke* [Munich, 1927–1956], I, 325.) This return from the world, however, was forced upon us primarily by Christianity. And without Christian self-consciousness, the history of self-reflection, which extends from Descartes through transcendental idealism to Husserl's Cartesian Meditations and Heidegger's analytic of *Dasein*, is unthinkable. "Idealism belongs entirely to the new world and does not need to conceal its indebtedness to Christianity for opening the hitherto blocked entryway." (Schelling, *Werke*, Vol. V, 64.)

tive relation with it. The world of nature is not *our* world, that is, a mere setting and evironment mediated by man. This world is and always will be self-grounded, *causa sui*, the ground of everything and the purpose of nothing, as it is for Spinoza, whom Feuerbach calls the "Moses of modern materialism." With respect to us, as men, nature is suprahuman, and not simply a-human or external or humanity. It is, to speak with Goethe's great sense of nature, "ever true, always right and error is invariably human."[14]

By his anti-Hegelian, and thus indirectly anti-Marxian, revalidation of nature in its immediacy, Feuerbach attempted a return to what metaphysics originally was and remained until Lucretius, namely the science of *physis*, of *natura genetrix*. "Philosophy is the science of actuality in its truth and totality; but the essence of actuality is nature (nature in the most universal sense of the word)." "*Philosophy must reunite itself with the natural sciences, and the natural sciences with philosophy*. This union, based upon reciprocal need and inner necessity, will be more lasting . . . and more fruitful than the *previous misalliance* between philosophy and theology."[15] There would be little sense in dwelling upon the banal and vulgar aspects of Feuerbach's naturalism ("Man is what he eats"), for these are obvious. Nor is his constant emphasis upon "sensuousness" of any importance in itself. Its importance lies rather in stressing our access to the world of nature by means of our living, world-open senses. The significance of the human senses is not merely "anthropological" but "ontological" as well.[16]

As the *all*-creative force, the *common* nature of all things, which the Greeks recognized as self-moving and self-productive, does not require, as do all human products, some external producer as its mediator. *For Hegel and Marx, on the other hand, that which produces itself is not nature but active spirit or working man in opposition to nature—whose spiritless or unhuman externality is first spiritualized and humanized by man.* The only fundamental insight which Marx derived from Hegel's *Phenomenology of Spirit* is that man produces his own world and hence his own self by the all-transforming activity of work. Whence, however, does man—either as subjectively active spirit or as actually productive man—derive this creative force which enables

[14] J. W. Goethe, *Gespräche*, ed. Biedermann (Leipzig, 1909), IV, 69. See also Vol. II, 40, and the following passage from *Maximen und Reflexionen aus Wilhelm Meisters Wanderjahren:* "For men have imposed law upon themselves without knowing what it was to which they were giving laws; nature, however, has been ordered by the gods. What men have posited is never quite appropriate, be it right or wrong; but what the gods posit—right or wrong—is always in its proper place."

[15] L. Feuerbach, *Werke*, II, 231 and 267.

[16] *Ibid.*, 324. With reference to Spinoza's *Deus sive Natura*, see *Werke*, Vol. VIII, 116ff.

him to possess the world by cultivating nature through his labor and imaginatively re-creating it according to his own purposes? This is a question which neither Marx nor Hegel was able to answer. They ascribe to active spirit, to man as a producer, a force which originally belongs only to nature, as *natura naturans*.[17]

3. Marx's Critique of Feuerbach

The first sentence of the First Thesis reads: "It is the main defect of all previous materialism (Feuerbach's included) that the object, actuality (sensuousness), is only grasped in objective form, or intuitively, and not subjectively, as sensuous human activity, as practice." Feuerbach's materialism views objective reality as standing vis-à-vis sensuous intuition, as having the character of an object. The basis for his interpretation lies in the fact that he does not understand sensuous intuition as a productive "sensuous-human activity," as practice, or, to express it in Hegel's terms, he does not dialectically comprehend that which stands over and against sense-certainty as "the other of itself." According to Marx, this active aspect of man which produces the object was neglected by the materialist tradition and only developed by the idealism of Kant, Fichte, and Hegel, even though these latter assumed that the active agent was the categorial understanding, the active I, or spirit, alienating itself to create a world. Feuerbach's materialism is a retrogression from the practice which idealism had already

---

[17] See Jan van der Meulen, *Hegel: Die gebrochene Mitte* (Hamburg, 1958), 258ff. It is here convincingly shown that Hegel underestimated the significance of nature and why, in taking his departure from self-positing spirit, he had to do so, even though the conceptual superiority of his over Kant's theory of nature enabled him to discover categories of "spirit" already present in organic forms of life: self-production, self-subsistence, self-differentiation. Despite these insights, nature remained for Hegel the "other" in relation to spirit. This may be seen already in the *Jenenser Logik, Metaphysik und Naturphilosophie*, ed. Lasson (Hamburg, 1923), 189. "Nature determined as the other, has its life in something other than life itself. . . ." Cf. *Logik*, ed. Lasson (Leipzig, 1934), I, 105: "Physical nature is an other which is such according to its own determination; it is the other of spirit. At first, this determination of nature is thus a mere relativity; it expresses no quality of nature itself but only a relation external to it. But since spirit is the true Something, nature in itself is accordingly no more than what it is vis-à-vis spirit; insofar as nature is taken to be for itself, its quality is therefore that of being the other in its self, being-outside-itself (in the determinations of space, time, and matter)." As an ontology of consciousness, Hegel's system presupposes that a self-systematizing development can only take place where spirit and consciousness exist. This development is consequently not to be found in the world of nature but only in world-history. Compare Gabler, *Kritik des Bewusstseins* (Leiden, 1901), 195ff., and especially M. Riedel, *Theorie und Praxis im Denken Hegels* (Stuttgart, 1965). See also Feuerbach, *Werke*, VIII, 26f. and 111.

worked out in theory; he does not manage to transform the idealist notion of practical activity into an actual, material activity, because he does not understand that human activity is both "critical" in that it alters the object as well as "objective," that is, productive of its own object. And it is this "practical-critical" and "revolutionary" activity of historical production which chiefly matters in the materialistic idealism of Marx. Marx therefore calls it "historical," or "practical," materialism and at times equates it with "communism." Feuerbach's materialism, on the other hand, is not concerned with anything historical or mediating and is therefore a naturalism unmediated by human society. "Insofar as Feuerbach is a materialist, he takes no account of history, and whenever he does concern himself with history, he is not a materialist. For him, materialism and history are poles apart."[18] And since history is political-social history, Marx criticizes Feuerbach for paying too much attention to nature and too little to the politics with which contemporary philosophy must align itself if it is to become true.

Since Feuerbach regards nature as a permanently existing object of sensuous intuition, objects take on the appearance of being immediately present in our theoretical vision, whereas they are really products of human industry and not of an already given, independent nature. The praxis of Marx's materialistic idealism is ultimately designed to realize an element of reason absent in existing society and to transform Hegel's proposition concerning the rationality of the actual into a fact. *The sphere of dialectical mediation within which Marx, following Hegel, finds his orientation is therefore not the world of nature but the world of history, and, accordingly, of man.* For the practical idealism of Marx, the primary and original world of nature is as external and accidental as it is for the speculative idealism of Hegel, and for the modern man of the industrial age it is as indifferent as those "coral islands of recent origin" which Marx probably read about in Darwin's travel book.[19]

For Hegel and Marx, the world of nature possesses no rationality because it lacks self-consciousness. Its actuality is minimal because it is only mediated and actualized by man. The "actuality" of which Marx speaks is one which is dependent upon man.

But it is not only the *world* around us which is a result of practical activity. This is also the case for the truth of theoretical knowledge. The Second Thesis reads: "The question whether human thought attains objective truth is not a theoretical but a practical question. Man

[18] MEGA, Sec. I, Vol. V, 34.
[19] *Ibid.,* 33ff.

must prove the truth, that is, the reality, of his thought in practice. The quarrel over the reality or unreality of thought isolated from practice is purely scholastic." Thus even the truth of theoretical knowledge is only elicited and verified in practice, that is, man recognizes reality only insofar as he makes and produces it—a thesis whose distant origin is found in the theological notion that knowledge and creation are at one in God. Marx himself returns once again to his second thesis in a footnote to *Capital*[20] where he cites Vico's proposition concerning the convertibility of the true and the self-made. Accordingly, truth is no longer understood as *adequatio rei et intellectus;* man's knowledge of his object is adequate because he has actually created it through practical creativity. Marx, unlike Vico, never asked how man could know a nature which he had not himself produced; this question fell outside the exclusively anthropological-social area of his interest. Only Engels attempted to extend dialectic to nature.

4. Feuerbach's Critique of Hegel's Dialectic of Sense-Certainty

We shall limit ourselves to the problem which is central to Hegel and Marx and which also embraces the question of history, namely the problem of mediation. When Feuerbach lays stress upon the "immediacy" of nature and sensuous experience, his very terminology is misleading and unduly open to attack. As is so often the case, language here fails to express what is meant, namely something positive and original. If the immediate were merely the *un*mediated or the *not yet* mediated, dialectic would triumph with ease. For, in the Hegelian sense, even the immediate can only exist for mediating thought. And the same inadequacy of language obtains for the words "infinite," "unconditioned," and "unconscious."[21] The meaning intended in talk about the "immediate" would be better expressed by calling it "that which shows itself," "that which directly gives itself" or, with reference to Husserl, "originary self-presentification."

Feuerbach challenges the fundamental principle of the Hegelian system: the *identity of thought and being,* which is the starting point as well as the goal of dialectical mediation. At the level of the *Phenomenology,* the road toward identity is a progressive *correspondence* of the subjective and objective aspect, beginning with the relationship

[20] Marx, *Das Kapital* (Hamburg, 1867), I, pt. 4, chap. 13.
[21] If the in-finite were merely the non-*finite*, the un-conditioned merely what is not *conditioned*, and the un-conscious merely what is not *conscious*, then these categories would have no positive meaning of their own.

between sense consciousness and object. An immediately present object corresponds precisely to the immediate consciousness and its sense-certainty. In this certainty, consciousness is an I only as a "pure this" and the object is likewise a "pure this." The individual knows what is individual (a this-here-now) just as, at the end of the course of experience, absolute knowledge corresponds to the absolute. And absolute *knowledge* is a knowledge *of the absolute* in precisely the same sense that immediate *consciousness* is a consciousness of *the immediate*.[22] By reformulating the difference between thought and being as a difference between knowing and the known, the difference itself is simply smoothed over, and not merely in the sense of reciprocal relation, but as a selfsameness brought to completion. From the very beginning, Hegel's system is governed by a fundamental proposition: the "identity of identity and non-identity"; and this proposition corresponds to the dialectical mediation of related terms in a supervening "third," that is, in their relationship as such. In this *quid pro quo* of immediate consciousness = consciousness of the immediate, and absolute knowledge = knowledge of the absolute, the whole problematic of dialectical mediation is spelled out in a language which in its very structure must be equally speculative-dialectical in so uniting what is disparate that it will not disintegrate. Whoever uncritically submits himself to this circle will find no escape. The prisoner of reflection can only make his way to freedom by means of a leap. And in 1839, with the publication of his *Critique of Hegel's Philosophy* in the *Hallische Jahrbücher*, Feuerbach made just such a leap. This work was followed up by the *Preliminary Theses for a Reform of Philosophy* (1842) and the *Principles of the Philosophy of the Future* (1843).

Contrary to Hegel's principle of speculative identity, Feuerbach insists upon the insoluble difference between thought and being (as well as between being and nothingness, singular and universal), because being (*esse*) is not merely being-thought but factual existence, or, to use Schelling's term, "*unvordenklich*." Actual being is a definite existence, here and now; thought and word are abstractly universal. The real existence of something shows itself to me and I can point to it; a being that has merely been thought cannot by itself prove any existence, despite Hegel's modification of the ontological argument.

---

[22] In an extraordinary fashion, this correspondence also determines the dialectical principle of the philosophy of religion: "Man has knowledge of God only insofar as God has knowledge of himself in man; this knowledge is the self-consciousness of God but it is just as much God's knowledge of man, and this, God's knowledge of man, is man's knowledge of God. The spirit of man, to know God, is simply the spirit of God himself." (Feuerbach, *Werke*, III/2, 117; Cf. III/1, 6 and 14). Cf. Wilhelm Purpus, *Zur Dialektik des Bewusstseins nach Hegel* (Berlin, 1908), 20.

But if Feuerbach's critique of Hegel's system of total mediation is to be understood, Hegel's dialectic of sense-certainty[23] must be presented in greater detail than in Feuerbach's critique itself. Even though our summary will be very abbreviated, simplified, and rough, it will nevertheless suffice to elucidate the dubious character of any dialectic[24] and the legitimacy of Feuerbach's critique.

It seems at first to sense consciousness that its object as well as its self are immediately given. Both the I sensuously conscious of a visible object and this object itself have the form of immediacy. They seem to confront one another as two things independent of any essential relation. On the one hand, there is my knowledge, on the other, an object alien to it; and although I indeed know the object, it nevertheless remains what it is even when it is not known. For sense-certainty, what is true and essential is not my knowledge but this object, since knowledge of an object is only possible when the object itself is first given to the knower.

Skeptically, Hegel now proceeds to examine whether the knowledge contained in sense-certainty is truly certain of its object and whether it is in any sense what it presumes to be. To this end, it is not at all necessary to reflect; it suffices simply to observe the objective certitude of sense-certainty in the same manner that sense-certainty itself maintains this certitude. Thus the question: "What is a 'this,' here and now?" This here, for example, is a tree. I turn around and this truth of sense-certainty has disappeared: the here is no longer a tree, but, for example, a house. "This tree" as well as "this house" are indifferent to the universal "this." To be sure, we still mean this definite individual tree and this definite individual house, but we are quite unable to say how we mean it, and language refutes our meaning when it turns out that the truth of sense-certainty is not the individual "this here" but an abstract universal "this." The same thing happens when instead of a "this-*here*" we consider a "this-*now*," for example, noon, day, night. Their in-different "being now" is not immediate but mediated because the abstract universal "now" is negatively determined through the fact that it is neither day nor night. The "now" is a negative "this," equally indifferent to both day and night, a universal pure and simple. The immediately concrete "this," day or night, merely plays along (*spielt nur beiher*); day and night are mere "examples" (*Beispiele*). The being of this-tree-here and of this-day-now does not remain something immediate, since sense-certainty in its very nature proves the universal to be the truth of its object; it takes, instead,

---

[23] In addition to Purpus, *op. cit.*, cf. Gabler's "die Erläuterung der Dialektik des Bewusstseins" in *Kritik des Bewusstseins* (Leiden, 1901).

[24] Heidegger characterizes it as a "genuine philosophic embarassment." He himself, relinquishing mediation, reduces the dialectic to "correspondences."

the form of something in which the process of mediation and negation is essential.

If one compares the relation in which knowledge and the object first stood with the relation they have come to assume in this result, it is found to be just the reverse of what first appeared. The object, which at first seemed to be the essential reality, has become the nonessential element, since the object, which was presumed to subsist even when we are not conscious of it, is no longer the universal. The universal is now our knowledge, which formerly seemed to be the nonessential factor. The object *is* only insofar as I *know* it. The truth of sense-certainty now lies in the I, in the immediate fact of my seeing. But the I, in turn is a universal I. No doubt I "mean" an individual I (me), but I am as little able to express its individuality as that of the here and the now; for when I say "I," I say "all I's." "Sense-certainty therefore discovers by experience that its essential nature lies neither in the object nor in the I and that the immediacy peculiar to it is neither an immediacy of the one nor of the other. For, in the case of both what I 'mean' is rather something nonessential; and the object and the I are universals, wherein that now and here and I, which I 'mean,' neither endures nor exists."

Thus the whole truth of sense-certainty—and only the whole is the truth—is not the disrelatedness of consciousness and object but rather their reciprocal relation, in accordance with which consciousness and object *together* undergo a change. This relation exists as a third term comprehending the two relating terms and merging them into a "conclusion." The apparent truth of sense-certainty has become stale through the dialectic of sense-certainty; for what seemed to be immediate, simple, and unequivocal, namely the "this" here and now, proves to be a "mediated simplicity or universality," mediated through thought and language.

> Language, however, is . . . the more truthful; in it we ourselves directly refute our own "meaning"; and since the universal is the truth of sense-certainty and language merely expresses this universal [Hoffmeister reads 'truth,' K.D.], it is not at all possible for us even to express in words any sensuous being which we "mean."[25]

This is precisely the point which Feuerbach challenges. Were Hegel really to enter the experience of sensuous consciousness and to shift the emphasis of the *Phenomenology* away from the *logic* of the phenomena, he would then have to acknowledge that sense-certainty in no way refutes itself by virtue of being thought and expressed

[25] G. W. F. Hegel, *Phänomenologie des Geistes*, ed. Hoffmeister (Hamburg, 1948), 82.

and he would have to recognize the reason why. "Language is here beside the point"[26]—"here," that is, in the realm of the senses.

> How could . . . sense consciousness find itself refuted or be refuted by the fact that individual being is inexpressible? Rather than a refutation of sense-certainty, sense consciousness takes this to be a refutation of language. Granting sense consciousness its own domain, its position is fully justified; otherwise, in the domain of life, we would have our *hunger* stilled with words instead of things. Sense consciousness therefore takes the entire first chapter of the *Phenomenology* to be nothing but . . . a word game which thought already *certain* of *itself* as truth plays with natural consciousness.[27]

Sense consciousness will never be talked into believing that its object is a universal "this" mediated by negation. "Hegel does not refute the here as an object of sense consciousness, differentiated for us from an object of pure thought; what he refutes is rather the logical here, the logical now. He refutes the *thought* of This-ness, the *Haecceitas*."[28]

> The *Phenomenology* is nothing but phenomenological logic.—This is the only point of view from which the chapter on sense-certainty is excusable. But this chapter is what it is because Hegel has not really projected and thought himself into sense consciousness, because sense consciousness is only an object in the sense of being an object of self-consciousness, of thought, because it is only the externalization of thought within self-certainty. Thus the *Phenomenology* or the *Logic*—for they amount to the same thing—begins by immediately presupposing itself, and accordingly with an immediate contradiction, an absolute break with sense consciousness. For it begins . . . not with the otherness of thought, but with the *thought of the otherness of thought*. Under these conditions thought is naturally certain of

[26] Cf. Feuerbach, 312. "In the beginning of the *Phenomenology* we encounter nothing but the contradiction between the *word*, which is universal, and the *fact*, which is always singular. And thought, which is exclusively based upon words, cannot overcome this contradiction. The word, however, is as little identical with the fact, as being when it is *pronounced* or *thought* is identical with actual being. If one should protest that—contrary to our standpoint—Hegel did not discuss being on the practical level but only on the theoretical one, it must be pointed out that the practical standpoint is very appropriate here. The question of being is after all a practical question, a question in which our being participates. . . . Being, grounded upon a multiplicity of such inexpressibles, is therefore itself inexpressible. The secret of being first discloses itself . . . where the Word terminates. If inexpressibility is therefore irrationality, then all of existence is irrational, since it is never anything but *this* existence. But existence is not irrational. Even without expressibility existence has its own sense and reason."

[27] *Ibid.*, 312.

[28] *Ibid.*, 312ff.

its victory from the outset—hence the humor with which thought makes a fool of sense consciousness. For the same reason, however, thought has not really refuted its opponent.[29]

The decisive objection which Feuerbach—much like Schelling and Kierkegaard—directs against Hegel's system of total mediation is that Hegel as a thinker begins with thought rather than with that precondition of all reflection which thought as such cannot anticipate; and that the *Phenomenology of Spirit* only seemingly and programmatically begins with the intuition of the simplest phenomenon, whereas it actually begins with the *logos* of the *Logic:* with self-thinking thought. Hegel begins with the *immediate* presupposition of philosophy as onto-logic, which, in turn, is onto-theology.[30] "There is, of course, an unavoidable discontinuity in the nature of science as such; it is however unnecessary that this discontinuity be unmediated. Philosophy mediates it by producing itself out of non-philosophy."[31] Philosophy must have the courage to call itself into question, instead of merely developing what it has posited in advance.

> The philosopher must incorporate into the very text of philosophy what Hegel reduced to a footnote, namely, the non-philosophical aspect of man, that which is against philosophy and opposes abstract thought. Only then will philosophy become a universal . . . irresistible power. Hence philosophy must not begin *with itself* but with its *antithesis,* with *non-philosophy.* The principle of *sensualism* is precisely this aspect of our nature which is distinct from thought, unphilosophical, and absolutely anti-scholastic.[32]

When Feuerbach takes recourse to sensuous intuition in order to regain an immediate access to nature, it is not because he lacks an understanding of the mediation, whose conditional truth is conceded in the realm of the "with-worldly" relations (I and Thou) and cultural-historical productions. His purpose is rather to break through a circle of thought caught up in reflection. He is also aware of the fact that the sensuous aspect of the senses—by which the object is, in the true sense of the word, "given" to us—is not the "immediate" in the sense which speculative philosophy attaches to the word, that is, something thoughtless and obvious. Immediate sensuous intuition is, on the contrary, subordinated to imagination and representation. Ordinarily, intuition does not intuit something as it is in itself but only as it is first imagined and represented. The true sensuous intuition first makes visible what is invisible to the uneducated eye.

[29] *Ibid.*
[30] L. Feuerbach, "Grundsätze der Philosophie der Zukunft," No. 6 in his *Kleine Schriften* (Frankfurt, 1966), uses this expression to characterize metaphysics.
[31] L. Feuerbach, *Zur Kritik der Hegelschen Philosophie,* 211, footnote.
[32] *Ibid.,* 211.

At first men only see things *as they appear to them,* not as they are; they see in things not the things themselves but only what they imagine them to be, and they ascribe their own nature to things, not distinguishing between an object and a representation of it. To the uneducated, subjective man, representation lies *nearer* at hand than *intuition,* for he is drawn *outside of himself in* in intuition whereas he *remains by himself* in representation. . . . Mankind has only very recently made a return to that sense of the *sensuous* which was present in Greece after the passing of the oriental dream world, i.e. an *unfalsified, objective,* intuition of the sensuous, i.e., the actual; and by this return, mankind has also come, for the first time, to itself.[33]

When, on the other hand, Hegel demands that one give up seeing and hearing to make real thinking possible, one might well ask how a thought could subsist without that attentive intuition of the thing in question in terms of which it corrects itself and lets itself be determined. Feuerbach, on the other hand, also realizes that our senses—even such lowly ones as taste and smell—are human and hence "spiritual."[34] "Universal consciousness" is itself already "spirituality"; man's sensuousness is full of sense. And, within the bounds of aesthetics, Hegel too has not contested this. Indeed, he has, more than anyone else, emphasized the point: " 'Sense'! This wonderful word, whose usage combines two opposed meanings. On the one hand, it signifies the organs of immediate apprehension, on the other, however, what we call sense: the meaning, the thought, the universality of a fact. And thus sense refers on one hand to the immediate exteriority of existence and on the other to the inner essence of this existence."[35] But the sensuous nature of incarnate man, which gives him access to the world of nature, is *by nature* already mediated with that which Hegel calls "Spirit" and takes as his unmediated point of departure.

The dubious character of idealism, both speculative and materialist, is bound up with its attitude toward nature. The model for theoretical as well as for practical mediation is not the primary world of nature, which produces and reproduces itself without human mediation, but rather the secondary world of active spirit, of working man,[36]

---

[33] Cf. G. W. F. Hegel, *Encyclopedia* § 449, *Zusatz,* concerning intuition and imagination.

[34] L. Feuerbach, *op. cit.,* 342. Cf. *Werke,* IV, 188ff. with reference to Descartes' *cogito.*

[35] G. W. F. Hegel, *Werke,* XII, 182f.

[36] The expressions "active spirit" and "working man" both refer to the same state of affairs. Work is, according to Hegel, the mark of man's spiritual nature (animals don't work). When Hegel speaks about the "work of the concept," this is no mere metaphor; it is a consequence of regarding comprehension itself as a process of "appropriating," "penetrating," bringing into the form of "universality." (*Philosophie der Religion,* III, 126).

who appropriates the world and makes it his own, that is, makes it into an environment. Whether a metaphysic originates in the world of nature or in the historically mediated world of man distinguishes ineradicably a mode of thought. And this distinction is especially clear when the methodological point of departure is the same, namely, the reflection of the world in our consciousness. Such is the case in Hegel and Descartes. With the common aim of realizing a complete skepticism, both have doubted the truth of sense-certainty and both have epitomized their doubt in a drastic example: Hegel with the disappearance of this tree here; Descartes with the disappearance of a piece of wax.

5. The Undialectical Critique of Sense-Certainty in Descartes

No ingenious process of reflection or contortions of language are required to understand Descartes' doubt in the truth of sense-certainty. Unlike Hegel, he does not use such terms as "the here" and "the now" to refer to what is here and now, and he never speaks of "the I." In Descartes, there is a complete equilibrium between what is said and what is meant. Everything is presented with great simplicity, reserve and easy precision, without paradoxical inversions and rhetorical effects, thus giving the reader the impression that—thanks to the universal distribution of "*bon sens*"—he himself could have thought and said it in exactly the same way.

Descartes' example is not merely a byplay, for the course of his thought does not venture into the speculative heights of independent thought processes. Doubt in the truth of sense-certainty is grounded in the basic self-certainty of the "*Je pense, donc je suis.*" But despite this certainty of the thinking self, it is nevertheless difficult to give up the opinion that the material things which we know by our senses are much more distinct than our invisible ego, taken exclusively as the agent of our consciousness. The human spirit is inclined to err in favor of what is external rather than keeping within the limits of the truth of self-certainty. "So be it! Let us slacken the reins of the mind once more, so that when the time is right we may draw them gently and control the mind more easily."[37] Let us take another look at the external objects with which we deal and are already acquainted. And not merely objects in general, but a very definite one, e.g., this piece of wax here.

> It was but recently taken from the hive; it has not yet lost the sweetness
> of the honey it contained, it still retains something of the fragrance

---

[37] This quotation and the following ones are taken from the concluding pages of Descartes' Second *Meditation*.

of the flowers from which it was gathered; its color, shape and size are readily apparent: it is hard, also cold, easily touched and if tapped with one's finger, it emits a sound. In short, it has everything which seems requisite for the most distinct acquaintance with any material body. But look! While I am speaking, the wax is taken near the fire; whatever taste it had is lost, its odor evaporates, its color changes, its shape is destroyed, it grows larger, it liquefies, it becomes hot, can hardly be touched and when tapped will no longer emit a sound: Does it nevertheless remain the same piece of wax?

What does remain of the piece of wax when all its properties (odor, color, shape, etc.) change and disappear? All that remains is a materially extended something which in turn admits of multiple differentiations according to the degree of heat that the piece of wax is exposed to. One must therefore admit that the enduring essence of the wax can only be grasped in thought (*solius mentis inspectio*) and not by means of the senses. Our thought, however, is led astray by words and linguistic usage. We are even caught up in words when we are not speaking, when we are silently considering what this piece of wax here really is. We say to ourselves: I *see* a piece of wax. We don't say: In thinking about its color, odor and shape, I judge that this body is a piece of wax. We therefore tend to conclude that the wax is known through the act of seeing and not exclusively through the insight of our understanding.

> But when I happen to look from a window at people passing by in the street, I find it natural to say, just as in the case of the wax, 'I see them'. And yet I see nothing but hats and coats under which machines might very well be hidden. I nevertheless judge that they are people. Thus what I presumed to see with my eyes I really know only through that ability to judge which dwells in my mind.

If one observes the naked wax, having, as it were, stripped off its clothes, it then becomes clear that its "waxness" is only grasped by means of thought, namely as *res extensa*. And now Descartes draws the slackened reins taut and returns to the thinking ego, which constructs the vanished world of sensibly visible things with mathematical ideas. The fact that I exist as one who sees was implied by my seeing the wax sensuously, and although I was mistaken about what I saw, it still remains certain that my consciousness of seeing exists, that this *cogitatio is* and that therefore I as a thinking being exist. What I notice in reference to the wax can be applied to everything that exists outside of myself. Thus, by analyzing the seeing of the wax, we discover at last the nature of our own mind.

> And behold! The goal which I sought I have finally attained, without any external assistance. For now that I know that material bodies

are not, properly speaking, conceived by the senses or the faculty of imagination, by being touched or seen, but solely through the understanding, by being grasped in thought, I clearly recognize that I can grasp nothing more easily and obviously than my own mind. But since one cannot readily relinquish the habit of a deeply rooted opinion, this seems an appropriate place to stop, that by prolonged meditation this newly gained knowledge may be more firmly impressed upon my memory.

Let us summarize the difference between Descartes' and Hegel's doubt concerning the truth of sense-certainty. Both make sense-certainty disappear in order to find its truth and both ask what is left after this disappearance. Hegel's answer is abstract: what remains is only the "universal" which is indifferent to everything that exists here and now; and finally, as the truth of the related terms, consciousness and object, a third term appears: the relation as such. Hegel's dialectic of sense-certainty challenges my immediate meaning and appeals to the greater truth of language, which always expresses the universal even when we mean the singular.

Since the very origin of Descartes' thought lay in mathematics and physics, he was protected from developing a confidence in language, and thus his answer to the question "what remains?" is not *abstractly*-universal. What remains essential in material things is their extension—something that cannot be seen but only thought by the *ego cogitans*, the undialectical, unequivocal, and one-sided basis for the reconstruction of the physical world out of mathematical ideas. Descartes' *Meditations* initiated a development which led to the foundation of modern physics and scientific technology; and his destruction of sensuous appearance, designed to bring about a mathematically universal science, is today of greater interest than ever, even though his definition of matter and his mechanical conception of the world have proved inadequate. And although the progress of science has left his conception of the living automaton far behind, this progress itself was nevertheless made in the direction which he pointed out.[38]

Hegel's dialectic of sense-certainty has had no scientific ramifications. Its goal was not to lay, according to the rules of the understanding, a new philosophical foundation for the construction of science, but rather to fulfill skepticism in the absolute knowledge of the absolute. The correctness and truth of Hegel's accomplishment cannot be proved, or refuted, or experimentally controlled. The "science" of the experiences of consciousness is speculative and has therefore nothing in common with science in the scientific sense of the word. This was already the case in Fichte's *Science of Knowledge*, whose "non-I" Hegel

---

[38] Cf. Paul Valéry, *Oeuvres I* (Bibl. de la Pléiade), 843ff. (Paris: Gallimard, 1957).

translates into "the other." If we finally ask ourselves: "What is this whole of Hegelian truth in which the senses lose their certainty?" we do not find an easy answer. It is an ingenious systematic construction, an unsurpassable edifice of conceptual reflection; and yet, in the midst of all this disobligingly pleasurable construction and progression, there is a wealth of genuine phenomenological insight concerning the spiritual world of man. Croce has set the precedent of distinguishing what is dead from what is living in the whole of Hegel's thought —he was followed by Dilthey, N. Hartmann, and T. Litt—, and whoever refuses to do the same, arguing that the whole alone is the truth, will also have to forego those real insights which the system itself tends rather to hide than sustain.

Confronting Hegel and Descartes, we find ourselves in a twofold dilemma. We are neither inclined to distrust on principle the testimony of our senses and their world-disclosing power in favor of a mathematico-physical construct, nor are we willing "to walk for once also on our head" with Hegel, trusting the seemingly cogent but really only persuasive course of speculative reflection. Only evidence, what is immediately illuminating, is cogent without being coercive. And since the human senses stem from the same origin as that which presents itself to them, one can assume that in every living being they are attuned to the corresponding appearance.[39]

[39] Cf. A. N. Whitehead, *Process and Reality* (New York, 1929), 219ff.: "There can only be evidence of a world of actual entities, if the immediate actual entity discloses them essential to its own composition."

HEGEL
AND HEIDEGGER

William H. Werkmeister

In his well-known book on Hegel, Walter Kaufmann has this to say about Heidegger's relation to Hegel:

> The prose of [Hegel's] *Logic* is worlds removed from the prose of Heidegger's, both in *Being and Time* and in *What is Metaphysics?*, which revolves around 'the nothing'; and Hegel's thought is, too. The distinction between being (*das Sein*) and beings (*Seiendes*) is common to both but comes from Aristotle. What Heidegger does with being and nothing is not merely different from what Hegel did with them; it is based on a total and unfortunate neglect of Hegel's discussion of these terms.[1]

[1] Walter Kaufmann, *Hegel* (New York, 1965), 213.

And Kaufmann adds, with special reference to Heidegger's later writings, that discussions of "the revelation of the nothing in the experience of anxiety" are "*not* excrescences of Hegel's spirit, but, on the contrary, examples of the sort of thing Hegel hoped to prevent henceforth by means of his discussion of being and nothing."[2]

One gathers from these statements that Professor Kaufmann sees Hegel and Heidegger as holding radically opposed views; that they do not even speak the same language. It is my contention that the real relation of the two thinkers to one another may be of a rather different nature; that, in fact, there is much of Hegel in Heidegger's basic position.

1

To begin with, it seems evident that even in the opening pages of *Sein und Zeit* there is a genuine appreciation of Hegel's work. As Heidegger sees it, what Plato and Aristotle achieved has persisted—and has persisted despite many alterations and "retouchings"—through all the centuries down to the *Logic* of Hegel. "And if Hegel finally defined 'Being' as the 'indeterminate immediate' and made this definition the basis of all further categorial explications of his *Logic,* he retained the perspective of ancient ontology" even though he stressed the multiplicity of the categories rather than the unity of Being."[3] It is the traditional metaphysics which, "becoming material to be reworked," "determined the foundations and the goals of Hegel's *Logic.*" (22) To be sure, since the days of Descartes, "the *ego cogito,* the subject, the 'I', reason, spirit, person" had all received attention but had "remained uninterrogated as to their Being and its structure." (22) Yet, Parmenides had already maintained that "Being is that which reveals itself in pure perceptive awareness, and only this seeing discovers Being. Primordial and genuine truth lies in pure intuition (*Anschauung*)." And it is this thesis, Heidegger adds, which is "the motivating conception" and the true basis of the Hegelian dialectic. (171)

And later on in *Sein und Zeit,* when discussing the nature of time, Heidegger states that in the philosophical tradition there is "a

[2] *Ibid.,* 214. Italics in original.
[3] Martin Heidegger, *Sein und Zeit* (4th ed., Halle, 1934), 2–3. The English translation, *Being and Time,* is by John Macquarrie and Edward Robinson (New York, 1962). Parenthesized numbers following indicate standard paging in the German volume. The translations are by the present author. Numbers preceded by *Enc.* refer to sections in Hegel's *Enzyklopädie der philosophischen Wissenschaften im Grundrisse,* ed. Bolland (Leiden, 1906).

noteworthy vacillation" as to whether time is to be regarded as "subjective" or as "objective." "In Hegel's interpretation of time both possibilities are brought to some degree of suspension." (405) But this, Heidegger finds, requires further elucidation, especially so since his own analysis of time differs radically from Hegel's.

Temporality, Heidegger tells us, is "constitutive" of the "there" in "being there," of the *Da* in *Dasein.* (408) The "there" is disclosed in "being there's" own temporality. (410) That is to say, being "thrown into the world," *Dasein* discovers "public time," first as the sequence of night and day which makes possible "dating" within "the nearest environmental context of events." "When the sun rises it is *time to.* . . ." (412) And so, in its temporality, *Dasein* has already discovered something like a "clock"—"something ready-to-hand which, in its regular recurrence, has become accessible in the expectant present." (413) But more than this, the time disclosed in "being there" is always understood as "time to. . . ." And particular "now there this and this" is in itself either "suitable" or "not suitable." In other words, the "now"—and this means "every modus of interpreted time"—is not simply a "now, there . . . ," but, as "this essentially datable now," it is "also essentially determined through the structure of suitableness or unsuitableness." (414) "Saying 'Now' is but the linguistic articulation of a making-present that reveals itself in its unity with what is retentively expected." (417) Measuring time gives time a distinctive public character; and only then do we come to know what we ordinarily mean by "time." (419)

Now the time "in which" that which is "at hand" "moves or rests" is not "objective"—if "objective" is taken to mean an in-itselfness. But neither is it "subjective"—if "subjective" is taken to mean "occurring in a subject." As Heidegger sees it, "world-time is 'more objective' than every possible object because as condition of the possibility of beings within a world, it is already 'objectified' with the disclosure that there is a world. But world-time is also 'more subjective' than every possible subject because it first makes possible the 'being' of the factually existing self." (419)

When Heidegger now turns to a discussion of Hegel's interpretation of time, he starts with the assumption that "the place within the system" at which an analysis of time is carried through can serve as a criterion for the basic conception of time that underlies the analysis. (42) He then finds that, "faithful to tradition," Hegel's analysis of time is presented in Part II of the *Encyclopedia of the Philosophical Sciences:* "Philosophy of Nature." Dealing more specifically with problems of mechanics, Hegel here links space and time in such a way that he can say that time is the "truth" of space. (*Enc.* §§ 254ff.) As Hegel puts it: "The negativity which, as point, relates itself to space and develops in it its determinations as line and surface, is, however, also for itself in the sphere of being-outside-itself, positing at the same time its determinations in the sphere of being-outside-itself but revealing itself as indifferent to the calm side-by-sideness [of the spatial points]. Thus posited for itself, [negativity] is time." (*Enc.* § 257) Thus, the "negativity as a side-by-side-ness," together with its retention as a "point-ness," is time. Each point in itself is a "now-here." "The point, thus, has reality in time." Conversely, the condition of the possibility of its positing itself is the "now."

But "time, as the negative unity of the being-outside-itself, is likewise something plainly abstract, ideal: it is that Being which, insofar as it is, is not, and insofar as it is not, is—it is intuited becoming." (*Enc.* § 258) The key idea here is that time is "intuited becoming." The being of time is the "now"; but insofar as, for another "now," every specific "now" is either "not yet" or "no more," time can also be regarded as non-being. As "intuited being," however, it is always understood as a "now." "In a positive sense," Hegel adds, "one can say of time that only the present is, the before and the after is not; but the concrete present is the result of the past and is pregnant with the future. The true present is thus eternity." (*Enc.* § 259, *Zusatz*)

This Hegelian interpretation of time Heidegger regards as representative of the "vulgar" conception of time. It "presupposes" that the "full structure" of the "now" remains "covered up and levelled" so that it can be intuited as something that is "at hand"—even though it is only an "ideal" something. (431)

If time is simply "intuited becoming," then neither the "coming into being" nor the "passing away" has a preference. Yet, Hegel also speaks of time as the "abstraction of devouring" (*Abstraktion des Verzehrens*) (*Enc.* § 258, *Zusatz*); and this, Heidegger maintains, is without question the most radical formula descriptive of our "vulgar" experience of time. Hegel, however, is sufficiently consistent in his thinking not to assign a preference to this "devouring" when he defines time. Such preference could find no justification within the Hegelian dialectic. Hegel's characterization of time remains purely abstract—abstract in a radical sense that lies even beyond the idea of a "flux" of time. "The most adequate expression of the Hegelian conception of time is the determination of time as negation of the negation, i.e., the negation of point-ness. In this formulation the sequence of 'nows' is formalized in the most extreme sense and is insurpassably levelled. And alone on the basis of this formal-dialectic conception of time is Hegel able to establish a connection between time and spirit." (432–433)

Whether or not this connection between time and spirit is justified is a question that does not concern us here. It is clear, however, that

Hegel's interpretation of time, as presented in the *Encyclopedia*, is radically different from Heidegger's; for it is Heidegger's thesis that temporality reveals itself in the very meaning of "being," as disclosed in "care": "The existential-ontological constitution of the totality of *Dasein* is grounded in temporality." (438) The disclosure of temporality, thus, makes the conception of Being at all possible. But Heidegger ends with a question: "Does *time* reveal itself as the horizon of *Being?*" (438)

Heidegger, as we have seen, restricted his interpretation of Hegel's conception of time to the relevant sections of the *Encyclopedia*. Hegel, however, dealt with the problem of time in other places also. To be sure, in the Preface to the *Phenomenology* he speaks of time as "the counterpart of space."[4] But he adds almost at once that philosophy "does not deal with a determination that is non-essential," and that "the real," that which is "self-establishing," "has a life within itself"; that "it is process that creates its own moments in its course," and that "the whole of this movement constitutes its positive content and its truth." (*Phen.* 105) This "bacchanalian revel, where not a member is sober" but which is "just as much a state of transparent unbroken calm" (*Phen.* 105), is hardly conceivable without an implied reference to time. It remains true, however, that in the whole of the *Phenomenology*, Hegel does not take up the problem of time as such. When he finally does refer to time (in the concluding eight pages of the lengthy book), he speaks of it somewhat enigmatically. "Time," he says, "is just the notion definitely existent, and presented to consciousness in the form of empty intuition." Spirit "necessarily appears in time"; and it appears in time "so long as it does not annul time." Conversely, time "appears as spirit's destiny and necessity, where spirit is not yet complete within itself." (*Phen.* 800)

Passages such as these but tend to give support to Heidegger's contention that his own interpretation differs radically from Hegel's— differs from it in its presuppositions, its self-disclosure, and its ultimate function in the structuring of Being. For Heidegger, temporality—and, therefore, time—reveals itself in the self-disclosure of *Dasein*. It reveals itself as the very meaning of *Dasein*, as essential to the "there." For Hegel, however, the situation is different. That whole swirling process of spirit "reflecting itself into itself" is distinguished into the intuitively apprehended pure notion, Time, and the content, the inherent, implicit, nature. (*Phen.* 801) The process "spirit accomplishes as actual History"; but Time, "intuitively apprehended," remains the external form

---

[4] G. W. F. Hegel, *The Phenomenology of Mind*, trans. J. B. Baillie (London, 1931, rev. ed.), 104. Parenthesized numbers throughout the remainder of this essay preceded by *Phen.* refer to pages in this volume.

of that process. And it is clear that as far as this conception of time is concerned, Hegel's thinking has as yet not liberated itself from the presuppositions of Newtonian mechanics. Heidegger's has.

2

The respective interpretations of time are but an obvious point of comparison of the basic views of Hegel and Heidegger. Much more important, however, is the interpretation of the "experience of consciousness" with which both men are dealing; and to a consideration of this problem I wish to turn next.

Heidegger gives us his reaction to Hegel's thinking in Chapter III of his *Holzwege*, entitled "Hegel's Conception of Experience." Let us take a look at this chapter. The discussion is based exclusively on the Introduction to Hegel's *Phenomenology of Mind*.[5]

Heidegger begins by quoting Hegel's Introduction in its entirety. He then analyzes it paragraph by paragraph, emphasizing that, for Hegel, philosophy is "the real cognition of that which in truth is."[6] What is significant for our purposes, however, is to examine the ideas which Heidegger regards as truly reflecting Hegel's ultimate position. And here we are told at once that, for Hegel, the Real is Spirit, and that "the nature of Spirit consists in self-consciousness." The real cognition [therefore] of that which exists as existing is the absolute cognition of the Absolute in its absoluteness." (118) But various problems arise here. To begin with, it is necessary to select a method which is suitable to absolute cognition. Descartes dealt with this, making self-certification rather than correspondence the criterion of truth. But it is necessary also to characterize the cognition of the Absolute as to content and limitations; and this Kant accomplished, setting limits to reason in its speculative employment. But now two possibilities must be admitted: either cognition is like an instrument which we employ in our relations with the real, or it is a "medium" through which the "light of truth" is disclosed to us. (119) Half-hidden in a subordinate clause is Hegel's statement that the Absolute in itself is with us and wants to be with us; and this being-with-us is "the light of truth which the Absolute itself radiates." (120)[7]

---

[5] References to the *Phenomenology of Mind* will be to the English translation, though are checked against the original text.

[6] Martin Heidegger, *Holzwege* (2d ed., Frankfurt, 1952), 117. Translations are by the present writer. Parenthesized numbers in this and the following eight paragraphs indicate pages in this volume.

[7] Cf. *Phen.*, 132–133.

Hegel now no longer uses the term philosophy but speaks only of science. "Philosophy is now the unconditioned knowledge within the knowledge of self-certainty. . . . The whole nature of philosophy is accomplished through the unconditional knowing of itself on the part of knowledge." (121) And in this sense "philosophy is *the* science." Its task is to view what is as that which is. "The unconditional knowing of itself, as the subjectivity of the subject, is the absoluteness of the Absolute"; and "philosophy is absolute cognition." (122) But Hegel had said: "This conclusion comes from the fact that the Absolute alone is true, or that the True is alone absolute." (*Phen.* 133) Heidegger, however, maintains that "these statements are made without further justification. They cannot be justified because no justification reaches down to their ultimate ground." In fact, it is they that posit what is ground for everything else. (124) And "truth in the sense of unconditional self-certainty alone is the Absolute." The phenomenology of Spirit is its presentation. (125)

Hegel and Heidegger both agree that it is difficult to accept this initial position, not because we stand outside the process of the self-revelation of absolute knowledge, trying to get in, but because we already are caught in the process and apprehend its "negative significance for us." We begin to understand that this process means "the ruin and overthrow" of the "natural consciousness" which, in the process, "loses its own truth." In our search for absolute self-certainty we find ourselves upon a "highway of despair"—upon a "pathway" that is "the conscious insight into the untruth of the phenomenal knowledge." (*Phen.* 135–136) Our "work" is "the distress of pain to endure the state of being inwardly torn, which *is* the in-finite relation in which the nature of the Absolute fulfills itself." (127)

Ordinary criticism of philosophical cognition, Heidegger continues, is "like the procedure of those who want to imagine an oak tree but take no notice of the fact that it is a tree." These critics "leave the impression of being in possession of all the essential conceptions, whereas every thing depends on first obtaining conceptions of the Absolute, of cognition, of Truth, of objectivity and subjectivity." (127 and *Phen.* 134) And at this point Hegel introduces his "decisive 'But' " (128): "But science, in the very fact that it comes on the scene, is itself *Erscheinung*." (*Phen.* 134)

"Erscheinen" means, first—so Heidegger points out, following Hegel—"appearing alongside" another kind of knowledge in the sense of "maintaining itself against it." But "erscheinen" means also to put in an appearance and in doing so to "point to another," to "something not yet apparent." That is to say, it means to be anticipatory of something that is itself not yet in evidence or that will never appear. (128) The "appearance" of science in its various phases is itself "the presence

of the Absolute"—a "presence" which consists in the Absolute's revealing itself step by step as what it is. (130) As Hegel puts it, the exposition of this revelation of the Absolute "may . . . be taken as the pathway of the natural consciousness which is pressing forward to true
knowledge." (*Phen.* 135) Philosophy itself is the process of the presen-
tational interpretation; and "natural consciousness will prove itself
to be only knowledge in principle or not real knowledge." (*Phen.* 135)
"The pathway is the conscious insight into the untruth of the phenomenal knowledge. . . . The series of shapes, which consciousness
traverses on this road, is . . . the detailed history of the process of
training and educating consciousness itself up to the level of science."
(*Phen.* 136) "The terminus is at that point where knowledge is no
longer compelled to go beyond itself." (*Phen.* 137)

Having followed Hegel's outline of his position thus far, Heidegger
now insists upon a clarification of the terminology to be employed.
The result is that a significant difference between Hegel's views and
Heidegger's views becomes apparent. As far as Hegel is concerned,
that which, in immediate presentation, is an object for consciousness
is "that which is" (*das Seiende*). Although actual, this *Seiende* is
neither true nor real; and it is not Being. Hegel uses the term "Being"
(*Sein*) as a name for what, in his sense, is as yet "untrue reality"
or "mere Being." (141–142) True Being (*das wahrhaft Seiende*) is
"the *ens actu*, the real, whose *actualitas* (reality) consists in the knowledge of that certainty which knows itself." (142) Only this certainty
can in truth "be" "all reality."

Heidegger, on the other hand, uses the term "Being" to designate
what Hegel (along with Kant) calls "object-ness" (*Gegenständlichkeit*)
and what, in addition, he represents as "true reality" and calls "the
reality of Spirit." (142) Heidegger, in other words, interprets "Being"
as "being present" (*Anwesen*) in "uncovert-ness" (*Unverborgenheit*).
"The being-ness of beings (*die Seiendheit des Seienden*) . . . is for
[him] only one—albeit a decisive—mode of Being." (142) This means
that, whereas Hegel's initial use of the term "being" made that term
in a strict sense inapplicable to "true Reality" or "Spirit," Heidegger's
use of the term does not entail similar limitations.

The difference thus indicated is of sufficient importance to deserve
further consideration. We therefore turn first to Hegel in order to
obtain a more detailed characterization of his position. What concerns
us here primarily is his discussion of the "truth of self-certainty"—an
issue that derives directly from Descartes' thesis that, in order to be
true knowledge, knowledge must be self-certifying or "self-certain."
If truth is "something other than consciousness itself," it "vanishes
in the course of our experience of it." (*Phen.* 218) "A certainty which
is on a par with its truth" is achieved only when "the certainty is

to itself its own object." "Being 'in-itself' and being 'for another' are here the same." (*Phen.* 218) With self-consciousness we have thus "passed into the native land of truth." (*Phen.* 219) "Knowledge of self" and "knowledge of an other" are now but "moments of self-consciousness"; and self-consciousness presents itself here as the process in which the opposition of those moments is removed and "oneness or identity with itself is established." (*Phen.* 220) "Being now no longer has the significance of mere abstract being." (*Phen.* 222) The "universal flux"—that is, the dialectic movement within the "self-related and self-existent self-consciousness" (*Phen.* 227)—is the self-revelation of Spirit. "It is the simple ultimate spiritual Being (*Wesen*) which, by coming at the same time to consciousness, is the real substance." (*Phen.* 375) In its "universal truth," self-consciouness is "a Being in and for itself" (*ein an und fürsich-seiendes Wesen*) (*Phen.* 457) and, as such, is "at once aware of being actual in the form of consciousness and present to itself as itself." (*Phen.* 458) "Spirit is thus the self-supporting absolutely real ultimate Being." (*Phen.* 459)

This fact is underscored when Hegel deals with the individual person in his relation to the universal. The individual, we are told, "moulds himself by culture to what he inherently is." "The extent of his culture is the measure of his reality and his power"; and the "concrete realization" of the "particular self" consists in "cancelling and transcending the natural self." (*Phen.* 515) This process, in which an individual raises himself to the cultural level, is "the development of individuality *qua* universal objective Being; . . . it is the development of the actual world" (*Phen.* 516)—that is, it is the process of making self-consciousness itself "actual and concrete." (*Phen.* 517; 649–650)

Separated from this process of self-actualization, "Being, pure Being," "has no differentiation either within itself or relatively to anything external." Having no discernible qualities, "it is pure indeterminateness and vacuity." "There is in it no object for thought." In fact, in its "indeterminate immediacy," this "Being" is the same as "Nothing, neither more nor less." Indeed, "Nothing" is "altogether the same thing, as pure Being."[8]

Hegel's thesis is thus quite clear. "Pure Being" is but an empty concept. It finds concretization and actualization only in the dialectic process in which, step by step, self-consciousness comes to self-certainty about itself as both, the subject and the object of cognition—a process in the course of which self-consciousness reveals itself to itself as what in truth it is: the whole of reality, the very essence of Spirit.

---

[8] G. W. F. Hegel, *Science of Logic*, trans. Johnston and Struthers (New York, 1929), I, chap. I, 94.

When next we turn to Heidegger's interpretation of "Being," we find that the approach and the perspective have changed; but is this a radical change? Or is the change more apparent than real?

Whereas Hegel did not explicitly raise the question as to the meaning of Being, Heidegger does raise it. He finds, however, that, in order to be guided in our investigation by the question itself, "the meaning of Being must already be available to us in some way."[9] But the most that can be said at the beginning is that "Being lies in the fact that something is, and in its Being as it is." (7) And of all the entities which "are," only one—"the inquirer"—can make Being "transparent" as his own "mode of Being," that of "*Dasein*," of "being there." As Heidegger puts it, "understanding of Being is itself a definite characteristic of *Dasein*'s Being." (12) And this "mode of Being" discloses itself in the very asking of the question. But more must be ascertained concerning the nature of *Dasein*.

Now "Dasein always understands itself by virtue of its own existence (*aus seiner eigenen Existenz heraus*)." (12) Its own existence, however, is such that, as a mode of Being, *Dasein* is capable of understanding "something like Being" (*so etwas wie Sein*). (17) But the approach must be "phenomenological." Ontology, Heidegger states, is possible only as phenomenology. (35) The "being of entities" can never be anything that "stands behind" the phenomena. I submit that this is an essentially Hegelian thought—although Heidegger here refers to Husserl rather than to Hegel. A difference between Heidegger and Hegel arises, of course, in the further interpretation of *Dasein*. For Hegel, *Dasein* is the concretization of self-consciousness in a basically rational cognitive progression from sensory data to the full realization of self-certainty, whereas for Heidegger it is essentially an emotional disclosure of "thereness" in its "anxiety," a "Being-in-the-world" (54)—which itself is but a form of knowing. (61) As Heidegger puts it: "In knowing, *Dasein* achieves a new status of Being (*Seinsstand*) toward a world which has already been discovered in *Dasein* itself." (62) Hegel's *Phenomenology*, I submit, but reveals the step-by-step progression of the process through which this "new status of Being" is achieved until we come to the full realization of self-consciousness as the self-identity of subject and object.

But while for Hegel this process is essentially cognitive and rational, for Heidegger it is of a different nature. "As one of *Dasein*'s possibilities of Being," he tells us, "anxiety . . . provides the phenomenal basis for explicitly grasping *Dasein*'s primordial totality of Being." (182; 183–190) More specifically, "as a state of mind, anxiety is a

[9] Martin Heidegger, *Sein und Zeit*, 25. Parenthesized numbers following and to the end of this section indicate pages in this volume.

primary mode of Being-in-the-world"; for it "individualizes and thus discloses *Dasein* as 'solus ipse.'" (188) It is illuminating, however, to compare these passages with Hegel's assertion (when speaking of the "bondsman") that, "in fear, self-existence is present within himself." (*Phen.* 239) But as far as Hegel is concerned, this individualizing fear is but one facet in a progressive dialectic that culminates in the actualization of the Absolute, whereas for Heidegger it is of the very essence of the whole of *Dasein*.

Hegel's analysis of the "unhappy consciousness" throws additional light upon this difference. To be sure, "the withdrawal of the emotional life into itself is to be taken in such a way that this life of feeling, in its own regard, *has* actuality *qua* particular existence. (*Phen.* 259) The feeling is "self-feeling" (*Selbstegefühl*), its "object" being "its own self." So far, however, the "inner life" of the self here involved remains "a shattered certainty of itself." (*Phen.* 259) Its particularity, nevertheless, has "the significance of *all* actuality"; and its "relation to actuality is the process of alteration or acting." (*Phen.* 260) "In work and enjoyment" the actual self "can readily forget itself." But, also, the individual may take a step beyond this level of *Dasein* (if I may use a Heideggerian term to express a Hegelian thought!) and may so relate himself to "absolute universal Being" as to reveal that, "in its particularity," consciousness is "inherently and essentially absolute, or is all reality." (*Phen.* 267) And it is at this point that, for Hegel, Reason supersedes feeling—a step not encountered in Heidegger's interpretation.

As Heidegger sees it, *Dasein*'s "Being-in-the-world" is disclosed in "anxiety" (*Angst*). Its activity (what Hegel called "the process of alteration or acting") takes the form of "taking care" (*Besorgen*)— an activity in and through which *Dasein* is "concerned with what-is-at-hand" and is thus "Being alongside entities within-the-world." Indeed, through "care" *Dasein* is "lost onto its 'world'"; and being "lost onto its world" (*verfallen*), it exists in "untruth." (222) On the other hand, "there is" truth "insofar and as long as *Dasein* is fully disclosed"; for, "as constituted through disclosedness" (*Erschlossenheit*)—that is, when it is not "lost onto its world"—"*Dasein* . . . is essentially in the truth." (226) "The Being of truth is thus connected primordially with *Dasein*"; and only because this is so "can anything like Being be understood." (230) The Being of *Dasein* thus plays a special role in our understanding of Being; but what "Being as such" (*Sein überhaupt*) is has so far not become clear. (231)

In Hegel's *Phenomenology* the dialectic inherent in the process of the self-unfoldment of the Absolute moves on to ever more far-reaching concerns of Reason until, in the end, the whole panorama in which Spirit "completes itself as a World-Spirit (*Phen.* 801) and comes to know itself "as Spirit." (*Phen.* 808) For Hegel, in other words, there is at every stage in the dialectic a pressing forward to a new and higher stage in which what has gone before is suspended in its one-sidedness, preserved in its essentials, and elevated to a new level until, in the end, the whole is preserved in dialectic progression in the Absolute. And it is the process as such which gives content and richness to the Absolute itself—to ultimate Being.

Heidegger sees no progression of this type. He puts it bluntly: "Attainment of the wholeness of *Dasein* in death is at the same time loss of the Being of *there*" (*Verlust des Seins des Da*). (237.) When someone has died, he still has Being; but it is the Being of "being-at-hand" which is characteristic of "corporeal things" only. "The *end* of the existent as *Dasein* is the beginning of that same existent as something-at-hand." (238–245) And where Hegel saw a progression of spiritual unfoldment beyond the death of the individual and as redemptive of the individual's own work and life, Heidegger sees death as "something impending" (250)—as something which *Dasein* cannot overcome; for *Dasein*'s very existence is a "Being-unto-death." "Death is the end of *Dasein* in its [that is, in *Dasein*'s] Being-towards-its-end." (259)

To be sure, Heidegger deals also with the ontological status of History. He could hardly avoid this problem because he maintained that "temporality" reveals *Dasein*'s "authentic-potentiality-for-Being-a-whole." (372) That is to say, for Heidegger, "*Dasein*'s Being is in principle historical"; and the "ontological structure" of history "has its roots in the historicality of *Dasein*." (392) But Heidegger's concern is with the interpretation of temporality *qua* temporality, not (as it was with Hegel) with the concretization of the Absolute in time; and he ends his discussion with the question: "Does *time* itself manifest itself as the horizon of Being?" (437) To this question he has no answer.

3

It would have contributed greatly to our understanding of Heidegger's relation to Hegel had Heidegger discussed in detail the issues I have touched upon here; but he has not done so. His further comments on the Introduction to Hegel's *Phenomenology* deal with other matters.

Thus, referring to what he calls Hegel's "first principle of consciousness"—"Consciousness is to itself its own *Begriff*" (*Phen.* 138)—he argues that the emphasis lies upon the "is"; for "it means: Consciousness itself achieves its own appearance-to-itself in such a way that, in appearing-to-itself it constitutes the place of the appearing—

a place which belongs to its own essence."[10] Hegel, however, continues that being its own *Begriff*, consciousness "immediately transcends . . . its own self"; that, "along with the particular there is at the same time set up the 'beyond.' " (*Phen.* 138) In thus destroying "its own limited satisfaction," consciousness suffers "at its own hands" and, faced with this fact, tries to "preserve for itself that which is in danger of being lost"—its own individuality; "but it can find no rest": "thought will agitate the thoughtlessness"; its "restlessness" will disturb "unthinking indolence." (*Phen.* 138) One looks in vain in Heidegger's writings for a penetrating analysis of these crucial passages, even though they are as crucial for Heidegger himself (or should be) as they were for Hegel.

Heidegger now turns to what he calls "Hegel's second principle of consciousness": "Consciousness supplies its own standard within itself." (*Phen.* 140) That is to say, consciousness is both, the criterion and the content of truth. Heidegger comments: "The way in which Hegel makes clear that both fall within consciousness leaves the impression of being a questionable game with words, and arouses a suspicion." (157) After all, criterion of truth and content of truth are not the same. It is by no means a matter of indifference as to which we call "concept" and which "object." If, at the level of the "natural consciousness," the "true" is called the "object," the latter is still object "for it"—that is, for natural consciousness. But if our knowledge is called "object," then knowledge (as that which "appears") is object "for us." The situation is similar when we consider the word "concept." The use of the terms "object" and "concept" is, thus, by no means arbitrary but is determined by the experiential situation. (158)

Hegel, of course, had added to his "second principle" that, "in what consciousness inside itself declares to be the essence or truth we have the standard which consciousness itself sets up, and by which we are to measure its knowledge." (*Phen.* 140) As I read this passage, it assumes the very distinction between "concept" and "object" the "obscuration" of which, according to Heidegger, entails a "questionable game of words." And when Hegel adds (what Heidegger regards as the "third principle"): "Consciousness examines and tests (*prüft*) itself" (*Phen.* 141), Heidegger concedes that "in examining and testing" (*im Prüfen*), the norm and that to which it is to be applied must both be present." "The nature of consciousness consists in the holding-together (*Zusammenhalt*) of both. (159) More specifically, "natural consciousness" is "immediate knowledge of an object taken as true," and is also "knowledge of its knowledge of the object." (159) "Knowledge

---

[10] Martin Heidegger, *Holzwege*, 148. Parenthesized numbers in the text from this point on, except those preceded by *Phen.*, indicate pages in this volume.

of the object and consciousness of that knowledge are the same and both, object and knowledge, are knowns (*Gewusstes*)"; and consciousness itself is "at the same time the one and the other." It is "in its very nature the comparison of the one with the other"; and "this comparing (*Vergleichen*) *is* the examination or testing." (159, 163) And consciousness *is* insofar as it comes to itself in its truth." (164) Heidegger thus agrees with Hegel on crucial points.

For Hegel, however, this "process of comparison," in which consciousness discerns its own ontological dimension within its ontic knowing, is "the *dialectic* movement . . . called *Experience*." (*Phen.* 142; Hegel's italics). As dialectic, experience is a process which, "by its very nature, can embrace nothing less than the entire system of consciousness, the whole realm of the Truth of Spirit." It does so in such a way that the "moments" of this Truth are "modes of consciousness" (*Gestalten des Bewusstseins*). (*Phen.* 144–145) It is in this sense, Heidegger concedes that "experience is the Absoluteness of the Absolute"; that it is the appearance of the Absolute in "absolvent self-appearance." (171) It is the process in and through which Absolute Consciousness "comes to presence" (*kommt zur Anwesenheit*) as itself, that is, as the "Being of beings" (*das Sein des Seienden*). (171)

But this conclusion Heidegger regards as merely the culmination of a subjectivism which stems from, and is rooted in, the Cartesian principle that "self-certainty"—and self-certainty alone—is the key to Absolute Truth. It is this subjectivism that Heidegger hopes to overcome in his own analysis of experience and of Being.

HEGEL
AND THE ORIENTALS

Kurt F. Leidecker

Friedrich Ueberweg, representative of "ideal-realism," once wrote that Hegel's philosophy of nature is the weakest part of his philosophy and thus could easily be made an object of ridicule. Others without number have accused Hegel more or less vituperatively not only of relative but of absolute ignorance in the fields of science and history and the empirico-concrete realm in general. They say he was completely oblivious to "facts," arbitrary, blind, and willfully engaged in distortions when it suited him. One must love Hegel, indeed, to survive these and other often justifiable onslaughts, together with the cynicism of a Schopenhauer among his more formidable critics.

Without question, the "mistakes" of Hegel in the empirical realm are disturbing and "fatal" in the sense of awkward and embarrassing, and one must live with them as every scientist lives with the mistaken notions and antiquated theories of his predecessors whose greatness is not in any way affected by what now appears as blatant "limitations" on their part. "Rectification of names," as the Chinese say, may be a better approach to Hegel's notions about the Orient. Nevertheless it is regrettable that such a mind was exposed to so many limitations as to cause distortions particularly in those areas where there could have been a meeting of minds.

When Hegel was working through the material which he wanted to utilize for his lectures he wrote to Ed. Dubec, a manufacturer in Hamburg, on December 22, 1822, that going through the quartos and octavos apparently dealing with China and India, was to him a "very interesting and entertaining business to have the peoples of the world pass in revue."[1] But he also revealed the fact, obvious in most of his seminars, that the introduction occupied the greater part of his time and that the end of the lecture series suffered in thoroughness because he had not been able to read and digest all that he wanted and needed to read and digest for an adequate treatment. Add to this the comparative sparseness of knowledge in his day, less serious in the case of China, more serious in the case of India and Indian philosophy and Buddhism, it must be admitted that Hegel worked under serious handicaps.

For Hegel history starts where myth leaves off, where the natural, arbitrary will of the individual is beginning to be negated in an incipient state, where Spirit, substantially in the form of absolute power, begins to dawn, where mere existence changes into a yet pristine ethical behavior.

These conditions he saw fulfilled in the Orient, but only in a modest way, for individuality had allegedly not turned inward to create for itself a realm of subjective freedom. While in "theocratic," patriarchical China the sphere of inwardness had not been able to attain maturity in a "motionless Oneness," in India, ruled "despotically" by a theocratic aristocracy, there was a wild, crazy reeling from extreme to extreme, a constantly roving, unfettered uneasiness.

China and Mongolia are typically Oriental, according to Hegel, but India already represents a first approximation to the West and can, in a few respects, be paralleled by Greece.

In Persia, on the other hand, with its theocratic monarchy, the transition becomes more articulate and, moving progressively, initiated the traditional world history, its spirit being "pure," "clarified," and ethically free.

[1] Quoted from *Briefe von und an Hegel*, Vol. II, 113, by Georg Lasson (ed.), *G. W. F. Hegel: Vorlesungen über die Philosophie der Weltgeschichte*, Vol. II (Leipzig, 1919), v.

Egypt, too, was for Hegel in the Oriental orbit and occupied a special place in that it spiritually entered the life of Greece.

On the basis of these descriptions which seem to us somewhat fantastic and unrealistic, how accurately did Hegel prognosticate the fate of the Orient and legitimize himself as a historian of civilization? It is nearly 150 years ago that he told his awed students that China was the only durable empire in the world, that India, too, was preserved by virtue of its indestructible *Gedankenlosigkeit* (literally: lack of thought; better, perhaps: thoughtlessness as to the past or future) but was essentially destined to be mixed, dominated, and suppressed. Of the empires of the Tigris and Euphrates only heaps of bricks are left because the Persian Empire, symbolizing the transition, was subject to decay, involving, of course, its immediate neighbors. But the realm of the Nile existed now only *under* the soil in its mute dead which are being carried off into all the world, and *above* the soil only in magnificent sepulchres.

The actual state of affairs today is nearly the perfect contradictory of what Hegel thought it would be. China is a progressive Communist country which has changed the most since adopting a Western political philosophy; India is independent and has become the largest democracy in the world; Iran, or Persia, has emerged as a modern state and has registered the most phenomenal economic progress in recent years; Iran's neighbors also have experienced a renaissance though at a much more modest pace; and Egypt is now more concerned with its fellahs than its mummies, submerging its unhappy past in urgent problems of the day which could establish it firmly *above* ground. In view of this, should we still read Hegel's evaluation of the Oriental world or consign it to oblivion?

Perhaps not Hegel should really be blamed for reading history so patently falsely. It must be borne in mind that with much effort and interest he studied nation after nation in their development which he then transcribed into his ideal scheme of the march of Spirit through history. He was the victim of the lack of perceptiveness of the parochial authors he read. They sensed and experienced the otherness of their own, Western, Christian civilization, and with his Christian bias it was not difficult for Hegel to put on and read with their spectacles. His informants seldom made the attempt to uncover the presuppositions of the Oriental cultures in certain thought patterns. On the contrary, they noted the oddities and let them stand, convenient targets for conversion, if possible. There was no penetration in depth, for among the welter of interesting and entertaining phenomena one did not look for depth. One only judged from a superior point of view.

It can be said that the linear view of history inspired by the Judeo-Christian scriptures which moves between creation and the events described in Revelation, was shared by and celebrated in Hegel its greatest triumph, but also its greatest and, perhaps, final defeat. In application to the Orient it proved itself wholly deficient for prognostication. The claim of having brought true freedom into the world[2] cost Christianity and Hegel dearly in loss of understanding the world, its peoples, and its development. It has caused both loss of face in the Orient as well. Spirit, it has turned out, does not move pompously through history. It works in humble and dark places. Its presence may be discovered everywhere, even in places and in eras where common sense is blind to it, as in the Indian caste system, to mention but one dramatic instance, which, being the evil it is, nevertheless inspires to seek freedom through discipline. Such understanding, of course, might not be expected of Hegel's informants, but we could have expected it of Hegel, the master of the dialectic.

For what Hegel has to say about Buddhism, we turn to his lectures of 1822 to 1823. He prefaced them by an excursion into the Indian spirit which drowsily and dreamingly, as he says, fritters itself away between two extremes, unbridled sensualism and the emptiest of abstractions, reducing reality to a perplexing servility. But there is another kind of dreaming, more simple, cruder and, therefore, not yet developed into the frenzied kind just mentioned, and that is in keeping with Buddhism, nay, *is* Buddhism we are to conclude.

That Buddhism is older than Brahmanism was, of course, an incorrect impression he received from literature; that it was not a reform movement was a correct one intuited by Hegel, yet incorrectly derived. Buddhism presented itself to him as a more "humane" religion than Brahmanism, and the forms it took in different countries, which would have been difficult to trace owing to the sparse information, were laid by Hegel to the confusedness of the Indian mind. If we now add that *nirvāna* in Hegel's mind is merely the "highest abstraction," blissfulness, yet is described as a state connected with death and the becoming of a Buddha, we are inclined to believe that the confusion was more Hegelian than a *hinterindisches* jumble.

How much more penetrating, understanding, sympathetic Schopenhauer's treatment of Buddhism! This archpessimist, "voluntarist," and charming egotist caught the spirit of Buddhism from imperfect reports, while the logical, if "pantragic," unctuous, sagacious Hegel rummaging through tomes of loaded history came up with platitudes and nonsensical allegations.

One curious by-product of Hegel's study of peoples and their customs outside the "peculiarly Chinese" was what he called the "Mongolian Principle," a synthesis, one might say, of Lamaism, Buddhism,

[2] See Bernhard Lakebrink, *Die Europäische Idee der Freiheit*, Part I (Leiden, 1968).

Shamanism, and a brand of abstractionist nihilism of Hegelian manu-
facture. Here we find discussions of the Chinese Fo, a *Schattierung*
(blend or shade) of Gautama the Buddha or Śakyamuni as the
Mahāyānists call him; the "dogma of metempsychosis;" "nothing" as
the principle and end of all things; the "nothing of finitude in general,
the *abstractum* of the highest being "which is not a god, not a spirit,"
but "that which is abstract and unconscious in itself, with indifferent
content whose nothing it is"; "a principle entirely complete or finished
(*fertig*), pure, simple, an eternal quiescence, motionless in which God
does not appear to man and whose essence consists in being without
activity, intelligence, soul or will."

It would, indeed, require a volume to "rectify the names" which
Hegel links with Buddhism and which according to modern painstaking
and unbiased researches require not only revision but reversal and,
thus, deserve to be forgotten along with the "Mongolian Principle."
No serious or competent writer on Buddhism today would even remotely countenance what Hegel wrote:

> Happiness consists of uniting oneself to nothing. The more man becomes
> like the stone, the tree, arrives at passivity, the more he is perfecting
> himself. . . . It is in indolence, destruction of all activity of the spirit
> that eternity, happiness consists. If man has arrived at that point,
> he is on perfect equality with Fo. The god is, furthermore, also imag-
> ined as the beyond, not as that which is true, what truth should
> represent for man. In man this emptiness should attain existence;
> he transports himself into this stage. This is approximately also what
> occurs in Buddhism, in Ceylon and in the land of Burmese.[3]

Here we see clearly the sternly theologico-dogmatically bound
interpretation of history resolve itself into an uncharitable account
of peoples and religions which contrasts with Herder's more gracious
philosophy of history. As Ernst Schulin writes in his *Die weltgeschicht-
liche Auffassung des Orients bei Hegel und Ranke*,[4] in Herder's dealings
with such peoples there lies a touch of pious love of neighbor, aside
from a veneration of that which is original and naive, a veneration
of the child which came to the fore during the German period of
genius, the classical age. Hegel uses, but Herder avoids, references
to Oriental despotism, a phrase still often met with in present-day
literature, substituting the gentler "father-authority." Herder, after all,
practiced empathy, Hegel the power of logic to which he bent history.
Oriental despotism for Hegel was an incontrovertible and universal

---

[3] G. Lasson, *op. cit.*, Vol. II, *Die orientalische Welt*, 334–335. The translation is by
the present author.
[4] (Göttingen, 1958), 6.

fact because he deduced it from the negative character of the deity, its "otherness," its abstractness, which, then, becomes power per se to which man can only react with submissiveness and servility.

It now appears that we have, after all, sat in judgment over Hegel. However, it seemed necessary as we were merely underlining that Hegel's ideal amalgam of Christianity and State for the realization of freedom and the full deployment of Spirit in its true nature was responsible for the distortions and contortions in the interpretations of world history, especially in the Orient which in the period of colonial expansion were not only not noticed as such, but were without much ado accepted and sanctioned. The ideology involved, however, is no longer popular nor valid if we interpret realistically contemporary developments in the Orient in the light of democratic and ecumenical thinking. That does not mean, however, that we have to agree with Hegel's fiercest critics who feel that he and his speculations belong strictly to the history of philosophy and we ought to be done with *Hegelei.* There are lessons to be drawn from all this which philosophers of culture might learn and profit by.

The amount of elucidation and discussion devoted to the Orient which we find in Hegel's lectures and writings in itself shows that he was wrestling here with quite formidable problems. They were not merely the ones connected with social and economic conditions, the emergence of Spirit in the objective form of a state, but they had to do with a religion and philosophy in a multiplicity of forms. It was, therefore, especially India which he had to draw into his purview.

It was rather easy for Hegel to get a sympathetic hearing when talking about India being in an inebriated and frenzied state (*Taumel*) when focusing his attention on the exotic religious behavior and irrational caste-bound customs, or the exaggerations, exuberances, and phantasmagorias with which epic and *purāṇic* literature is so replete. However, there came to be known, gradually, in Hegel's own time, also more sober yet romantic matter, and Western stories and fairy tales were traced to India. Most important of all, one had discovered theological and metaphysical literature which demanded a reassessment of Hindu intellectual and spiritual capabilities as well as comparisons with Western speculations in the same fields. The lofty and philosophical character of the Hindu documents, as it appeared in translation after translation from the Sanskrit, was eliciting a deep interest and demanded also that Hegel come to grips with it. So powerful was the appeal that Hegel himself came close to compromising his own convictions. For while the (Christian) believer, such as himself, was loath to discuss the reasonableness or unreasonableness of his belief, he was under compulsion to reduce the positive dogmas of Western religion to reason also "only because he wished to satisfy (*Genüge leisten*) the 'stranger' (*den Fremden*), will say, the unbeliever," as reported by Hermann Glockner.[5]

Also from another point of view Hegel owed it to himself and to his hearers to advance from the abstract and general in his subtle condemnation of the Eastern peoples, especially the Hindus whom he had characterized as submerged in "thoughtless Oriental perception" (*gedankenloser orientalischer Anschauung*), to a more concrete evaluation. For the Romanticists were speaking exuberantly of Indian love lyrics, and religious dramas, poets—including his own esteemed Goethe—turned to India in unrestrained admiration, and even students of theology were looking for new light to the land of the Ganges. From day to day India gained in recognition as the homeland of wisdom and religion and at last supplanted China as the source of philosophy in the opinion of the intelligentsia of the age. Affinities were discovered in language, religion, metaphysics, aesthetics, which could not be dismissed so bluntly as the curiosities of a far-off people. India was no longer "*belanglos*" (of no consequence). Indeed, one even discovered order and system in their thinking, qualities which the Kantian particularly would appreciate. Above all, India no longer presented the image of an arrested phase of the World Spirit, but seemed to make a bid for having a more thorough knowledge of its being than even the West had.

Some four years or so before his death Hegel was given an opportunity to justify his position more thoroughly in the face of a changing attitude toward the Orient brought about by Romanticism in particular. He did so with éclat and show of comprehensive scholarship and with as little overt condescension as he could manage. The occasion was the appearance, in Berlin, in the year 1826, of Wilhelm von Humbolt's treatise *Ueber die unter dem Namen Bhagavad-Gita bekannte Episode des Mahabharata*. Hegel reviewed it in the *Jahrbücher für wissenschaftliche Kritik*, January 1827, columns 51–63, and October 1827, columns 1441–1492.

Hegel's lengthy discussion would seem at first sight to be a tribute to von Humboldt. But so great was his display of acquaintance with the foreign, particularly English literature dealing with the philosophical poem that it quasi buried the accomplishments of the German scholar under an avalanche of analytical remarks extending even into the minutiae of philology and topping it off with metaphysical observations intelligent only to a Hegel student, that von Humboldt's original appreciation of his having undertaken the review of his book

[5] Hermann Glockner, *Hegel*, Vol. II, *Entwicklung und Schicksal der Hegelschen Philosophie* (Stuttgart, 1958), 55.

changed—and rightly so—to keen disappointment. The reviewer complained that in the *Bhagavad Gītā* there are mixed "philosophy and fable, genuine with spurious matter, what is ancient with what is modern," but he added another dimension in the shape of his own subtleties and thus obfuscated an already complicated discussion which turned out to the discredit of von Humboldt who, it must be owned, had a better understanding of this famous composition than did Hegel.

A full examination of Hegel's stand regarding the *Bhagavad Gītā* would have to be very lengthy and certainly prove him wrong in several respects. But attention may be called to the final remarks which soften Hegel's previous views about Indian religion and spirituality. He deigned to observe that some "superficial ideas of Indian religiosity and its contents" must be given up and supplemented by an exploration of the "ever more documented peculiarities of the Indian spirit." This, of course, was a distinct gain in the direction of a better understanding of Indian thought on Hegel's part, but it was by no means sufficient or adequate. For Hegel insisted, all facts to the contrary,[6] that Brahma is the empty, murky One (*das leere, trübe Eine*), the deficient (*das Mangelhafte*), which is without distinction of subjectivity and objectivity, is wholly abstract and—*mirabile dictu*—spiritless (*geistlos*). Contemplation and devotion (*bhakti*), so intimately associated with the *Bhagavad Gītā*, also did not meet with any understanding from Hegel, not to mention pantheism of which he had total and unkind misconceptions.

There are indications, however, in Hegel's works that the contrast between East and West, though frequently discussed with brutal frankness, might not have been conceived as absolute. After all, it is the One Spirit that works in both hemispheres, and lethargy, formless, empty thinking can be encountered in the West also, while it is acknowledged by him[7] that rationalistic tendencies are likewise present in the East, though they never advanced to the stage of systematization. The admission is weak, to be sure, but nonetheless quite significant.

[6] See the oft-quoted Vedāntic passage: *Pūrṇamadah pūrṇamidam pūrṇāt pūrṇamudacyate | pūrṇasya pūrṇamādāya pūrṇamevāvasiṣyate,* which should be scrutinized in conjunction with Hegel's dialectical system. It has been translated, or, rather transliterated freely as follows by Swami Yatiswarananda (*The Divine Life, Its Practice and Realisation* [Mylapore, 1944,] 344): "That which is Brahman—the all-pervading Self in all—is infinite [*pūrṇa* actually means full, abundant, complete, perfect, entire]. And This which appears as the universe, but is all-pervading in Its real nature, is infinite. This differentiated Brahman emanates from the undifferentiated Brahman, but does not give up Its real nature. Rising above all limiting adjuncts, that which appears as the conditioned ever remains the unconditioned infinite Brahman."

[7] Glockner, *op. cit.,* Vol. I, *Schwierigkeiten und Voraussetzungen der Hegelschen Philosophie* (Stuttgart, 1954), 63.

The suspicion, thus, steals itself into our minds that Hegel needed the Orient for the sake of historical and dialectical consistency. This all the more when we scrutinize some of this harsh pronouncements about Indian thought and philosophy which are quite unverifiable and were not shared even in his day by those very authorities whom he quoted, nor by the Romanticists who took pride and joy in having found soul brothers in the Orient. It is not true that Orient and Occident are moments of the Spirit, as Hermann Glockner has said,[8] whose antagonism brings about a coming-to-itself. A less uncompromising stand would have made Hegel a world citizen in the fullest sense of the word. What he accused the Orientals of, that they want nothing to do with what is not in agreement with their own nature, that they shove it aside or fight it and subject it or submit to it if possessing greater might, is the very attitude inherent in Western and Christian thinking and therefore in his own. One is almost tempted to turn Hegel against himself or change the signs in order to get the correct perspective. For it is the Hindu who is tolerant of other views, and anyone studying the great civilizations of the East can certainly not come to the conclusion that all Orientals sought quiescence and abhorred change.

There are two sentences in particular which reconcile Hegel, unbeknown to himself, to Indian thinking in its basic complexion. One is: Truth is the whole and the whole is becoming (*das Wahre ist das Ganze und das Ganze ist ein Werden*). Brahman, too, is a dynamic totality, *ein seiend Werdendes*. It scintillates in its actuality and beckons in its myriad possibilities. It is never frozen being, it is never identifiable with the part.

The second pronouncement is that in Christianity hate should turn to love. This is to be the result of the *verkehrte Welt*, the world turned upside down or inside out, as he has it in the *Phenomenology of Spirit*. This should be compared with what the Buddha said: Hate does not cease by hate, hate ceases by love. Christianwise, hate is part of the natural, right-side-up world, and you have to negate it in order to make it a better world; Buddhistwise, you do not negate, invert, convert, or turn this world upside down, you do not fight evil, you assume the positive attitude or accept and live the reality of the "better" world. Seen in this light, charges of irrationalism, emptiness, abstractness, *Geistlosigkeit* (lack of spirituality), *Gedankenlosigkeit*, fall to the ground of their own dead weight.

It is now incumbent on us, *diese Hegelschen Ideen aufzuheben*, that is, to reduce, store away, or raise these ideas of Hegel's. No one is a better guide here than Hegel himself and his faithful interpreter,

[8] *Ibid.,* 72.

Hermann Glockner, who clarifies his relative and absolute idealism on the basis of his own writings.[9] The relativist idealist is, according to Hegel, "one immersed in battle." The absolute idealist is also immersed in battle, but he is more, for he is "both fighter and the battle itself." This is unadulterated Upanishadic thought, a perfect description of *brahman*, the ultimate Vedāntic principle, so beautifully interpreted in Ralph Waldo Emerson's poem "Brahma," a transcription of verses found in the *Upanishads* and the *Bhagavad Gītā:* "I am the doubter and the doubt, and I the hymn the Brahmin sings. . . ." It seems almost imcomprehensible how Hegel could, on the one hand, exemplify in himself the very personification of Indian Vedāntic thought and, on the other hand, be the classic misinterpreter of Indian thought and psyche. And yet it is understandable on the basis of, nay, from the core of the dialectic itself.

The question may, of course, be asked would Hegel, had he possessed a better knowledge of Indian philosophy, have acknowledged his affinity as did Schopenhauer when he discovered identities with his own thinking in the *Oupnekhat* and in Buddhism? Would he have been overjoyed or would he have jealously guarded the insight he had won and gone on in his own lumbering, ponderous way? As Iwan Iljin[10] has so admirably shown, Hegel's philosophy wavers between *dualism in a disguised form*, and *the attempt to "strike" the empirico-concrete* deliberately. His all-too-cautious circumspection and his quest of contentment—which seemed to have been one of his prime objectives in life as it was in his marriage—often stood in his own way of being what Iljin credits him with: that logical visionary and panlogistic clairvoyant.

If Hegel has any meaning for us today he and his philosophy must become subject to the dialectic itself as Hermann Glockner also suggests.[11] In this respect Iljin's work on Hegel's philosophy as a contemplative theory of God is the most significant and enlightening one especially for unfolding for us the implications of Hegel's dialectical system in comparison with Indian thinking as it reached its peak in the Vedānta as modified and modulated by various thinkers. Thus, it is not to the *tours de force* of the *Philosophy of History* that we have to look to get insight, but to the Hegelian system in its mature state which in Iljin's masterful presentation is absolutely comparable to ultimate metaphysical notions in the Indian system.

Hegel's historical studies in which he took such pride, together with his analysis of the empirical, concrete world, are far from truth

---

[9] *Ibid.*, 309ff.
[10] Iwan Iljin, *Die Philosophie Hegels als kontemplative Gotteslehre* (Bern, 1946), 358.
[11] Glockner, *op. cit.*, Vol. I, xxvi.

or reality, although they had a *Wirklichkeit* for him. Somehow he failed to look, or did not want to look at this area or phase of the Spirit from the absolute point of view, *sub specie aeternitatis*, in order to fit it into the historical schematism of Western theology and thus endow it with a sort of truth escaping, as it were, the criticism directed at a Kant, the *Alleszermalmer*. As a matter of fact it was this phase of the Hegelian philosophy which attracted the Hegelians in America[12] in that it did not destroy the world as structured in Christian theology, but preserved it. Even if the *brahman* of Indian philosophy should find appreciation along with other concepts of Indian philosophy, it could always be and was interpreted as "negative unity."

So far as Hegel himself was concerned, he redeemed himself in his panlogism from the sins he committed in his history of the Orient. It is in his panlogism where Indian thought, Taoism, Buddhism, and all the rest can find adequate representation and appreciation. The dialectic is the greatest and permanent achievement of Hegel and within its context he can be and was the trailblazer for the synthesis between Orient and Occident. Hegel, here, transcended himself and has *aufgehoben* the empirico-concrete phase of his philosophy. Spirit and freedom having achieved new dimensions within the last century and a half, have placed us at a vantage point which Hegel could not himself have occupied and which in his servility to dominant dogmas of his time he did not even faintly envisage. The Orient in its modern states has demonstrated that Spirit can become objective in its midst. Through political, educational, and cultural activities in innumerable institutions and organizations the will of the individual is set free, except where a new type of bondage, as in Communism, supplants the rigors of family and caste. In that some Oriental countries have developed a national spirit, the will of the individuals has created even substantiality for the state.

Hegel wanted to be a pantheist, as Iljin has shown,[13] but he did not succeed. Perhaps he lacked the courage of the Oriental thinkers; yet he did say in the *Philosophie des Rechts* that God made everything, even at its worst. And thus it is up to us to complete Hegel in a more daring and more comprehensive and more comprehending conception of man not only as a historical entity, but as an eternal moment in that very contemplation or *Versenkung*, which he, with limited vision, criticized.

[12] See the relevant passages in Leidecker, *Yankee Teacher: The Life of William Torrey Harris* (New York, 1946).
[13] Iljin, *op. cit.*, 381.

HEGEL'S ABSOLUTE
AND THEISM*

F. La T. Godfrey

This paper is a study of the relation of Hegel's Absolute to Theism. It is an attempt to unite Hegel's Idea with the God of religion, and to show that the pure thought-determinations of Hegel's *Logic* exibit the ground plan and purpose of the world, and thus presuppose an Absolute Author. If this thesis can be established, a basis in pure Thought is provided for a speculative knowledge of God, and theism will be grounded on pure reason. Hence I ask the Hegelian to recon-

* Though his name does not appear in this essay, I must pay tribute of thanks to the late Professor Macran who made Hegel live in Dublin. My best thanks are due too, to Professor A. A. Luce who kindly read my typescript and gave me many valuable suggestions.

sider his Absolute and the theologian to give credence to the gospel of pure thought.

Pure thought for Hegel is a process in which progressive advance is made from concepts shown to be abstract apart from their opposites to a concrete concept which contains both in a distinct unity; as empirical examples, we may see black and white as both based on grey, and agent and patient united in the idea of mutually dependent agents. Hegel's *Logic*, which systematically applies this method of deduction, to which I will refer later, is a definite exposition of the essential concepts which constitute the structure of nature and mind. These concepts of being, starting from the most abstract, quality and quantity, form a system of totality in which each has its place, supporting those above and supported by those below it in the logical order; similarly, in a business house, the ground floor is the base and also the end, for here are the offices for the sake of which the house exists. Thus, in the last section of the *Logic* physical and chemical objects are seen to be in themselves abstract and incomplete, and they find their concrete basis in living objects, and life is fulfilled in minds which have an intrinsic claim to value and truth. Accordingly, we live in a world whose structure and purpose are known by pure thought, and the world is not an aggregate of individuals nor the result of blind forces. My thesis is that, if we read the *Logic* rightly, we must regard its content as the thought of a divine creator, who is distinct from the world but manifests his purpose in it. We will then have certain pure knowledge of the God of theism, as Absolute Personality and Providence, the Author of the world and eternally concerned with it. Hegel does, as we shall see, frequently speak of the Absolute in these terms, using the language of religion; but his strict doctrine as a philosopher is a metaphysic which finds the Absolute in a monistic pantheism, in which God is the world force or spirit immanent in the world and coming to self-consciousness only in the minds of men who are conscious of it as the Absolute.[1]

[1] In his smaller *Logic*, which is the first part of the *Encyclopedia*, Hegel clearly distinguishes between the God of religion and the God of philosophy. He says: "Truth is the object of Logic . . . God is truth. . . . The form of feeling [in religion] is the lowest in which spiritual truth can be expressed. The world of spiritual existences, God himself, exists in proper truth only in thought and as thought." (*Enc.* § 19, *Zusatz*) Also, we read: "The term 'Objective Thoughts' indicates the *truth*—the truth which is to be the absolute *object* of philosophy, and not merely the goal at which it aims." (*Enc.* § 25) Professor Findlay calls attention to a passage in the *Encyclopedia* (§ 564) "where God is said to be God only in as far as He knows Himself, where this self-knowledge is said to be God's self-consciousness *in Man* and to be *Man's* knowledge of God, which develops into Man's self-knowledge *in* God." (*Hegel: A Re-examination* [London, 1958], 342).

It is clear that such an Absolute cannot be identified with the God of theism, to whom we must attribute the attributes of an absolute Subject, whom we can know as not only present in the world but as the Divine Being distinct from it. I contend that this God, whom Hegel as philosopher relegates to religion, is the true and logical outcome of his *Logic*.

We suppose, accordingly, that theism has the difficult task of combining immanence and transcendence, and we should see that neither doctrine is complete without the other. Both doctrines are developments from the immediate consciousness of God which Hegel holds is present in all rational beings. (*Enc.* § 2) For in all thought we are conscious of subject and the objective world together and in distinction from one another. Hence, while we may pay explicit attention to one, the unity which is the ground of both is always present in out minds.

It is sufficient for our purposes to note that the God of primitive religion is animistic, vaguely conceived as distinct from nature and mind and at the same time present in them, both transcendent and immanent. We are concerned with definite theories of God, not with the varieties of religious experience, but with trying to relate Hegel's Absolute, which he frequently speaks of as God, with theistic doctrine. Theological doctrine, when it has outgrown animism, tends to emphasize transcendence but is forced also to recognize immanence. On the other hand immanentist doctrine may so emphasize the identity of God as the universal being with the world as to deny transcendence. Hegel's Absolute seems to be the logical climax of immanentist theory, and I hope to show that it is incomplete without recognition of God as distinct from the world, but author of it.

We must consider in turn (1) transcendence in deism and in traditional theism, and (2) doctrines of immanence.

1. Transcendent Doctrines

Both deism and traditional theology assert a transcendent Deity with existence of his own quite distinct from that of all finite beings; for all things in space and time and all individual subjects, nations and institutions are finite existences, and they, together with the order which we see in the world, call for a permanent cause outside them. This is the transcendent Deity, who must be one, self-sufficient, infinite and eternal.

Deism is the simplest form of transcendent doctrine. The Deity is regarded as the unknown cause of the world, as, for example, by eighteenth-century writers of the Enlightenment like Hartley and Priestley, followers of Locke, who gives the Deity power to punish the wicked and to reward the righteous.[2] But we must ask, how, if he is transcendent and self-sufficient, external to the world, can he be its cause or concerned with it, and how can he be known by finite beings, who can only predicate finite attributes of him? The difficulty of sheer transcendence is apparent in Herbert Spencer's unknowable Power which manifests itself in the universe.[3] Can a purely transcendent Being express itself in the world? Christian philosophers, such as St. Augustine, saw this difficulty and denied the opposition between God and the world by regarding Him as Creator of it, both matter and form, space and time.[4] Christian theologians developed the well-known cosmological and physicotheological and ontological arguments of the divine activity in proving the existence of the God of theism.

These arguments of rational theology are so familiar to philosophers from Kant's criticisms of them that I will not elaborate them, but it may be useful to contrast Kant's viewpoint with that of Hegel. Since, for Kant, thought by itself is empty and knows nothing without a content of sense, our knowledge is limited to objects of experience in space and time.[5] We may and indeed we must think of God, but we cannot know him or determine his nature. Hence, for Kant, God who transcends our world of experience cannot be known through human cognition.[6] For Hegel, on the other hand, all knowledge is a level of thought, and pure thought apart from sense can determine the universal Being, and show that the rational and the ideal is the real. For God, in Hegel's strict view as a philosopher, is not a transcendent Being apart from the world, but "Reason immanent in it," an impersonal system of "objective thoughts" which actualizes itself at different levels in nature which is a "system of unconscious thought," and in mind. (*Enc.* § 24 and *Zusatz*)

Rational theology further claims to determine by thought the attributes of the divine nature, and theologians are again faced with the problem of knowing a transcendent being. Moses Maimonides declares that all predicates assigned to the Deity, wise, good, omnipotent, and so on, are equivocal or nominal and have no real meaning; for all predicates are drawn from the world of finite things.[7]

This is negative theology, but theologians do require positive knowledge of God's nature. Is this possible, if God as infinite is a transcendent inscrutable X, the negation of human predicates? Aquinas

[2] John Locke, *An Essay Concerning Human Understanding*, IV, 10.
[3] Herbert Spencer, *First Principles* (London, 1867), 46.
[4] Augustine, *De Civitate Dei*, XI, 6.
[5] Immanuel Kant, *Critique of Pure Reason*, B 75.
[6] Ibid., B 612ff.
[7] Moses Maimonides, *The Guide for the Perplexed*, trans. Friedlander (London, 1904), pt. I, chap. 58.

and many modern theologians meet the difficulty by predication by analogy;[8] we may say that a predicate, *a*, is related to God as *a* is related to finite things, this predication leaving God in himself as transcendent, for we should distinguish between the meaning of a predicate, for example, wise, as applied to a finite or infinite object. To illustrate:

i.   Intellect (a) is related to God (X) as intellect is related to man (Y). We may compare this case of analogy with one in which X and Y are both finite.

ii. Steering (a) is related to statesmen (X) as it is to pilots (Y). In this case, we know both X and Y and can compare them and see the identity, intelligent direction. But, if X is transcendent and unknown, we cannot say that a is related to X as a is related to Y, and the relation of a to Y will throw no light on X. This analogical knowledge appears to link the idea of the Infinite X with the finite by a middle term, for example, intelligence; this is possible, if we have positive knowledge of God and can compare infinite and finite intelligence.

But, if we start with God as a transcendent X, a finite middle term will not give knowledge of Him. Accordingly, unless the theistic philosopher who relies on analogical predication can assume some degree of positive knowledge of God, he will "oscillate," as Professor Copleston says, "between anthropomorphism and agnosticism."[9]

This dilemma leads us up to Hegel's viewpoint. He holds that we have immediate knowledge of God as the Supreme Being, ground of subject and objective world, as immanent in the world and in our thought, and that reflective thought can determine it. (*Enc.* § 2) I think that we may at least agree that theology can hardly build on a basis of skepticism where transcendence is emphasized at the expense of immanence or on an opposition between faith and reason.

2. Doctrines of Pure Immanence

These theories affirm that God is all, and we may distinguish two main forms:

(a) The divine principle is indifferently omnipresent in all events and particular things of nature, storms, hills, animals and men, and all are equally appearances of God. We may see this idea in Hinduism and also in the doctrine of Stoicism which affirms that God is present everywhere and at all times; hence the wise man will not be disturbed by fear or desire, for after all everything is really perfect. As Alexander Pope says in his *Essay on Man:*

[8] Thomas Aquinas, *Summa Theologica* (London, 1911), I, XII, Qu. 10.
[9] Frederick Copleston, *Contemporary Philosophy* (London, 1963), 96.

> All are but parts of one stupendous whole
> Whose body Nature is, and God the soul; . . .
> Breathes in our soul, informs our mortal part,
> As full, as perfect in a hair as heart.

Such a doctrine posits the reality of particular things as appearances of God without grounding them on his identity, thus equating God with phenomena.

(b) The complementary immanentist theory may be called abstract monism. If God is all, and God is simple Identity, we must regard the Supreme Being as an indifferent indeterminate Absolute; it is the Identity and ground of all diversity and opposition. We see this in the infinite substance of Spinoza, to which Hegel often refers. Its essential attributes for intellect are thought and extension, but as infinite substance it remains the identical energy behind them, when we abstract from their peculiar determinations, as we must do to arrive at substance; for all determinations are negations like points on a line, and substance being positive must be indeterminate.

If the identity of the Absolute is thus emphasized against diversity, immanence turns into empty transcendence; it is self-refuting, for, as pure identity, nothing proceeds from it; it is opposed to the world of nature and mind, and hence it is not infinite or absolute. The Absolute, to be absolute, must be the self-determining ground of nature and mind.

Hegel clearly distinguishes his Absolute from the God of pantheism, whether present equally in all things or the abstract substance of which things are negations or passing modes.[10] For Hegel the Absolute is subject not substance.[11] It actualizes itself in a graded order of reality and value as shown by the dialectic of reason; this order culminates as subject in the minds of men who are conscious of it as the Absolute. Hegel, in fact, gives us concrete monism, the concrete system of categories of the *Logic*, the Idea; he calls this system the Absolute, the self-realizing universal which, taking on the forms of space and time, is the world-force or spirit actualized in nature and mind. (*Enc.* § 20) This again is immanentist doctrine, for the world is the manifestation of the absolute system of thought-determinations which have no existence except as the ground of nature and in finite minds who think them.

Before we can relate Hegel's Absolute to theism, we must first briefly (a) consider his method of pure thought, and (b) sketch the content involved in his Absolute as thought by us in the *Logic*.

[10] G. W. F. Hegel, *Philosophy of Religion*, trans. Speirs and Sanderson (London, 1895), I, 96ff. and 214ff.
[11] G. W. F. Hegel, *Phenomenology of Mind*, trans. Baillie (London, 1931), 15; *Werke*, II, 14.

(a) Hegel's Method

(i) Its General Validity

In Chapter VI of his *Logic* (*Enc.* §§ 79–83), Hegel sets out the essential features of his dialectical method; it consists of three moments, which he calls abstract understanding, negative reason, and positive speculative reason. The understanding entertains some concept as true by itself, negative reason points out opposition and contradiction in it, and positive reason rethinks the concept, reconciling the opposition in a concrete idea without importing any external content. This triadic procedure, the best-known example of which is the advance from being through nothing to becoming, is the basis of Hegel's method; by it pure being, the first concept of the *Logic*, is progressively determined, the synthesis of each triad or a deduction from it being the starting point of the next triad. Such in general is Hegel's method, but as the dialectic of thought proceeds, opposition tends to become less tense, for opposition decreases as more comprehensive syntheses are reached. Hegel insists that pure thought develops the implications of pure being quite autonomously without debt to content given by experience. (*Enc.* § 12) In fact, pure thought is free from all the doubts and uncertainties of experience and if we can get pure thought to function, the result is certain knowledge, the a priori equipment of our minds which we can bring to light by reflection.[12]

Hegel's dialectical method in the *Logic*, by which the idealist proceeds independently of experience from abstract to concrete Truth, has been a stumbling block to many. For example, Professor Findlay in his sympathetic *Hegel: A Re-examination* tells us that this method does not give validity of proof. He says that the concepts of the *Logic* are only a sequence of linguistic recommendations which cannot claim truth or validity,[13] but on the next page he bids us not to give too subjective an interpretation to the terms of the *Logic*; for he goes on to tell us that the *Logic* as the study of thought determinations is also a study of things as they really are. But we may reply that this is the principle on which pure thought depends, and to grant

---

[12] This idea goes back to Plato, who in the *Phaedo*, tells us that thought should turn its back on experience and develop the truth out of its own resources. The method of advance by dialectic of double negation is really Hegel's discovery, though Fichte's thesis, antithesis, synthesis was probably a stimulus to him. We may also recall St. Augustine's saying: "Do not go outside yourself; retreat within yourself, truth resides in the inner man (*in interiore homine habitat veritas*)." (*De Vera Religione*, chap. 39, 72.)

[13] J. N. Findlay, *Hegel: A Re-examination* (London, 1958), 151.

this is to allow the general validity of the method, apart from matters of detail which may call for correction. Idealists, indeed, from Parmenides onwards have held that being and thought are identical, so that being is what we *must* think it to be. How then are we to think the necessary contents of thought which constitute the ultimate determinations of thought and being? Hegel's answer is by the dialectical method of pure thought. It seems clear, as Kant showed, that deductive process in metaphysics tends to be dogmatic, as in Spinoza, and while induction may claim to establish an hypothesis, since it is based on contingent experience, it cannot give us universal and necessary truth. If we dismiss pure thought and assume like Kant that thought in itself is analytical, empty of content, and can know nothing, metaphysic is reduced to fiction.

Assuming, then, the general validity of the dialectic, we must ask, does it establish the Absolute as Reason or thought, which in itself is the "self-actualizing universal" (*Enc.* § 6 and § 20), and which exists only as it develops itself in space and time at different levels until it reaches consciousness in man? If this is the Absolute reached by dialectic, we must concede that it is pantheistic doctrine and can be no partner in theism. We will first consider the dialectic process, and later, questions arising from the content of the *Logic*.

(ii) The Dialectic Process as Our Subjective Process

I believe that the dialectical process, of which the moments are understanding, negative and positive reason (*Enc.* §§ 79–83), is the process by which we, as possessing potential reason, see the totality of ultimate thought-content. We apprehend it as a totality of different levels of truth, reality, and value as it is unrolled for us when we adopt the attitude of pure thought; we are the spectators of this continuous system of thought-determinations which constitute the essence of things. I reject Hegel's view of the thought-content of the *Logic* as the self-actualizing, self-developing Absolute. We must look on it as a panorama of different levels of thought revealed to us in the process of the dialectic. I hope to argue later that this content is the thought-plan of the Absolute as Absolute subject, or to use Aristotle's phrase, *Active Reason*.

We should not import what appears to imply temporal notions into the logical relations of the concepts of the *Logic*. The earlier categories are incomplete appearances, what we by dialectic apprehend first, so that any account of being which views it as thought developing, growing, and sprouting is misleading. We must look to the end and see the last category, rational personality, as completing what is actual, but we must remember that the other categories, while inadequate views of the actual, are necessary links in a chain, and have their rightful places in the system. To regard the later categories as in some way products or growths from the earlier is to forget that while the earlier are abstract without the later, they are means to the later.

To suppose that this system of thought in the *Logic* is anything but a totality or that we should think it as Hegel says, as a *self-actualizing universal* (*Enc.* § 20), seems to be a mistake and to confuse our developing view of the content with a supposed actual develpoment of it. This is a fundamental point, for on it the issue between a pantheistic and theistic interpretation of the *Logic* depends. Hegel states his own doctrine in a well-known passage in the Preface to the *Phenomenology of Mind:*

> The truth is the whole. The whole, however, is merely the essential nature reaching its completeness through the process of its own development. Of the Absolute it must be said that it is essentially a result, that only at the end is it what it is in very truth; and just in that consists its nature, which is to be actual, subject, or self-becoming, self-development.[14]

In the Introduction to the lesser *Logic*, Hegel speaks of the content of logic as that which "producing itself within the precincts of the mental life has become the *world*, the inward and outward world, of consciousness." (*Enc.* § 6) F. H. Bradley, on the other hand, tells us that there is no development in the Absolute which is perfect and complete.[15] We may not agree with Bradley's account of the Absolute, but it seems impossible to regard it as something which develops from stage to stage, so that at point A it is not B, and at point B it is not C.

We talk quite naturally of the passage in the *Logic*, from A to B and from B to C, and from C to D from, for example, mechanism through chemism to teleology, life, and mind. But this passage is really the subjective passage which we must make in thinking these categories which are logically related as abstract to concrete factors of being, where each factor has its place and function in the total system; we cannot identify being with the last category, although it best displays the nature of being; for while rational personality is the climax, end, and purpose of them, it cannot stand apart from the other modes of being which exist for it.

If, then, it is clear that the thought-content of the *Logic* is not a self-developing system, we will not regard it as the Absolute which develops itself by stages in and as the world. To say that the Absolute is self-actualizing universal which develops in space and time, from

[14] Hegel, *op. cit.*, 17.
[15] F. H. Bradley, *Appearance and Reality* (London, 1897), 499.

unconscious impersonal states to conscious personality in man, is really to regard it as a finite thing, which grows and develops like an oak tree which grows from an acorn or like a man who grows from an infant. But such development and self-actualization are only possible because the finite exists within an environment in harmony with it, and which it can include in itself. In fact, growth and development belong to the finite which as singular combines particularity with universality, and so can express in its limited way the universal system within which it exists.

Being then, we will say, in the *Logic* consists of a system of thought-determinations related in dialectical order, where what we may call the lower are means to the higher and in the highest an absolute end, rational personality, is thought. We should not assimilate it to an organism like a tree or a human being, or regard it as a living individual as Plato, probably metaphorically, speaks of his system of Ideas in the *Timaeus* (30b); for it is not a finite existent thing, but a perfect system of thought-content. We may think of it as Plato's hierarchical system of Ideas constituting the *Idea of the Good* which is beyond existence but is the metaphysical basis of nature and mind. What Plato only suggests in abstract form in Book VI of the *Republic* (for example, 509) seems to be worked out in pure thought in Hegel's *Logic*, and we have here the nonempirical scheme of the world. In what way is it relevant to theism? While Hegel calls it the Absolute, the self-actualizing universal, I hope to show that we should relate it to an Absolute Subject who combines intellect and will, and that we should think it as the content of God's thought of the essence of nature and mind.

(b) Content of the Logic

I must now attempt, as suggested above, a brief sketch of the content of this system of thought. The lowest levels of thought-content (*Enc.* §§ 84–111) are those of quality and quantity characteristic of sense perception; they lead to categories of reflection, in which the scientific understanding is at home (*Enc.* §§ 112–159), where essence and appearance, identity and diversity are related in various ways, as in the ideas of thing and its properties, form and matter, force and its manifestations. The final category of reflection is that of substances in reciprocal reaction with one another. Hegel's dialectical advance from reciprocity to the Notion (*Begriff*) is one of his most striking and valuable discoveries, and we shall return to it later. (*Enc.* §§ 155–159)

We see now a new level of being, subjectivity, the universal which includes difference within itself and remains universal, identical, and independent, that is, singular. (*Enc.* § 163)

The third section of the *Logic* develops the idea of the Notion, as subjective, objective Notion and Idea, the unity of objectivity and subjectivity. (*Enc.* §§ 213–244) The doctrine of the subjective Notion displays the formal activity of the subject as self-organizing by means of judgments and syllogisms. This activity, as exercised apart from objects, is empty and abstract and must lead to the idea of Notion as subjects.

The object deduced is simply being in which subjectivity, as self-organizing unity of universal, particular and singular, as far as is conceivable, is negated. We now see what, according to Hegel corresponds with Leibniz's *Monad* (*Enc.* § 194), the singular exclusive object which professes to be an absolute existence by itself without doors or windows, but which, as merely one of such objects, is necessitated from without. We may, perhaps, compare it with the displaced person who has lost his freedom and subjectivity and is treated like a parcel, the contradiction of independence combined with dependence. In the dialectic of the object, starting with mechanism, objects externally and indifferently related, we see subjectivity, mutual dependence, gradually restored in chemism and teleology in life, which is indifferently both subject and object. In the living individual, the externality and indifference of diversity of the object are in principle overcome. (*Enc.* § 216) The result is the *realized end*, the living individual subject-object. Its content, the parts, exist as interdependent, and form a totality, distinct from one another but inseparable. Each part is a differentiation of its whole and accomplishes the ends of the whole. They exist for it, and it exists in them. Life, then, is the form of the body, and the body is alive through its form, by which it is a totality. Hence the living individual is what Kant calls *an end of nature* for the sake of which its members as organs exist;[16] it is a self-realizing individual, existing by means of them and its environment.

We have reached the Idea, the sphere of truth in which objectivity is brought into harmony with subjectivity in life and mind, and the good or final value is realized. (*Enc.* § 213) Life is consummated in mind, in which subject and object are mediated in the Idea as theoretical and practical; empirical cognition and conduct from different angles aim at progressively achieving this harmony. Empirical knowledge, starting with the apparent opposition of the objective world to the subject, constructs an inner world of knowledge on the assumption that nature is intelligible and subject to its concepts. For, if it is assumed with Kant that the opposition of subject and object is ultimate,

---

[16] Immanuel Kant, *Critique of Judgment* (Berlin, 1790), § 64.

knowledge is only phenomenal and we have subjective idealism. Practical activity, volition, as Kant's goodwill, which acts only from the idea of pure law or duty, sets up its ideal of the good as real and necessary against the actual world of contingent events inner and outer, with the result that the ideal remains unrealized and the goodwill accomplishes nothing. But, if we remember that the world is real and intelligible and that intelligent will is in action, we see that the will does positively alter natural subjective tendencies and physical nature in accordance with its practical principles of right, for in action the opposition between subject and object is overcome.

If we, then, survey pure being at the level of mind, we find that the empirical dualism of subject and object is continually overcome, and mind works in a world of nature which is not alien to it but is the field for its activity. Nature, though distinct from mind, is continuous with it at a lower level of thought-content, and its externality and incoherence as seen in mechanism, chemism, and life present a problem for the cognition and practical activity of mind. But idealism shows that the problem is set to be overcome, and that mind continually constructs a second world of nature in which truth and value are established; if anyone doubts this, he should look around him at the manifold achievements of civilization. The whole world is based on a system of ultimate thought-content, and its *ratio essendi* is the progressive realization of rational experience. The absolute Idea unites the theoretical Idea which posits the reality of the actual world with the practical Idea which posits the reality of the ideal of the subject. (*Enc.* § 235) The result is concrete monism; for being is now seen to be a concrete system of thought present in different levels of reality and value in the world, and it appears at the end as the truth, personality, in which there is identity of objectivity with subjectivity, the final term in the dialectic of being.

The Ontological Status of the System of Pure Thought

Being then is thought, the ground of subject and object. Thought is the system of the categories. Should we say that this system of pure thought *is* the Absolute Being, the self-determining ground of nature and mind? Here again, we have the immanentist doctrine that the Absolute is pure thought-content which develops itself dialectically in space and time through different levels of being, reaching finally minds which are conscious of it. Thought makes nature and mind and thinks itself in us. Hence, when we think thought as the Absolute metaphysical principle, we should say that it is really not we who think it, but rather that thought is the real subject which thinks itself in us. The Truth, then will be one Absolute subject, the identity of individuals who think the categories as absolute; to see the Truth they must negate the individual differences of particular men; for reality consists of pure thought-content which has reached consciousness of itself in them.

Here we see the paradoxical result of the doctrine of pure thought-content as the absolute self-determining ground of nature and mind. For this theory, the Absolute is impersonal, unconscious thought, the system of the categories culminating in the idea of personality or spirit, and self-actualized in individual persons who consciously identify themselves with this universal Absolute Spirit. The religious consciousness is then transcended in the mind of the philosopher, and the idea of the personal God of theism must be regarded on this doctrine as metaphorical language, for the Absolute as personality does not exist except in individual persons who as philosophers think the system of the categories as the absolute. Professor Stace puts this point well: "The Absolute *is* the categories. We must not say that the Absolute is something which somehow has the categories, for this," Stace thinks, "would involve a mysterious thing-in-itself to which the categories apply in an external fashion."[17]

The result is a form of pantheism which reduces God and man to an impersonal system of thought-content. This avoids a transcendent Absolute, but it seems that it cannot carry the weight of both nature and mind, and Hegel himself appears at times to refer it to the God of theism. I will cite some such passages later, but my main contention is that the thought-content of the *Logic*, as the ground of the world, necessarily implies an Absolute Subject, distinct from finite human subjects.

I have already argued that we should not regard the dialectical process of the *Logic* as the self-developing movement of objective thought-content; I hold that we should think the dialectic as the method by which we gradually discover the pure thoughts which constitute different levels of the system of being. If we view the continuous system of the categories as a totality, that is, as the ultimate scheme of reality, it will be seen that they involve an Absolute Subject, whose thoughts they are, and not merely a human or finite thinker, as the immanentist doctrine supposes. We may call this Subject transcendent, but it is known by us as the Thinker of the categories, and hence it is not externally related to them.

We may first ask: Is the status given to nature in Hegel's system consistent with the immanentist theory of the categories? The category of cognition is realized in human subjects, but cognition, including both knowledge and conduct, cannot be realized apart from physical objects and life; here we have thought-determinations prior to minds

[17] W. T. Stace, *The Philosophy of Hegel* (London, 1924), 77ff.

and having a level of being of their own. As Hegel says, nature in mechanism, chemism, and teleology has an immediate being of its own in the system of the categories apart from and prior to cognitive subjects. (*Enc.* § 193) Nature, then, in space and time is an object of possible experience for us to think and act in, and our thinking does not constitute it as a possible object of experience, but alters it in many ways, so that we make a second nature from the first.

If thought-content implies a subject, then thought-content of the world which is not known by us and which has an immediate existence relatively independent of us, implies an absolute Thinker or Subject; nature, as an object of possible thought for us, must be an actual thought-content prior to our thinking it, and is therefore thought by an absolute Subject. The pure concepts of the Object realized in space and time, inorganic and organic, stars, mountains, trees, fishes, and so on, objects of perceptual experience and studied by natural science have an existence logically and temporally prior to finite minds; Hegel is quite clear about this in his *Philosophy of Nature.* (*Enc.* § 248, *Zusatz*) Hence, they must, as thoughts, be objects of an absolute Subject, who as active Reason, constitutes them as objects for our potential reason. I conclude, then, that the system of the categories implies an absolute Thinker, who through them constitutes both nature and finite minds, and thinks the whole world eternally, for it can hardly be said to exist, if there are only finite subjects.

Hegel's accounts of the Notion seem to support this point of view, and I will refer to them later. (*Enc.* §§ 160–165) The idea of God as the eternal Thinker of the categories and through them the creator of the world is also supported by a well-known passage in Hegel's Introduction to his larger *Logic*. Hegel says:

> Logic is consequently to be understood as the System of Pure Reason, as the Realm of Pure Thought. *This realm is the Truth as it is, without husk in and for itself.* One may therefore express it thus: that this content *shows forth God as he is in his eternal essence before the creation of Nature and of a Finite Spirit.*[18]

Those, like Stace, who hold to the immanentist doctrine would regard this language as metaphorical and religious, and to be understood by the philosopher as meaning that the Idea is the Absolute essence which passes into the form of space and time and produces nature out of itself.[19] I must reply that we should regard the Idea as the plan of the world and not as a self-actualizing universal.

I welcome Professor Findlay's description of the *Logic* as the con-

---

[18] G. W. F. Hegel, *Wissenschaft der Logik, Werke,* IV, 46; *Science of Logic,* trans. Johnston and Struthers (London, 1929), I, 60.
[19] Stace, *op. cit.,* 303ff.

ceptual "blue-print" of nature and mind.[20] I take this phrase in a metaphysical sense as the basic blueprint of the world, discovered by pure
thought. But surely we should say that a blueprint involves a thinker
who is the author of it, distinct from any of the terms in it? Should
we not say that this system of thought-determinations is God's plan
of the world and that it reveals a purpose to which nature is subordinate, human rational activity, coming to a climax in art, religion,
and philosophy, in which man is conscious of God as Supreme Being?

I think that those who hold the metaphysical doctrine of immanence should show what sort of being can be ascribed to the system
of the categories when there is no finite mind which thinks them.
We have already seen that nature both logically and in time comes
before finite minds, and we cannot say that men or other finite beings
have always thought the system of the categories consciously or unconsciously. Should we not say that they exist *ante rem*, as the thought-
content of the Absolute Subject who thinks them as his blueprint of
the world, realized progressively in space and time?

Finite minds can certainly think this scheme of things and as universal subjects, possessing potential reason, regard themselves as its
final term; but the scheme itself seems to involve Providence as its
author, Active Reason, absolute Spirit, who eternally thinks it and
manifests Himself in the world through it. Theism may well accept
Hegel's Idea, the thought-content which is the ground of nature and
mind, if we regard it as the content thought by the absolute Subject
as the basis of the world. Hegel himself, as in the passage just quoted,
does frequently express this idea, combining theism with the immanence of the categories as the divine thoughts realized in the world.
Those who hold the nontheistic doctrine of the Idea explain away
such references to an absolute Thinker as expressions of religious language to be superseded in philosophy. My purpose is to try to reconcile
the God of religion with the Absolute of philosophy, theism with Hegel's
Logic.

It is clear that Hegel has great sympathy with religion and in
particular with Christianity. I will now cite four passages in which
he uses in the *Logic*, religious language of God as Providence and
Personality:

(1)   To say that the world is ruled by Providence implies that de-
      sign . . . is the active principle, so that the issue corresponds to
      what has been foreknown and forewilled. (*Enc.* § 147, *Zusatz*)

(2)   We conceive the world to ourselves as a great totality which is created
      by God, and so created that in it God has manifested himself
      to us. We regard the world as ruled by Divine Providence, implying

[20] Findlay, *op. cit.*, 20.

that the scattered and divided parts of the world are continually brought back, and made conformable, to the unity from which they have issued. (*Enc.* § 213, *Zusatz*)

(3) Divine Providence may be said to stand to the world and its process in the capacity of absolute cunning. God lets men do as they please . . . but the result is the accomplishment of—not their plans, but his." (*Enc.* § 209, *Zusatz*)

(4) It is true that God is necessity, or as we may also put it, that he is the absolute Thing: He is however no less the absolute person. That he is the absolute Person however is a point which the philosophy of Spinoza never reached. (*Enc.* § 151, *Zusatz*)

In such passages, Hegel speaks of the Absolute as not merely immanent and self-actualizing thought-content but as transcendent Subject manifesting himself in the world through the categories. The language of these quotations may be regarded as pictorial, but they result in giving plausibility to the idea of thought-content as the ground of the world by linking it with the personal God of theism, who has an existence of his own distinct from nature and mind, but manifests himself by his "divine decrees" in the world. (*Enc.* § 163, *Zusatz*) This line of thought substitutes for a self-actualizing self-developing Absolute immanent in nature and mind, the idea of Providence revealing himself in the scheme of the world.

It is also remarkable that Hegel in speaking of the transition of the *Logic* of pure thought to the *Philosophy of Nature* tells us that the Idea "*resolves* (*sich entschliesst*) to let the 'moment' of its particularity . . . go forth freely as Nature." (*Enc.* § 244) At this important point of his philosophy, Hegel has recourse again to the diction of theism.

If we accept Hegel's doctrine that the categories of the *Logic* are the Absolute, then in some way nature, being in space and time and infected by contingency, must be deduced from the Idea. Stace discusses this problem, and he concludes that the deduction is invalid.[21] This is a well-known difficulty. It is clear that, if the system of the categories is the Absolute, nature and mind must be deducible from it; for otherwise, the categories would be only subjective or human forms of thinking, the dialectic showing that some are more coherent than others. Hegel insists that they are objective, not simply because we must think them, but because pure thought is the metaphysical principle of the world, and Reason pure and impassive, as Anaxagoras said, governs the universe. (*Enc.* § 24, *Zusatz*)

Hence it is necessary for Hegel to deduce nature and also mind from the system of categories. We must be satisfied not only that the dialectic process is valid but also that these universal thoughts are objective and have real being prior to nature and to human subjects

[21] Stace, *op. cit.*, 306ff.

who are latecomers into the world. Now, I would urge, this is only possible, if they are eternally thought by an Absolute Subject as the ground plan or essential structure of the world. Granting this, we can agree that the categories of the *Logic* must be actualized in the spatiotemporal world, and that the world of nature will exhibit this logical order. I will deal with this question below in considering Hegel's *Philosophy of Nature.*

The theist will be asked whether the idea of an absolute Subject is really contained in the *Logic* and consistent with it, or is it foisted in at the end to make good alleged deficiencies of the immanentist doctrine of the Idea? We may reply that the *Logic* shows that being for pure thought is a definite system of thought, whose end is the realization of rational personality, and that it is reasonable and necessary to regard this plan as "the divine decrees" of an Absolute Subject. It might be wise to leave the argument at this point; but it seems that I should show that the idea of an Absolute Subject is not an *ad hoc* last-minute addition *ab extra* to the dialectic. I believe that we may find logical evidence for it, if we remember that the Idea is the complete account of the Notion, in which subjectivity is introduced in the *Logic.*

The sphere of the Notion brings us to the standpoint of philosophy; this means that the viewpoint of concrete monism or absolute idealism is opening out for contemplation. I must quote Hegel's striking words in introducing the Notion.

> No doubt the Notion is not mere Being, or the immediate: it involves mediation, but the mediation lies in itself. . . . The Notion is the genuine first; and things are what they are through the action of the Notion, immanent in them, and revealing itself in them. In religious language we express this by saying that God created the world out of nothing. In other words, the world and finite things have issued from the fulness of the divine thoughts and the divine decrees. Thus religion recognizes thought and the Notion to be the infinite form, or the free creative activity, which can realize itself without the help of a matter that exists outside it. (*Enc.* § 163, *Zusatz*)

If it is said that these statements are metaphorical, and that Hegel has chosen to speak in the language of religion instead of the philosophical diction of impersonal thought-process, I would reply that he really had no option. For at the level of the Notion actualized in the Idea it is manifest that the being studied by pure thought is a divine scheme which reveals the purpose of an Absolute Subject. The following considerations should make this clear.

In the doctrine of the Subjective Notion, Hegel shows that the subject is a self-organizing person, and that he cannot realize himself on the formal basis of judgments and syllogisms apart from the objective world deduced in the objective Notion. The subject is actualized as a person at the level of the Idea, in which he exercises knowledge and conation in harmony with the objective world of nature and other persons. As Hegel points out, freedom is actualized at this level of being (*Enc.* § 158); thus, so far as mother and son act as related by reciprocal rights and duties in the family, their actions are recognized as necessary, but as they are not externally determined, they are free. For freedom means doing deliberately what is right as involved in membership of the social life, and we may see this freedom in the very determined man who acts from a moral or social purpose. To act as a self-contained unit is to act as a thing or imperfect subject; a man as self-organizing subject has liberty to do this, but he will then be at loggerheads with other persons, who will confine his liberty of action. We see, then, that the world does not consist merely of interacting objects and living individuals, but it is a system in which persons can live and develop in peace subject to the ethical law whose purpose is to promote rational personality in all its aspects. This law is not externally imposed on the individual, and he does not impose it on himself as an isolated individual, but he accepts it as he accepts all good things which are necessary for life and are included in the plan of the world. As Hegel says, Christian ethic is based on the principle of personality (*Enc.* § 163, *Zusatz*), and personality involves a metaphysic of the world which comes to light in the Notion and Idea.

I have here emphasized the practical side of the finite subject as an ethical will with intrinsic value, for it is evident from this viewpoint that we cannot merge the individual with others in a common universal subject which thinks the Absolute, and that we must reject a pantheism which is an impersonal system of thought-content indifferent to individual persons. We say above that this is the paradoxical result of Hegel's immanentist doctrine. We must rather think the Notion and Idea, from which we and the world proceed, as a system of divine thoughts whose purpose is the development of persons in what Aristotle calls moral and intellectual virtue, science, art, religion, philosophy. We acknowledge our debt to Hegel for his discovery of the content of pure thought. But we reject his view of it as consisting of thoughts unthought until we think them. We maintain that they are the master-thoughts of the absolute Thinker.

The Unity of Philosophy and Theology

The *Logic* is the core of Hegel's philosophy; it is actualized in space and time as is shown in his *Philosophy of Nature* and his *Philosophy of Mind*. We must finally consider these second and third members of this trilogy in relation to theism.

We have regarded the Idea of the *Logic* as the plan of the absolute Subject for the world, and there should now be no difficulty in the deduction of nature. We should think of the divine Personality actualizing in space and time his scheme for the realization of rational persons. Hegel showed in the subjective Notion that subjective activity exercised apart from objects is abstract and empty (*Enc.* § 193), and we must similarly agree that the pure divine thoughts of the *Logic* must be realized in the objective world. The actual world differs from the pure scheme by its spatiotemporal form, as we have seen, and this form is the medium through which the universals *ante rem* are expressed in the world of particular facts. We must affirm this two-way relation between the universal scheme and particular existent things, so that the rational of the *Logic* and the real dealt with by empirical science are inseparable, but distinct. We can accept the general agrument of Hegel's *Philosophy of Nature* which shows that the laws of the natural sciences correspond with the categories of the objective Notion; it should, of course, be brought up to date on the lines suggested, for example, by Professor Errol E. Harris in his *Foundations of Metaphysics in Science* (London, 1965).

In the *Philosophy of Mind*, Hegel shows a wide knowledge of religious experience. He tells us that the content of religion and philosophy is the same, both being cognition of the Absolute; but while the form of the religious consciousness is feeling (*Anschauung*) and imagination (*Vorstellung*), the form of philosophy is pure thought.[22] The philosopher then thinks this thought-content as the self-actualizing universal which is present in nature and mind in unconscious and conscious states, and which is finally conscious of itself in the man who thinks it as such. Hence, although the religions consciousness is given by Hegel an important place in human life, since it is unreflective it is liable to criticism, and its content is given a different form by the philosopher who takes over theological teaching and gives immanentist versions of theological doctrines. Hegel, accordingly, transcends the theism of religion by pantheism in philosophy.

But if we can link, as I have suggested, Hegel's Idea with theism, speculative theism should be possible as the ground common to the philosopher as metaphysician and to the theologian as concerned with the truths and problems of religious experience. I will only suggest a few points. The liberty of the individual is secured, for it is involved in subjective activity as distinct from externally necessitated action, and this may be said to imply the possibility of evil, the refusal of

[22] G. W. F. Hegel, *Philosophy of Religion*, edition cited, I, 118ff. The present author has used Wallace's translation of the lesser *Logic* and the translations of (a) The *Phenomenology* by Baillie, and (b) *Science of Logic* by Johnston and Struthers.

man to recognize his place in the divine scheme of the world. Doctrines of grace and redemption will not be explained away, and the end of man will consist not simply in affirming identity with an impersonal system of thought but in personal union with a personal God.

We have identified the content of the *Logic* with the purpose of God as Active Reason, and I must now show that we should think the divine Personality as both transcendent and immanent in the world. He is transcendent as eternally thinking this plan as that on which nature and mind depends. If we remember that his purpose is being continually and progressively realized, we shall see that He is also immanent in the world. There is nothing strange about this, for the finite person, too, is similarly both transcendent and immanent, as the unity of universal and particular; as universal, he is the constant central self which identifies itself with certain dominant purposes and ideas belonging to its scheme of life and which transcends and directs what is particular. As immanent, he realizes this universal self in particular activities which express his inner nature. Of course, with the finite person, the ideal with which he identifies himself may be very imperfect and subject to change, and he may continually fail to apply it. But in the absolute Personality there is no variableness, and, since the divine scheme is the eternal basis of the world, it is always being realized. Hegel's *Philosophy of History*, which deals with the progressive realization of human free personality, gives us an empirical report of this.

It may be objected that, as our knowledge of human persons is always imperfect, so our knowledge of the divine Being must oscillate between anthropomorphism and agnosticism; we may reply that it is, of course, difficult, as any biographer will agree, to have certain knowledge of particular persons, for we must depend on our experience of their behavior and on what they, perhaps wrongly, tell us about their inner guiding ideas and principles. But we must remember that our knowledge of God is not merely hypothetical or based on experience, however convincing and important this may be. The philosopher-theologian has pure intellectual knowledge of the Truth mediated by dialectic, and this knowledge is implicit in every thinking being.

Speculative theism may then recognize that its transcendent God is known not merely vaguely, as in mystical religions, nor merely by feeling, imagination, or analogy, but by the philosophical consciousness in the pure thought of the divine plan of the world, which reveals God as the absolute Personality and Providence, both transcendent and immanent.

HEGEL
AND THE RATIONALIZATION
OF MYSTICISM

Frederick C. Copleston

1

In the preface of his *Philosophy of Right* Hegel maintains that a philosophy is its own time apprehended in thought.[1] It is not the philosopher's business to create an imaginary world of his own. His task is to understand the present and actual as subsuming the past in itself, as the culmination (up to date) of a process of development.

Among the phenomena, the structure and development of which the philosopher can try to understand, is religion. And from one point of view at any rate religion can be regarded as a particular expression of the human spirit. Thus in the *Phenomenology of Spirit* and in the *Encyclopaedia of the Philosophical Sciences* religion forms the subject-matter of a particular section, while Hegel's lectures on the philoso-

[1] "*so ist auch die Philosophie, ihre Zeit in Gedanken erfasst.*" *Werke*, VII, 35.

phy of religion form a series alongside other series, the lectures on the philosophy of history, on art and on the history of philosophy.

It would be a mistake, however, to conclude that the philosophy of religion is peripheral to Hegel's main line of thought. He tells us roundly that the subject-matter both of religion and philosophy is "God and nothing but God and the self-unfolding of God."[2] Moreover for Hegel the philosophy of religion is not simply reflection about religion from outside. Obviously, the development of religious beliefs and practices constitutes an historical phenomenon about which the philosopher can reflect, even if he does not accept any of the religions which he is considering. And Hegel certainly devotes a good deal of space to reflection about the historical development of religion. But he does so from the point of view of one who believes that Lutheran Christianity is the highest expression of religion, at any rate up to date. For Hegel the philosophy of religion is religion attaining the level of reflective self-awareness and self-understanding. This is why he thinks himself justified in maintaining that he is simply carrying further the programme of St. Anselm and other mediaeval theologians, the programme of "faith seeking understanding." The instrument of understanding which Hegel employs is, of course, absolute idealism. And it is clearly arguable that what he regards as the process of understanding Christianity is really the process of transforming the Christian religion into idealist metaphysics. But this does not alter the fact that Hegel looks on himself as engaged in solving problems which arise out of a religion of which he is an adherent.

What is it that Hegel wishes to understand, to express in the language of philosophy? I select one basic problem, the relation between the world and God, between finite things and the infinite divine reality.

An obvious question is this. Why, or with what right, does Hegel assume in the first place that there is an infinite, a divine reality? It seems to me that there are two things to be borne in mind. In the first place Hegel enrolled in his youth in the Protestant theological faculty at Tübingen. It is indeed a notorious fact that his initial reaction not only to the theological lectures delivered at Tübingen but also to the Christian religion itself, as developed by the Apostles and their successors, was far from favorable.[3] The point is, however, that Hegel

[2] "Der Gegenstand der Religion wie der Philosophie ist *die ewige Wahrheit* in ihre Objectivität selbst), Gott und Nichts als Gott und die Explication Gottes." *Werke*, XV, 37.

[3] See *Hegels Theologische Jugendschriften*, ed. Herman Nohl (Tübingen, 1907), and *Dokumente zur Hegels Entwicklung*, ed. J. Hoffmeister (Stuttgart, 1936). There is an English translation of some of Hegel's early writings on religion, *Early Theological Writings*, trans. T. M. Knox, with introduction by R. Kroner (Chicago, 1948). Paul Asveld's *La Pensée religieuse du jeune Hegel* (Louvain, 1953) is relevant.

came to philosophy from theology. This meant in effect that he assumed that Christian belief was in fact true, in some sense at any rate of the word "true"; and that he then tried, by means of philosophical reflection, to exhibit what we may call the "inner truth" in religious belief.[4] In the second place Hegel was convinced that from the philosophical point of view the finite is not intelligible except in the light of its relationship to an infinite whole, which is the ultimate reality. His philosophy is therefore concerned with exhibiting the nature of the ultimate reality rather than with trying to prove its existence.

The problem which I have selected for consideration can be expressed in this way. In the religious consciousness, as it manifests itself in both Judaism and Christianity, we find God objectified. God is set over against Nature and the finite subject. In other words, an opposition is asserted between God and the world, God and man. For Hegel, this opposition cannot be anything but repugnant to speculative philosophy. On the one hand, if the alleged infinite is set over against the finite, so as to exclude it, how can it properly be described as infinite? Again, if the finite is set over against the infinite, is it not absolutized, with the result that the infinite becomes a superfluous hypothesis? In fine, pictorial theism, with its God "out there" or "up there," cannot satisfy the reflective mind.

Yet how can we overcome in thought the opposition between the finite and the infinite, between the world and God, between man and God? In Christianity there is indeed a synthesis, an overcoming of the estrangement of the finite subject from God. But this synthesis is lived rather than thought. The difficulty lies in thinking it, in constructing a genuinely philosophical theism. If on the one hand we use the term "God" as a label for the Many in their given empirical existence, this is tantamount to embracing atheism. For the word "God" would then refer simply to the class of finite things, the existence of which is not denied by the atheist. If on the other hand we declare the Many to be illusion, this is equivalent to embracing what Hegel describes as "acosmism."[5] In neither case can we be said to have solved the problem at issue. What we have done is to eliminate one of the factors (in the first case God, in the second case the world) which need to be brought together in a unity which at the same time preserves a distinction.

---

[4] With Leibniz we can already find a tendency to find an "inner truth" in Christian beliefs. With Lessing, in his mature thought, this tendency is much more marked. But whereas Lessing did not think of himself as a Christian, Hegel came to think of himself as a champion of Christianity, even if it is pretty obvious that in his developed system Christianity is transformed into exoteric Hegelianism, as McTaggart puts it.

[5] This is what Hegel understands by pantheism when he denies that he is a pantheist.

Hegel's problem, as actually raised and treated by him, has obviously to be seen in the light of the presuppositions involved in his adherence to the post-Kantian idealist movement. And, in my opinion, the spirit and demands of the romantic movement are also relevant factors. At the same time there is a real sense in which the problem to which I have been referring is a contemporary problem. We have only to think, for example, of Dr. J. A. T. Robinson's famous book *Honest to God* and of its author's attack on pictorial theism, with its God "out there." There are, of course, contextual differences. For instance, one of Dr. Robinson's themes is the apparent growing irrelevance of the concept of God when seen in the light of such factors as the growth of the scientific outlook and of depth psychology. But the differences can, I think, be exaggerated. It would be an obvious anachronism to attribute to Hegel a knowledge of depth psychology and of psychological explanations of the felt need for religion. But Hegel was by no means unaware of the way in which the God "out there" can appear as a superfluous addition to the world. "Science," he remarks, "thus forms a universe of knowledge which has no need of God, lies outside religion and has, directly, nothing to do with it."[6] In any case Dr. Robinson's basic problem seems to me to be similar to that of Hegel. How are we to think of God if we are not to think of him as a super-person over against the world? In the language of Paul Tillich we can speak of both Hegel and Dr. Robinson as trying to make the transition from "God" to *God*.

2

In the notes which form the so-called *Fragment of a System* of 1800, Hegel expresses a serious doubt whether philosophy is capable of thinking, of conceptualizing that is to say, the unity-in-difference between the divine spirit and the human spirit which is lived, but not clearly thought, on the level of Christian love. Philosophy is a process of thinking; and thought posits an object over against itself, an object about which we think. Further, discursive thought, working with the categories of traditional logic, asserts antitheses, such as that between the infinite and the finite, which it is unable to overcome. "Infinite" means "not finite"; and there is an end of the matter. The same idea seems to be re-echoed in a recent book by Dr. Robinson when he asserts that to express the overcoming of dualism (between Creator and creature) "within the logic of non-contradiction is of course finally impossible."[7] Hegel's conclusion is that "philosophy

[6] "Die Wissenschaft bildet so ein *Universum der Erkenntnis*, das für sich Gottes nicht bedarf, *ausserhalb der Religion* liegt und mit ihr direct nichts zu schaffen hat." *Werke*, XV, 32.
[7] J. A. T. Robinson, *Exploration into God* (London, 1967), 141.

therefore has to stop short of religion because it is a process of thinking."[8]

Every student of Hegel is aware that the philosopher very soon looked to dialectical thinking to accomplish what was impossible for a "static" logic which posited antitheses and then was unable to overcome them. It is not so obvious, however, that Hegel was concerned, in part, with thinking through, with raising to the level of pure conceptual thought, a relationship between the finite spirit and God which he regarded as having found expression in the paradoxical utterances of religious mystics. I am not indeed prepared to follow Richard Kroner in describing Hegel as a "Christian mystic, seeking adequate speculative expression."[9] For it seems to me extravagant to speak of Hegel himself as a mystic, whether Christian or otherwise. But when Professor W. T. Stace maintains that Hegel endeavored to turn the mystical idea of identity-in-distinction into a logical concept,[10] and when Mr. G. R. G. Mure writes of Hegel's "strenuous and uncompromising effort, which has no serious parallel, to rationalize and to bring to light the mystic union of God and man proclaimed by men such as Meister Eckhart and Jacob Böhme, to reveal it as a union through distinction for which the whole world is evidence,"[11] they are saying, I think, what is quite true. Hegel was doubtless hostile to the taking of short cuts in philosophy by substituting appeals to intuition or to mystical insights in place of the patient effort to understand and to express the truth in a systematic way. Moreover, his sarcastic references in the preface to the *Phenomenology* to Schelling's insistence on approaching the Absolute by the "negative way" are well known. But it by no means follows that Hegel did not regard mystical writers as having given expression, even if in paradoxical form, to valid insights which the philosopher should try to conceptualize, exhibiting their universal significance.[12] In point of fact he quotes Meister Eckhart to the effect that "the eye with which God sees me is the eye with which I see him; my eye and his eye are one. . . . If God were not, I should not be; if I were not, he would not be either."[13] Hegel further remarks that the older theologians among whom he numbers Eckhart had, as

[8] G. W. F. Hegel, *Early Theological Writings*, trans. T. M. Knox (Chicago, 1948), 313.

[9] *Ibid.*, 8. (In Preface by Richard Kroner.)

[10] In his *Mysticism and Philosophy* (London, 1961).

[11] *The Philosophy of Hegel* (London, 1965), 103.

[12] For example, if a religious mystic writes simply of an exceptional state of union between the soul and God, Hegel would see in what the mystic says a general metaphysical truth about the relation between the finite and the infinite.

[13] "Das Auge, mit dem mich Gott sieht, ist das Auge, mit dem ich ihn sehe, mein Auge und sein Auge ist eins . . . Wenn Gott nicht wäre, wäre ich nicht, wenn ich nicht wäre, so wäre er nicht." *Werke*, XV, 228.

he puts it, a better grasp of "this depth"[14] than their modern successors. So I do not think that it is at all far-fetched to represent Hegel as trying to give philosophical expression to a mystical insight.

3

Now perhaps I have given the impression that in my opinion Hegel regards the sphere of religion as concerned only with feeling and with emotive language. This impression would, however, be erroneous. In his phenomenological analysis of the religious consciousness Hegel does indeed allow for the basic importance of immediacy, of feeling, the feeling of dependence for example. But he is very far from equating religion with feeling. In his view thought and knowledge are essential to the development of the religious consciousness. He tells us, for example, that "knowledge is an essential element of the Christian religion itself";[15] and he insists on the truth of the Christian dogmas. It is indeed true that for Hegel the mode of thinking characteristic of the religious consciousness is pictorial thought. And inasmuch as philosophy, in his view, converts pictorial thought into pure conceptual thought, we can say that for Hegel philosophy demythologizes the content of religious belief. At the same time it must be added that he regards this process of demythologization as starting within the religious sphere; in, that is to say, the course of the historical development of the religious consciousness and its self-expression. In other words, even though Hegel asserts a distinction between the modes of conception characteristic of the religious consciousness and of speculative philosophy, he also asserts a continuity. This is why he feels entitled to make the claim, to which I have already referred, that he is continuing the task of theologians such as St. Anselm, and why he thinks himself justified in making such statements as that philosophy "only unfolds itself when it unfolds religion, and when it unfolds itself it unfolds religion."[16]

This point, namely that there is continuity as well as distinction between the modes of conception characteristic of the religious consciousness and of speculative philosophy, has, I think, a certain importance for the understanding of Hegel. We are told, for example, that if we ask "what is God?" or "what does the term *God* signify?," we are trying to grasp the nature of God in thought, and that "the nature of God as grasped in thought"[17] is what is called in philosophy the

[14] "diese Tiefe," *ibid.*

[15] "Das *Erkennen* liegt daher in der christlichen Religion selbst." *Werke*, XV, 35.

[16] "(Die Philosophie) explicirt daher nur sich, indem sie die Religion explicirt und indem sie sich explicirt, explicirt sie de Religion." *Ibid.*, 37.

[17] "(Das Absolute), die im Gedanken gefasste Natur Gottes." *Werke*, XV, 42.

Absolute. Hegel thus translates talk about God into talk about the Absolute or transforms the concept of God into that of the Absolute. And we may thus draw the conclusions that according to Hegel the religious consciousness projects the ultimate reality into the celestial sphere in the form of a personal transcendent being out there, over against the world and the human spirit, whereas philosophy rejects this externalization of God and conceives the ultimate reality as the all-comprehensive Life, the self-actualizing Absolute. Though, however, there is certainly some truth in this account of the matter, the account is defective or inadequate. For it neglects the fact that, according to Hegel, the truth of the fundamental unity between the finite spirit and the divine spirit finds expression in the Christian religion in such doctrines as those of the historic Incarnation, the indwelling of the Holy Spirit in the Church, the Eucharist and the communion of saints. In other words, what philosophy does is not to supply a truth of which religion has no inkling but rather to present the truth as following from the nature of the Absolute instead of presenting it in the form of contingent propositions, depending for their truth on historic events which might or might not have occurred.

To put the matter in another way, at the time of the Enlightenment it was generally agreed, both by opponents and defenders of Christianity, that the Christian religion stood or fell according as it was able or unable to make good certain historic claims. Hegel, however, is trying to show that Christian beliefs are true independently of these historic claims. This means, of course, that Christianity is presented, to use McTaggart's phrase, as exoteric Hegelianism, while absolute idealism is presented as esoteric Christianity. And the natural conclusion is that the fall of absolute idealism would entail the fall of Christianity. For absolute idealism, according to Hegel, is Christianity, in its cognitive aspect at any rate, when in possession of full self-understanding. This is indeed an idea which most Christian theologians would hardly receive with enthusiasm. And understandably so. But the point which I am trying to make here is simply that Hegel does not separate the concept of truth from religious statements and attach it only to philosophical statements. Religious statements can be true. And when the philosopher expresses their truth in a different form, it is the same truth which he is presenting. That is to say, in Hegel's opinion the truth remains the same.

Now if we consider the sort of statements to which Hegel refers in the writings of mystics such as Eckhart, it is clear that they assert a unity between God and man, between the finite spirit and the divine spirit. At the same time it is clear that they do not assert the reducibility of the concept of God to the concept of man. Whatever may seem to be the literal meaning of some of Eckhart's utterances, the general line of his thought makes it quite clear that he had no intention of asserting that "God" and "man" are convertible terms. It is also clear, I think, that mystics such as Eckhart did not assume that a realization of the unity between man and God is something given from the start. Rather is it something to which the human spirit can attain, though it does not necessarily do so. In other words, there is a unity-in-distinction which the human mind can grasp or apprehend, though it does not always or necessarily do so.

These, it seems to me, are some of the ideas to which Hegel thinks that he has given expression in terms of absolute idealism. In the first place the Hegelian Absolute is clearly not reducible without residue to the human mind. For it is the One which, though not temporally prior to the Many, manifests itself or expresses itself in the world. In Hegel's opinion, the national State, considered as an organic whole enduring in time, is irreducible to any given set of citizens, to those, for example, who are living here and now. In an analogous manner the Absolute is irreducible to any given set of finite things, including finite minds. The Absolute or God is, in St. Paul's words, he in whom "we live and move and have our being." (*Acts* 17:28)

In the second place, just as the national State does not exist apart from its citizens but in and through them, though at the same time it is more than the sum of them, so does the Absolute exist in and through the Many, immanent in them while comprising them within its own life.

In the third place, though the Absolute must be defined as self-thinking thought (for this is what it is in essence, as Aristotle saw), it must also be conceived as a dynamic process of self-actualization. When Hegel asserts that "of the Absolute it must be said that it is essentially [a] result, that only at the end is it what it is in very truth,"[18] and that the Absolute is "the essence which completes (or actualizes) itself through its own development,"[19] I think that he means precisely what he says. That is to say, the Absolute comes to know itself in actuality in and through the human mind as its vehicle. But when Hegel says that "God knows himself in the finite spirit,"[20] it is not any and every sort of knowledge to which he is referring. He is referring above all to the knowledge of God in religion and philosophy. It is this knowledge which from another point of view is God's knowledge of himself. "Finite consciousness knows God only in so

---

[18] "Es is von dem Absoluten zu sagen, dass es wesentlich *Resultat*, dass es erst am *Ende* das ist, was es in Wahrheit ist." *Werke*, II, 24.

[19] "(Das Ganze aber ist nur) das durch seine Entwicklung vollendende Wesen." *Ibid.*

[20] "(Wir haben also hier die Religion der Manifestation Gottes, indem) Gott sich im endlichen Geiste wiess." *Werke*, XVI, 192.

far as God knows himself in it."[21] That is to say, at the level at which the finite spirit becomes the vehicle of the divine self-knowledge it rises above its particularity and becomes in actuality a moment in the divine life. The divine self-knowledge is not reducible to any individual's knowledge of God; but the individual's knowledge of God is a moment in the process of the Absolute's return to itself in self-reflection.

Awareness of the identity-in-distinction which obtains between the human spirit and the infinite spirit is not something given from the start. Just as we cannot come to know the true nature of the universal in general except by first objectifying it as a reality apart from particulars (as in the traditional interpretation of Platonism), so the human mind cannot come to know the true nature of God except by first objectifying him as a personal transcendent being "out there," over against the world and man. This is a dialectically necessary stage in the process by which the universal spirit comes to see itself, in and through the human mind, as the one reality, the Alpha and Omega. As we have noted, Hegel believes that the true view of God is expressed in the Christian dogmas in the form appropriate to the religious consciousness. What philosophy does is to exhibit the unity between the human spirit and God, not as a privilege gratuitously bestowed upon some men but rather as a truth which follows from the nature of reality itself. It exhibits spirit, manifesting itself in the religious and philosophical development of mankind, as "the living process by which the implicit unity of divine and human nature becomes actual and attains concrete existence."[22]

4

From what I have been saying it should be clear that I accept neither the right-wing interpretation of Hegel, according to which God in himself is to be conceived as enjoying self-knowledge independently of all creation, nor the interpretation which pretty well identifies the position of Hegel with that of Feuerbach. As for the right-wing interpretation, I am, of course, aware that in his very favorable review in the *Jahrbuch für wissenschaftliche Kritik*[23] of K. F. Göschel's book of aphorisms, Hegel refers with approval to Göschel's statement that

---

[21] "Das endliche Bewusstsein weiss Gott nur insofern, als Gott sich in ihm weiss." *Ibid.*, 191.

[22] Der Geist ist daher der lebendige *Process*, dass die an sich seyende Einheit der göttlichen und menschlichen Natur für sich und hervorgebracht werde." *Werke*, XVI, 210.

[23] G. W. F Hegel, *Werke*, XVI, 276–313.

God in himself is self-knowledge in itself, while as knowing himself in creatures God is self-knowledge outside himself. But though I may be wrong, I do not think that Hegel really commits himself to saying more than that the divine essence must be defined as self-thinking thought. As for the identification of Hegel's position with that of Feuerbach, Hegel is not concerned, as Feuerbach was, with transforming theology into anthropology, with reducing God to man. He is concerned with bringing God and man together by employing the concept of identity-in-distinction. This was, I think, seen by Kierkegaard. The Danish thinker's picture of Hegel as producing a *tertium quid*, a fantastic metaphysical abstraction, absolute thought, in which both God and man disappear, may be a caricature, but it at any rate expresses Kierkegaard's recognition of the fact that Hegel does not aim at a reduction without residue either of God to man or of man to God.

Hegel might perhaps be described as a panentheist by intention.[24] Needless to say, he is not concerned with overcoming theism in the sense of imaginative representations of God as an old man on a throne beyond the clouds. The theism to which he tries to give consistent philosophical expression already recognizes God as infinite spirit. And what Hegel endeavors to accomplish is to think the relation between the infinite and the finite in such a way as to allow the infinite to fill, as it were, all reality while at the same time a distinction is preserved. If we take pantheism as representing the concept of identity and theism that of distinction, Hegel's aim is to show how the two concepts, which appear antithetical, can be reconciled at a higher level. All things are "in God," moments in the divine life; but God, as the One, is not simply reducible to "all things," to the Many. To give, however, a clear statement of this idea is no easy task. And it is arguable that the result of Hegel's reflections is so ambiguous that it is questionable whether it can be properly described as theism of any kind, unless the meaning of the term is extended well beyond what seems to be permitted by ordinary usage. This is why I suggest that Hegel might be best described as a panentheist "by intention."

5

The ambiguity of the results of Hegel's philosophizing is a point which merits a little amplification. As we have noted, he regards the

[24] In an interesting article entitled "Hegel as Panentheist," Robert C. Whittemore notes that "the term 'panentheism' seems not to have been part of Hegel's theological vocabulary, although it was current in Germany in his time." [*Studies in Hegel* in Volume IX of Tulane Studies in Philosophy (The Hague: Nijhoff, 1960), 134.] Whittemore argues, however, that Hegel was in fact a panentheist.

philosopher as concerned primarily with the problems which arise out of his contemporary world. And in the sphere of religion he mentions this problem. "There was a time when all knowledge was knowledge of God."[25] That is to say, there was a time when knowledge of God himself was considered the highest form of knowledge and when knowledge of the world was thought to be in some sense knowledge of God, that is, of God's handiwork. In the modern world, however, scientific knowledge of finite things has increased to such an extent that the sphere of the knowledge of God has been progressively contracted. Indeed, "it is a matter of no concern to our age that it knows nothing of God. On the contrary, the belief that this knowledge is not even possible passes for the highest degree of insight."[26] Hegel, however, believing that the real is the rational and the rational the real, that God is the supreme reality and hence the supremely rational (or, rather absolute reason itself), and that the rational must be penetrable by reason, insists that the essence of God can be known by the human reason. In fact it is not altogether unreasonable to say that the task which Hegel proposes to the philosopher is that of attaining by philosophical reflection to what the mediaeval theologians called the beatific vision of God and which they reserved for heaven. This idea, however, should be clearly absurd if God were represented as a transcendent reality of such a kind that we know of him, as Aquinas put it, what he is not rather than what he is. Given therefore Hegel's conviction of the power and scope of the human mind, he has, so to speak, to bring God down from his state of transcendence and at the same time to elevate man. And this means in effect two things. First, what traditional Christian doctrine represents as the free creation of a world by a transcendent creator must be represented, from the philosophical point of view, as a divine self-exteriorization which is essential to the divine life. Secondly, man's knowledge of God and God's knowledge of himself must be depicted as two aspects of one reality. Hence Hegel can say that "without the world God is not God."[27] That is to say, the essence of the Absolute as self-thinking thought is not actualized in concrete reality except in the sphere of spirit which requires the sphere of Nature as its necessary presupposition. And in the sphere of spirit man's knowledge of God is God's knowledge of himself.

Now Hegel himself did not think of this doctrine as equivalent to the elimination of God. Individual human beings perish, but the

[25] "Es hat eine Zeit gegeben, wo alles Wissen Wissenschaft von Gott gewesen ist." *Werke*, XV, 52.
[26] "Es macht unserm Zeitalter keinen Kummer mehr, von Gott nichts zu erkennen, vielmehr gilt es für die höchste Einsicht, dass diese Erkenntnis sogar nicht möglich sei." *Werke*, XV, 53.
[27] "Ohne Welt ist Gott nicht Gott." *Werke*, XV, 210.

One remains. The individual's knowledge of God, considered precisely as knowledge possessed by this individual, is transitory; but the development of the religious consciousness in general continues. The universal mind lives in and through particular minds; but while particulars are transitory, the universal abides. At the same time there is no great difficulty in seeing the force of the contention that Hegel's theory is well on its way to becoming a recommendation to look on the world in a special way, namely as one organic and developing whole which, with the emergence of man and the subsequent growth of scientific knowledge, can be represented as coming to know itself in and through the human mind.

In other words, a plausible case can be made for representing Hegel's philosophy of religion as a stage in a process in which the concept of God is progressively eliminated. Hegel, it may be said, undertakes a demythologization of Christian doctrine.[28] But the result of his own philosophizing is a cloud of metaphysical mystification which is subsequently dissipated by naturalism and positivism. Hegel saw the problems arising out of traditional theism. But he was unable to solve them, not because he lacked ability, but because they are insolu-

---

[28] Professor Emil Fackenheim has asserted that "Hegelian philosophy of religion is not demythologizing or antisymbolic. It is transmythological and transsymbolic." [*The Religious Dimension of Hegel's Thought* (Bloomington, Ind.: 1967), 161.] But I doubt whether there is much, if any, substantial difference between what Fackenheim says and what I intended to suggest above. As the term "demythologization" is associated with the Bultmannian theology, I qualified my suggestion by the phrase "it may be said". In any case it is not my intention to suggest that Hegel wished either to get rid of the forms of thought characteristic of Christian doctrine or to change them *within the sphere of religion*. He did not. On the contrary, he insisted on the Christian dogmas *as true*. But in so far as philosophy expresses the same truth in a supposedly more adequate form (more adequate, that is to say, from the point of view of the speculative philosopher), it seems to me that the religious representation of the truth can reasonably be described (again from the point of view of the speculative philosopher) as "mythical". Fackenheim speaks of transrepresentation. I agree that this is what Hegel is trying to do. Even if, however, Hegel himself would not use the word "myth", I do not see why we should not use it. A modern *theologian* who pursues a policy of demythologization is not necessarily out to destroy "myth" and leave a blank or emptiness. For he may be primarily concerned with substituting for what he considers outworn representations of religious truth representations which he believes to be more expressive and effective in relation to the modern mind. Whereas, however, this process takes place within *theology*, this is not the case with Hegel. With him there is, as Fackenheim puts it, a "transfiguration of faith into philosophy". The question then arises whether religious truths, when they have been "transfigured" or "demythologized" (in the sense of being lifted from the language of religion into that of philosophy), do not become different doctrines. Hegel of course was convinced that the content of truth was the same, though the form of expression differed. But it does not necessarily follow that Hegel was right in thinking this.

ble. If therefore religion is to be preserved, it has to be separated from talk about God. Or, if the word "God" is retained, it must be given a meaning which involves no reference to an alleged transcendent being of any kind. We can thus see in the contemporary Death-of-God theology the spiritual heir of Hegelianism, even if Hegel himself would not have been prepared to recognize it as such.

6

If this point of view is adopted, it follows that the statements about God which were made by men such as Meister Eckhart and which evidently impressed Hegel were not about God at all, about God, that is to say, as an existent reality. Suppose, however, that we believe that the claim of religious mystics to have enjoyed knowledge by acquaintance of a reality which is identifiable neither with Nature nor with the finite spirit and which is in some sense the only "true" reality cannot be simply dismissed. Or suppose that we believe that God is inescapable in the sense that a One reveals itself as the attracting goal of the human spirit's movement towards an ultimate unity or as the hidden ground of the demands which impose themselves upon us in the recognition of ideal values in relation to the successive situations which call for action in the world. If we have beliefs of this kind, we could, I suppose, pursue a policy of Wittgensteinian silence and refrain from trying to state their content. But if we choose to speak, we shall need the word "God" or some equivalent term.

Once, however, we begin to speak, we encounter the sort of problems which Hegel encountered, such as the problem of stating the relation between the world and God. As this relation is presumably unique, we might designate it by the symbol X. But though the construction of a purely artificial language might conceivably be of some use in academic discussion, provided that we could state some rules for the manipulation of the selected symbols, it would be useless for general communication and for exhibiting the relevance of our beliefs to human life and society. Hence in practice we are inevitably thrown back on ordinary language. And this means in effect that we have to use counterbalancing analogies and "projections," by means of which we try to grasp and state that which cannot be adequately grasped and stated. To anyone who believes that all that can be said can be said clearly, this is not a satisfactory state of affairs. But it is an essential characteristic of this particular language-game, talk about God. And if we try to eliminate it by translating talk about God into the language of the absolute idealism of Hegel or into that of logical positivism, we shall soon find ourselves talking about something else, about the world when looked at in a special way, or about man, no longer about God. In fine, Hegel attempted, in my opinion, to do what cannot be done, namely to make plain to view what can only be simply apprehended through the use of analogies and symbols.

A final point. The analogies and projections which we use tend to get a grip on the mind, holding it captive and leading it to imagine that it understands more than it does. The mystical writers, however, such as St. John of the Cross, remind us of the inadequacy of our conceptual representations of God, of the shortcomings of our language in this region of thought. To employ once again a phrase of Paul Tillich, it is the religious mystics who most strikingly exemplify the movement of the human spirit from "God" to *God*. But this, I think, is a feature of mysticism of which Hegel failed to appreciate the significance.

HEGEL'S IDEAS
ABOUT TRAGEDY

Walter Kaufmann

Hegel did not have a Procrustean "theory of tragedy" but illuminated many tragedies more' than any other philosopher before or after him. We shall first weigh and refine Hegel's two major suggestions about Greek tragedy, and then we shall consider his comments on Shakespeare's tragedies.

Unlike Sophocles, who enjoys special protection—deprecating him would be a misdemeanor—Hegel and Nietzsche are outlaws, and taking a passing potshot at them is widely considered good form. To say or insinuate that Hegel did violence to all the many men and subjects he discussed, bending the past to his own will and forcing facts to fit into his system, is the academic equivalent of a politician's waving a flag or invoking the Pilgrim Fathers; such gestures require no historical research.

F. L. Lucas' travesty of Hegel's views on tragedy is unusual only insofar as it is longer than most.[1] Kitto is exceptionally brief but equally unfair to Hegel when he considers Antigone's character: "where the blemish is there, only Hegel can tell us."[2] So much for Hegel's theories. One would scarcely gather from Kitto's comment that Hegel called "the heavenly Antigone, the most glorious figure ever to have appeared on earth."[3]

The point here at issue is the heart of Hegel's contribution to our understanding of tragedy. Plato wanted the poets to represent men "in every way good."[4] Aristotle countered with his conception of *hamartia*, arguing that it is shocking rather than tragic when good men go from happiness to misfortune. Although Aristotle himself stressed the importance of the action and the plot above that of character, his fateful notion of the tragic flaw or error led generations of critics and playwrights to focus their attention on the so-called tragic hero. It even led some interpreters of the *Antigone*, including Kitto, to argue that Creon is the hero of the play.[5] If one approaches the play in the traditional manner, one has to deny either that Antigone is "outstanding in virtue"—this is the usual approach—or that she is the heroine.

Hegel's understanding of Greek tragedy far surpassed that of most of his detractors. He realized that at the center of the greatest tragedies of Aeschylus and Sophocles we find not a tragic hero but a tragic collision, and that the conflict is not between good and evil but between one-sided positions, each of which embodies some good.

This immensely fruitful suggestion does not commit Hegel to find any blemish in the heavenly Antigone. Her character is not at issue any more than Creon's; their positions are. It is obviously possible to love and admire her, or to thrill to Luther's courage at Worms, or to Thomas More's rare fusion of wit and integrity, without accepting their views, the principles for which they willingly risked everything. Least of all does our admiration for a human being who suffers or dies clinging stubbornly to his ideas entail the judgment that there is no good at all in the position of those who oppose him.

[1] F. L. Lucas, *Tragedy: Serious Drama in Relation to Aristotle's Poetics* (New York, 1962), 57–60. It is followed by briefer but no less sprightly caricatures of Schopenhauer (61ff.) and Nietzsche (62ff.). What is typical is that the level of these passages is so far beneath the rest of the book.

[2] J. Kitto, *Greek Tragedy* (3d rev. ed., Garden City, N.Y., n.d.), 133.

[3] G. W. F. Hegel, *Geschichte der Philosophie, Werke*, XVIII, 114. This and all succeeding translations from Hegel's writings are by the present author.

[4] Plato, *Laws*, 660.

[5] To be sure, "Creon's part is half as long again as Antigone's" (Kitto, *op. cit.*, 130); but, the herald's part in *Agamemnon* is half as long again as Agamemnon's, Cassandra's is twice, Clytemnestra's four times, and the Chorus's ten times as long.

All this ought to be obvious; yet Hegel's detractors have generally chosen to ignore, if not implicitly deny, it. Why? One reason may be found in the reluctance to face up to Sophocles' philosophical dimension. Once we admit that "the most glorious figure ever to have appeared on earth" went to her doom without any comfort, that the catastrophe was final and unmitigated, and that the playwright did not take this to be atypical of our world—the traditional image of the cheerful Sophocles collapses. His world view was terrifying, and most critics would rather not think about it. According to the accepted view, Sophocles was a pious man of utterly conventional opinions who happened to have three great talents—writing poetry, creating characters, and fashioning plots. That way he did not disturb anybody's sleep, and in gratitude for that he was conceded not mere talent but true genius. The most poignantly tragic poet was misrepresented as a mere craftsman and then, as if to compensate for this indignity, flattered endlessly.

This development can be traced back to Aristotle. Hegel breached the framework Aristotle had laid down in chapter 13 of the *Poetics*. He opened up new vistas. But several ways were found to meet this threat. One continued to look for a flaw in Antigone, either ignoring Hegel altogether or claiming that this was what his view came down to. Or one claimed that Hegel had sided with Creon, and that this proved him a wicked man who could safely be ignored. Or—the most common stratagem—it was suggested that Hegel's view of tragedy could safely be ignored because it had been based exclusively on *Antigone*.

Two points seem to support the last claim. *Antigone* furnishes a splendid example of a tragic collision in which some good may be found on both sides, and Hegel apparently loved this play more than any other tragedy.[6] But his exceptionally deep feeling for *Antigone* did not come from any sense that it was the *only* tragedy to support his generalizations; it was prompted by his admiration for the heroine and his susceptibility to the theme of a sister's love for her brother. To rebut the usual view of the matter, we must for a time leave Sophocles and show briefly how well Hegel's concept of the tragic collision illuminates some of the masterpieces of Aeschylus and Euripides. Indeed, eventually we shall see that it fits them much better than it fits *Antigone*.

Unlike Aristotle, Hegel was far from basing his view of tragedy almost exclusively on Sophocles. The tragic poet whose world view most closely resembled Hegel's was Aeschylus. One could not wish for more perfect illustrations of collisions in which neither side is

---

[6] G. W. F. Hegel, *Werke*, XIII, 51 and XIV, 556.

simply wicked and some moral claims are present on both sides than we find in the *Oresteia* and *Prometheus*. Indeed, the very words "right collides with right" are encountered in *The Libation Bearers*.[7]

Not only was Aeschylus more interested in these rival claims than in the characters that put them forward, but the Prometheus trilogy and the *Oresteia* represent elaborate attempts to give both sides a hearing before working out a satisfactory solution that does justice to both sides.

In these two trilogies both sides relent in the end and the outcome is joyous; *The Suppliants* was probably of that type, too. In the *Seven* neither side relents in the least, and the brothers destroy each other; but there is no implication that one of them is good and the other evil; on the contrary.

Aeschylus' *Persians* and Euripides' *Trojan Women* show that not all Greek tragedies were of this nature, but most of Aeschylus' works were, and so were some of Euripides' masterpieces. Touched by the wand of Hegel's concept of collision, the perennial enigma of Euripides' *Bacchae* is solved.

Nietzsche's suggestion that Euripides "finally ended his career with a glorification of his adversary," Dionysus,[8] is as misguided as the rival theory that in his last play the old poet launched his fiercest attack on the evils of traditional religion. Both interpretations assume falsely that the conflict is between a good and a bad side, and go on to ask which side the poet meant to be the good one.

Must the poet either denounce reason, criticism, and sobriety or be blind to the claims of passion, ecstasy, and enthusiastic vision? Dry and dull as it may sound if said in one short sentence, a life without reason turns men into beasts, and a life without passion and vision is a living death. Like Sophocles in *Antigone*, Euripides associates the claims of feeling with the female; but he goes much further than Sophocles in avoiding any semblance of a black-and-white contrast. What makes for tragedy is the relentless one-sidedness of both antagonists. The poetic power of the *Bacchae* permeates the symbolic force of the incredible conclusion: prudent fear of passion becomes prurient, and the man blind to the sweeping beauty of irrational experience is destroyed by those who, abdicating reason, revel in the blindness of their frenzy; yet such passion is not alien to him but the womb from which he sprang, as close to him, though Pentheus does not know it, as Jocasta to Oedipus. Pentheus and Agave, his mother, were played

---

[7] 461: Arēs Arei xymbalei, Dikāi Dika.

[8] F. Nietzsche, *Birth of Tragedy* (my translation), § 12: 82. This misinterpretation may owe something to the influence of Schopenhauer, who had called *The Bacchae* "a revolting fabrication for the benefit of pagan priests." (*The World as Will and Idea*, Vol. 2, chap. 37.)

by the same actor. And Agave is the sister of Semele, the mother of Dionysus.

In the chapter on "The Apollinian and the Dionysian" in his *Psychological Types*, C. G. Jung claimed that he had scored an advance over Nietzsche by noticing that "the urges dammed up in civilized man are terribly destructive and much more dangerous than the urges of primitive man who, to some degree, gives constant vent to his negative urges." Not only did Nietzsche realize this; the point is so far from being new that we may consider *The Bacchae* its classical illustration. Agave and the other Bacchae who dismember her son are not barbarians but hypercivilized scoffers whom Dionysus punishes by making their frenzy utterly bestial.

To seek flaws or errors of judgment in Pentheus is pointless, though both are easy to find; for the tragedy revolves not around a single tragic hero but around a conflict between two one-sided views.[9] Precisely this it has in common with the most admired tragedies of Aeschylus and Sophocles.

Euripides' *Hippolytus* prefigures the conflict of the *Bacchae*. The chaste Hippolytus, insensitive to the claims of love, falls prey to passion run rampant, not yet represented by the mother, as in the last play, but by his stepmother. Not only is there wide agreement that these two tragedies are unsurpassed by any of Euripides' other plays, but in the poet's prologue to *Hippolytus* we are told expressly that the youth will be destroyed for his exclusive allegiance to Artemis and his failure to respect Aphrodite also; both are divine, and a man should heed both.

Hegel is not committed to the view that *all* tragedies entail a tragic collision of this type. Far from claiming, for example, that Racine's *Phèdre* furnishes another illustration, Hegel said in his lectures that it was a

---

[9] After writing this, I found much the same view of this play in E. R. Dodd's excellent introduction to his edition of Euripides' *Bacchae* (Oxford, 1944): Euripides' "favourite method is to take a one-sided point of view, a noble half-truth, to exhibit its nobility, and then to exhibit the disaster to which it leads its blind adherents—because it is after all only part of the truth" (xliii). And William Arrowsmith, in his introduction to his own translation, which is based on Dodd's volume, speaks of "a head-on collision between those who, for all their piety, represent the full-blown tyranny of popular custom and conforming tradition and the arrogant exemplar of the ruthlessly antitraditional mind." (536). It might seem that both men are expounding Hegel; but Hegel's name is not one to conjure with, and neither of them so much as mentions him!

Similarly Dodds says: "The first modern writer who understood the Dionysiac psychology was Erwin Rohde; his *Psyche* (1st ed.; Leipzig, 1891–1894; English translation, 1925) is still the fundamental book" (ix)—as if the closest friend and mentor of the young Rohde, Nietzsche, had never existed.

silly feature of the French treatment of Racine to give Hippolytus another amour; that way it is no longer a punishment of love as a pathos that he suffers but a mere mishap that he is in love with a girl and therefore does not oblige another female, who is, to be sure, the wife of his father, but this ethical obstacle is obscured by his love of Aricia. Hence the cause of his destruction is no longer his injury or neglect of a universal power as such, nor anything ethical, but something particular and accidental.[10]

In his influential lecture on "Hegel's Theory of Tragedy," A. C. Bradley, the brother of F. H. Bradley, the British "Idealist" philosopher, said:

> It will be agreed, further, that in all tragedy there is some sort of collision or conflict—conflict of feelings, modes of thought, desires, wills, purposes; conflict of persons with one another, or with circumstances, or with themselves; one, several, or all of these kinds of conflict, as the case may be. . . . The essentially tragic fact is the self-division and the intestinal warfare of the ethical substance, not so much the war of good with evil as the war of good with good.[11]

Since A. C. Bradley was one of the foremost interpreters of Shakespearean tragedy, this "theory" is better known in the English-speaking world than its origins in Hegel. Bradley's version is admirably compact—a single lecture of barely over twenty pages, compared to scattered pages in Hegel's *Phenomenology of the Spirit* and in his lectures on aesthetics, on philosophy of religion, and on the history of philosophy. Moreover, Bradley writes clearly and the text of his lecture is authentic, while Hegel's style is exceptionally difficult, and the posthumously published lectures were put together by students who, drawing on notes taken in different years, provided not only their own transitions, not indicated as such in the text, but often also their own organization of materials that Hegel had, at different times, presented in different arrangements. For all that, Bradley's version has the same fatal fault that distinguished British "Absolute Idealism" from Hegel's philosophy: The Bradley brothers, like most of the major British philosophers, were unhistorically minded.

My orientation is more historical and open-ended than Hegel's. Anglo-American Idealism does not have the least appeal for me. What I find in reading Hegel is not "the block-universe eternal and without a history,"[12] but a singularly restless and at bottom quite unsystematic

---

[10] G. W. F. Hegel, *Philosophie der Religion, Werke*, XVI, 134 (ed. Lasson), XIII.2, 167; *Philosophy of Religion*, trans. Speirs and Sanderson (London, 1895), II, 265. The passage is found in Hegel's own manuscript.

[11] A. C. Bradley, *Oxford Lectures on Poetry* (Oxford, 1950), 70.

[12] William James, *A Pluralistic Universe* (New York, 1909), 310. Although he felt that Hegel's mind was essentially "impressionistic," James nevertheless projected Anglo-American Absolute Idealism into Hegel.

spirit that is scared of its own pluralistic bent and tries, never twice in the same way, to organize the chaos of its observations, insights, and ideas. Every such attempt is systematic to a fault, but superseded by a new outline in the next edition, or the next time Hegel gives the course.

Given antiquarian interests, one would have to go beyond the standard versions of the lectures, reconstructing the development of Hegel's views. At the very least, one would have to collate remarks in widely different places. In a monograph on Hegel that would be appropriate and well worth doing, but my concern here is altogether different.

Hegel says hundreds of things that are open to criticism. But to find fault with many of the dicta in his lectures would be pointless for many reasons. The wording is often due to his students; and even when it is his own, *all* lecturers say a great deal that does not stand up well under scrutiny. When the lectures are neither written out nor meant for publication, it is petty to try to score off them. Detailed criticism might be justified if the Hegelian corpus were widely revered as authoritative; but the situation is more nearly the opposite, and amassing objections would be like carrying nails to the crucifixion, on Saturday.

Hegel's treatment of *Antigone* in the *Phenomenology* strikes me as quite absurd at many points.[13] But Hegel made a few central suggestions that advance our understanding of tragedy more than anything else written since Aristotle; and my concern is with illuminating these ideas.

Let us agree, then, not to speak of "all tragedy" and "the essentially tragic fact," as Bradley does, committing ourselves to argue that *The Trojan Women* and a large number of other tragedies are in fact *not* tragedies or to assimilate them forcibly to paradigms on which they were not modeled. Let us rather recall that Greek tragedy had roots in Homer's *Iliad*, where the noble clash with the noble and no hero is evil, and that Aeschylus sublimated the contests of Homer into moral collisions. Some of Euripides' tragedies stand in this same tradition, while others represent different types of tragedy. To suppose, as Bradley does, that a few general principles must apply to all tragedies, including Shakespeare's, is historically blind; Shakespeare's spirit was not nourished on Aeschylus nor even mainly on the *Iliad*. The Christian influence cannot be ignored, and Christianity had taught for centuries that not only evil but also evil human beings did exist.

Nor are tragic collisions central in all of Sophocles' plays. Neither *Ajax* nor *The Women of Trachis*, neither *Electra* nor *Oedipus at Colonus* illustrates this concept at all clearly, though if one is com-

---

[13] See W. Kaufmann, *Hegel* (Garden City, N.Y., 1965), § 30.

mitted to this notion one can, of course, water it down the way Bradley does until something at least remotely like it can be found in these plays, too. Rather, we should admit that tragedies differ greatly, that Hegel's concept strikingly illuminates the *Oresteia* and *Prometheus*, *Hippolytus* and *The Bacchae*, and that it is also of some help—though much less so—when we come to *Antigone, Oedipus Tyrannus,* and *Philoctetes*.

In *Oedipus Tyrannus*, for example, Hegel did not analyze the moral conflicts, and he did not note the curse of honesty or the emphasis on the dark side of justice, but his approach facilitates such discoveries rather better than Aristotle's reflections on various kinds of plots do. Hegel gets us away from Aristotle's fateful claim that the protagonist must not be outstanding in virtue and from the inveterate prejudice that each tragedy has one hero—two notions that have profoundly damaged Sophoclean criticism to this day. Hegel himself never made the most of these insights, but no other philosopher did better.

Before we bring out the gravest fault of Hegel's concept of the tragic collision, let us introduce his other, closely related and no less influential contribution to our understanding of Greek tragedy. Hegel suggested that external accidents, such as sickness, loss of property, and death should arouse no interest other than

> eagerness to rush up and help. If one can't do that, images of woe and misery merely tear our heart. Truly tragic suffering, on the other hand, is imposed only on active individuals, as the consequence of some act of their own that is no less justified than it is fraught with guilt, owing to the collision it involves; and they are also answerable for it with their whole self.[14]

This dictum is entirely applicable only to tragedies built around a tragic collision, like *The Libation Bearers* and *Prometheus, Hippolytus, The Bacchae,* and *Antigone*. It also illuminates some tragedies in which right does not clash with right: *The Persians,* for example. But Hegel clearly implies that the sufferings of Euripides' Trojan women are not "truly tragic"; and this suggestion has been taken up not only by Bradley but also by several twentieth-century philosophers. Again, the root evil consists in an attempt to assimilate all tragedies to a single model, instead of admitting how much tragedies differ.

While I find Hegel's conception of "truly tragic suffering" objectionable and too narrow, it is of interest not only because of its great influence but also because it points the way toward a much needed refinement of the ancient idea of *hamartia*. Those who wish to give Aristotle the benefit of every doubt may wish to say that Hegel merely

[14] G. W. F. Hegel, *Aesthetik, Werke,* XIV, 532.

specifies the nature of error that leads to the suffering—one-sidedness—although Gerald F. Else believes that Aristotle meant an error
about the identity of a close relative.[15] But Aristotle's reason for at-
tributing *hamartia* to those who suffer and are destroyed was that
he considered totally undeserved suffering shocking rather than tragic.
Hegel's twin concepts of tragic collision and tragic suffering facilitate
a subtler insight into innocence and guilt. Prometheus and Orestes
commit no error of judgment and are not flawed characters, yet Hegel's
dicta apply to them.

We must make a crucial distinction between *tragic guilt* and *moral
fault*. Those raised on the tragic flaw too often balk at recognizing
innocent suffering; following Aristotle, they consider it shocking; and
though in life it stares them in the face, they do not wish to admit
it in literature. Like Job's friends they impute moral faults. But a
man's destruction may be brought about by his choice, his act, his
heroism, though he is morally admirable.

Consider Kafka's *The Trial* and *The Castle*. The hero of the former
approaches (not too closely) the passivity of the man in the parable
that is told in chapter 9 of *The Trial*. Denied admission—it does not
matter to what—the man in the parable settles down outside the gate,
makes occasional inquiries, and wastes his whole life. Similarly, the
hero of *The Trial* allows the information that he is under arrest—which
in fact he is not—to ruin *his* life. He makes no further attempt to
live after his own fashion. The hero of *The Castle*, on the other hand,
is often blamed for being such an activist. Even if this juxtaposition
should be a little too neat, we ought to see that Kafka retains our
interest by establishing a close connection between each hero's decision
and destruction—but that this does not mean that they deserve their
fate.

One of the reasons for the perennial fascination of *Oedipus
Tyrannus* is that the question of the hero's guilt and the connection
between his own acts and his suffering keeps haunting us. Oedipus
is an active individual through and through. His suffering is a direct
consequence of his past deeds, done before the play begins, and of
his decisions in the play. At every step he was justified. He killed
Laius in self-defense; after liberating Thebes from the Sphinx, he was
asked to marry Jocasta and become king; and his insistence to push
the inquiry that cannot be abandoned without subjecting Thebes to
further deaths from plague is wholly admirable. *Morally*, he is not
at fault, yet he is guilty of parricide and incest.

He blinds himself not by way of confessing, contrary to fact,
that he was wrong to push his inquiry, and that those who had

[15] Gerald F. Else, *Aristotle's Poetics: The Argument* (Cambridge, 1963), 379ff.

counseled him to stop were right. Neither does he immediately plead his own innocence or marshal extenuating circumstances. Poetically, that would have made for a less tragic, a less powerful conclusion; morally, it would have been less heroic.

In his *Philosophy of Right*, Hegel comments:

> The *heroic* self-consciousness (so in the tragedies of the ancients, of Oedipus, etc.) has not yet proceeded from its solidity [*Gediegenheit*] to the reflection on the difference between *deed* and *action*, between the external event and premeditation and knowledge of the circumstances, or to the fragmentation of the consequences; it accepts its guilt for the whole range of the deed. (§ 118)

Hegel's development of this idea in his lectures on aesthetics is worth quoting too:

> Oedipus has slain a man in a quarrel, which could easily happen in the circumstances of that age and was not considered a crime. He did not know that this violent man, who barred his way, was his father; neither did he know that the queen he later married was his mother; but once the misfortune was revealed, he, as a heroic subject, accepts all the consequences of his first deed and atones for parricide and incest.[16]
>
> The self-reliant solidity and totality of the heroic character does not wish to share the guilt and knows nothing of this opposition of subjective intentions and objective deeds and consequences, while the implications and ramifications of modern actions are such that everybody tries to push all guilt as far away from himself as possible. Our view is more moral in this respect, insofar as in the moral realm the subjective aspect of knowledge of the circumstances and good intentions constitutes a central element of action. In the heroic age, however, the individual was essentially one, and whatever was objective was and remained his, if it had issued from him; hence the subject also wants to have done entirely and alone whatever it has done . . .

Hegel's perceptive comments show incidentally how Sartre's existentialism revives the heroic ethos of Sophocles. A man is his deeds and his life, and to plead that one's intentions were better than one's works is, according to Sartre, a mark of bad faith. While it is inhumanly harsh to judge others that way, we are inclined to admire those who see themselves that way.

This double standard suggests some confusion. Our distinction between tragic guilt and moral fault does not go far enough. "Guilt" is not the right word where guilt feelings are not appropriate; and we do

---

[16] G. W. F. Hegel, *Werke*, ed. Lasson (1931), Xa, 266: from the lectures of 1826. The immediately following paragraph is found on the same page, but had been published earlier: Lasson reprints it from Hotho's edition, and it is also to be found in *Werke*, ed. Glockner, XII, 257ff.

not really admire those who harbor such feelings in a situation in which they are not to be blamed. The *mot juste* is not tragic guilt but tragic *responsibility;* for responsibility, like pride, is something one can *take.*

It is not particularly reasonable to take pride in being an American, an Athenian, or Oedipus; and if it takes the form of boasting it is even odious. Nor is it particularly reasonable to take responsibility for being an American, an Athenian, or Oedipus; and if it takes the form of wallowing in guilt feelings it is neurotic. But pride can mean that we accept high standards and feel that behavior and accomplishments considered satisfactory by others will not do for us. Similarly, responsibility can be free of guilt feelings and can mean that we define our field of action. Thus pride and responsibility can be future-oriented and, as it were, two sides of the same outlook.

To return to Hegel, he did not have a "theory of tragedy." He brought to the discussion of Greek tragedy the concepts of tragic collision and "truly tragic suffering," and he suggested that in some sense the protagonists brought their suffering on themselves, were guilty, and accepted their guilt. These ideas illuminate many of the best Greek tragedies; but not all Greek tragedies are built around a tragic collision, not all the suffering in Greek tragedy is "truly tragic" in Hegel's sense, and not all the protagonists accept their guilt, as Oedipus does in the Tyrannus and as Hegel may have thought—mistakenly— Antigone did.[17] Deianeira does; but Electra and Philoctetes see themselves as suffering innocently, and their sufferings are not "truly tragic," according to Hegel. Indeed, many modern writers under Hegel's influence would deny that they are tragic at all. Finally, Hegel does not distinguish as sharply as we would between tragic responsibility and moral fault.

Oedipus' blindness in the end is poetically powerful because it brings out his spiritual blindness up to that point. That he blinds himself is in keeping with his active stance throughout. Sophocles does

---

[17] G. W. F. Hegel, *Phänomenologie des Geistes* (1807 edition), 412; *Werke*, II, 361; *Phen.*, trans. Baillie, 491. A similar passage in Hegel's discussion of Socrates' trial is more cautious, but really quite pointless unless it is again assumed that Antigone admits her error. Hegel suggests that Socrates ought to have proposed a fine for himself, admitting his guilt; and then Hegel goes on: "Thus we see the heavenly Antigone, the most glorious figure ever to have appeared on earth, go to her death in Sophocles; in her final words she posits as the one possibility: 'If this pleases the gods that we, we confess that, since we suffer, we erred' " (*Aesthetik, Werke,* XVIII, 114).

Eric C. Woodcock, in his "Note on Sophocles' *Antigone,* 925, 296" (*Classical Review,* 43 (1929), 116ff.), translates these lines: "Nay, then, if these things are pleasing to the gods, and if I have sinned, I will acquiesce in my fate." In any case, Antigone continues: "But if the *hamartia* is on the other side, may they then suffer no more evil than they unjustly inflict on me."

not show him to us as a victim, a plaything of wanton gods, a
Gloucester, but a heroic figure to the last. Still, Oedipus does not blind
himself after weighing his life in the balance, finding himself guilty,
and deciding that this is the proper punishment. Such a view of the
matter would be as far from Sophocles' intentions as it would be to
have Oedipus blinded by Laius' servants, as in Euripides' lost *Oedipus*.
Sophocles' hero is neither a pathetic creature who suffers monstrous
injustice—a forerunner of Woyzeck—nor is he found in the end to
deserve cruel punishment. Rather he realizes all at once that the king
whose murderer he seeks and has cursed, was killed by him; that
he has killed his father; that the woman whom he married and who
bore his children was his mother; and that by pushing his investigation
to the end he has driven her to suicide. Seeing her dead body, he
plucks the clasps from her robe and blinds himself. When he emerges
from the palace, blind, our feeling is *not* that justice has been done
at last. Rather that moment holds more terror than words can convey.
At that point Carl Orff's music for the play reminds us what Aeschylus'
and Sophocles' music may have added to the tragedies we know.[18]
In the end righteous indignation and retributive justice are called into
question, and the impact is shattering.

Hegel's concepts do not plumb the depths of Oedipus' despair.
Still, they come incomparably closer to the spirit of Greek tragedy
than Plato or Aristotle did, and they are also superior to those of
Schopenhauer and other more recent philosophers.

Before proceeding further we must bring out the fatal flaw of
Hegel's conception of the tragic collision, for this helps to account
for the fact that it applies better to the two more philosophical tragic
poets than it does to Sophocles. Hegel assumed not only that in such
conflicts some good was to be found on both sides but also that both
sides were *equally* justified.[19] In the plays by Aeschylus and Euripides
that I have given as examples this may be so; in Sophocles it never is.

If only at first glance, Aristotle's doctrine of the tragic flaw or
error seems to apply to Shakespearean more than to Greek tragedy.
On the other hand, Hegel's concept of tragic collision, though familiar
in the English-speaking world through the discipleship of A. C. Bradley,
a. major Shakespearean critic, fits Greek tragedy far better than did
Aristotle's principles, but it is not very illuminating when applied
to Shakespeare.

---

[18] There is no play I have seen in more different productions. The Hölderlin translation, with Carl Orff's music, in Vienna, October 12, 1962, was incomparably the
best and altogether magnificent. (It had its American broadcast premiere October
30, 1967, at 9 P.M., on WRVR.) But the power of this tragedy even in mediocre
productions constitutes part of what I have called "The Riddle of Oedipus."
[19] "*Gleichberechtigt*," for example, *Werke*, XIV, 567.

In Greek tragedy, which was modelled on the *Iliad,* claim clashed with claim. In *Othello,* the noble hero and his innocent wife are undone by Iago's perverse wickedness. In *Lear,* Cordelia returns to England in the end with the forces of light, which vanquish the forces of darkness, but in the process she herself and her old father are destroyed along with her evil sisters. Lear and Gloucester are not innocent, but Goneril and Regan are clearly not intended to have any valid claims, any more than Iago. Edmund, like Iago, has motives, and he resembles Richard III in having an almost attractive vitality, but even if all three have grievances, there is no right on their sides. Macbeth is incomparably more appealing, but his murders are totally unjustified. Nor are we made to feel that Hamlet's uncle has any right whatever on his side.

Thus *Hamlet, Othello, Lear* and *Macbeth* are not constructed around the moral conflict between two parties who have some legitimate claims but are too one-sided. Shakespeare's greatest tragedies are significantly different from *The Oresteia* and the Prometheus trilogy, *Antigone* and *The Bacchae.* Hegel himself realized this, but Bradley, who lacked Hegel's keen historical sense, did not do justice to this difference, and in his essay on "Hegel's Theory of Tragedy" tried to assimilate Shakespeare to the Greeks.

Hegel proceeds historically and, in his lectures on aesthetics, first discusses ancient tragedy, making the points we have discussed, and then contrasts modern, and especially Shakespearean, tragedy with that of the Greeks:

> The heroes of ancient classical tragedy encounter situations in which, if they firmly decide in favor of the one ethical pathos that alone suits their own finished character, they must necessarily come into conflict with the equally justified ethical power that confronts them.[20]

"Equally" is wrong. Hegel's term is *gleichberechtigt,* but Zeus in *Prometheus* and Creon in *Antigone,* or those who advise Oedipus, in the *Tyrannus* to cease inquiring, are not morally on a par with the three heroes. Even so they represent some moral claims and are not comparable to Iago, Goneril, or Claudius. In the very next sentence, Hegel introduces his contrast with the characters in modern tragedy. By "modern" I mean post-medieval, after 1500. Hegel's infelicitous word is "romantic," which he uses as a technical term.

> Romantic characters, on the other hand, stand from the outset in a wealth of more accidental circumstances and conditions, within which one could act this way or that, so that the conflict that, to be sure, is occasioned by external preconditions, is essentially grounded

in the *character*. The individuals in their passion obey their own character, not that it is substantially justified, but simply because they are what they are. Of course the Greek heroes also act in accordance with their individuality, but in the best ancient tragedies this individuality is necessarily, as mentioned previously, a self-contained ethical pathos. In modern tragedy, on the other hand, the character in its peculiarity decides in accordance with subjective desires and needs, external influences, etc., and whether he chooses what is justified or is led into injustice and crime, remains a matter of accident. Here ethical claims and character *may* coincide; but this congruity . . . still would not constitute the *essential* basis and objective condition of tragic profundity and beauty.

As for the more specific differences between these modern characters, few generalizations are possible, considering the immense variety permitted in this area. I shall therefore touch only on the following principal points.

The first distinction that strikes us immediately is that between abstract and therefore formal characterizations on the one hand, and individuals who confront us as concrete and living human beings, on the other. To illustrate the first type, one might particularly cite the tragic figures of the French and Italians, who, having been inspired by imitation of the ancients, may be considered more or less as mere personifications of certain passions for love, honor, fame, domination, tyranny, etc. Of the motives of their actions and the degree and nature of their feelings they certainly speak with a lavish display of rhetoric and much declamatory art, yet this manner of explication reminds one more of Seneca's failures than of the dramatic masterpieces of the Greeks.

After a brief general characterization of Spanish tragedy, Hegel continues:

> The greatest masters, on the other hand, in the depiction of full individuals and characters are the English, and among them, in turn, Shakespeare excels all others and is almost beyond reach. For even when some merely formal passion, as, for example, the lust to rule in *Macbeth*, or jealousy in *Othello*, claims the whole pathos of one of his tragic heroes, nevertheless such abstractions do not consume the full reach of the individuality; even given such a determination, his individuals still remain whole human beings. Indeed, the more Shakespeare, using the infinite breadth of his world stage, moves toward the extremes of evil and absurdity, the more—as I have mentioned previously—he refuses to drown even the figures on these ultimate boundaries in their limitations, without the riches of a poetic dowry; instead he gives them spirit and imagination, and by virtue of the image in which they contemplate themselves objectively, in theoretical reflection, like a work of art, he makes them free artistic creators of themselves; and thus, given the full virility and faithfulness of his character studies, he knows how to interest us quite as much

in criminals as in the most vulgar and insipid louts and fools. The way his tragic characters express themselves is similarly individual, real, directly alive, supremely manifold, and yet, when it seems necessary, of such sublimity and striking power of expression, of such fervor and inventiveness in images and metaphors produced on the spur of the moment, of such rhetoric, bred not in schools but by true feeling and the consistency of character, that, in view of this fusion of direct vitality and inner greatness of soul, one will not easily find another modern dramatist who could be placed beside him. Goethe, in his youth strove after a similar faithfulness to nature and particularity, but without such inner force and height of passion, and Schiller came to cultivate a violence whose tempestuous expansion lacks any real core.

A *second* difference among modern characters concerns their *firmness* or their inner *vacillation* and division. The weakness of indecision, the back and forth of reflection, the weighing of the reasons that should influence the decision, are occasionally found even among the ancients, in some of Euripides' tragedies. . . . In modern tragedy such vacillating figures are encountered frequently, especially types who experience two passions that send them from one decision, one deed, to another. . . . Even though tragic action depends on a collision, the projection of this discord into a single individual is always awkward in a number of ways.[21]

It should be clear that Hegel, so far from forcing the rich variety of tragedies into a tight, preconceived system, or applying a few bone-dry triads to whatever history offers him, combined wide learning and deep insight with a pluralistic bent. His native tendency was to consider an abundance of empirical materials, to try saying something interesting about whatever he discussed, and to approximate a lawless alternation of essays and aphorisms. Since he disapproved of the German romantics' lack of discipline, he found it difficult in the extreme to finish any books.

His first attempt, the *Phenomenology of the Spirit*, published when he was thirty-six, was presented as the first part of a system, of which the second part never appeared; the conception of the book changed radically while he wrote it; and it still bears the imprint of his native, highly unsystematic bent. In his second attempt, the *Logic*, he achieved a far greater degree of order, by the ingenious device of labeling his constant digressions, many of them fascinating essays, "Notes." In the first volume of the *Logic* he interspersed over thirty "Notes"; and by the time he reached the third and final volume, he was doing something altogether different from what he had done in the first two. After that he stopped writing books. He published two more volumes,

[21] G. W. F. Hegel, *Werke*, XIV, 567–570.

to be sure,—both of them syllabi marked clearly on the title page "To be used in connection with his lectures." The great bulk of his posthumously published collected "works" is due to the inclusion of his lectures, published by his students, largely on the basis of their own notes. Finding that he never adhered to the same order twice, they not only collated notes of different years but felt free—for example, in the lectures on aesthetics—to impose systematic arrangements of their own.

Coming back to tragedy now, it is plain that Hegel had a lively appreciation of Shakespeare's tragic art; it is much less plain whether Hegel had a theory of tragedy. To be precise, he had ideas about tragedy, he offered interesting observations on specific plays—always brief, hardly ever as much as a page at a time—but he did not develop anything that one could call a theory of tragedy if one means by a theory more than a loose collection of ideas and passing comments. Least of all did he have the kind of theory that those thinking they know all about him expect of him. It would have been tedious to interrupt our quotations from his lectures by pointing out again and again how much his dicta fly in the face of common misconceptions about Hegel. This is also true of the following comments, which begin at the bottom of the page from which we quoted last:

> But what is worst is if the vacillation and change of the character and the whole human being becomes the principle of the whole presentation—as it were, as a crooked dialectic of art—and the truth is supposed to be to show that no character is really firm and sure of himself. The one-sided aims of particular passions and characters, to be sure, may not be realized without being contested in any way, and even in everyday reality the response of the environment and of the individuals opposing them do not spare them the experience of their finitude and untenability. But this conclusion . . . must not be placed right in the individual himself, as a dialectical mechanism; otherwise the subject, as this particular subjectivity, is merely an empty and indeterminate form that does not coalesce organically with any determination of aims or of the character. Just so, it makes a difference if the change in the whole inner condition of a man appears as a consistent consequence of his peculiarity, so that what develops and comes out had been present in his character all along. Thus in Shakespeare's *Lear*, for example, the original folly of the old man grows into madness while, similarly, Gloucester's spiritual blindness is changed into actual physical blindness, in which his eyes are finally opened to the true difference in the love of his two sons.
>
> Shakespeare, above all, furnishes, as against this presentation of vacillating and bifurcated characters, the most beautiful examples of figures who are firm and consistent, and who, precisely by so resolutely clinging to themselves and to their aims, destroy themselves. Not justi-

fied morally but carried only by the formal necessity of their individuality, they allow themselves to be lured to their deed by external
conditions, or they blindly plunge into it; and then they hold out
in it by sheer force of will, even if now they do what they are doing
only from necessity, to maintain themselves against others or simply
because they have reached the pass they have reached. The emergence
of the passion that, though it implicitly accords with character, had
not erupted so far but now unfolds—this course and progression of
a great soul, its inner development, the painting of its self-destructive
fight against circumstances, conditions, and consequences—is the major
content in many of Shakespeare's most interesting tragedies.[22]

It is widely supposed that Aristotle was, unlike Plato, a great
empiricist who collected a vast amount of data and based his ideas
upon these; and the constant mention of specific tragedies in the *Poetics*
seems to bear this out—though there was a time when Aristotle was
associated with scholasticism and rationalism and considered the
archenemy of modern empiricism. Hegel, on the other hand, is almost
universally decried as a Procrustes. But the more we quote from him,
the clearer it should become that his first concern is to do justice to
his data—in this case, Shakespeare's tragedies. His attitude toward
Shakespeare is infinitely more humble than Aristotle's toward
Sophocles, not to speak of Aeschylus or Euripides. Hegel does not say:
there are four kinds of plots, and this one is the best, and that the
worst; and now let us give marks to *King Lear* and *Hamlet*. Rather
he asks what is the crux "in many of Shakespeare's most interesting
tragedies."

He goes on to say that

> The last important point still to be discussed concerns the *tragic conclu-*
> *sion* toward which the modern characters are moving, as well as the
> kind of tragic *reconciliation* that is permitted by this point of view.

Since the heroes are different from those of Greek tragedy, the conclusion is different too:

> Macbeth, for example, the elder daughters and sons-in-law[23] of Lear,
> the President in [Schiller's] *Kabale und Liebe* [Cabal and Love, 1784],
> Richard III, etc. etc., deserve for their abominations nothing better
> than they receive. This kind of conclusion usually proceeds in such
> a way that the individuals are broken as they dash against an extant
> power in whose despite they wanted to execute their particular aim.

---

[22] *Ibid.*, 570–572.
[23] Whether this plural (*Tochtermänner*) represents an oral slip in one of Hegel's
lectures or a mistake in a student's notes, H. G. Hotho might have caught it
when he published the lectures: Albany succeeds Lear.

Hegel gives some examples from Schiller's and Goethe's plays[24] and continues:

> On the other hand, the tragic conclusion is presented merely as the effect of unfortunate circumstances and external accidents that might just as easily have turned out differently, bringing about a happy ending. . . . Such a course can take a great deal out of us, yet it merely appears horrible, and one immediately confronts the demand that the external accidents should accord with what constitutes the true inner nature of these beautiful characters. Only in this way can we feel reconciled, for example, to the destruction of Hamlet and Juliet. Viewed externally, Hamlet's death seems to be brought about accidentally through the duel with Laertes and the exchange of the rapiers. But in the background of Hamlet's soul, death lurks from the beginning. The sandbank of finitude does not suffice him; given such sorrow and tenderness, such grief and such nausea over all the conditions of life, we feel from the outset that in this abominable environment he is a lost man whom inner disgust has almost consumed even before death comes to him from outside. The same applies to *Romeo and Juliet*. This tender blossom [Juliet] does not find the ground on which she has been planted agreeable, and nothing remains to us but to lament the sad evanescence of such beautiful love, which, like a tender rose in the valley of this accidental world, is broken by the rough winds and thunderstorms and the infirm calculations of noble, benevolent prudence. But the sorrow that thus overcomes us is only a painful reconciliation . . .[25]

Detailed evaluations of Hegel's generally very sensitive comments both on Shakespeare in general and on particular plays would serve little purpose, for these are obviously passing observations in lectures, and the really crucial point here is to establish the tenor of Hegel's remarks. He was plainly untroubled by distinctions between philosophy and literary criticism, and those who nowadays favor the ploy "but is that philosophy?" should face the fact that Hegel spent most of his time in the last decade of his life, when he was a professor at Berlin, giving lectures that were, for the most part, "not philosophy."

Even if we applaud his many insights and feel pleasantly surprised by the lack of any insistence on a tight system, we cannot finally allow Hegel's *aperçus* to pass without all criticism. Oddly, the most important objection is that Hegel is too unsystematic. At this level

[24] G. W. F. Hegel, *Werke*, XIV, 572ff. Here the only English translation informs the reader that Goethe's Götz "goes to ground." Readers with little German realize, no doubt, that Götz "geht . . . zu Grunde," that is, he perishes.

[25] G. W. F. Hegel, *Werke*, XIV, 573ff. Five more words conclude this sentence and paragraph: *"eine unglückselige Seligkeit in Unglück."* Without sufficient regard for the multiple play on words, this might be rendered: a miserable bliss in misfortune.

serious discussion is scarcely possible. What is needed is a more sustained analysis of a few tragic poets and of some specific plays. And if it should be said that this, too, is not philosophy, one might reply: far better to do this and do it well than to add to "the dreariness of aesthetics."[26] Moreover, it is surely relevant to philosophy when such analyses show how traditional philosophers went wrong. Some knowledge of philosophy enables one to see, too, where many literary critics, untrained in philosophy, have failed.

In conclusion, we must still take note of one point that Hegel makes in the paragraph following the last one we have quoted. Here he indicates that he prefers a happy ending—other things being equal.

> When nothing else is at stake except this difference, I must confess that I, for my part, prefer a happy conclusion. And why not? For prizing mere misfortune, only because it is misfortune, above a happy solution, there is no other reason but a certain elegant sensitivity that feeds on pain and suffering, finding itself more interesting in the process than in painless situations, which it considers everyday affairs. If the interests themselves are of such a nature that it really is not worthwhile to sacrifice individuals to them who, without renouncing themselves, could give up their aims or come to terms with each other, then the conclusion need not be tragic. One must insist on the tragic nature of conflicts and solutions where this is necessary to vindicate a superior view. But when there is no such necessity, mere suffering and misfortune are in no way justified. This constitutes the natural reason for *plays* and *dramas*, which are intermediate between tragedies and comedies.[27]

Here, as we have seen, Hegel is closer to the great Greek tragic poets than are the critics who sneer at him for his supposed lack of feeling for tragedy. Moreover, Hegel is far from censuring *Antigone* or *Oedipus Tyrannus*, or Shakespeare's tragedies. What he does say is that catastrophic endings must be justified, as they are in these cases. But the main point of his remarks at this point is plainly to provide a transition to "*plays* and *dramas*, which are intermediate between tragedies and comedies"; and he recognizes, as too many twentieth-century critics do not, that most modern plays are neither tragedies nor comedies.

Even so, Hegel's reference to "a certain elegant sensitivity," though perhaps amply justified in its time—the age of the restoration after the Napoleonic wars, when German romanticism was decaying— seems dated in the era after World War II. We no longer think of everyday life as painless, and misfortune and catastrophe no longer

---

[26] This is the title of an essay by J. A. Passmore, *Mind*, 60 (1951), 318–335.
[27] G. W. F. Hegel, *Werke*, XIV, 574ff.

seem exotic and "interesting." Rather we tend to wonder whether any large-scale image of life that eschews tremendous suffering or, after including it, depicts a happy ending is not necessarily untrue to life and at best entertaining. So dark seems reality to us that yet more darkness on the stage may not be what we want; but serious plays with happy endings do not help because they have a false ring. The solution that meets with the widest favor is black comedy of some sort, whether theatre of the absurd or not—an image that depicts the horrors we know from reality but makes us laugh at them.

AFTER HEGEL*

Franco Lombardi

1. Introduction: Our Ambivalent Relationship with Hegel and Hegel's Ambiguity

There is perhaps no thinker who excites so many mixed feelings as Hegel. In general, Hegel is at the root of that complex we call the modern world. He has, however, displeased his immediate disciples whom we shall call the ungrateful sons of Hegel,[1] as well as philosophers of another temper of mind, for example, Bertrand Russell.[2] Hegel is fast becoming a remote thinker, and the age he lived in is beginning to look like the prehistory of mankind.

---

* Translated from the Italian by B. P. Keaney.
[1] See section 4, below.
[2] Cf. B. Russell, *History of Western Philosophy* (New York, 1945), 730–746.

Contemporary Italian philosophy shares all these mixed feelings. As early as 1933,[3] when the Hegel Congress was held in Rome, there were obvious differences between the situation in Italy and elsewhere. In the Netherlands, for example, Hegelianism was the embodiment of orthodoxy. For almost a century and a half, whilst Italy suffered the pains of Nation-birth, Hegel inspired the Italian philosophical scene, but that inspiration was subjected to Italianization and reshaped to deal with the actual problems dominating European thought.[4]

The foregoing remarks serve to show how complicated the situation is and why this complication is increased by the two streams of Italian Neo-Hegelianism one of which emphasizes continuity with tradition while the other has broken with and is in contrast to that tradition.[5] However, if the different national currents for all their individuality of flow and origin join and build up the more general image of man's predicament within the universe, this is also due to Hegel's philosophical thought.

The ambivalent feeling is not confined to the specifically philosophical world but is also characteristic of the more embracing political and social sphere. Here one cannot affirm that the philosophical approach of an epoch, and by that I mean the essential characteristics of its critical philosophical thought, is not distinct from man's more general approach to the Real which we have dubbed his outlook on the Universe.

Looked at from a more philosophical standpoint, Hegel represents the last great philosophical "Summa." This was not just another philosophical system. (The last one, as it turned out, since after Hegel the rebellion against all systems has flared up and Croce and Gentile can be considered as merely late runners.[6]) It was a system which attempted to contain all thought and all reality in the *Logos*, and that from Creation through the time of Georg Wilhelm Friedrich Hegel and for all eternity. Hegel's was the last great system which attempted to resolve not only philosophy but also science, not only theology but also the science of man, art, and economics, the doctrine of the State, sociology and so on. Hegel accomplished this by means of an Idea,

---

[3] See the proceedings: *Verhandlungen des dritten Hegel Kongresses vom 19 bis 23 April in Rom* (Tübingen, 1934). Concerning that conference, see also F. Lombardi "Intorno al concetto della dialettica," *Giornale Critico della filosofia italiana* (1933), 110–126; 208–231; and "Razionalità, dialettica e libertà," in *Memoria Accademica* (Naples, 1933), 56.

[4] See section 6, below.

[5] See F. Lombardi "Continuità e rottura, che cosa resta oggi della filosofia?", in *De Homine*, Vol. 11–12, 169–228. Reprinted in F. Lombardi, *Il senso della storia ed altri saggi* (Florence, 1965).

[6] See section 6, below.

which although a priori, nevertheless develops through the external world and through the historical development of man's thought. It should not be forgotten that when Hegel decided on the grounds of his "dialectical thinking" that there were three rings of Saturn and only three, he was not more original than, say, Simplicius interpreting Aristotle. The whole "development" is enclosed within the definite compass of an Idea, namely "that which is."[7] In this last respect, Hegelian speculation is the butt of contemporary thought, and this confrontation began immediately after Hegel.

Hegel, on the other hand, is the man who first accepted the mass and wealth of ethical, social, and political matter as part of philosophical reflection. His system has been likened to a nut, the shell of which has to be broken to obtain the kernel, or, to a bone, the hard external surface of which has to be broken through to obtain the marrow. And what a marrow! The Germans aptly describe it as *Löwenmark*. All subsequent thought drew upon Hegel, not only the political thought of Marx, Treitschke, Labriola, and Croce, but also the historical thought of Jellinck, with its reflections on law, and the aesthetics of Francesco de Sanctis. Wherever you find a keen sense of "the real" and of thought immanent in Being plus the revival of Machiavelli's realism—there at the root you will find Hegel's philosophy. These problems may well be beset with difficulties. Hegel has been identified, not always correctly, with Prussian and Germanic "Realism," and many regard Nazism as the culmination of this movement. Today we are in the throes of a not always enlightened revival of Enlightenment Ideals, and with a defense—which is not always critically founded—of the "Natural" basis of the State. But these problems will not be solved merely by going back to a time before Hegel.[8]

2. The Double-Faced Image of Hegel in the History of Speculative European Thought

Before Hegel, philosophy investigated the meaning of the True, the Good, the Beautiful, the nature of the human intellect and the structure of our thinking. It was fashionable to dwell philosophically *sub specie aeterni* and to reject the contingent and the mundane of history. Hegel is the first to present a philosophy which can account for the variety of different truths which philosophers throughout history have introduced.[9] The problem of the understanding of different

[7] See section 3, below.
[8] See section 11, below.
[9] See the reference in note 12, below.

cultures in which Dilthey, Weber, and Simmel were participants was started in this way.[10] Today the same question is examined not only diachronically but also synchronically, and is known as the question of "other cultures" or more ambiguously the problem of "Cultural Relativism."[11]

This development led to questions on the nature and task of philosophy. Hegel undoubtedly put forward the premises of the revolution in philosophy,[12] and later Croce,[13] profiting from the development inspired by the master's thought,[14] did the same with compelling clarity.

Hegel stretched, so to speak, the very same concept of thought he had inherited from Plato and Aristotle onto the course of history.[15] This he did by means of "Dialectics." Metaphorically speaking, the result was that the philosopher's cap (*die Mutze*) was doffed (*emporgehoben*) to the heaven of concepts. Technically speaking, the result was the division of the concept into Thesis, Antithesis, and Synthesis, so that both truth and reality became self-contradictory.

A series of difficulties followed, and they require individual consideration. The most immediate result, however, was the unhappy marriage of philosophy with history and of both with moral philosophy, sociology, and politics. This, however, has no immediate connection with the notion of the philosopher's commitment or the unity of thinker and philosopher with his role as person and politician. Yet one cannot deny that there was an unnecessary confusion of political, sociological, historical, and philosophical problems. This confusion stemmed from a fundamentally wrong notion of the meaning of Dialectic and of the nature and task of philosophy.[16]

3. The Defects of the Hegelian Dialectic

The first flaw is that the system is static. This defect stems from the first category in Hegel's *Logic*, namely, Being, Not-being, and Be-

[10] Cf. the following note. On the notion of culture, see section 4, below.

[11] A critical approach to the problem can be found in F. Lombardi, "Il relativismo culturale," in *De Homine*, Vol. 17–18, an introductory essay to the issue of cultural anthropology.

[12] See, simply as an instance, G. W. F. Hegel, *Grundlinien der Philosophie des Rechts, Werke*, VII, 18ff.

[13] Concerning Croce, see footnote 36.

[14] See sections 4 and 6 of this essay.

[15] For a clarification of this criticism see sections 9 and 10 below. A more detailed criticism can be found in my volume, *Le origini della filosofia europea nel mondo greco* (Asti and Rome, 1954).

[16] See section 12, below.

coming. This criticism can be collated with that found in Trendelenburg, Schelling's Berlin lectures, in Kierkegaard, and also in Feuerbach. There are traces of the same criticism in Kuno Fischer,[17] who influenced the Italian Bertrando Spaventa[18] and who in turn influenced Gentile.[19] Fischer's criticism, and Spaventa's and Gentile's even more so, are connected with the polemic between the Hegelian Left and Right on the place of the *Phenomenology* in Hegel's system. The relevant issue in this struggle was whether thought is an *ens in se,* which would mean that God is prior to the world, or whether God only reveals himself in and through human thought in such a way that the *Logos* lives and manifests itself in the act of thinking. If the latter interpretation were correct, then it would appear difficult to defend the view that phenomenology was prior to and a necessary preliminary introduction to the system.

The second flaw is that the dialectical movement is only possible insofar as the truth-content of the thought is settled by dialectically contrasting the same truth in two propositions and resolving the contrast in "a superior truth" of the synthesis. This explains the necessary logistical nature of the process. Feuerbach, Marx, and Kierkegaard have discussed this defect. When Croce, who had been taught the Herbartian distinction by Antonio Labriola, wanted to oppose this reduction of all values to the "logical" value of the truth of thought, he considered reforming the dialectic of opposites by replacing it with a dialectic of distinct grades of the human spirit. This was the cause of the argument between Croce and Gentile,[20] namely whether distinct or opposite grades should be used in the dialectic. The equivocal nature of the quarrel stems from the fact that both parties in line with Hegel and Marx favored a dialectic of the truth-content of thought either by emphasizing the content of thought obtained by the dialectical process, or, in the case of Croce, by determining the content of the activity of the thinking-subject through the various "forms" or "moments" of its expression in Art, Logical Thought, Economic, and Ethical Willing.

The third flaw in Hegelian dialectic is that by insisting that

---

[17] For a discussion of these criticisms see F. Lombardi, *Ludwig Feuerbach* (Florence, 1935) and *Søren Kierkegaard* (Florence, 1936; 1967). [For a convenient translation of a collection of materials on the Feuerbachian criticism of Hegel see *Writings of the Young Marx on Philosophy and Society*, edited and translated by Loyd D. Easton and Kurt H. Guddat (Garden City, N.Y., 1967), 151–495.—Ed.]

[18] See the article by Bertrando Spaventa published by Gentile in *Giornale critico della filosofia italiana*.

[19] See Giovanni Gentile, *La riforma della dialettica hegeliana* (Palermo, 1923). Cf. also Gentile's remarks as editor of Spaventa's previously cited article.

[20] See "Una discussione fra filosofi amici," in B. Croce's *Conversazioni critiche*, Vol. 2 (Bari, 1924).

thought was constantly developing and is in a process of becoming, it insists on a contradiction. The process of becoming means that every truth put forward, even the truth of the process of becoming, will eventually deny and contradict itself. The only other alternative is that thought will somehow reach a conclusion and by so doing will seal the development of thought and thus deny the law of dialectical development and becoming which was promulgated as necessary and real. The point to be stressed here is that thought seals its own development and thus concludes the historical development. There is a reference to this in Kuno Fischer[21] but it was Marx who not only analyzed but tried to solve the problem. The solution which Marx offered was that the Hegelian Idea, instead of representing the conclusion of the historical development, was no more than a "moment" that in its turn would be denied by the other factor present,—the positive factor of the proletariat. In the words of Engels, the proletariat would attain the ideal of classical German philosophy or liberty, namely that the end of *finis* remains a speculative ideal and the practical result would be a reintegration of man who was not only intellectually estranged and alienated but had been reduced in his work to a monetary and an exchange pawn. Marx himself, however, does not escape the trap which he set for Hegel. The contradiction that there is an end to historical development is found in Marx, although with the latter it is on the historical and factual level rather than on the critical and ideological plane. Marx thought that man's refound paradise would be that socialist society where not only the dynamism of human law and history would come to a halt, but the State itself and the interior dynamism of its sects and parties, with their diverse interests, would be at a full stop. After fifty years of history, however, the collectivist society is still changing. Gentile tackles the problem from a different angle.[22] Later on, Bergson and Croce took up a similar position. Gentile affirmed the infinite historical development of thought. The basis for his view is itself a contradiction. Gentile maintained that the sign of a philosophical system's decadence was when the "active thought" became "past thought," and this decadence could only be overcome by a thought which was actual, unique, and immanent.

The fourth and last flaw in the Hegelian dialectic is that although Hegel tried to do justice to the "concrete" and "the particular," it is the "concrete" and "the particular" in their relation to the totality and not in their individual instances in time. In other words, what is real is ouside of time. This last criticism was also the criticism of F. H. Bradley who, sinning more against the Hegelian spirit than

---

[21] See F. Lombardi, *Ludwig Feuerbach* (Florence, 1935).
[22] See section 6, below.

the Hegelian letter, concluded that history was an "appearance," while "reality" was outside of time.[23]

Hegel is significant in that he inaugurated the problem and the study of a justification of "man's becoming" and the "becoming of history"; yet, just when he should have confronted the eternal to defend the particular in Time, just then there reappears "the unmoved truth of the Idea." Under the features of Hegel we discover the face of Augustine.[24]

4. The Ungrateful Sons of Hegel

Feuerbach wrote rather sententiously that "Hegel represents the Old Testament of the new philosophy" and that whereas Hegel had found philosophy in reason, it was now time to find reason in man.[25] Feuerbach's contention was that speculation had succeeded in making man stand on his head, and that now man must stand on his feet. Even Feuerbach, however, considered man somehow outside space and time, and it was Marx who planned to lead man back into society and history. The question now was, what was the best way for the individual man, who is always the member of a society and a citizen of his time, to transform his contemporary material world and to construct an elaborate world of thought whose very center would be found in Marx's world of progress, namely the economically and politically structured society in which man lived. The religious problem which troubled Feuerbach was seen by Marx as an ideological problem, and the latter wished to inject into the so-called "Absolutes of Value" some of the social and economical infrastructure of a particular society and culture.

Comte tackled the problem in France and invented the term "milieu," a term which had had its origins in astronomy before its adoption by biology. The problem discussed by Marx and by Comte is still relevant and deals with the relation between the individual and his milieu, between the thinker and his time, between moral values, truth, and society and between philosophy and sociology.

The same period saw the demythologizing of history. Hegel had conceived History with a capital H which described the creation and eschatological conclusion of the History of the World: it now became a story of the infinite number of human facts none of which could

---

[23] See F. H. Bradley, *Appearance and Reality* (London, 1902), 469; also Josiah Royce, *The World and the Individual* (New York, 1901), Series II, Lecture III.

[24] F. Lombardi, *Nascita del mondo moderno* (Florence, 1967), 161ff. (French translation, Paris, 1958; German translation, Cologne, 1961).

[25] See my volume on Feuerbach cited in footnote 17.

be foreseen and all of which depended on their being known. This inspired, despite the contrary interest in discovering the laws regulating the world, the opinion that history was an infinite and unforeseeable development and this led to the view that every fact was unique in its individuality. This was Bergson's opinion, and in holding it he was both the opposer and supporter of Positivism.

In Germany, discussion centered on the individual nature of the fact, the relation of truth and value to a definite "culture," the relativity of culture, and the demand for absolute standards or for a standard of "human validity" in truth and value. Both Dilthey and Max Weber were busy in this field as also was Simmel, who, however, pursued a line different from that of Meinecke and of Tröltsch.

The Ciceronian concept of *"cultura animi"* gave way in eithteenth-century France to "civilization" understood in the sense of "becoming civilized" or of the advance of enlightenment and primarily the advance of the material means and instruments of progress. In Britain, and later in the United States, these ideas were understood in "civilization" with particular emphasis on "civilized laws." The French "Culture" became *"Kultur"* in German, and in Burckhardt's book *Die Kultur der Renaissance in Italien* there was a second new word, namely Renaissance, which was unknown to Hegel, but which was used by Michelet.[26] *"Kultur"* was misunderstood by the Italian translator of the book and was translated as *civiltà*. *"Kultur"* is the sum total of the values of a definite epoch and society, and both term and what it represents are greatly respected in Germany. Weber brought the term to the United States, where it became the American and sociological "Culture" and signified the complete result of all the descriptions of a definite group or society. This last meaning today prevails in Europe and Italy, and thus the term has changed its meaning three times in three generations. The term "culture" has a wider significance in the general social and democratic sphere and illustrates the general approach of American Society and that society's thought.[27] With the increasing interest in "other" cultures, societies, and civilizations, the problem now becomes a problem of Cultural Anthropology, and the question of "Cultural Relativism"[28] reappears. The problem, then, is still the same: the relation of Truth to diverse truths and to history or, in other words, the problem of the relation between

---

[26] See my *Nascita del mondo moderno*, 51n. and 77.

[27] See F. Lombardi, "L'America o il mondo nuovo, in filosofia," originally an introduction to a book by several authors entitled *Il pensiero moderno in America* (Turin, 1955), now in my *Filosofia e Società* (Florence, 1967), 309ff.

[28] Cf. the article cited in note 11 above and also "Assolutezza vera e falsa della verità," Chapter One of my *Concetto e problemi della storia della filosofia* (Florence, 1969, 3d ed.), § 3.

individual and society, the absolute qualities of Truth and Value and their validity and relationship with the development of man. This is the problem inaugurated by Hegel.

Anglo-Saxon society saw the problem from its traditional empirical and democratic standpoint, maintaining that both language and politics showed that only individuals are real whereas the universal concept is not. The theologian Duns Scotus maintained this before Bacon and Dewey. This same tradition nursed Darwin and his disciples. Darwin maintained that time and change were not mental constructs as Hegel had said but were facts and so Darwin revived the Bergsonian concept of duration. In our contemporary understanding of change or time as duration or fact, all of us are first and foremost Darwinians and not Hegelians.

In the medical world, Freud has discovered beyond the observable phenomenon of man the power of the obscure and unconscious motivations of our earliest formation, in particular, from the prenatal world and from the world of sex. We are unknown to ourselves, and our ability to think is a very small luminous island which occasionally flashes through and emerges from the deep mist of our species.

The nineteenth century and even more the twentieth, are characterized by the rebellion against reason, and this rebellion takes the aspect of a reaction against Hegel. Metaphorically, it is the rebellion of the slaves against the goddess "Reason," which resulted in the goddess being replaced by her enemies, namely Naturalism, Determinism, Irrationalism, Existentialism, Freudianism. The trends of the twentieth century from Marxism and Positivism to the philosophies of Life and of the Unconscious, to those more or less Existential, represent in some way the rebellion of the ungrateful sons against their father Hegel. The rebellion consists of the various reflections of those whom Hegel fed and who revolted against their father and breadwinner by pursuing the spirit of the teaching in a manner not intended by the teacher.

5. A Historical Summary of More Recent Philosophical Thought

The writer is of the opinion that in a more general view of the history of philosophy, cultural history should be analyzed differently.[29]

---

[29] See "La 'filosofia occidentale' e il pensiero indiano," in my *Filosofia e società* (Florence, 1967), 369ff. Concerning this whole paragraph, see "La palude" in *Il senso della storia ed altri saggi* (Florence, 1965), 137. A French translation appeared in *Revue Philosophique* for 1966, 451–462.

The period to be considered is that from 1890 to the present day. One could begin on either side of the Rhine—either with Bergson or with Husserl. "Filmlike" is the term which characterizes this period. Impressionism in painting was the prelude to the fall from grace of the portrait and the emphatically anthropomorphical classical art of Greece and Rome.[30] "Filmlike" [*filmico*] is a simile for "continuum" and illustrates a reaction against the traditional empirical concept of the "fact." Bergson, for instance, fought against the "concept" and against "logical thought," which he claimed broke up the continuity of intuition. The new culture is characterized by the following terms which offer a further explanation of "filmlike": Duration, Continuity, Interrelation, and Historical Blocks [*blocco storico*]. In Italy, Gramsci borrowed the last term from Georges Sorel, who had taken it from Bergson, and it characterizes the Marxism of Gramsci and that of Geörg Lukács (in his *Class Conscience and Class Struggle*). The same metaphor is valid for the various forms of Existentialism and for the various developments in Marxism and in Catholic thought. An example of the last would be Bontadini's stand for the neoclassical against traditional metaphysics. Lastly, the new physics of Werner Heisenberg would appear to support the doctrine of continuity or of interrelation between subject and object and among subjects themselves.[31]

This was a reaction both against the laws and mechanical theories of Positivism and against the Subjective Idealism which attempted to justify the so-called consequences of Kantian philosophy, namely the denial of the thing-in-itself. The assumption now was that although an object must have a subject, the reverse is true as well, and that all subjects are interrelated. Bergson's use of the term *"d'emblée"* and Heidegger's use of *"mit da"* illustrate this assumption. This solution favored by all "concrete" philosophers would prevent the errors of positivism and idealism. It might also provide the easiest solution to the problem of the relation between individual and milieu. But this solution would dissolve the problem and not solve it. Merleau-Ponty and the later Sartre are exempt from this criticism. That this solution is facile is evident firstly because the transcendental originality of the subject often recalls the unexorcised spectre of solipsism, and secondly because it does not solve the old problem revived by Engels of the relation between the individual and history and the relation between economics, history, and society.[32]

[30] For this idea see my volume *Aforismi inattuali sull'arte* (Florence, 1965), especially 45ff.

[31] On Heisenberg, see my essay "De Homine" in *La posizione dell'uomo nell'universo* (Florence, 1963), 151ff.

[32] Cf. J. P. Sartre, *Critique de la raison dialectique* (Paris, 1960; Italian translation, Milan, 1965).

6. The Development of Thought after Hegel (Feuerbach
and Marx and the Young Hegelians of Naples; the Development
of Hegelian Thought in Italy)

The young Marx put the problem this way: According to Hegel,
historical development concluded with the Hegelian Idea, and that
for Hegel was synonymous with the Prussian State. How shall history
progress now? The answer has already been given. The same Idea
is brought down from its dizzy heights and somersaulted into its contrary, the proletariat. The net result will be the reintegration of man
and the realization of the ideal of classic German philosophy, namely
liberty. Such was the opinion of the young Marx. After 1870, the
publication of the *Gotha Program* brought a new turn in German
socialism and the meeting of Marx, Engels, and Lassalle inspired new
legislation on labor and the development of the industrial society. The
immediate revolutionary goals of the "Communes" in 1848 were left
behind when the education of the masses produced the proletarian
dictatorship which dealt the deathblow to history. With regard to
philosophy, Engels wrote and Marx accepted that all philosophy was
reduced to methodical dialectics and logic.[33] Engels and Marx had discussed whether Russia would be the leader of Western Society or
whether she would have to run the inevitable gauntlet of industrialism
whose only exit was capitalism and death. Lenin discovered, during
the First World War, the importance of the positions of power, and
he maintained against Marx, who was in this and other respects a
child of the nineteenth century, that politics precedes and conditions
economics and not vice versa. But this is the climate and principle
of the twentieth centruy in contrast to the historical character of the
nineteenth century. What characterizes the period from Bakunin to
Lenin is the belief in the parallel between tactical principles and Russian unity between thought and praxis. Yet for both Marx and Lenin
the revolution is and remains the eschatological conclusion and end
of the history of mankind or rather the conclusion of the prehistory
and the beginning of mankind.

In the 1840s, a group of young men in Naples received the recently published volumes of Hegel. These students were from Calabria,
and when they returned from Naples to their place of origin, the local
people nicknamed them "Begriffi" because of their frequent use of
the word *"Begriff."* In addition to the more orthodox representatives
of Hegelian thought, for example, Antonio Tari, who specialized in

---

[33] F. Engels, *Anti-Dühring* (Leipzig, 1878; trans. Burns, London, 1934).

Aesthetics, and Augusto Vera, there were other philosophers, for example, Bertrando Spaventa, Francesco de Sanctis, Salvatore Tommasi, Antonio Labriola of the "Left-wing" of Hegelianism. They emphasized the trend already present in Germany away from the theological problem of the Divine origin of the world and instead toward the understanding of the evolution of nations. It was this side of Hegelianism which the young de Sanctis favored, and while still an exile in Zürich, he proposed that the Idea should come down to the level of the individual and history. Bertrando Spaventa was the uncle of Benedetto Croce (on Croce's mother's side) and was also related to Gentile through Donato Jaia. Francesco de Sanctis returned to Naples in the 1860s after the unification of Italy and, as Minister of Education, was responsible for University reforms. Salvatore Tommasi was a physiologist who espoused Naturalism after 1870 and engineered the change of bias from Idealism to Positivism in the University of Naples. Antonio Labriola left Hegelianism to become a follower of Herbart; he then favored *Volkspsychologie* and finally embraced historical materialism and Marxism. Marxism as he saw it was not a historical scheme or design although—and this was more precisely formulated by his young friend and disciple, Benedetto Croce—it was a rule of historical interpretation. These thinkers left the closed boundaries of systematic philosophy and became literary critics, doctors, historians, and politicians; but they all preserved a regard for Philosophy comparable to that of the veil of the soul in Dante's *Picarda*.[34]

Benedetto Croce was familiar not only with the thought of Francesco de Sanctis and Antonio Labriola but with Positivism and the writings of Marx when he began to write around the turn of the century. He was familiar with Marx through his correspondence with Sorel and his daily contact with Labriola, and he also knew the thought of Bergson. It was, however, during the years 1903 and 1904 that Croce seriously studied Hegel. Croce's problem was similar to Bergson's, namely the problem of infinite historical development. It was also similar to that put by De Sanctis, who stressed the novelty and uniqueness of works of art and of history.[35] Where Bergson had recourse to intuition, Croce favored the view of a general concept of art which not only accounted for every work of art but in order to be *the* philosophical concept of art could not be totally exhausted in any single work of art. He also suggested a similar general concept of the State and maintained that every concept which endeavored to describe the

---

[34] On these thinkers see F. Lombardi, *La filosofia italiana negli ultimi cento anni* (Asti and Rome, 1958).

[35] For a re-evaluation of Croce's thought see F. Lombardi "Noterelle in tema di linguaggio," in *Aforismi inattuali sull'arte* (Florence, 1965).

infinite history of man could not be explained away by a particular or by the totality of particular historical facts.[36]

Croce thus advanced a new interpretation of the concept and task of philosophy and its relation to history. The philosopher was linked with the historian, the art critic, the psychologist, the sociologist, the moral philosopher, and the politician.

Giovanni Gentile, inspired by Donato Jaia and Bertrando Spaventa, was at odds with Croce from the beginning by emphasizing Dialectics.[37] Between 1909 and 1912,[38] he reaffirmed the principle of the subjectivity of reality which said that the unique Thought is the same as the unique Reality and that Thought is present each time the thinking subject says "I." Gentile attempted to reform the Hegelian Dialectic,[39] and his attempt was similar to Croce's at least in some respects. Instead of posing the *Logos* first, then out of it nature and finally phenomenology, Gentile, similarly to Croce, claimed that the Absolute is always actual; that is, reality is eternal and is so in the full complement of its connotations. Reality is not defective insofar as it cannot be said that any particular moment could be outside it. Understood thus, the *Logic* of Hegel becomes Phenomenology; the *logos* becomes actual thought; God, or the Absolute, becomes history. This process takes place, for Croce, according to the four modes of the Spirit: Art, Logic (or Historical Judgment), Economics, and Morals, and for Gentile in the thinking subject's saying "I."

So Croce and Gentile continued to be faithful to the traditional

---

[36] See Benedetto Croce's *Filosofia della pratica* (Bari, 1909; English translation, London, 1913). Notice the distinction drawn by Croce between philosophy of the practical and practical philosophy. See also what is said on the diversification of States and governments. Regarding the concept of art, read Croce's criticism of de Sanctis in "Un problema critico," in *Ariosto, Shakespeare e Corneille* (Bari, 1920), 5.

[37] See Gentile's review of Croce's *Aesthetics* in *Frammenti di estetica e di letteratura* (Lanciano, 1921), 136ff., 149ff., 162ff.; Gentile's "Intorno all'idealismo attuale," in *Saggi critici*, Vol. 2, (Florence, 1927) concerning "Una discussione fra filosofi amici" (cited above in footnote 20). On Gentile, see F. Lombardi's *La filosofia negli ultimi cento anni* (Asti and Rome, 1958), 409ff.

[38] See G. Gentile "Le forme assolute dello spirito" (1909) an appendix to *Il modernismo e i rapporti tra religione e filosofia* (Bari, 1909); "L'atto del pensare come atto puro," in *La riforma della dialletica hegeliana e altri scritti* (Messina, 1913). In the same book can be found "Il concetto della storia della filosofia," "Il circolo della filosofia e della storio della filosofia" (1909), "Il metodo dell'immanenza" (1913), "L'esperienza pura e la realtà storica" (1915). See also Gentile, *Teoria generale dello spirito come atto puro* (Pisa, 1916); English translation, *The Theory of Mind as Pure Act* (London, 1922), and *Sistema di logica come teoria del conoscere* (Pisa, 1909). [For a valuable introduction to the thought and writings of Giovanni Gentile, see Professor H. S. Harris's Introduction to his translation of Gentile's *Genesis and Structure of Society* (Urbana, Ill., 1960), 1–63.—Ed.]

[39] See his *La riforma della dialettica hegeliana e altri scritti* (Messina, 1913).

doctrine of a universal or rational a priori concept. Kant had "intuited" this as a transcendental concept and Hegel had made it an "absolute." It must be said in the latter's defense, however, that in accordance with the claimed consequences of Kantian philosophy and in agreement with the limits which Kant had given to the problem,[40] he did not merely deny the existence of the "thing in itself" but developed a dialectical system of thesis, antithesis, and synthesis which provided a more comprehensive idea of "truth." If one maintains this philosophy one ought to assume that there is nothing outside of thought. One should accordingly accept Gentile's view and say not only that the Universal Thought thinks in me—be it Reality or the Absolute Subject, but also that I, an empirical individual born of woman, am not reality. Were this so, philosophical truth would hold a monopoly over scientific truth, and both the process of history and the process from God, or the Absolute, would rest in the same sanctuary. The idealistic doctrine of Hegel which equated the Real with the rational further distinguished reality into existential and accidental and this led to its manipulation as a justification within the general context of history for the processes of Fascism. From 1925 onward, Croce, both as a man and as a politician, did everything to prevent this; but it was in vain.

Let us now cast a quick glance back at the immediate consequences of Hegel's thought. According to Feuerbach the legacy Hegel left was a Philosophy of Reason. Feuerbach himself intended to relate reason to man. Marx did not consider man as abstractly as Feuerbach, and his intention was to place man back in society and history. We have said that Positivism naturalized the sacramental Hegelian idea of history: this criticism was particularly relevant to Bergson, who stressed the individuality and uniqueness of historical fact and emphasized "intuition" in opposition to Croce's "concept." Naturally this aroused questions on "what the task of philosophy is" and "what is the nature of thought."[41] But Croce had behind him not only Positivism and Bergson but also de Sanctis and Labriola. Hegelianism, which is or could be presented as the problem of the divine creation of the world, was now reduced to the problem of man-made history. The spirit of Croce's philosophy was to understand the history we made, and that of Gentile's was the account of history contained in saying "I." Both ran counter to a "Philosophy of the Spirit" which, although it gave the impression of respecting the unique individuality of history and the unique individuality of the empirical subject, nevertheless sacrificed both event and subject to a Universal Subject or Universal Thought. Thus in Italy there were two streams of Hegelian philosophy. One form of Neo-Hegelianism donned a more worldly and human

---

[40] See F. Lombardi, *Kant vivo* (2d ed., Florence, 1968).
[41] See section 9 below.

apparel; the other exhibited the tendency to accept the Hegelian and metaphysical nature of Being, with its doctrine of the Spirit of the world, as the *logos* or immanent reason of historical development. This latter side can be compared to a theology turned upside down or to a justification of historical development in the theological sense.

It remains to be said that the philosopher attuned to "Being" begins to reflect on his own experience of the world and of the progress which such an experience promotes. In brief, Hegelianism and Neo-Hegelianism in Italy ultimately reached an extreme position which is best characterized by the phrase, "Hegelianism turned upside-down."

7. Annotations: Points of Tension in Italian Philosophy

One of the points of tension or of internal conflict in the philosophies examined above is the contrast between the emphasis laid on the idea of individuality and the importance assigned in fact to it. And perhaps greater tension arises in the phenomenon that the more the view of an infinite development of history was advanced, the more the "infinite categories" were favored as against the "fixed," the "a priori" categories of Aristotle, Kant, and ultimately Hegel. However, we find that all this infinite development (which, according to Gentile, should deny itself) had to remain contained and be a prisoner of the four categories of Croce or of the three of Gentile, and these categories were once again a priori and eternal.

The same thing is evident if we consider the two points of view on the task of philosophy. One view stresses the "pure" concept which relates to all the historical manifestations of this concept without being identified with any particular one. The other view holds the "pure" concept in a more defined way, either psychological-historical-political in nature or sociological and more generally metaphysical. This makes it impossible for the individual human sciences to know their scope and limits. And one last point: the distinction made by Croce between philosophy and theoretical thought in general on one side, and politics and practice on the other, were contradicted in fact by the undue intermingling of philosophy and politics in both Croce and Gentile. So it is just as easy to see the philosophy of Hegel in his reactionaries as it is in his most conservative disciples.

8. Two Possible Ways of Understanding What Thought Is: The Aristotelian and Traditional Doctrine of What Is Thought. Greek Thought and Hegelian Speculation. The Antinomies of Speculative European Thought

There are only two possible ways of understanding what "thought" is. The first is Aristotle's and can be sketched as follows.

Suppose that on one side of a table we have the particular empirical data of sensation and on the other side, in a box, what Aristotle calls the "categories." I shall select from the box, with the aid of a pair of pincers, the appropriate predicate term or category; and thus subject and object would be synthesized in the "judgment."

It is evident that one cannot assume that this universal corresponds to the data of sensation in the judgment, unless (and here Kant would be dogmatic) we presuppose that the thing-in-itself has what Aristotle calls "Form"; in other words, the universal which is welded with the "*synolon*" of the individual.

The historical gap between Aristotle and Kant was increased by the critical epistemology of the British empiricists and it was Kant's problem to find out in what way the universal propositions of science which were not analytical but a priori could be related to experience. The classic example which Kant offered was Galileo's law of the inclined plane,[42] and the interpretation offered was that the law of the inclined plane was true of experience because that same experience was subject to the transcendental principles of reason. This was a valid law of interpretation and valid for all men: it did not possess, however, "objective validity," as this would require a knowledge of things in themselves. Despite the overtures of Kant his Transcendental Idealism became the Absolute Idealism of Fichte and Schelling, and the reason for the transition was that it was not possible to have a direct knowledge of the "thing-in-itself," nor to infer it as the cause of sensation for the category "cause" only applied to the phenomenal world. So the thought of man (rather Thought and the Universal Idea in us) would not only intuit and categorize experience but would in a certain sense be guilty of dissimulation. The following citation from a Latin poet aptly describes Fichte's subject: *Fingit creditque* (It fictionalizes and it believes).

The consequences of the Aristotelian view are many. Here is one of them. Thought according to Aristotle represented "the thing in itself as it is in itself" and could not err in its representation. Otherwise the act of knowing could not guarantee truth.[43] Similarly, because thought was concordant with reality, it could understand the possibility of communication between subjects, and it can at least be argued that there is of necessity one thought, numerically speaking, which is the

[42] See F. Lombardi, *op. cit.*, and the essay on Galileo in *Galilei, Calvino, Rousseau* (Florence, 1969).

[43] Aristotle, *Metaphysics*, VI, § 4, 1.3. Cf. *De Interpretatione*, chap. I, 16a, 1.12. Error is not in sensation *qua* sensation, nor is it in the thought or in the concept *qua* thought or sensation, but only in so far as we join or disjoin them with things with which they ought not to be joined or disjoined. And across the centuries Croce. On Croce see F. Lombardi, *Il concetto della libertà* (3d ed., Florence, 1966), 36.

sole universal, rational a priori thought in the individual without being of the individual.

This is even more evident in Plato. Aristotle, despite his efforts to state a metaphysics of the individual was constrained to the universal by the premises of his Logic. In Plato, the soul which sees the immaterial and eternal ideas, is itself immaterial and eternal. The soul which sees the ideas (comparable later to the Active Intellect of Aristotle or of Averroes, the Pure Reason of Kant) is as much related to the body as thought is to experience and ultimately its origin is different from that of experience.[44]

A further consequence revolves around what is meant by liberty. Traditional speculation has understood liberty (ultimately still conceives it so even when it denies it) in the sense of seeing its Independence, its metaphysical nature, as a reality of the soul or spirit, of an immaterial nature over against the materialism of the world or the body. Halfway through the eighteenth century—to be precise, after Hegel—this mythical description of liberty was discarded, mythical in the sense that it disregarded instances of space and time, but only insofar as it was a question of reversing yet maintaining the terms of the problem, namely of the more or less material dependence of the spirit on the body.

The same comment holds good with regard to the contraposition (or mere autonomy) between empiricism and rationalism or later between idealism and positivism in this context: that the former addressed man and his own experiences, whereas the latter was concerned with the "a posteriori"—not unlike the situation where someone denies his belief in God, yet professes his belief in the Devil.

Likewise, the mythical concept of an Absolute Truth, which is a truth abstracted from time and from place, is denied and is hurled down from its pedestal. This took place immediately after Hegel and obtains today. With the death of Absolute Truth, Truth itself died; in its place came the ill-defined concept of "Ideology" (Marx) or the affirmation that man recites terms and concepts and is a *homo faber* and is not a *homo teoreticus* (Dewey). Science itself does not seek grand theoreticians but practically minded men. It is permissible for anyone to doubt whether that is said merely because the concept of a mythical truth fixed once and for all and dogmatically "objective" is confused with that truth which man brings about as a result of laborious constructs through the hundreds and thousands of years of his own history—the ever-increasing coherent and well-founded concept of what he thinks of the world.

As long as one clings to the traditional concept of thought, one

[44] This is Kant's expression. Compare the passages as indicated in the commentary to Kant in F. Lombardi, *Kant vivo* (Florence, 1968).

cannot put forward the progressive development of science. The philosopher, according to Aristotle, following a deductive and a priori procedure, is more capable of understanding the essence of the world than it would be possible by attempting a quantitative and inductive study which yields no valid proposition to which he can commit himself—on the basis of the old a posteriori—in experience. Likewise, the modern idealist does not leave any possibility of true knowledge to the scientist, for on his view no reality subsists about which we ought to advance such knowledge—of which, by hypothesis, we are ignorant.

But as long as the traditional concept of what thought is prevails, it is no longer possible, not even in general, to attempt a history of thought understood as a history of the entire cultural world of man. The thought about which Aristotle talks here is adamantine in its truth and, like a diamond, its truth neither changes nor corrupts even when it is thrown into the mud of the human current. Should it change in part or whole it would not be thought but perhaps an opinion or a new thought.[45] An attempt was made by Hegel to introduce, or rather to include in this same unfalsifiable thought, the seed of becoming and thus of progress. Once again we run into the same difficulty as we had above with the Hegelian concept of "Dialectic." And another point comes to the fore, namely that Hegel works with the ancient doctrine of the concept as a universal rational a priori thought which would per se be other and diverse from experience. It does not matter that Hegel asserts here that his is not the subjective thought of Kant or Fichte only because he has swallowed up so much of the world by erecting a universal Idea. It is a fact that he has devoured the whole world just as a boa constrictor devours a donkey, and the progress of the victim through the serpent's body is a gradual one. Indeed, the mainspring or the force of the Idea, the law of its becoming, is once again "the concept" of the "Begriffi." This mainspring is still of a logical nature or a dialectical logistic nature which was not enough to satisfy the physiologist Salvatore Tommasi when he wished to give an account of his discipline by it.[46]

Taking up a point which we have just mentioned, namely a point on the antinomy existing between empiricism and rationalism and on the question of Science, should we not reduce it more simply and perhaps simplistically to an operational question? It is thus not a question of delimiting and circumscribing the ambit and the territory of the scientist, which is to stick to the facts, but rather of what he can experiment with and define. Hence if the same scientist wishes to render an account of what he does and of the reasons or even of the

[45] This is still, according to Croce, a "pseudo-concept."
[46] Salvatore Tommasi, *Il naturalismo moderno* (Bari, 1913). On him see F. Lombardi *La filosofia italiana negli ultimi cento anni* (Asti and Rome, 1958).

more profound motives which guide him in his endeavor and wishes to construct a concept or model of the state of things, then one just cannot get away with a half man (*dimidiatus vir*). For this same man who researches, reconstructs, and thinks is still a unique individual and a unique thinker, whether he concentrate on philosophy or his own specialty which may inspire him to the periphery of our world of experience. But such experience is always the center of a circumference and implies a concept of his own world, and thus Positive Knowledge, Historical Knowledge, or Scientific Knowledge is advanced.[47]

9. The Overthrow of the Understanding of What Thinking Is

We shall return now to the image we gave above of Aristotle's procedure, which was that of putting on one side the data of experience and on the other side choosing by means of pincers from the box containing the twelve categories. Our purpose will be to see what account better corresponds with our synthesis or the judgment. (We must note that in regard to the categories, whether they be of Aristotle, Kant, or Hegel, they are always a priori, fixed once and for all, and always valid.)[48]

And our purpose will be to see the manner of our speaking in this area and what goes on when I think, and to find a terminology which best fits the work in hand; let it be known that I have already chosen it. This is rather like the Saint who was commanded by the Prior of the monastery not to perform too many miracles and to that end was requested by the Prior always to ask permission to perform a miracle. The Saint, seeing a poor fellow falling from a second story window exclaimed: "Hold it, until I get permission."

To formulate the most simple word requires choosing a genus or concept from an infinite number of not yet definite ones, which I weave, so to say, into the thread of my discourse. Thus thinking, which in effect is my thought in act, is the bridge linking the concept to the word.

Let us say that this is a bridge, and *sui generis* like a vaulted archway, resting on one side on the word which I have now given and which is defined in my speaking it, and which projects itself in the direction of the term I am about to speak, like the subject-predicate relation. On the other side this bridge rests on a term or a base which is not explicitly there and which I do not take up with the pincers. (Recall the image we attributed to Aristotle.) Yet I move to grasp it or, if you wish, to evoke it, insofar as I pronounce it and formulate it.

[47] See the following treatment in section 9.
[48] See section 7 above.

To put it another way, I formulate the most simple of words insofar as my thought and thinking (or the "bridge" which we mentioned above) advances as if *per ignes* in a halo of infinite or as yet indefinite possibilities which lie within every word I formulate and pronounce.

My pronouncing the word I choose indicates the context of the choice which I have just described as a bridge. The context is manifold; the choice is unique. "Mediation" is the relation of the process of thinking in act between the given word (O) and the word which I am about to utter (S).[49] And we use the term "mediated" for the relation or the process of reflection undergone by the subject recollecting himself (A), his act of bridging the gap between subject (O) and predicate (S), and being conscious of this recollection (C). The fact that recollection or what I call the "mediated" is possible gives the word I am going to say a value because it "films" my process of building a bridge from one word to another. The word I speak and the proposition I formulate are true if and only if there is a choice and I choose this actual world in preference to the other alternative. (According to the syllogistic scheme, A is either A or is non-A,[50] but it is not the case that A is not A; therefore, A is A, or more succinctly, "It is the case that A is A insofar as it is not the case that A is not A".) Insofar as the whole sphere of my potential total experience turns and reflects on itself, that is its own convalidation. Ultimately the word that I utter and the proposition I formulate illustrate my compatibility with the totality of my experience.[51]

This signifies that every reflection manifests not only our past experience but also the "possible" and therefore the entire system of our intellectual and moral thought. He alone can affirm that he has seen a flying donkey whose world allows the possibility of a flying donkey. If this were not the case a new fact or new experience would be subject to rusty and old-fashioned criteria of validity. A fact is what we always maintain as fact until the contrary is proved, and it therefore denotes at the very least a certain world of values. The gods of Olympus have not crumbled because the mountain peak has been captured by man, but because the human and spiritual conscience of man has been elevated and is no longer prepared to recognize itself in them.

If this is true, it is also true that Galileo did not find confirmation of the Law of the Inclined Plane in experience, according to Kant's interpretation. The net of concepts adequately represent the facts, and

---

[49] Cf. the diagram at the end of the present section.
[50] See what Gentile says in *Sistema di logica* on judgments and syllogisms.
[51] Cf. what Kant has to say on the real as that which is congruent with the totality of experience.

the facts are so as they are represented. The law formulates and predicts as it builds a bridge and intertwines new relations (*intelligit*) with hithertofore unrelated experience, or else it gathers together and forms an alliance with that experience (*cum-capit*—it comprehends) and at some time formulates and relates to a "new experience," a word, a formula, a law. And this is the concept.[52]

Every word, insofar as it is a genus or per se general term, covers an area of experience in a term which we call the concept. The *cum-capio* is the gathering together, and consequent on this is the comprehension or formation of the concept. Language is accordingly symbolical. The process and its symbolism are valid for the simple terms and concepts with which a child describes his world, and for the more sophisticated and complex expressions through which an adult pursues the process of more coherently and more closely uniting himself with the world of his experience.

Each word and concept is at the center of experience, and it is the center and its circumference which represent the total experience of the subject. The same parallel is valid for the different levels of immediate experience and the levels of language which express them.[53] The distinction between ordinary language and scientific language is a distinction in degree of our thought's uniting with experience. The same analogy holds for the distinction between positive scientific thinking and philosophical thinking. The first turns toward the periphery of our experience, while the second returns toward the center. Both indicate the interior coherence of thought. The model we have proposed shows that both scentific thought and philosophical reflection have the same center and the same periphery and that the former does not lack interiority or internal criticism nor the latter knowledge of the world or experience. The perspicacity and sagacity of scientist and philosopher will allow both to stress the area relevant to their research.

The following model illustrates the point:

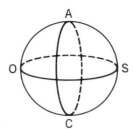

---

[52] See my essay on Galileo as cited above in note 42.
[53] See the treatment in section 10 to follow.

What we have said, above, illustrates that I am the actual individual person who I am. I am a witness to myself in my acts, and this "I" is always the word in a language, the member of a group, and the citizen of a society. Thus I am a social animal. The situation is not such that there is the private individual and alongside or apart from him is society or the public. Just as language is interior to and consubstantial with the word, so the "public"—and that is why we can say "we"—is interior to and more interior to us than we are to ourselves.[54]

10. Continuation of the Greek and Traditional Concept of "Intelligence"

We shall briefly refer to the model of thought given above. In selecting or formulating the word I am going to say, I think, as it were, within the thought which I advance. I do not "know," however, either the word which I have given or the "abstract" which I am going to say. In other words I know what we have called, above, the very content of my thought, what we know when we are thinking of it or when we are conscious of it or consciousness itself (C). It is important at this point to repeat that I do not "know" the very process of thought, that is, I do not "know" whether I stand attentively and vigilantly within my thought, more or less exercising self-control over it. What I do is I think.

Hence it is obvious that the model presented, besides describing discursive thought or speech, clarifies what happens whilst and as long as I talk. It can therefore throw some light on the nature of the intelligent activity of the individual at a more or less conscious level; it will illuminate what is the basis of such an activity, the basic activity of the organism and of life.

In pronouncing the most simple word I am the performer and I am aware of all the processes of brain and body, from those which move the lips and the tongue to those through which I breathe and which cause my heart to beat. When I become too emotional, my heart leaps to my throat, and impairs my ability to breathe and speak. In order to pronounce a word, on the other hand, and even whilst pronouncing it, I do not first think of the word and then take the wheel of discourse. I may, of course, first reflect with myself and then decide that I talk. These are but two of the processes which I

[54] See F. Lombardi "Noterelle in tema di linguaggio" in *Aforismi inattuali sull'arte* (Florence, 1965), where a distinction is drawn between the present and Saussure's models.

realize in myself in thinking, and they have their parallels in the brain and organism because it is my whole person-unity who thinks. If thinking is a free act (which it is if it has the value it has[55]), it is to be noted that I do not have an adequate comprehension, far less a scientific knowledge, of the acts of my brain. It is only of late that studies of brain-processes have been possible, and the final scientific word on what happens when I think has not yet been given.

This description of the Greek concept of "intelligence" is a description of a discursive or logical intelligence which expresses itself in words. We have seen this Greek concept too often, and perhaps the Greek thinkers are themselves responsible for its interpretation as an a priori rational universal which accompanied the word without identifying itself with the act by which it was mentally formed.

The potential of this discursive or logical intelligence is perhaps a more profound intelligence which stimulates my speaking (and makes me realize myself in my brain-processes and in my whole organism) and which lies within the critical dialectics of my intellectual activity or of that more or less intentional and conscious self-movement which does not necessitate my speaking out or my speaking to myself when it moves me. Once again, this time from the psychological standpoint, I am ignorant of what goes on.

Generally speaking, the first difficulty we meet is terminological. The fixed language of Greek speculative thought has an anthropomorphic ring, especially when we consider the words "understanding," "intelligence," etc., and we ourselves have fallen prey to this anthropomorphism when we have talked of the understanding of nature, of life, of things, etc. *Lacrimae Rerum!*

The fundamental difficulty is the relation between the mechanical world and "life." Analogically the same difficulty occurs when we try to distinguish vegetative life from animal life and both from human life.

11. The Concept of Liberty. The State and the Individual. The Subjects and the Subject of History

We ought not to hedge around what is generally called "Liberty." The problem once again is the difference between the purely mechanical world and the world of life, between vegetative life and animal life, and finally between "human liberty" and "moral liberty."[56]

This problem was tackled by Bergson. He regarded the brain as

---

[55] See section 9, above.

[56] See F. Lombardi, *Il concetto della libertà* (Florence, 1966), 145ff.

a "telephone office," but maintained that human liberty in the strict sense only occurred when there was an increase in the number of mental convolutions. The number of convolutions defined liberty, and since the monkey did not have that definite number, the monkey did not possess liberty. Two questions now arise: First, How does this transition take place? Second, Can one legitimately conceive "liberty" rooted in necessity? It may be said that those who favor determinism and extend its control to our "inner liberty" are the victims of an out-of-date terminology. But this is too facile a solution and establishes nothing. What would have to be established would be the validity of concepts like "liberty in crisis," "structured liberty," and "responsible liberty."[57] We may say at this point that liberty is the "*ratio essendi*" of Truth.

We have maintained the view that saying a simple word involves my whole corporeal and mental activity. When I utter a valid word, this indicates my control over all the forces of my world, spiritual and physical. I do not succeed in formulating a "valid word" when I am spiritually distracted in sorrow or when the physical forces of my world so interact on my body that I cannot control the unity which is "me." We may call this Liberty which enables me to recollect and control myself in acting intelligently and as a unity, Responsible Liberty, or Liberty which has a job to do. It is "Structured Liberty" because it is the power to act of an individual unit of body and soul who has matured and has grown through education and through the favorable generation-selections. It is "Liberty in crisis,"[58] as it delivers a sentence and makes a decision.

This concept of "Liberty" shows that we are not isolated individuals and indicates that we ought not to try and understand the social aspect by allowing the totality to override the individual, or by allowing the latter to suffer, as Hegel does, at the hands of history, or as Durkheim does by overemphasizing Society, nor should we drown individuality in the confusion of the so-called concrete philosophy.

On the contrary, I succeed in acting insofar as I am aware of the world situation which I more or less accept or which I intend to change. I change it only when I succeed in seeing things as they are, that is, when I accept the relation between my original and still abstract "intention" and "the concrete force of things." Our action with the concrete world is always a compromise. This is as true of Alexander cutting the Gordian Knot with his sword as it is of Punch, who thinks he has taken his revenge when he hurls insults at those

---

[57] See F. Lombardi, "La morale e la storia" in *op. cit.*

[58] Compare what has been said previously about choice and see my *Problemi della libertà* (Florence, 1966), 15ff.

who have beaten him. In every case we make ourselves responsible for a world which we approve of insofar as we accept it or at least insofar as (perhaps which a mental reservation about our actions tomorrow) we do not act toward its immediate destruction.

12. Hegel and Ourselves. The Dialectical and Dialectics. The Task of the Philosopher, the Psychologist, the Historian, the Scientist, the Politician. Historicity and Non-Historicity. The Human Rationale of History

The view which we have proposed above may be described as a reflective criticism or dialectic of life, of the conscious activity of man and of his thought. The concept of dialectic is partly Hegelian and partly anti-Hegelian.

Hegel's view of dialectic consists in a rational assessment of the interior spirituality of man's acting and not only of man's thinking. By so doing, Hegel wished, and I think justly, that man would realize one state of himself, (thought or action) as a value by the subject contrapositing something as a nonvalue.

Our view or the model we proposed is dialectical, yet it is possible to show—and this has already been done in part—that it is not an Hegelian dialectic.[59]

Traditionally since Hegel, dialectic has meant the instituting of a discourse, generally of an historical or psychological-political-sociological nature, characterized by opposing theses dialectically to provide a synthesis. This method could be used to oppose theses of a specifically philosophical character or to oppose theses of various schools of philosophy so that a synthesis and eventually a synthesis of the whole history of philosophy could be attained and thus this method would produce a history of unique truth.[60] This method could also be used in other fields of human endeavor, for example, literature. Another terrain which this method could explore would be a dialectic of the formal activities of the human spirit whereby a "logistical"

---

[59] Note the first of the criticisms levelled against the Hegelian dialectic and see also what has been said on choice and against the Aristotelian model of the act of thinking. When I utter a word I thereby follow the dialectic of thought. On the other hand, according to the Aristotelian model assumed in the Hegelian dialectic, it cannot be understood how the predicate could at the same time be posed and taken away. Cf. F. Lombardi, *Il mondo degli uomini* (Florence, 1967), II, 51ff., and *Dopo lo storicismo* (Asti and Rome, 1955), 315ff.

[60] G. Gentile "Il concetto della storia della filosofia" and "Il circolo della filosofia e della storia della filosofia," in *La riforma della dialettica hegeliana* (Messina, 1913).

synthesis of the truth could be reached. The same methodology could be applied to show the progress of human history and society by offering a synthesis of the various theories which have opposed each other in the story of man and his world.

The above type of discourse is undoubtedly possible and valid on the historical as well as the psychological level, provided, of course, that it is offered as a "working hypothesis" and not as a fixed scheme of interpretation. This is a confirmation of the distinction made between the discourse and concept of the philosopher and that proper to the psychologist, the historian, the scientist, the politician, and so on.[61]

The above remark, however, must be seen in reference to the Hegelian concept of liberty, which, as we have explained previously, was promulgated in heaven accompanied by a celestial fanfare worthy of a universal judgment, and later was reduced to an earthly status purporting to rationalize human nature and the individual. Hegel conceived liberty to be identical with the Necessity of a rational nature. For this reason he could say that the real is rational and the rational is real. That is why the Hegelian concept said too much and yet too little.

The same criticism may be made against Hegel's idea of the effectiveness of the will and our responsibility in the world. His *"coacti tamen voluerunt"* would sanction slavery on the plea that the slave accepts and respects the will of his master.[62]

If we extend the interpretation of Hegel to the reinterpretation of those who followed him and apply it to the latter's account of historical processes, which reduced the world to a man-made world, then the Author of history is not even an upside-down God, but universal thought. Even though I make a thousand mistakes every day, yet I cannot waive aside my responsibility to the world, which, as far as I am concerned, I create insofar as I accept it, or at least I do not endeavor to bring it to its end.

So presented, it is possible to accept or reject Hegel's discourse on the rationality of history. He could talk of a Reason which would display itself across history, and the individual would be the dupe of Reason's astuteness.

Humanity continually gives reasons for its progress in history. Humanity's superiority to the animal world is not the favor of a divine transcendence or immanence which guides it, but is the result of man's

---

[61] I have insisted on this in all my writings. See for instance *Il mondo degli uomini* (1st ed., Florence, 1935), II, 25f.

[62] Cf. the relevant passages from Hegel as mentioned in my *La libertà del volere e l'individuo* (Milan, 1941).

ability to acknowledge what is good. Good in this context does not mean the absolute good but the better good in a given situation, the diagonal good which crosses various interests and possible values in a particular epoch and in a particular society.[63]

For the same reason there is not a unique subject of history, nor a universal thought or reason which talks univocally through all and on behalf of all: everyone talks and forms concepts as an individual of a particular group, of a particular culture, and as a citizen of his time, and he must renew his time and set it in progress, and this he achieves by reunderstanding his world, and by reformulating it in a language of individual words. Thus the truth which each one of us formulates is potentially universal and tends to confront the truth put forward by others and make itself in fact and in principle universal. Copernicus formulated his words in his time and coined a motto which was inscribed at the beginning of his book: "This book will wait for its reader." Everyone who is humble and proud of his thought can make this motto his own.

Humanity, which has gone through the stone, the bronze, and the iron ages, and which has been busy for the last fifty years in making an assessment of its civil order and of civilization in general, can wait, and, if civil living is given time, then, despite the unhappy lot of some individuals, humanity will continue to advance, and the historical progress of the world is assured.[64] This history is the history of great men, the history of small men, the history of the forgotten and the unknown multitudes, all of whom have contributed to the construction of this edifice of human civilization.

13. Our Relation with Hegel from the Stand-point of Post-Hegelian Social and Political Development[65]

Our feelings toward Hegel are mixed not only from the philosophical point of view but also from our status as men in the world. Philosophical problems and their solutions are only one side of the prism which symbolizes the human problems of an epoch, and the philosopher must not forget his role as a man of this world.[66]

Hegel adopted the enlightened eighteenth century's idea of progress, which he called Reason, and he gave to thought and to history a dialectical character. Marx adopted the messianic and apocalyptic

---

[63] Cf. "La morale e la storia," § 11 in *Il concetto della libertà* (Florence, 1966).
[64] Cf. the passage in Vico to which Croce often comes back. On Vico, see F. Lombardi "L'uomo G. B. Vico" in *De Homine*, Vol. 28.
[65] See section 1, above.
[66] See F. Lombardi, *La posizione dell'uomo nell'universo* (Florence, 1963).

mantle of his race, and, linking Hegel with Saint-Simon, threw it with placating indulgence toward the sea of a reintegrated and redeemed humanity. The same "motif" is found in the three *'étages'* of Comte. The program of Gotha continued the movement at a trotting pace which gradually accelerated to a full gallop when proletariat rule heralded the revolution.

The beginning of this century showed a change. There were doubts about the optimism which surrounded the evolutionary and rational progress of the nineteenth century. There was the rise of individualism; there was the uprising of Activism or the appearance of irrational currents which persevered in Europe till the dawn of World War I.

Lenin differed from Marx in this respect that the latter believed that Economics conditioned Politics whereas the former believed the opposite. Lenin learned well the importance of the balance of power and of the control of power, and under his tutelage and sway the revolution passed from the barricades of city squares to the discipline and uniformity of an organized party. It was now a question of the militia and the masses. It is interesting to note that the term "masses" is found only in one context in the nineteenth century, namely in a book written around the time of Marx's youth entitled *Die Freien.* Thanks to Bakunin, who favored democratic centralization, party politics revived, and the slogan was "Russian more than red," and this replaced the so-called Strategy of History which was the legacy of Marx and of the whole nineteenth century.

The Second International finished, theoretically, with the first World War, and its death resulted from the fact that the war did not divide the socialist movements. Socialism became National Socialism between the wars, and this period was characterized by economic and labor problems which in Germany and in Italy found their solution in the war.

The Spanish Civil War characterized a new period. Among the nations, the new frontier was not vertical but horizontal, forming two countries in every nation. Another new factor was the appearance of a new feeling for the individual and of his right to life and tolerance.

The economic theory of Keynes signaled the new, free, and programmed society of tomorrow. The old-fashioned socialism of Marx, which was the solution offered by the nineteenth century, derived its strength from the overproduction of "free enterprise" and the resultant social, economic ills and unemployment. Marx himself maintained that the progressive reduction in salaries would result in money ending up in the hands of the few: all these ills could only be avoided by nationalizing industries and communications. The new political-economic theory seemed to reduce the chances of financial crises and gave the State the chance to intervene more subtly in the national economy by planning economic growth and by nationalizing the country's great industries. Democratic collectivity, industrial participation, the development of a socialism not intent on war, all these seemed to indicate that basically every economy should be a market economy defined by consumer demands. As the ills of both economies become apparent and demand new solutions, so, despite the atmosphere of the "iron curtain" and the "cold war"—an atmosphere which has characterized much of the international scene—it seems certain that despite their differences in depth, both economies will converge rather than diverge toward the new society of tomorrow.

The more society progresses, the more the premises, both on a national and on an international scale of nineteenth-century socialism and of Marx, have to be modified.

The more capitalism developed, the more society, already characterized as *"Lumpenproletariat"* and in the hands of capitalistic contractors, became varied and divided. Now there are the varied classes of technicians, aristocrats, proletarians (condemned by Lenin), managers, captains of industry, the anonymous. Capital is divided among the great mass of consumers and becomes more and more distantiated from effective and exclusive management direction. In the socialist societies problems arise for which Marx provided no solutions either because these problems did not then exist, or they were not foreseen, or they stemmed from problems which were adjourned for future reference. The following are typical examples:

The conflicts between sectorial and group interests, between town and country; between industry and a more or less specialized and industrialized Agriculture; between vested and consumer interests; between the "new politicians" and the technologists and industrial directors; and between the new group with power and the great mass who aspire to power and more luxury by their own efforts. Politics also undergoes change in evolving industrial society, and the development of mass communication media has transformed state and government. For different reasons, but in both types of society, the politician must become more technical and professional and cannot be compared to the nineteenth-century politician who could still be in the "Sundays of Life" and at intervals in his professional duty the *"vir probus dicendi peritus"* according to the Ciceronian tradition. Political parties tend to become more and more organized and in the grip of the party propaganda machine. They become more and more distinct from the nineteenth-century politician and from the system itself whether it be socialism, liberalism, etc. The programs of individual members of different parties can be the same, and the proof of this is that it is no longer possible to divide by a vertical line the programs of the Democrats and the Republicans in America, the Labour and Conservative parties in Britain, the Social Democrats and the Christian Democrats in Germany, etc.

This does not mean that there is no difference between the two parties. The new parties tend to supplant the multiplicity and diversity of the parties of the old stamp which today regard themselves as "Parties of Opinion" opposed to the new "Parties of the Mass." The difference lies in their defense of one or other part of society, of those who possess more, of those who possess too much, and of those who possess nothing or who possess too little and desire to possess more; and there are also differences in how they go about executing their policy: some are for conservatism, others for change, others for liberty, and others for justice; and there are the realists and the utopians.

In all instances politics today is different from nineteenth-century politics. The contemporary sort does not associate too much with ideology and system and concentrates on solving the actual political and economic problems of society; to do this it has far more need of the positive sciences than it has of philosophy.[67] Politics today has given itself to the masses and must therefore seek the *slogans* which will mass-communicate and invent new "Hidden Persuaders" whose guile is the art of technical propaganda. The old problems of political representation, of the relation between politics and economics, between political or dialectical representation of the parties and corporative representation, between formal liberty and jurisdiction, between the state and society, or between legal government and real society,—problems which date not only from the time of Rousseau, for example, the general will and the will of the people—and problems which date not only from Hegel, who saw them in nostalgic reference to the German or National State, as also did Fichte and the "nostalgics" of every age, but also problems from the time of Tocqueville and Burckhardt, from the well-founded discussions of the guilds or the Fabian Society, from the trade unions of France and Italy and the workshop counsels of Gramsci and Gobetti. These problems continue to arise in new situations and with a new urgency even if the solutions which from time to time are shown in perspective (for example, the recent student movement and its request for representation in assembly deliberations) do not manifest much political fantasy and an adequate knowledge of the historical precedents of the problem and the actual difficulty—or incongruence—of the proposed "solutions."

Now, after the Second World War and within the last ten years, we have three worlds: the industrially developed countries of the American-European world; the industrialized countries of Russian and

[67] Cf. F. Lombardi, "La filosofia e le scienze morali," in *Filosofia e società* (Florence, 1967), 29ff.

Eastern Europe; and the industrially underdeveloped countries of the third world, which the China of Mao seeks to lead. The relationship between the second world and the third world is perhaps best seen in the relation between the second world, which Lenin created, and the third world of Mao. Lenin overthrew the nineteenth-century's relation between economics (history) and politics (the intervention of the individual). Mao promoted the revolutionary transition from city to country, promoted the "army" as protagonists for the revolution which carried "the good news," and represents a fundamentally different psychological structure—the Orient. The East has no traditional or historical link with the European city-state or borough; but it has a link with the grass roots, for example, in China, the community of a Chinese village. The village has no "citizens," but the individual is a member of and a participant in the community, with all the advantages and disadvantages which go with such a situation. He is an individual (in this sense he is essentially private and not political), but is at the same time more of a group animal. It is this latter fact which illustrates the lack of *Discordia Concors* or "Party Dialectics" in Oriental political life. This lack of "citizenship," this lack of "dialectics" is also found in Eastern Europe; and wherever it is found, there would appear to be a convergence in the person's self of "the little father complex" of politics, of religion, and of truth and philosophy.

14. The New Reality and the Ethos of the Society of Tomorrow

The growth in human population, in methods of transportation, the facility of means of communication, the development everywhere of industrial societies—all these contribute to "the open society" and the crises which dog the traditional values of an individual nation.

It is perhaps worthwhile to compare the traditional values of the Occident and the Orient. Its cradle in Greece inspired the former to be a dynamic society, to favor activity and development; through the stages of the city-states and their burgher classes, through the period of Enlightenment and the French Revolution, Western society won its way to the new industrial society and the dream of Becoming of Age or of progress. With the development of the American consumer society, it continues to create new markets, new values, new fashions, from day to day and from month to month. The Orient, on the other hand, is characterized, as Cattaneo has said, by an immovable and withdrawn society inspired by contemplation rather than action Eternity rather than Time. Pasternak—in contrast to the nineteenth-century myth of Faust and the mirage of a redeemed humanity for whom the dying Faust pleaded that the play stop—indicates the projection of enduring value of the star-studded sky, which he compares to the eyes of the wounded Andrew in Tolstoy's *War and Peace*, above and beyond the phenomena of politics and part of the same history of mankind.

The *Ethos* of our times is much more varied and complex than that envisaged by the nineteenth-century Hegel, for whom history's development had a unique sense. The age of history which is the nineteenth century whose second half saw social values appear is now the age of humanity, in which the values of East and West, of contemplation and action, are intermingled. Contemporary society is fraught with the struggle between active involvement through society and the independence of the individual, the struggle between time and eternity. There are always "mores," and the players change positions constantly; yet it would appear true that the individual becomes more independent and private when he becomes related beyond the confines of society and "closed" national cultures with the whole of humanity.

The barriers between nations have been removed and the closed national cultures which gave the individual the security of traditional values have become open. Ideological conformance will restore neither security nor value. It is in opening himself up to the whole of humanity that the contemporary person will find himself and so his security and value.

This new outlook, which embraces humanity as a whole, will, we hope, re-emphasize the spiritual autonomy and critical independence of the individual. At the same time the conquest of the country by the city, the conquest of distance by speed, will encourage our dominion over space, and will therefore increase our chances of privacy and solitude, both of which are at a premium in the grotesquely built industrial towns of today. Man is more likely to be an individual among three thousand and more millions of individuals. There can no longer be an individual or a nation, as Hegel thought, who would be able to carry the Idea or represent the Spirit of the World more or less on horseback. The earth has been photographed from the moon and is seen in her true light as perhaps the only one of the millions of stars and planets which is inhabited. Remembering what we have said about the "cuspidal" society of the Middle Ages, with its absolute values in truth and morality and religion, we may say that the people of tomorrow will gradually acquire an awareness of the infinite smallness and grandeur of man—who constantly through history tries to reconquer or reconstruct values—and will seek the permanence of the elementary and fundamental values of man, as these are the deepest currents which course the sea of humanity, the sea whose surface ripples with the opinions and actions of individuals.

A SELECT BIBLIOGRAPHY*

Robert L. Perkins
with
Warren E. Steinkraus

I. Hegel's Own Publications

Collected Works

1832–1845, *Werke*, 18 vols. edited by a group of his former students including P. Marheineke, J. Schulze, L. Henning, E.

* The selections in this listing that are about Hegel, besides containing some important older citations, include materials that are typical and representative of recent scholarship in several countries. There are many additional articles, for example, in the *Hegel-Studien* and *Hegel-Archiv*, that are not listed herein. For an illuminating clarification of the editions and availability of Hegel's works, the reader is referred to Walter Kaufmann's *Hegel* (1965), 469–478.

The beginning student will find items under the heading "Some General Studies" most useful. An exhaustive bibliography of writings about Hegel, which presently contains 5000 items, is in preparation under the direction of Professor Joseph Flay of Pennsylvania State University. It will contain a computerized index of authors and subjects arranged by language and date.

Gans, H. Hotho, L. Michelet, and F. Förster (Berlin). Volumes I–VIII contain the writings published by Hegel during his lifetime. The remainder are based on students' lecture notes.

1927–1930, *Sämtliche Werke, Jubiläumsausgabe,* 20 vols. ed., Hermann Glockner. This is a republication of the foregoing with slight modifications. The 1935 and later editions include a *Hegel-Lexikon.* It has been reprinted as recently as 1964. Widely available.

1911–   , *Sämtliche Werke, Kritische Ausgabe.* The first fifteen volumes were edited by Georg Lasson and after his death in 1932, the work was continued by Johannes Hoffmeister, who added three more volumes by 1939. He has been succeeded by various editors. This edition is still in process (Leipzig and Hamburg). It contains four volumes of letters in *Briefe von und an Hegel.* Several volumes such as the *Encyclopedia* and *Phenomenology* have appeared separately in more exact critical editions.

A new multivolume critical edition of the works is underway and will be published by Felix Meiner Verlag of Hamburg.

Other Volumes

Hoffmeister, Johannes, ed., *Dokumente zu Hegels Entwicklung,* Stuttgart, 1936.

Nohl, Hermann, ed., *Hegels Theologische Jugendschriften,* Tübingen, 1907.

II. English Translations

The Phenomenology of Mind

Trans. by J. B. Baillie, 2 vols., London, 1910. Revised one-volume edition, 1931.

A translation and commentary of the *Preface* has been made by Walter Kaufmann and appears in his *Hegel* (1965), 368–459. A translation of the Introduction has been made by Kenley Dove and appears in Heidegger's *Hegel's Concept of Experience,* New York, 1970.

The Science of Logic

Trans. by W. H. Johnston and L. G. Struthers, 2 vols., London, 1929.

Trans. by A. V. Miller, London, 1969.
The second part of this work, "Essence," was translated with
a commentary interpolated into the text by W. T. Harris
in his *Hegel's Doctrine of Reflection*, New York, 1881. Sections of the third part of this work were translated by H. S.
Macran in two publications, *The Doctrine of Formal Logic*,
Oxford, 1912, and *Logic of World and Idea*, Oxford, 1929.

The Encyclopedia

Though complete translations of this work into French (by A.
Vera in 1863) and into Italian (by B. Croce in 1923) have
existed for a number of years, there is at present no single
edition of this work in English, but its three major parts
have been translated, the second only very recently.

I. *The Logic of Hegel*

Trans. by William Wallace, Oxford, 1874.

II. *The Philosophy of Nature*

Trans. by A. V. Miller, New York, 1970.
Trans. by M. J. Petry, 3 vols., London, 1970.

III. *The Philosophy of Mind*

Trans. by William Wallace, Oxford, 1894. Reprinted 1969.

Gustav Mueller has translated large sections primarily of the
1817 edition of the *Encyclopedia*, New York, 1959, and has
provided a helpful running commentary, but it is not a complete translation.

The Philosophy of Right

Trans. by S. W. Dyde, London, 1896.
Trans. by T. M. Knox, Oxford, 1942, This edition includes the
students' notes and valuable comments by the translator. A
slightly revised edition appeared in 1945 and a paperback
edition in 1967.
Selections from this work have been earlier translated by J.
Macbride Sterrett under the title *The Ethics of Hegel*, Boston,
1893.

Lectures on the Philosophy of History

Trans. by J. Sibree, London, 1858. Reprinted often.

The Philosophy of Fine Art

Trans. by F. P. B. Osmaston, 4 vols., London, 1920.
A new translation of this work is presently in progress by
T. M. Knox.

Lectures on the Philosophy of Religion

Trans. by E. B. Speirs and J. B. Sanderson, 3 vols., London,
1895.

Lectures on the History of Philosophy

Trans. by E. S. Haldane and F. Simson, 3 vols., London, 1892.

Early Theological Writings

Trans. by T. M. Knox with an Introduction by R. Kroner,
Chicago, 1948. Reprinted in paperback, New York, 1961. This
volume is based on the main body of H. Nohl's *Hegels
Theologische Jugendschriften.*

Political Writings

Trans. by T. M. Knox, with an Introduction by Z. A. Pelcyzn-
ski, Oxford, 1964; 1969. Includes material not translated elsewhere such as "Über die englisch Reformbill" and "Die
Verfassung Deutschlands."

Letters

A selection of letters to and from Hegel has been translated
by Walter Kaufmann and appears in his *Hegel* (1965),
298–345.

There are useful books of translated selections edited by Jacob
Loewenberg, *Hegel Selections*, New York, 1929; and by Carl
J. Friedrich, *The Philosophy of Hegel*, New York, 1953. Various extracts are to be found in *German Classics of the 19th
and 20th Centuries* and also in issues of *The Journal of Speculative Philosophy. Hegel Highlights*, edited by Wanda Oryn-
ski, New York, 1960, also contains selected extracts.

III. Writings about Hegel

1. Some General Studies and Introductions

a. Books

Adorno, Theodor W., *Aspekte der Hegelschen Philosophie*, Berlin, 1957.

Adorno, Theodor W., *Drei Studien zu Hegel*, Frankfurt, 1963.

Baillie, J. B., *The Origin and Significance of Hegel's Logic: A General Introduction to Hegel's System*, London, 1901.

Bröcker, Walter, *Auseinandersetzungen mit Hegel*, Frankfurt, 1965.

Caird, Edward, *Hegel*, London, 1883; reprinted, Hamden, Conn., 1968. One of the best brief outlines of Hegel's thought.

Coreth, Emerich, *Das Dialektische Sein in Hegels Logik*, Vienna, 1952.

Croce, Benedetto, *What Is Living and What Is Dead in the Philosophy of Hegel*, trans. from the 1906 Italian edition by D. Ainslie, New York, 1915. The German edition of this volume (Heidelberg, 1909) contains over fifty pages of bibliographical material on Hegel. Reprinted, New York, 1969.

Cunningham, G. Watts, *Thought and Reality in Hegel's System*, New York, 1910.

von Dooren, W., *Het Totaliteitsbegrip bij Hegel ei zijin Voorgangers*, Assen, 1965.

Findlay, J. N., *Hegel: A Re-examination*, London, 1958.

Fischer, Kuno, *Hegels Leben, Werke und Lehre*, 2 vols., Heidelberg, 1901.

Fleischmann, Eugène, *La Science Universelle ou la Logique de Hegel*, Paris, 1968.

Garaudy, Roger, *La Pensée de Hegel*, Paris, 1966.

Gentile, Giovanni, *La Riforma della Dialettica Hegeliana e Altri Scritti*, Messina, 1923.

Glockner, Hermann, *Der Begriff in Hegels Philosophie*, Tübingen, 1924.

Glockner, Hermann, *Hegel*, 2 vols.: *I Die Voraussetzungen der Hegelschen Philosophie; II Entwicklung und Schiksal der Hegelschen Philosophie*, Stuttgart, 1929; 1940.

Grégoire, Franz, *Etudes Hégéliennes: Les Points Capitaux du Système*, Louvain, 1958.

Haering, Theodor, *Hegel, sein Wollen und sein Werk*, Leipzig, 1938.

Harris, William T., *Hegel's Logic*, Chicago, 1895; reprinted, New York, 1969.

Haym, Rudolf, *Hegel und seine Zeit*, Berlin, 1857; reprinted, Hildesheim, 1962.

Heiss, Robert, *Die Grossen Dialektiker des 19 Jahrhunderts: Hegel, Kierkegaard, Marx*, Berlin, 1963.

Hook, Sidney, *From Hegel to Marx*, New York, 1936; reprinted, Ann Arbor, 1962.

Hyppolite, Jean, *Logique et Existence. Essai sur la Logique de Hegel*, Paris, 1953.

Kaufmann, Walter, *Hegel: Reinterpretation, Texts and Commentary*, Garden City, N.Y., 1965. Contains valuable biographical information and useful bibliographical material.

Kojève, Alexandre, *Introduction à la Lecture de Hegel*, Paris, 1947. Abridged English edition, trans. by J. Nichols, Jr., and edited by Allen Bloom, New York, 1969.

Kroner, Richard, *Von Kant bis Hegel*, 2 vols., Tübingen, 1921.

Lenin, V. I., *Cahiers sur la Dialectique de Hegel*, tr. H. Lefebvre and N. Guterman, Paris, 1967.

Litt, Theodor, *Hegel: Versuch einer Kritischen Erneuerung*, Heidelberg, 1953.

Löwith, Karl, *From Hegel to Nietzsche*, trans. from the 1941 German edition by David E. Green, New York, 1964.

Mackintosh, R., *Hegel and Hegelianism*, Edinburgh, 1913.

McTaggart, J. M. E., *Studies in the Hegelian Dialectic*, Cambridge, 1896; reprinted, New York, 1964.

McTaggart, J. M. E., *A Commentary on Hegel's Logic*, Cambridge, 1910; reprinted, New York, 1964.

Merker, Nicolao, *Le Origini della Logica Hegeliana (Hegel a Jena)*, Milan, 1961.

Moog, Willy, *Hegel und die Hegelsche Schule*, Munich, 1930.

Mueller, Gustav E., *Dialectic*, New York, 1953.

Mueller, Gustav E., *Hegel: Denkgeschichte eines Lebendigen*, Bern, 1959.

Mueller, Gustav E., *Hegel: The Man, His Vision and Work*, New York, 1969.

Mure, G. R. G., *An Introduction to Hegel*, Oxford, 1940.

Mure, G. R. G., *A Study of Hegel's Logic*, Oxford, 1950.

Mure, G. R. G., *The Philosophy of Hegel*, London, 1965. A short book for the general reader.

Niel, Henri, *De la Mediation dans la Philosophie de Hegel*, Paris, 1945.

Noël, Georges, *La Logique de Hegel*, Paris, 1897.

Palmier, Jean M., *Essai sur la Formation du Système Hegelien*, Paris, 1968.

Pringle-Pattison, Andrew Seth, *Hegelianism and Personality*, Edinburgh, 1883. (Sometimes listed under Seth.)

Rosenkranz, Karl, *Kritische Erlaüterungen des Hegel'schen Systems*, Königsberg, 1840; reprinted, Hildesheim, 1963.

Schwarz, Justus, *Hegels Philosophische Entwicklung*, Frankfurt, 1938.

Soll, Ivan, *An Introduction to Hegel's Metaphysics*, Chicago, 1969.

Stace, W. T., *The Philosophy of Hegel*, London, 1924; reprinted, New York, 1955. A highly useful outline of the general system.

Stirling, J. H., *The Secret of Hegel*, London, 1865; reprinted, Dubuque, Iowa, 1967.

Thulstrup, Niels, *Hegel*, Copenhagen, 1967.

Travis, D. C., ed., *A Hegel Symposium*, Austin, Texas, 1962. Contains essays on differing topics by Travis, C. J. Friedrich, S. Hook, H. Motekat, G. Mueller, and H. Rehder.

Trendelenburg, Adolf, *Die Logische Frage in Hegels System*, Leipzig, 1843.

Tulane Studies in Philosophy, *Studies in Hegel*, The Hague, 1960. Contains seven essays on varied themes by A. Brinkley, J. K. Feibleman, M. Franklin, P. G. Morrison, A. Reck, R. C. Whittemore, and E. G. Ballard.

Ulrici, Hermann, *Über Princip und Method der Hegelschen Philosophie*, Halle, 1841.

Vera, Augusto, *Introduction à la Philosophie de Hegel*, Paris, 1855.

Wahl, Jean, *La Logique de Hegel comme Phenomenologie*, Paris, 1965.

Wallace, William, *Prolegomena to the Study of Hegel's Philosophy*, Oxford, 1894; reprinted, New York, 1968. This is primarily concerned with the smaller *Logic* of Hegel and originally appeared in a one volume edition with the author's translation of the first part of the *Encyclopedia* in 1874.

Weil, E., *Logique de la Philosophie*, Paris, 1967.

b. Articles and Chapters

Adorno, Theodor W., "Erfahrungsgehalte der Hegelschen Philosophie," *Archiv für Philosophie*, 6 (1959), 67–89.

Barion, Jakob, "Dialektik der Natur und Geschichte," in *Erkenntnis und Verantwortung*, ed. J. Derbolav and F. Nicolin, Düsseldorf, 1960.

Bar-on, Zvie, "Hegels logische Kategorien," *Iyyun*, 14–15 (1963), 89–119.

Bergmann, Frithjof H., "The Purpose of Hegel's System," *Jour. of History of Phil.*, 2 (1964), 189–204.

Berndtson, Arthur, "Hegel, Reason and Reality," *Phil. & Phen. Res.*, 20 (1959), 38–46.

Brunet, Christian, "L'ontologie dans l'*Encyklopädie* de Hegel," *Rev. de Metaphysique et de Moral*, 65 (1960), 449–462.

Dilthey, Wilhelm, "Die Jugendgeschichte Hegels," in *Gesammelte Schriften*, Vol. 4, Berlin, 1921.

Dulckeit, Gerhard, "System und Geschichte in Hegels Philosophie," *Zeit. für Deutsche Kulturphilosophie*, 4 (1937), 25–61.

Edlin, Gregor, "Dialektik und Komplementarität," *Studia Philosophica*, 24 (1964), 66–89.

Findlay, J. N., "Some Merits of Hegelianism," *Proc. Aris. Society*, 56 (1955–1956), 1–24.

Flach, Werner, "Hegels dialektische Methode," *Hegel-Studien*, Beiheft 1 (1964), 55–64.

Fleischmann, Jakob, "Objektive und subjektive Logik bei Hegel," *Hegel-Studien*, Beiheft 1 (1964), 45–54.

Foster, M. B., "The Opposition between Hegel and the Philosophy of Empiricism," *Verhandlungen des dritten Hegelkongresses* (Tübingen/Haarlem, 1934), 79–96.

Garaudy, Roger, "Contradiction et Totalité dans le Logique de Hegel," *Rev. Philosophique de la France et de l'Etranger*, 89 (1964), 67–79.

Godfrey, F. La T., "Hegel's Dialectic in Historical Philosophy," *Philosophy*, 16 (1941), 306–310.

Grégoire, Franz, "Hegel et l'Universelle Contradiction," *Rev. Phil. de Louvain*, 44 (1937), 36–73.

Groll, M., "The Self-movement of the Notion in Hegel's Philosophy," *Iyyun*, 12 (1961), 83–166.

Guéroult, M., "Hegel sur l'Antithètique de la Raison Pure," *Rev. de Metaphysique et de Morale*, 38 (1931), 413–439.

Gutièrrez, Girardot R., "Què es Dialectica?", *Mito. Revista Bimestral de Cultura*, 6 (1960), 100–118.

Hall, G. Stanley, "Notes on Hegel and his Critics," *Jour. Speculative Phil.*, 12 (1878), 93–103.

Henrich, Dieter, "Hegels Theorie über den Zufall," *Kant-Studien*, 50 (1958–1959), 131–148.

Henrich, Dieter, "Anfang und Methode der Logik," *Hegel-Studien*, Beiheft 1 (1964), 19–35.

Hessing, J., "Das Wahre in der Philosophie Hegels," *Verhandlungen des Zweiten Hegelkongresses*, Tübingen/Haarlem, 1932.

Kaufmann, Walter, "The Hegel Myth and Its Method," *Phil. Review*, 60 (1951), 459ff.

Kline, George L., "Some Recent Reinterpretations of Hegel's Philosophy," *The Monist*, 48 (1964), 34–75.

Kopper, J., "Reflexion und Identität in der Hegelschen Philosophie," *Kant-Studien*, 58 (1967), 33–53.

Kosok, Michael, "The Formalization of Hegels Dialectical Logic," *Inter. Phil. Quarterly*, 6 (1966), 596–631.

Kroner, Richard, "Zur Problematik der Hegelschen Dialektik," *Hegel-Studien*, 2 (1963), 303–314.

Kubeš, Miloslav, "Hegels Auffassung der Rolle von Zeichen und Symbol in Erkenntnisprozess," *Filosofický Časopis*, 12 (1964), 521–528.

Lakebrink, Bernhard, "Causalität und Finalität bei Hegel," *Freiburger dies Universitatis*, 11 (1963–1964), 103–115.

Landgrebe, L., "Das Problem der Dialektik," *Marxismusstudien*, 3 (1960), 1–65.

Langlois, Jean, "Note sur Hegel et le Principe de Contradiction," *Sciences Ecclésiastiques*, 11 (1959), 99–110.

Lenk, Kurt, "Dialektik und Ideologie," *Archiv für Rechts-und Sozialphilosophie*, 49 (1963), 303–318.

Lobkowicz, Nicholas, "Abstraction and Dialectics," *Rev. Meta.*, 21 (1968), 468–490.

Marcuse, Herbert, "Actuality of Dialectic," *Diogenes*, 8 (1960), 80ff.

Maurer, Johannes, "On the Fundamental Problem of Hegel," *Unitas*, 17 (1938), 278ff.

Merker, Nicolao, "Questioni e momenti della Genesi della Logica Hegeliana," *Rivista Critica di Storia della Filosofia*, 18 (1963), 89–95.

Mueller, Gustav, "The Hegel Legend of 'Thesis-Antithesis-Synthesis,'" *Jour. of the History of Ideas*, 19 (1958), 411–414.

Nador, György, "Hegel über den Empirismus," *Ratio*, 6 (1964), 134–139.

Peperzak, Adrien T., "Existenz und Denken im Werden der Hegelschen Philosophie," *Scholastik*, 38 (1963), 226–238.

Pöggeler, Otto, "Hegels Jenaer Systemkonzeption," *Philosophisches Jahrbuch*, 71 (1963–1964), 286–318.

Rossi, Pietro, "La Diallettica Hegeliana," *Rivista di Filosofia*, 49 (1958), 283–333.

Smith, John E., "The Relation of Thought and Being: Some Lessons from Hegel's *Encyclopedia*," *The New Scholasticism*, 38 (1964), 22–43.

Tran Duc Thao, "Le 'noyau rationnel' dans le Dialectique Hégélienne," *La Pensée Revue du Rationalisme Moderne*, 119 (1965), 3–34.

Van der Meulen, Jan, "Begriff und Realität," *Hegel-Studien*, Beiheft 1 (1964), 131–139.

Wahl, Jean, "Une Interpretation de la Logique de Hegel," *Critique*, 79 (1953), 1050–1071.

Walsh, W. H., "Hegel and Intellectual Intuition," *Mind*, 54 (1945), 49–63.

2. Phenomenology of Spirit

Bloch, Ernst, "Das Faustmotiv der Phänomenologie des Geistes," *Hegel-Studien*, 1 (1961), 155–171.
Contri, Siro, "La Coscienza Infelice nella Filosofia Hegeliana," *Theorein*, 2 (1961), 42–65.
Dove, Kenley R., *Toward an Interpretation of Hegel's Phänomenologie des Geistes*, New Haven, 1965. Dissertation.
Gauvin, Joseph, "Entfremdung et Entausserung dans la Phénoménologie de l'Esprit de Hegel," *Archives de Philosophie*, 25 (1962), 555–571.
Haering, Theodor, "Die Entstehungsgeschichte des Phänomenologie des Geistes," *Verhandlungen der Dritten Hegelkongresses* (Tübingen/Haarlem, 1934), 118–138.
Heidegger, Martin, "Hegels Begriff der Erfahrung," in *Holzwege*, Frankfurt, 1952. Translated into English as *Hegel's Concept of Experience*, New York, 1970.
Hyppolite, Jean, *Genèse et Structure de la Phénoménologie de l'Esprit de Hegel*, 2 vols., Paris, 1946.
Kursanow, G. A., "Hegels 'Phänomenologie des Geistes,'" *Deutsche Zeitschrift für Philosophie*, 10 (1962), 1451–1460.
Loewenberg, Jacob, *Hegel's Phenomenology: Dialogues on the Life of the Mind*, LaSalle, Ill., 1965.
Nink, Caspar, *Kommentar zu den Grundlegenden Abschnitten von Hegels Phänomenologie des Geistes*, Regensberg, 1948.
Pöggeler, Otto, "Zur Deutung der Phänomenologie des Geistes," *Hegel-Studien*, 1 (1961), 255–294.
Roeder von Diersburg, Egenolf, "Konstante und varible Hilfsbegriffe in Hegels Phänomenologie," *Archiv für Philosophie*, 13 (1964), 50–70.
Royce, Josiah, *Lectures on Modern Idealism*, New Haven, 1919. Lectures VI, VII, and VIII are on the *Phenomenology*.
Schmitz, H., "Der Gestaltbegriff in Hegels Phänomenologie des Geistes und seine Geistesgeschichtliche Bedeutung," in *Gestaltprobleme der Dichtung*, Bonn, 1957.
Stiehler, Gottfried, *Die Dialektik in Hegels 'Phänomenologie des Geistes,'* Berlin, 1964.
Totaro, Francesco, "Tempo e Storia nella 'Fenomenologica dello Spirito' di Hegel," *Revista di Filosofia Neo-Scolastica*, 57 (1965), 448–482.

Tran Duc Thao, "La 'Phénoménologie de l'Esprit et son sontenu réel," *Les Temps Modernes*, 3 (1947), 492–519.

Wahl, Jean, *Le Malheur de la Conscience dans la Philosophie de Hegel*, Paris, 1951.

3. Nature and Science

Alexander, Samuel, "Hegel's Conception of Nature," *Mind*, 2 (1886), 495–523.

Baer, Reinhold, "Hegel und die Mathematik," *Verhandlungen des zweiten Hegelkongresses*, ed. Wigersma (Tübingen/Haarlem, 1932), 104–120.

Bosio, Franco, "Le antinomie kantiane della totalita cosmologica e la lors critica in Hegel," *Il Pensiero*, 9 (1964), 39–104.

Braun, Hermann, *Realität und Reflexion: Studien zu Hegels Philosophie der Natur*, Heidelberg, 1960.

Brecht, Stefan, *The Place of Natural Science in Hegel's Philosophy*, Cambridge, 1959. Harvard dissertation, including answers to Hegel's critics.

Chlebik, Franz, *Kraft und Stoff, oder der Dynamismus der Atome aus Hegel'schen Prämissen*, Berlin, 1873.

Christensen, Darrel E., "Hegel's Phenomenological Analysis and Freud's Psychoanalysis," *Inter. Phil. Quarterly*, 8 (1968), 356–378.

Collingwood, R. G., "Hegel: The Transition to the Modern View of Nature," in *The Idea of Nature* (Oxford, 1945), 121–132.

Durck, Johanna, *Die Psychologie Hegels*, Bern, 1927.

Fialco, Nathan, "Hegel's Views on Mental Derangement," *Jour. Abnormal & Soc. Psych.* 24 (1930), 241–267.

Harris, Errol, "The Philosophy of Nature in Hegel's System," *Rev. Metaphysics*, 3 (1949), 213–228.

Harris, William T., "Philosophy of Nature," *Jour. Speculative Phil.*, 5 (1871), 274ff.

McTaggart, J. M. E., *Studies in Hegelian Cosmology*, Cambridge, 1918.

Meyerson, Emile, *De l'Explication dans les Sciences*, Paris, 1921. Primarily concerned with Hegel's Philosophy of Nature.

Ritchie, D. G., "Darwin and Hegel," *Proc. Aristotelian Soc.*, 1 (1891), 55–74.

Steverding, B., "Hegels Naturphilosophie," *Physikalische Blätter* 17 (1961), 437ff.

Whittemore, Robert C., "Hegel's 'Science' and Whitehead's 'Modern World,' " *Philosophy*, 31 (1956), 36–54.

Wigersma, B., "Der dialektische Zusammenhaus der Physikalischen," *Verhandlungen des dritten Hegelkongresses* (Tübingen/Haarlem, 1934), 251–269.

4. Ethics, Social and Political Philosophy

Avineri, Shlomo, "Hegel and Nationalism," *Rev. Politics*, 24 (1962), 461–484.

Avineri, Shlomo, "Hegel's Views on Jewish Emancipation," *Jewish Social Studies*, 25 (1963), 145–151.

Balaguschkin, E. G., "Sozialer Aspekt der Familie in Hegels Philosophie des Rechts," *Studien zur Hegels Rechtsphilosophie in USSR* (Moscow, 1966), 94–127.

Beyer, Wilhelm R., "Aktuelle juridische Hegeliana," *Archiv für Rechts-und Sozialphilosophie*, 47 (1961), 227–243.

Binder, Julius, "Die Freiheit als Recht," *Verhandlungen des ersten Hegel-Kongresses* (Tübingen/Haarlem, 1931), 146–210.

Brightman, Edgar S., "Hegel's Influence in the Contemporary Situation," *Crozer Quarterly*, 12 (1935), 47–56.

Chamley, Paul, "Les origines de la pensée économique de Hegel," *Hegel-Studien*, 3 (1965), 225–261.

Darmstaedter, Friedrich, "Das Naturrecht als soziale Macht und die Rechtsphilosophie," *Sophia* (Italy), 5 (1937), 212–235.

Dubsky, Ivan, *Hegels Arbeitsbegriff und die Idealistische Dialektik*, Prague, 1961.

Flechtheim, Ossip K., "Hegel and the Problem of Punishment," *Jour. History of Ideas*, 8 (1947), 293–308.

Fleischmann, E., *La Philosophie Politique de Hegel*, Paris, 1964.

Fleischmann, Jacob, "Hegel's Theory of the Will," *Studies in Philosophy*, 6 (1960), 268–315.

Foster, Michael B., *The Political Philosophies of Plato and Hegel*, New York, 1965.

Gentile, Giovanni, "Il Concetto dello Stato in Hegel," *Verhandlungen des zweiten Hegelkongresses*, ed. B. Wigersma (Tübingen/Haarlem, 1932), 121–134.

Giese, Gerhardt, *Hegels Staatsidee und der Begriff der Staatserziehung*, Halle, 1926.

Goldstein, L. J., "The Meaning of 'State' in Hegel's 'Philosophy of History,' " *Phil. Quarterly*, 12 (1962), 60–72.

Grégoire, F., "Hegel et la divinité de l'Etat," *Actes du IIIe Congres des Societés de Philosophie* (Louvain, 1947), 247–253.

Grégoire, F., "L'Etat Hégélien est-il totalitaire?" *Rev. Philosophique de Louvain*, 60 (1962), 244–253.

Holz, Hans Heinz, *Herr und Knecht bei Leibniz und Hegel; Zur Interpretation der Klassengesellschaft*, Berlin, 1968.

Hook, Sidney, "Hegel Rehabilitated?", *Encounter* 24 (1965), 53–58. A series of comments followed: S. Avineri, "Hook's Hegel"; Z. A. Pelczynski, "Hegel Again"; and S. Hook, "Hegel and his Apologists."

Hyppolite, Jean, *Studies in Marx and Hegel*, trans. from the French by J. O'Neill, New York, 1969.

Kaufmann, Walter (ed.), *Hegel's Political Philosophy* New York, 1970.

Kelley, George A., "Notes on Hegel's 'Lordship and Bondage,'" *Rev. Metaphysics*, 19 (1966), 780–802.

Knox, T. M., "Hegel's Attitude to Kant's Ethics," *Kant-Studien*, 49 (1957–1958), 70–81.

Lakebrink, Bernhard, "Freiheit und Notwendigkeit in Hegels Philosophie," *Hegel-Studien*, Beiheft 1 (1964), 181–192.

Larenz, Karl, "Hegel und das Privatrecht," *Verhandlungen des zweiten Hegel-Kongresses*, ed. Wigersma (Tübingen/Haarlem, 1932), 135–148.

Lasson, Georg, *Einleitung für Hegels "Schriften zur Politik und Rechtsphilosophie,"* Leipzig, 1923.

Lasson, Georg, *Einleitung zu den Grundlinien der Philosophie des Rechts*, Leipzig, 1930.

Ludz, Peter C., "Dialektik und Ideologie in der Philosophie Hegels," *Archiv für Rechts-und Sozialphilosophie*, 47 (1961), 133–146.

Lukács, Geörgy, *Der Junge Hegel: Über die Beziehungen von Dialektik und Oekonomie*, Zurich, 1948.

Lukács, Geörgy, *Der Junge Hegel und die Probleme der Kapital-istchen Gesellschaft*, Berlin, 1954.

Marcuse, Herbert, *Reason and Revolution; Hegel and the Rise of Social Theory*, 2d ed., Boston, 1960.

Mehta, Urajendra R., *Hegel and the Modern State; An Introduction to Hegel's Political Thought*, New Delhi, 1968.

Munson, Thomas N., "An Interpretation of Hegel's Political Thought," *The Monist*, 48 (1964), 97–111.

Nicolin, Friedhelm, "Hegels Arbeiten zur Theorie des subjektiven Geistes," *Erkenntnis und Verantwortung*, Düsseldorf, 1960, 356–374.

Peperzak, Adrien T., *Le Jeune Hegel et la Vision Morale du Monde*, The Hague, 1960.

Perkins, Robert L., "The Family: Hegel and Kierkegaard's Judge Wilhelm," *Hegel-Jahrbuch* (1967), 89–100.

Piontkowskij, A. A., "Zur Frage der politischen Wertung der

Hegelschen Rechtsphilosophie," *Studien Zur Hegels Rechtsphilosophie in USSR* (Moscow, 1966), 1–24.

Reyburn, Hugh Adam, *The Ethical Theory of Hegel*, Oxford, 1921.

Riedel, Manfred, *Theorie und Praxis im Denken Hegels*, Stuttgart, 1965.

Riedel, Manfred, "Hegels Kritik des Naturrechts," *Hegel-Studien*, 4 (1967), 177–204.

Ritter, Joachim, *Hegel und die Französische Revolution*, Frankfurt, 1965.

Ritter, Joachim, "Personne et Propriété selon Hegel," *Archives de Philosophie*, 31 (1968), 179–201.

Rosenzweig, F., *Hegel und der Staat*, 2 vols., Munich/Berlin, 1920.

Röttges, Heinz, *Der Begriff der Freiheit in der Philosophie Hegels*, Cologne, 1963.

Smith, Constance I., "Hegel on War," *Jour. History of Ideas*, 26 (1965), 282–285.

Sobotka, Milan, *Die Idealistische Dialektik der Praxis bei Hegel*, Prague, 1965.

Suter, Jean-Francois, "Tradition et Revolution," *Hegel-Studien*, Beiheft 1 (1964), 307–325.

Topitsch, Ernst, *Die Sozialphilosophie Hegels als Heilslehre und Herrschaftsideologie*, Neuwied/Berlin, 1967.

von Trott zu Solz, Adam, *Hegels Staatsphilosophie und das Internationale Recht*, Göttingen, 1967.

Walsh, W. H., *Hegelian Ethics*, New York, 1969.

Weil, Eric, "Die Säkularisierung der Politik und des politischen Denkens in der Neuzeit," *Marxismusstudien*, 4 (1962), 144–162.

Weil, Eric, *Hegel et L'Etat*, 2d ed., Paris, 1966.

Wein, Hermann, "Der Ursprung der Lehre vom objektiven Geist bei Hegel," in his *Philosophie als Erfahrungswissenschaft*, (The Hague, 1965), 73–81.

Wenke, H., *Hegels Theorie des objektiven Geistes*, Halle, 1927.

5. Philosophy of Religion

Adams, G. P., *The Mystical Element in Hegel's Early Theological Writings*, Berkeley, 1910.

Albrecht, W., *Hegels Gottesbeweis*, Berlin, 1958.

Asveld, Paul, *La Pensée Religieuse du jeune Hegel*, Paris, 1953.

Bernstein, Ulrich, "Hegel's Lutheran Background," *Rev. of Religion*, 3 (1904), 276–305.

Bruaire, C., *Logique et Religion Chrétienne dans la Philosophie de Hegel*, Paris, 1964.

Christensen, Darrel, ed. *Hegel and the Philosophy of Religion: The Wofford Symposium*, The Hague, 1970.

Dulckheit, G., *Die Idee Gottes im Geiste der Philosophie Hegels*, Munich, 1947.

Fackenheim, Emil L., *The Religious Dimension in Hegel's Thought*, Bloomington, Ind., 1968.

Garaudy, Rodger, *Dieu est Mort, Etude sur Hegel*, Paris, 1962.

Glockner, H., "Hegels Kritik des Christentums," *Zeitschrift für deutsch Kulturphilosophie*, 5 (1938), 17–47 and 118–169.

Haushalter, Walter M., Mrs. *Eddy Purloins from Hegel*, Boston, 1936.

Henrich, Dieter, *Der Ontologische Gottesbeweis*, Tübingen, 1960.

Hyppolite, Jean, "Le Tragique et le Rational dans la Philosophie de Hegel," *Hegel-Jahrbuch 1964*, 9–15.

Iljin, Iwan, *Die Philosophie Hegels als kontemplative Gotteslehre*, Bern, 1946.

Kaufmann, Walter, "Hegel's Early Antitheological Phase," *Phil. Review*, 63 (1954), 3–18.

Kimmerle, Heinz, "Zu Hegels Religionsphilosophie," *Philosophische Rundschau*, 15 (1968), 111–135.

King, A. R., "Immortality in the Thought of Hegel," *Methodist Review*, 109 (1926), 212–224.

Kojève, Alexandre, "Hegel, Marx et le Christianisme," *Critique*, 1 (1956), 339–366.

Lakebrink, Bernhard, "Die Freiheit in Gott," *Rückschau und Ausblick* (Cologne, 1962), 166–181.

Lasson, Georg, "Hegels Religionsphilosophie," *Verhandlungen des zweiten Hegelkongresses* (Tübingen/Haarlem, 1932), 183–193.

Lauer, Quentin, "Hegel on Proofs for God's Existence," *Kant-Studien*, 55 (1964), 443–465.

Löwith, Karl, "Hegel and the Christian Religion," in Löwith's *Nature, History, and Existentialism* (Evanston, Ill., 1966), 162–203.

Major, Ladislav, "Zu Hegels Religionsphilosophie," *Filosofický Časopis*, 12 (1964), 495–528.

Merlan, Philip, "Hegel: 'Cur deus homo?,' " *Sitzungsberichte des 12 Internationalen Philosophiekongresses*, 12 (1961), 319–326.

Mueller, Gustav E., "Fünf Ursprunge von Hegels Religionsphilosophie," *Studia Philosophica*, 22 (1962), 60–82.

Munson, Thomas N., "Hegel as Philosopher of Religion," *Jour. of Religion*, 46 (1966), 9–23.

Mure, G. R. G., "Hegel, Luther, and the Owl of Minerva," *Philosophy*, 41 (1966), 127–139.

Raju, Poola, *Thought and Reality* (Hegelianism and Advaita), London, 1937.

Schmidt, Erik, *Hegels Lehre von Gott*, Gütersloh, 1952.

Schoeps, Hans-Joachim, "Die ausserchristlichen Religionen bei Hegel," in his *Studien zur unbekannten Religions- und Geistesgeschichte*, Göttingen, 1963.

Schweitzer, Carl G., "Die Glaubensgrundlagen des Hegelschen Denkens," *Hegel-Studien*, Beiheft 1 (1964), 237–238.

Splett, Jorg, *Die Trinitätslehre G. W. F. Hegels*, Munich, 1965.

Sterrett, J. M., *Studies in Hegel's Philosophy of Religion*, New York, 1890.

Vancourt, R., *La Pensée religieuse de Hegel*, Paris, 1964.

6. Philosophy of Art

Badaloni, Nicola, "G. W. F. Hegel, Estetica," *Critica Marxista*, 2 (1964), 211–221.

Brelet, Gisèle, "Hegel et la musique moderne," *Hegel-Jahrbuch 1965*, 10–26.

Bukofzer, Manfred, "Hegels Musikästhetik," *Deuxieme Congres International d'Esthetique et de Science de l'Art*, 2 (1937), 32–35.

Fleischmann, Jacob, "Hegel's Concept of Romanticism," *Iyyun*, 9 (1958), 121–138.

Glockner, Hermann, "Die Ästhetik in Hegels System der Philosophie," *Verhandlungen des zweiten Hegelkongresses*, ed. Wigersma (Tübingen/Haarlem, 1932), 149–167.

Heimsoeth, Heinz. "Hegels Philosophie der Musik," *Hegel-Studien*, 2 (1963), 161–201.

Kaminsky, Jack, *Hegel on Art*, Albany, 1962.

Kedney, John S., *Hegel's Aesthetics*, Chicago. 1892.

Knox, Israel, *The Aesthetic Theories of Kant, Hegel and Schopenhauer*, New York, 1936.

Kuhn, Helmut, "Die Vollendung der klassischen deutschen Äesthetik durch Hegel," in *Schriften zur Ästhetik* (Munich, 1966), 15–144.

Morawski, Stefan, "Hegels Ästhetik und das 'Ende der Kunstperiode,'" *Hegel-Jahrbuch 1964*, 60–71.

Negri, Antimo, "La similitudine nella poesia drammatica secondo Hegel," *Rivista di Estetica*, 5 (1960), 105–112.

Pöggeler, Otto, "Hegel und die griechische Tragödie," *Hegel-Studien*, Beiheft 1 (1964), 285–305.

Rohrmoser, Gunter, "Zum Problem der ästhetischen Versöhnung Schiller und Hegel," *Euphorion*, 53 (1959), 351–366.

Teyssedre, Bernard, *L'Esthetique de Hegel*, Paris, 1958.

7. Philosophy of History

Christensen, Darrel E., "Nelson and Hegel on the Philosophy of History," *Jour. History of Ideas*, 25 (1964), 439–444.

Collinet, Michel, "The Idea of Progress in the Nineteenth Century," *Diogenes*, 9 (1961), 98ff.

Cottier, Marie-Martin, "Hegel, la théologie et l'histoire," *Revue Thomiste*, 61 (1961), 88–108.

Crites, Stephen D., "Fate and Historical Existence," *The Monist*, 53 (1969), 14–39.

Heimsoeth, Heinz, "Politik und Moral in Hegels Geschichtsphilosophie," in his *Studien zur Philosophiegeschichte*, (Cologne, 1961), 22–42.

Hyppolite, Jean, *Introduction à la Philosophie de l'Historie de Hegel*, 2d ed., Paris, 1968.

Lasson, Georg, *Hegel als Geschichtsphilosoph*, Leipzig, 1920.

Lukács, Geörgy, *Geschichte und Klassenbewusstsein*, Berlin, 1923.

Marcuse, Herbert, *Hegels Ontologie und die Grundlegung einer Theorie der Geschichtlichkeit*, Frankfurt, 1932.

Maurer, Reinhart K., "Hegel et la Fin de L'histoire," *Archives de Philosophia*, 30 (1967), 483–518.

Morris, G. S., *Hegel's Philosophy of the State and of History*, Chicago, 1887.

Munk, Arthur W., "The Problem of the Philosophy of History: Hegel and After," *Philosophical Forum*, 3 (1945), 19–22.

Papaioannou, Kostas, "History and Theodicy," *Diogenes*, 14 (1966), 38–63.

Vanni Rovighi, S., *La Concezione Hegeliana della Storia*, Milan, 1942.

8. History of Philosophy

Baron, R., "Dialectica et humanisms chez Plato et Hegel," *Giornale di Metafisica*, 20 (1965), 142–149.

Behler, Ernst, "Friedrich Schlegel und Hegel," *Hegel-Studien*, 2 (1963), 203–250.

Copleston, Frederick, *A History of Philosophy*, Vol. 7, London, 1963. Treatment of Hegel on pages 159–247.

Croce, Benedetto, "La Place de Hegel dans l'Histoire de la Philosophie," *Rev. de Métaphysique et de Morale*, 46 (1938), 211–224.

Earle, William, "Hegel and Some Contemporary Philosophers," *Phil. & Phen. Research*, 20 (1960), 352–364.

Easton, Loyd D., *Hegel's First American Followers*, Athens, Ohio, 1966.

Foucher de Careil, L. A., *Hegel et Schopenhauer*, Paris: 1862.

Gadamer, Hans-Georg, "Hegel und die antike Dialektik," *Hegel-Studien*, 1 (1961), 173–199.

Girndt, Helmut, *Differenz des Fichteschen und Hegelschen Systems der Philosophie*, Bonn, 1965.

Gray, J. Glenn, *Hegel's Hellenic Ideal*, New York: 1941; reprinted as *Hegel and Greek Thought*, New York, 1968.

Harris, Henry S., "Hegelianism of the 'Right' and 'Left,'" *Rev. Metaphysics*, 11 (1958), 603–609.

Heidegger, Martin, "Hegel et les Grecs," *Cahiers du Sud*, 45 (1958), #349, 355–368.

Horn, Joachim C., *Monade und Begriff. Der Weg von Leibniz zu Hegel*, Munich, 1965.

Ilting, Karl-Heinz, "Hegels Auseinandersetzung mit der aristotelieschen Politik," *Philosophisches Jahrbuch*, 71 (1963–1964), 38–58.

Kummel, Friedrich, *Platon und Hegel zur Ontologischen Begrundung des Zirkels in der Erkenntnis*, Tübingen, 1968.

Lakebrink, Bernhard, "Der Platonismus und die Hegelsche Metaphysik," *Dialektik und Dynamik der Person* (Cologne and Berlin, 1963), 239–251.

Litt, Theodor, "Goethe und Hegel," *Studium Generale*, 2 (1948), 413–427.

Löwith, Karl ed., *Die Hegelsche Linke*, Stuttgart, 1962.

Lübbe, Hermann, ed., *Die Hegelsche Rechte*, Stuttgart, 1962.

Maier, Josef, *On Hegel's Critique of Kant*, New York: 1939.

Orsini, G. N. B., "Feuerbach's Supposed Objections to Hegel," *Jour. History of Ideas*, 30 (1969), 85–90.

Perkins, Robert L, "Two Nineteenth Century Interpretations of Socrates: Hegel and Kierkegaard," *Kierkegaard-Studiet*, 4 (1967), 82–87.

Pochmann, Henry A., *New England Transcendentalism and St. Louis Hegelianism*, Philadelphia, 1948.

Prauss, G., "Hegels Parmenides Deutung," *Kant-Studien*, 57 (1966), 276–285.

Stenzel, J., "Hegels Auffassung der Griechischen Philosophie," *Verhandlungen die zweiten Hegelkongresses*, ed. Wigersma (Tübingen/Haarlem, 1932), 168–183.

Swieżawski, Stefan, "Hegel und die mittelalterliche Philosophie," *Archiv für Philosophie*, 10 (1960), 24–78.

Takeuchi, Yoshinori, "Hegel and Buddhism," *Il Pensiero*, 7 (1962), 5–46.

Verene, Donald P., "Kant, Hegel and Cassirer," *Jour. History of Ideas*, 30 (1969), 33–46.

Walsh, W. H., "Hegel on the History of Philosophy," *History and Theory*, 4, Beiheft 5 (1964–1965), 67–82.

Weiss, Frederick G., *Hegel's Critique of Aristotle's Philosophy of Mind*, The Hague, 1969.

9. Phenomenology and Existentialism

Bense, Max, *Hegel und Kierkegaard. Eine Prinzipielle Untersuchung*, Cologne, 1948.

Castro, Lopez, O., "Dos puntos de partida el filosofar: Hegel y Husserl," *La Palabra y el Hombre*, 7 (1964), 32–44.

De Waelhans, Alphonse, "Identité et différence: Heidegger et Hegel," *Rev. Internationale de Philosophie* 52 (1960), 221–237.

De Waelhans, Alphonse, "Phénoménologie Husserlienne et Phénoménologie Hégélienne," in his *Existence et Signification*, Paris, 1958.

von Hagen, Eduard, *Abstraktion und Konkretion bei Hegel und Kierkegaard*, Bonn, 1969.

Hartmann, Klaus, *Sartre's Ontology: A Study of Being and Nothingness in the Light of Hegel's Logic*. Evanston, 1966.

Kopper, Joachim, "Sartres Verständnis der Lehre Hegels von der Gemeinschaft," *Kant-Studien*, 52 (1960–1961), 159–172.

Lessing, Arthur, "Hegel and Existentialism, on Unhappiness," *The Personalist*, 49 (1968), 61–77.

Major, Ladislav, "Heidegger und Hegel," *Filosofický Časopis*, 12 (1964), 539–546.

Merleau-Ponty, Maurice, "L'existentialism chez Hegel," *Temps Modernes*, 1 (1945), #7, 1311–1319.

Navickas, Joseph L., "The Hegelian Notion of Subjectivity," *Inter. Phil. Quarterly*, 8 (1968), 68–93.

Puligandla, Ramakrishna, "Similarities between the Phenomenologies of Hegel and Husserl," *Phil. Quarterly*, 18 (1965) 127–143.

Radermacher, Hans, *Kierkegaard's Hegelverständnis*, Cologne, 1958.

Ramsey, Paul, " 'Existenz' and the Existence of God: A Study of Kierkegaard and Hegel," *Jour. Religion*, 28 (1948), 157–176.

Ricci Garotti, Loris, "Heidegger *contra* Hegel?", *Il Pensiero*, 8 (1963), 303–326.

Schrader, George A., "Hegel's Contribution to Phenomenology," *The Monist*, 48 (1964), 18–33.

Smith, Christopher, "Heidegger, Hegel and the Problem of Das Nichts," *Inter. Phil. Quarterly*, 8 (1968), 379–405.

Thulstrup, Niels, *Kierkegaards Forhold til Hegel og til den Spekulative Idealism Indtil 1846*, Copenhagen, 1967.

Wahl, Jean, "Hegel et Kierkegaard," *Verhandlungen des dritten Hegelkongresses* (Tübingen/Haarlem, 1932), 236–250.

10. Marx and Marxism

Apel, Karl-Otto, "Reflexion und materielle Praxis" (Zur erkenntnis-anthropologischen Begrundung der Dialektik zwischen Hegel und Marx), *Hegel-Studien*, Beiheft 1 (1964), 151–166.

Avineri, Shlomo, "The Hegelian Origins of Marx's Political Thought," *Rev. Metaphysics*, 21 (1967), 33–56.

Ballestrom, Karl G., *Die Sowjetische Erkenntnismetaphysiks und ihr Verhältnis zu Hegel*, Dordrecht, 1968.

Barion, Jakob, *Hegel und die Marxistische Staatslehre*, Bonn: 1963.

Bekker, Konrad, *Marx's Philosophische Entwicklung, sein Verhältnis zu Hegel*, Zürich, 1940.

Cerroni, Umberto, "La critica di Marx all Filosofia hegeliana del diritto publico," *Rivista Internazionale di Filosofia del Diritto*, 38 (1961), 281–308.

Dupre, Louis K., *The Philosophical Foundations of Marxism*, New York, 1966.

Fetscher, Iring, "Hegel et le Marxisme," *Archives de Philosophie*, 22 (1959), 323–368.

McLellan, David, *The Young Hegelians and Karl Marx*, London, 1969.

Riedel, Manfred, "Grundzüge einer Theorie des Lebendigen bei Hegel und Marx," *Zeitschrift für Philosophische Forschung*, 19 (1965), 577–600.

Simon, Josef, "Zum Problem einer 'Philosophie der Tat.' Text und Literatur zur nachhegelschen Philosophie in 19. Jahrhundert," *Hegel-Studien*, 3 (1965), 297–320.

Touilleux, Paul, *Introduction aux Systèmes de Marxe et Hegel*, Paris, 1960.

Tucker, R. C., "The Symbolism of History in Hegel and Marx," *Jour. Philosophy*, 54 (1957), 144–145.

CONTRIBUTORS

SHLOMO AVINERI (b. 1933) is Senior Lecturer in political theory at the Hebrew University of Jerusalem. A graduate of the Hebrew University and the London School of Economics, he was visiting lecturer at Yale University during 1967–1968. In addition to important articles on Hegel, Marx, Thomas More, and other subjects, he is the author of *The Social and Political Thought of Karl Marx* (1968), the translator of Marx's *Early Writings* into Hebrew, and editor of the forthcoming *Karl Marx: Writings on Colonialism and Modernization* (1969).

FREDERICK C. COPLESTON, S. J. (b. 1907) is Professor of the History of Philosophy both at Heythrop College in England and at the Gregorian University in Rome. Educated at Oxford University, he entered the Society of Jesus in 1930. In addition to many articles and seven books, he is best known for his distinguished eight-volume *History of Philosophy* (1946–1966). Among his other books are *Friedrich Nietzsche, Philosopher of Culture* (1942), *St. Thomas and Nietzsche* (1944), *Medieval Philosophy* (1952), *Existentialism and Modern Man* (1948), and *Contemporary Philosophy* (1956).

KENLEY ROYCE DOVE (b. 1936) is now an Assistant Professor of Philosophy at Yale University after having taught two years at Williams College. He received his doctorate from Yale University and spent 1967–1968 in Berlin under a Morse Fellowship doing research on Hegel. His translation of the Introduction to Hegel's *Phenomenology of Spirit* was published in 1970.

JOHN N. FINDLAY (b. 1903) formerly held the chair of Philosophy at Kings College in London and is now Professor of Philosophy at Yale University. He was educated at Transvaal University College in South Africa and at Oxford University. A leader in the movement to restore interest in the thought of Hegel, he is well-known for his *Hegel: A Re-examination* (1958) and for his Gifford Lectures at the University of St. Andrews (1964–1966). In addition to many articles, his writings include *Meinong's Theory of Objects* (1933), *Values and Intentions* (1961), *Language, Mind and Value* (1963), *The Discipline of the Cave* (1965), *The Transcendence of the Cave* (1967), and *Ascent to the Absolute* (1970).

F. La T. GODFREY (b. 1891) was educated at Dublin University where he is now Senior Dean and Senior Fellow of Trinity College and honors lecturer in Mental and Moral Science and lecturer in the History of Philosophy. He was a student of the prominent Hegel scholar of some decades ago, H. S. Macran. In addition to an essay on Hegel's dialectic in historical philosophy, he has published articles on numerous themes in *Hermathena* over a period of years.

ERROL E. HARRIS (b. 1908) is currently Professor of Philosophy and chairman of the department at Northwestern University. Educated at Rhodes University College in South Africa and at Oxford, he has also taught at the universities of Witwatersrand, Edinburgh, and Kansas. He has been a Bollingen Research Fellow, a Ford Foundation Research Fellow, and a National Science Foundation Research Fellow. Past President of the Metaphysical Society of America, he has published six books and twoscore articles in various journals, several on Hegel. His learned volumes include *Revelation Through Reason* (1958), *Nature, Mind and Modern Science* (1954), *The Foundations of Metaphysics in Science* (1965), *Annihilation and Utopia* (1966), and the forthcoming *Hypothesis and Perception.*

JEAN HYPPOLITE (1907–1968) Until his death, Professor Hyppolite held the chair of the history of philosophical thought at the College de France in Paris. He is well-known for his work on Hegel, not only by articles, but by his distinguished two-volume translation of the *Phenomenology* into French (1939–1941). In addition he has written *Genèse et Structure de la Phénoménologie de l'Espirit* (1946), *Logique et Existence. Essai sur le Logique de Hegel* (1953), *Etudes sur Marx et Hegel* (1955; (English translation 1969), and *Introduction à la Philosophie de l'Histoire de Hegel* (1968).

WALTER KAUFMANN (b. 1921) was educated at Williams College and at Harvard University and is now Professor of Philosophy at Princeton University. In addition to numerous articles in various journals including several on Hegel, he is the author of a series of distinguished volumes including *Nietzsche* (1950), *Critique of Religion and Philosophy* (1958), *From Shakespeare to Existentialism* (1959), *The Faith of a Heretic* (1961), *Hegel: Reinterpretation, Texts and Commentary* (1965), and *Tragedy and Philosophy* (1968). He has translated ten of Nietzsche's works and is the editor of *Hegel's Political Philosophy* (1970).

SIR T. MALCOLM KNOX (b. 1900) was Principal of the University of St. Andrews in Scotland from 1953 until his retirement in 1966. From 1936 to 1953 he held the chair of Moral Philosophy at that school and earlier he was lecturer and then fellow of Jesus College at Oxford University. He was knighted in 1961 and has received honorary degrees from the universities of Pennsylvania, Edinburgh, Dundee, and Glasgow. His noteworthy translation of Hegel's *Philosophy of Right* appeared in 1942, and has several times been reprinted. He also translated Hegel's *Early Theological Writings* (1948) and *Hegel's Political Writings* (1964). He has recently been a Gifford Lecturer at the University of Aberdeen and these lectures have been published in two volumes, *Action*, and *A Layman's Quest* (1968). Sir Malcolm is presently working on a translation of Hegel's *Lectures on Aesthetics*.

KURT F. LEIDECKER (b. 1902) is Professor of Philosophy at Mary Washington College of the University of Virginia. Educated at Oberlin and the University of Chicago, his special field is Oriental philosophies and the intellectual relations between the Orient and the West. Among his books are *A Sanskrit Grammar, Royce and Indian Thought* (1931), and a life of the St. Louis Hegelian William Torrey Harris entitled *Yankee Teacher* (1946). In addition, he has published translations of Nietzsche's letters, some of Heidegger's essays, and a work of Paracelsus plus many articles on Indian Philosophy and on Buddhism.

FRANCO LOMBARDI (b. 1906) is currently President of the Faculty of Letters and Philosophy at the University of Rome, where he has also been Professor of Moral Philosophy and of the History of Philosophy. Editor of *De Homine*, he is author of many books including *Ludwig Feuerbach* (1935), *Sören Kierkegaard* (1936), *Nascita del mondo moderno* (1953), *Ricostruzione filosofica* (1956), *Il concetto della liberta* (1966), and *Kant vivo* (1968). His major works are now available in an eighteen-volume edition published in Florence. He is a member of the National Academy of Lincei in Italy and is a contributor to the *Encyclopedia of Philosophy*.

KARL LÖWITH (b. 1897), now living in Switzerland, is emeritus Professor of Philosophy from the University of Heidelberg. A lifelong scholar of the history of thought his many distinguished volumes include *Jakob Burckhardt* (1936), *Meaning in History* (1949), *Heidegger: Denker in dürftiger Zeit* (1953), *Wissen, Glaube und Skepsis* (1956), *From Hegel to Nietzsche* (1964, from the 1941 German edition), *Vorträge und Abhandlungen* (1966), and *Nature, History and Existentialism* (1966). He has also edited *Texte der Hegelschen Linken* (1961).

GUSTAV EMIL MUELLER (b. 1898) studied at Heidelberg and London universities and received his Ph.D. from the University of Bern in 1923. A lifelong student of Hegel, he taught for a time at the University of Oregon, but in 1930 he began a professorship at the University of Oklahoma which continued until his recent retirement. In addition to numerous articles on philosophy, he has written plays, stories, and poetry. Among the books he has written are *Interplay of Opposites; a Dialectical Ontology* (1956), *Hegel, Denkgeschichte eines Lebendige* (1959), *Plato, the Founder of Philosophy as Dialectic* (1963), *Origin and Dimensions* (1965), and *Hegel: The Man, His Vision and Work* (1968). In 1959, he translated and annotated major portions of the 1817 edition of Hegel's *Encyclopedia.*

ROBERT L. PERKINS (b. 1930) is Professor of Philosophy and Chairman of the department at the University of South Alabama. Currently Secretary of the Hegel Society of America, he has had several articles published on the thought of Kierkegaard and Hegel and was a participant in the Fourth International Hegel Conference in Prague in 1966. He is the author of *Søren Kierkegaard* (1969).

WARREN E. STEINKRAUS (b. 1922) has been Professor of Philosophy at the State University College of New York in Oswego since 1964, having formerly taught at DePauw University and Union College in Kentucky. He received his doctorate under the late E. S. Brightman at Boston University. In addition to articles in sundry journals, he has contributed essays to the *Encyclopedia of Philosophy*, Ginsberg's *Critique of War*, and Christensen's *Hegel and the Philosophy of Religion*. He edited *New Studies in Berkeley's Philosophy* (1966).

WILLIAM H. WERKMEISTER (b. 1901) is presently Professor of Philosophy at the University of Florida in Tallahassee and was formerly Director of the School of Philosophy at the University of Southern California and Editor of *The Personalist.* He has also taught at the University of Nebraska, and at Harvard and has been a Lecturer at Bonn, Cologne, Giessen, and Hamburg. In addition to many articles, his published works include *A Philosophy of Science* (1940), *The Basis and Structure of Knowledge* (1948), *A History of Philosophical Ideas in America* (1949), *Outlines of a Theory of Value* (1959), and *Theories of Ethics* (1961).

Dr. Albert Richer, who translated the article by Jean Hyppolite, is a professor of Modern Language at Framingham State College in Framingham, Massachusetts. Dr. Bernard P. Keaney, who translated the essay by Franco Lombardi, received his doctor's degree from the Gregorian University in Rome and was formerly at the State University of New York College in Oswego.

NAME INDEX

SUBJECT INDEX